THE
EVERYTHING
GUIDE TO STARTING
AN ONLINE BUSINESS

Dear Reader,

Business fundamentals have not changed in the past several decades. Even though Facebook and Twitter didn't exist in 1993, companies still sold products or services, they still had to meet payroll, and they still had to pay taxes. While the tools have changed—and the opportunities have grown around them—profit still equals revenue minus costs.

I wrote this book because these basics are sometimes forgotten by would-be online entrepreneurs. This book is full of practical, use-it-today knowledge that can help you tool up for success—and mitigate your risks. I hope to bridge the gaps of your business knowledge, and help you to understand the nuances of online business. Finally, I include some of the most advanced online strategies, from CRM to SEO to social media.

So congratulations on taking the leap to starting your own business—or at least thinking about it. There is no better feeling than that of being in control of your destiny. Sure, owning your own business is hard work, but if you have to work, why shouldn't you be rewarded for your efforts?

See you online,

Randall M. Craig

(@RandallCraig)

Welcome to the EVERYTHING® Series!

These handy, accessible books give you all you need to tackle a difficult project, gain a new hobby, comprehend a fascinating topic, prepare for an exam, or even brush up on something you learned back in school but have since forgotten.

You can choose to read an Everything® book from cover to cover or just pick out the information you want from our four useful boxes: e-questions, e-facts, e-alerts, and e-ssentials.

We give you everything you need to know on the subject, but throw in a lot of fun stuff along the way, too.

We now have more than 400 Everything® books in print, spanning such wide-ranging categories as weddings, pregnancy, cooking, music instruction, foreign language, crafts, pets, New Age, and so much more. When you're done reading them all, you can finally say you know Everything®!

QUESTION

Answers to
common questions

FACT

Important snippets
of information

ALERT

Urgent
warnings

ESSENTIAL

Quick
handy tips

PUBLISHER Karen Cooper

MANAGING EDITOR, EVERYTHING® SERIES Lisa Laing

COPY CHIEF Casey Ebert

ASSOCIATE PRODUCTION EDITOR Mary Beth Dolan

ACQUISITIONS EDITOR Lisa Laing

DEVELOPMENT EDITOR Katie Corcoran Lytle

EVERYTHING® SERIES COVER DESIGNER Erin Alexander

Visit the entire Everything® series at *www.everything.com*

THE
EVERYTHING®

GUIDE TO STARTING
AN ONLINE BUSINESS

The latest strategies and advice on how to
start a profitable Internet business

Randall Craig

Adams Media
New York London Toronto Sydney New Delhi

*Dedicated to my family, who have shared my journey
starting numerous online businesses over the years.*

Adams Media
An Imprint of Simon & Schuster, Inc.
57 Littlefield Street
Avon, Massachusetts 02322

An Everything® Series Book.
Everything® and everything.com® are registered trademarks of Simon & Schuster, Inc.

ADAMS MEDIA and colophon are trademarks of Simon and Schuster.

For information about special discounts for bulk purchases, please contact Simon & Schuster Special Sales at 1-866-506-1949 or business@simonandschuster.com.

The Simon & Schuster Speakers Bureau can bring authors to your live event. For more information or to book an event contact the Simon & Schuster Speakers Bureau at 1-866-248-3049 or visit our website at www.simonspeakers.com.

Manufactured in the United States of America

10 9 8 7

Library of Congress Cataloging-in-Publication Data has been applied for.

ISBN 978-1-4405-5530-5
ISBN 978-1-4405-5531-2 (ebook)

The Everything® Guide to Starting an Online Business contains material adapted and abridged from *The Everything® Start Your Own Business Book, 4th Edition,* by Judith B. Harrington, copyright © 2012, 2010, 2006, 2002 by Simon & Schuster, Inc., ISBN 13: 978-1-4405-0407-5.

Contents

Top 10 Tips You'll Learn about Online Business

1. How to avoid the usual pitfalls of a start-up business.

2. How to determine when your business idea will become profitable.

3. How to assess risk and, even better, how to manage it.

4. How to put together a business plan.

5. Ideas on how to finance your start-up.

6. Enough technical lingo to know what you need—and what you don't.

7. How to use social media effectively.

8. Which online business activities you should avoid.

9. Advanced concepts for converting browsers to buyers.

10. Tips for keeping your business in the winner's circle after it's up and going.

Introduction

WELCOME TO YOUR NEW CAREER. Each day that you go into your new office, there will be something new: e-mails from prospects asking a product question or suppliers pitching new services; calls from your developer asking about a software upgrade; partners looking to do joint marketing; and your family asking when you will be joining them for dinner.

With the possible exception of this last point, every day is usually completely different. That is why running your own online business is so much fun. With everyone asking you questions, it is sometimes challenging when you don't have the answers. Too many businesses fail precisely because the owner didn't invest in himself first. Simple investments, like the time you are spending reading this book, can give you the know-how from hundreds of online start-up experiences.

Reading a book, though, won't make you successful—only your hard work will. There are many models of success, from making a few dollars in the evenings, to building a completely online business, to using the web as another channel for a traditional business. There are even businesses that serve other online businesses: web designers, developers, and writers, to name a few.

What type of business should you start? Generally, people are more successful if they focus on the intersection of their skills, their passion, and the market. What unique skills do you have? What do you really enjoy doing? And is there a market for your service or product? What you think your business is about might not be where your business ends up. Unlike manufacturers or large retailers, online business carries the benefit of much lower capital investment; as you learn, it is easier to pivot the business in the direction of higher sales. Whatever your scale of operation, the job of finding an idea, then growing it to reach your goals is like none other. It truly is a journey of discovery—but with a big financial reward.

Starting and running a business requires a great deal of knowledge. Setting realistic goals for yourself and your business—weekly, monthly, quarterly, and annually—is critical to success. Build step by step, and focus on getting the business off the ground rather than getting lost in dreams of a lavish lifestyle sometime in the future.

Become familiar with who your customers are—their likes and dislikes. Reading trade publications (every industry has them), networking with other online entrepreneurs, joining organizations, reading and writing blogs in your field, and connecting in social media are all different ways to stay in touch with the people who will make or break your business—your customers. Good customer relations are critical to any successful business!

As you read this book for the first time, note the areas that are beyond your direct experience. These spheres require more detailed study, but they also may point out where you need help from a college course, mentor, consultant, or a business partner. This book takes a general approach that you can apply to your unique situation. You will find specifics on tasks such as writing a business plan, calculating the break-even point where your business becomes profitable, and converting browsers to buyers. You'll also find, as you are going through the book, that you may actually know more than you originally thought. Welcome to your new career!

CHAPTER 1

Setting the Stage!

Making your start in a new business, even if it is only new to you, can be one of the most thrilling and rewarding experiences of your life. No one sets off expecting to fail, nor should you. Success will only be yours though if you follow through with preparation, diligence, guts, risk taking, and perseverance. Read on to see if you are ready to launch your idea.

Self-Evaluation

While it is true that starting and running a business is difficult, it's done all the time, and done very successfully, by many individuals who have built empires large and small. Building a business is done by Wall Streeters and by everyday people who simply want to be their own bosses. Google, Apple, Microsoft all started very small—Apple in a garage.

Before you even consider starting your own business, you need to determine whether you're the right person for the job. Would you hire you? The position in question involves being your own boss and running the show, which includes marketing, sales, customer service, and possibly maintaining an inventory, supervising other employees, bookkeeping, planning, and establishing investor relations. Most importantly, the job hinges on your ability to make many key decisions, some on short notice, and the effectiveness of your people skills, since nearly every online business involves interaction with others. You may be skilled in all of these key areas, but if you aren't, you'll either have to find other people who can assist you or tool up yourself.

Here's a list of traits and characteristics that will help you run a business successfully:

- The ability to gather facts and make important decisions
- The ability to stay motivated, even when the business starts off slowly, as most businesses do
- Good organizational skills
- Good communication skills—verbal and written
- A base understanding of web technology
- A stick-to-it drive that keeps you working long hours to get the job done
- Physical stamina to weather the long hours and lack of sleep that may be part of the job, especially in the early stages of the business
- The ability to get along well with many different types of personalities
- A diplomatic manner of harnessing or managing anger and frustration
- Confidence in your skills, knowledge, and abilities to run a specific type of business
- Confidence in your ability to find the answers to questions you don't yet know
- The ability to be firm or flexible, as required, so you can make adjustments or changes in your plans
- The ability to successfully balance a business life and a personal life

The last item on this list is the toughest one. Many entrepreneurs report that the toughest transition is moving from a 9 A.M. to 5 P.M. job, to a 5 A.M. to 9 P.M. job. While running a business takes many hours and extreme dedication, if you sacrifice everything else in your life, you will eventually have regrets. A business is not worth building if you can't stick around to see it prosper.

ESSENTIAL

You will need to know every aspect of your business, not just the areas that involve your particular interests or strengths. Even if you delegate some tasks, such as bookkeeping or inventory management, you will need to be aware of how things stand at all times. Sometimes small mistakes can sink an otherwise sound business. As you read through this book, highlight the areas that need more attention. Don't get blindsided.

Be honest with yourself and determine how many of the previously listed skills and talents you possess. How many do you see yourself learning? How many indicate the need for a business partner (or partners) to fill the void? How many simply do not describe you? If it's more than 40 percent, then you may not be ready right now to go into your own business. It's better to make that determination early on.

Pros of Starting Your Own Business

If you aren't looking to reach a goal by opening up a business, then why go through all the trouble? As it turns out, there are quite a lot of pros associated with being an entrepreneur. Here are a few:

- You are your own boss. No longer are you working for someone else. You only have to answer to yourself (and your investors, the bank, the IRS, and regulatory agencies). You get to make the big decisions for a change.
- The sky's the limit. Working for yourself may afford you the opportunity to make more money than working for somebody else. The risks are greater, but the potential rewards are too.
- You can prove yourself. You have the opportunity to use your skills, abilities, and creativity to do things your way. You can fully use your skills, including ones that your former workplace may have stifled.

- You'll be involved in all areas of the business—from funding and finance to many of the smaller daily details.
- You'll take pride in promoting and marketing your own company—there is a special feeling you get when touting your own business.
- You can make money while you sleep. One of the unique aspects of most online businesses is that the company—or website—continues to earn twenty-four hours a day, seven days a week. There is tremendous satisfaction when you wake up in the morning and see a number of transactions . . . and money in your bank.
- You decide where to locate your business. Tired of commuting an hour or more every day in slow-moving traffic to get to the office? Now you can set up the office closer to home—or in your home.
- The chance of a big payday. Beyond the income that you earn along the way, you may eventually sell the company.

From the design of the website and company logo to the sales strategy and marketing plan, it's your call, your ball game, and your business. Like a roller coaster ride, starting a business has the proverbial ups and downs—and that's what makes it fun.

ALERT

You'll see many websites about earning money with little effort. Don't believe them. If there was a way to make a fortune that easily, the promoters would be doing it themselves—not trying to sell the concept to you.

Cons of Starting Your Own Business

Whenever there are pros, there are offsetting cons. In the previous section, you saw some of the positive aspects of starting your own business. It's important also to be aware of some of the negatives:

- You don't get a guaranteed salary or paycheck. There is always a financial risk involved in starting a business. Not only may you not make money for some period of time, you will have to invest your own money into the business. It may be some time before you're in a position to pay yourself. Depending on the type of business, it often takes several years before you show a profit.

- **Everything's all on your shoulders.** While it's good to be the king during times of prosperity, you will also occupy the throne during lean times. Along with making the exciting and fun decisions, you'll also have some tough decisions, such as choosing which of two employees to lay off because you can't afford to keep them both on the payroll.
- **You can't please everyone.** When you work for someone else, you may be able to excel in the art of making your boss happy, or even thrilled, with your performance. As the boss, however, there will be occasions when you won't be able to make everyone (or anyone) happy. Keeping customers satisfied, employees feeling valued, and investors happy can be a dicey balancing act.
- **You only have the 168-hour week.** There are 168 hours in a seven-day week. You may find yourself sacrificing other aspects of your life to work a good portion of those hours. If finances allow, you can hire people to handle much of this work. However, you will need to train them, review their work, and maintain some control over all areas of the business.
- **You are both president . . . and janitor.** While having a fancy title on your card may give you prestige, a founder's job also includes taking out the garbage, cleaning the washrooms, going to the post office, boxing inventory for shipping, and anything else that you can't afford others to do. If you're not willing to get your hands dirty, then starting a business might not be for you.
- **Growing pains are common.** Some businesses grow smoothly while (most) others experience growing pains. These are the times when there may be a drop-off in progress because the market, industry, or economy slows down, or because competition heats up.

Some of these points may not seem so challenging, and some of them may be show-stoppers. Remember, your friends and family will be on the entrepreneurial ride with you—ask them what they think of both the pros, and the cons.

Before You Start

Some of the most successful entrepreneurs will tell you that if they had realized what they were getting into, they probably would have lost the nerve to start their businesses in the first place. Other business owners say that they wish they had thought it all through more carefully and been able to foresee some of the pitfalls of running a business. To get a basic feel for the road that lies ahead, it's important to ask yourself three basic questions.

ALERT

As crazy as it sounds, it's possible to bring a product to market too soon, before customers know they need it. You also don't want to be too late coming to market. The last thing you want to do is invest in launching a product or service if there is no ready market for it. Investigate the market to find if it is the right time and place for your idea before investing too much time and money in your plan.

What Are My Goals?

Yes, you want to make money, but how much and how fast? Do you see yourself running a small online service business, or do you hope to become the next Google? Is this a business you hope to pass to your children after you retire, or do you hope to build a successful business over the next few years, sell it, and retire to some exotic locale? Are you looking at altruistic goals? There are many goals beyond the obvious one of making money. And how will you know if you have created a successful business if you have nothing by which to gauge success?

How Well Do I Understand Business?

You don't need to be a regular reader of the *Wall Street Journal* to open a business. Eight-year-olds who can barely read can set up a lemonade stand and rake in some cash on a hot day. However, it's important that you understand business principles as they pertain to your business concept. Do you have a basic understanding of bookkeeping, paying taxes, paying employees and vendors, signing contracts, making deals, marketing, and operating in accordance with state, local, and county rules, laws, and regulations? Because we are talking about an online business, it also means understanding the basics of web technology. You don't have to know how to do all of this before you start, but you will need to research—and learn along the way.

How Will Running a Business Impact My Life?

Can you emotionally and financially roll with the uncertainty a business faces until it shows a profit? Can your family handle it? Will you be able to maintain a life outside of the business? How motivated are you?

You need to assess how well you can balance the many demands of a business, emotionally and physically, with the rest of your life. You need to be able to have a life away from your business; otherwise, you'll lose all perspective. If you neglect other areas of your life, such as family and health, in the end the business will also suffer as a result. If running a business means sleepless nights and ulcers, then perhaps the security of working for someone else isn't so bad after all.

The Upside of a Down Economy

Economists can tell you about business cycles that produce prosperity and times of economic retraction. When you are considering starting your business it is important to have a solid understanding of what is happening in the larger economy overall. It is more challenging for start-ups when credit is tight, consumers hold back, and online competitors come from everywhere. Yet whenever there is economic change, there is opportunity—especially online. Here are some of the special considerations for starting a business when times are tough.

Test Your Concept for the Times

Every idea has to be put into context. In tough times, families might not be able to afford a trip to Disney, but will look for value online. A shopping referral site that focuses on discounts in a specific niche may be more successful than a "lifestyle" site selling luxuries.

Consumers Still Need Basics

Can you become a discount resource for everyday items? You may have to trim your margins, but online businesses do not have the overheads that weigh down traditional businesses. Even in prosperous times folks like a bargain.

Squeezed Out? Jump Back In

Perhaps you find yourself on the wrong side of "right sizing" at your now former employer. If your job gets cut, this can be the push you need to bring your talent to the marketplace. Sometimes customers will follow a valued relationship, which can set you up with clients immediately.

ALERT

Your former employer may take a dim view of your "stealing" customers and employees for your new venture. Make sure you aren't on the wrong side of any agreements that you've signed—or the law.

Take the Long View

You, of course, need to make business decisions based on the current economic climate. When you are considering launching your game plan in slower economic times, remember that eventually the economy will pick up. Your business concept must be elastic enough to flourish in good times and bad.

Adapt Your Funding Plan

There are additional pressures for this part of the business launch when credit is tight and even angel investors—usually well-off individuals who look for early stage opportunities to put their money into—look long and hard at possible investments. It is not impossible to put together the monies you will need, but you may need to give yourself more time for this part of the planning effort. It may be necessary to think creatively about more resources for funding—without jeopardizing the ultimate success and health of the business. Later in this book you will learn more about putting funding in place.

Know What You Don't Know

Often, the best way to get a feel for what to do is by being aware of what not to do. Instead of making mistakes and learning the hard way, you can learn from the mistakes of others. In the sections below, you'll find some advice to help you avoid the pitfalls and common mistakes that often go along with starting your own business.

Determine Your Target Audience

Too often, when asked whom their business will appeal to, people starting an online business say "everybody." Unfortunately, while you would like everyone to be a customer, it is virtually impossible—and unreasonably expensive—to attract everyone. Most businesses cater to a particular segment of the population, whether it's baby boomers, new moms, coffee drinkers, athletes, kids, or some other group. You need to determine your primary target audiences to be successful.

Don't Act Impulsively

Not doing the proper research is a big no-no. You need to know all about the business you're entering. Learn all the details. Spend time checking out competitors, banks, suppliers, consultants, and so forth. Know what permits and licenses you need to obtain. Save yourself headaches later by being prepared up front. That being said, many entrepreneurs rely on their "gut" to make decisions. Nothing wrong with that—but doing some research will reduce your risk considerably.

Have a Marketing Plan

There are plenty of ways to spread the word that you're in business. However, all of these methods take planning. You may have the best product or service in the world, but if you don't market it, no one will know about it.

Don't Ignore the Competition

How will you know if your prices are competitive if you don't know what your competitors are up to? Check out your competition before you open your doors for business. Get a feel for what your competitors are doing, how successful they are, and what you can do differently to carve a niche for yourself.

Watching the competition isn't just a question of their pricing either. How do they advertise? How do they deliver their products or services? What is the tone of the writing on their websites? What technology are they using? While copying the competition isn't the goal, learning from them is.

FACT

Keeping an eye on your competition should be an ongoing exercise. You should always be looking for that little something extra to set you apart from the crowd. It might be lower prices, unique products, or deluxe service. However you do it, you need to distinguish yourself from others offering the same goods or services.

Don't Underestimate Your Time Frame to Profitability

Having a sound business plan, being aware of the competition, meeting the needs of your customers, and executing a solid marketing strategy can make your business successful sooner rather than later. However, it takes time to build a reputation and gain repeat customers. During that time, you will exhaust a great deal of funding. Don't ignore the numbers. If they tell you that it should take three years to show a profit, then don't start spending "profits" in the first six months before you have any. Too many businesses (particularly those that are web-based) have made the mistake of spending paper profits. Remember that banks and venture capitalists look at profit-and-loss statements; eyeballs don't pay the rent—real dollars do.

Don't Cut the Wrong Corners

While you don't want to spend money foolishly, you need to carefully determine where to save and where to spend. Spending a fortune to create a product, then saving money by not having an advertising or marketing campaign is a colossal waste of your efforts. Cutting the sales force may save you money, but cripple your revenues. Find the right places to save money.

Focus on People, Not Just Technology

Just because you're starting an online business doesn't mean you should be blinded by technology; it's not a substitute for good relationships with your suppliers, customers, and employees. Technology tools make success possible, but people make it happen.

Don't Bite Off More Than You Can Chew

Many businesses are built in phases, and for good reason. You only have so many hours in the day and so much money in the bank. Too often, entrepreneurs will spread themselves so thin that they don't have the capacity to be successful. Start with a fixed number of products or services, aim for a narrower market niche, or build only a certain part of your technology. Start small, prove your concepts, and let your business grow.

Think Like a Businessperson

If you're going to be an entrepreneur, you need to think like one. You need to be able to establish and maintain many relationships in a professional business manner, including those with suppliers, customers, investors, and the bank. You must feel confident in a leadership role, being able to motivate and manage employees successfully. Present yourself professionally, offer the short version of what your business is all about, and conduct yourself maturely without letting your emotions take control. You also need to hone your networking skills. Use social media to stay connected—people expect it.

You also need to be driven, confident, and focused. Initially, your business will seem like a 24/7 proposition. Even during nonbusiness hours, you will focus on aspects of the business and constantly be thinking of ways you can improve it. You need to be able to act and react when necessary. For example, you may be on vacation when you get a message that your major supplier has gone out of business. You instantly need to find another supplier to make delivery deadlines. As a start-up, you're never completely away from a business.

And finally, you need to think like a successful entrepreneur by continually looking for new opportunities and figuring out how you can use them to your advantage. Look for what is being done well, what can be improved upon, and what is lacking or missing in your field. You will become much more critical of other goods and services and may find yourself thinking as a consumer advocate.

ESSENTIAL

It's important to realize your strengths and weaknesses so you can hire people to handle various areas for you. An artist might want to run an Internet retail business selling his art over the web. He may not be versed in the technical aspects of the Internet, however, and should bring in someone who is able to set up and maintain the website.

Are you really ready to be an entrepreneur? Here's a list of questions to ask yourself to measure your progress:

- How well can you formulate new business strategies and research them? Can you easily draw new ideas for your business from other areas of your life?
- Can you present your business to others in an enticing, succinct, and compelling manner?
- Are you able to establish and maintain relationships that benefit your business?
- Do you have ways to regularly keep in touch with prospects and clients?
- Can you take feedback and criticism without being defensive?
- Are you able to present a consistently positive image of your business and motivate your employees or staff to do the same?
- Can you earn the respect of your employees or staff?
- Are you able to make customers or clients feel special?
- Can you motivate yourself to stay focused even when things go wrong?
- Can you generate excitement in others and rally your employees, family, neighbors, and friends around your business venture?
- Can you tolerate the risks that come with starting your own business and remain focused on the long-term goal of turning a profit?
- How well can you spot potential opportunities to enhance your business?
- How good are you at staying abreast of new developments in your chosen industry?
- Do you know how to keep accurate records and do you have the discipline to stay on top of them?
- Can you gauge how much your products or services are worth in the market?
- Do you have the skills for working with a budget?

- Can you stay focused on tracking your cash flow weekly or monthly?
- Can you find ways to maximize profits through modifications of the business?

These are just some of the questions that you should ponder while teaching yourself to think like an entrepreneur. The areas in which you're strongest may be those that point you toward one type of business as opposed to another. For example, a people person will be more likely to open a retail business or service business that deals with the public than someone who is a skilled artist and is not interested in dealing directly with loads of customers or prospective customers.

If you've read this section and you're concerned, don't be: you've just identified a few activities that you need to work on before you take the plunge. Address these concerns by trying the following:

- Take a course to get up to speed.
- Volunteer in a community leadership role.
- Find a mentor.
- Take on a partner with some of these attributes.
- Decide not to leave your job just yet, but look for opportunities to learn these skills on your current employer's dime.

Even just reading this book is a big step, as these pages explore many different facets of growing a successful online business.

Talk to the Experts

It's very hard to build a business in a vacuum. The feedback, suggestions, and opinions of others can be extremely valuable in getting a business off the ground. In fact, companies pay large sums of money for studies and focus groups that answer a lot of their key business questions before they present goods or services to the public.

Advisors need not be successful businesspeople. They can be friends or even relatives who simply promise to provide objective opinions. You might even put together an advisory board to discuss ideas with as they arise. Here is a white paper—a short document that explores a topic—that has more on the subject: *www.budurl.com/onlineadvisory*.

Whatever route you choose, be ready to ask many questions. Keep thinking of new angles to approaching your business, and bounce them off other people. Ask others to play devil's advocate. The more alternatives you consider, the more likely you'll be to find the ones that are best for your business.

Don't think about asking questions only as you are working through the initial planning either. An advisory board or mentor will be invaluable throughout the life of your business. Keep them up-to-date, so that any questions that you do ask will have context.

QUESTION

What are small business development centers (SBDCs), and how can they help?
Small business development centers are quasi-government agencies located across the country. Usually based in college or university settings, their mission is to coach business owners and teach them how to solve specific problems. Classes and workshops are offered and individual counseling can be scheduled.

Plan Your Exit Strategy Now

Thinking about leaving your business before it has even been hatched may seem counterintuitive. Yet, it is one of the most important planning steps you will make. Eventually you will no longer be involved in the business; whether you are savoring your newly fattened bank account or are pushing up daisies, an end will come.

One aspect of an online business's exit strategy that is different than a traditional business's exit strategy is the technology. Consider: if you can identify the technology architecture that is used by your potential acquirer, then technology will be one less barrier for the new owner to surmount. At the same time, if your business might be purchased as a way to acquire talent, then it would be more valuable if your team already knew the acquirer's base technology.

As time goes on, you will want to revisit your exit strategy and make adjustments accordingly. Be ready for your harvest.

CHAPTER 2

How Much Time Will You Spend?

This is one of the most important questions as it will determine the type—and sometimes the success—of the business that you eventually start. For example, if you are looking to start your online business in the evenings, then you only have so many hours that will be available to you. If you decide to work six days (and evenings) each week, the story is very different. Neither is wrong, just different. The important thing is to make a decision—and understand the implications.

Make Money in Your Spare Time

Who doesn't like the idea of a few extra bucks in his pocket? Trading in time in front of the TV for time online, and ending up with a second payday each week sounds alluring indeed. If you do have spare time (that you want to give up), you may be interested in one of the following options.

Supplement Your Day Job

Are you happy doing what you do each day, but are looking to make some money on the side? Or maybe, you are concerned about your job security, and see an online business as a contingency plan, just in case. Whatever the reason, the business that you choose should be one that can properly be fitted into the time that is available. Having a second source of income will give you a higher standard of living—with the job security of your current position.

Another aspect of supplementing your day job is the time that it will take you to achieve your new business's goals. As the time that you devote is somewhat limited, you shouldn't expect instant returns.

Be careful to avoid online businesses that move beyond the time that you have available. If you begin to work on your online business during the day, your employer will take a dim view of your daytime extracurricular activities. The whole question of your relationship to your current employer is quite important. If you are thinking of setting up a business that is partly related to your current employer's business, be careful. Have you signed any agreements that preclude being involved in something that is competitive? Would someone (a client, prospect, investor, etc.) see an ethical issue with your competing against your employer? What legal risks might you be exposed to?

Transition to a New Career

Are you fundamentally dissatisfied with your current job? Perhaps you aren't appreciated for your efforts? Or maybe you have been passed over for a promotion, and think that you could do better elsewhere?

If this is the case, you may see an online business as your exit plan: while you are working during the day for someone else, you are spending your nights and weekends planning (and executing) the transition to your own full-time business.

How do you know when to actually quit your day job to focus on your online business full time? Some ideas:

- When it is so busy at night that the only way to find more time to build the business is to take hours from the day. (Consider asking your current employer for a permanent reduced work schedule—e.g., a four-day week.)
- When you have earned enough money from your new enterprise that you no longer need the day job. Don't forget to put some money away for a rainy day. The entrepreneur's mantra is that if you don't make money, you don't eat.
- When you can no longer stand to go into the office every day. It takes motivation to be an entrepreneur; if you leave your day job completely drained and demotivated, you won't have the energy to be successful at night.
- When you are unable to make deals with partners and suppliers on a timely basis because you are only available during the evenings, and they are only available during the day.

An online business is a great exit plan, but leaving too soon means taking a higher risk than you really need to.

Test-Drive an Idea

One of the magical attributes of many online businesses is that so little capital is required to start them up. An online business allows you to test-drive a concept with very little time and financial cost. If the concept shows promise, then investment can follow. Manufacturers, on the other hand, must invest in a factory and pay for inventory and logistics, product development, and human resources, just to begin.

The idea of a test-drive for your online business is simple: take your concept, set up an online storefront to showcase your products and services, do some basic marketing, and learn. At the very beginning, the test-drive is really no more than market research. If it appears that there is an opportunity, then setting up a low-cost website will let you gauge the market directly. More importantly, the test-drive will teach you about the market—helpful when you don't have much direct experience in the sector.

Here's an example: During the day, you are an analyst at a bank; you might be very good at financial analysis, ratios, and bank policies, but you know nothing about buying or selling crafts. You are hoping to sell crafts in an online store, and your market research shows that there is a demand. (Remember, this is just an example!)

To test-drive this concept, you make a deal with a local artist to sell her goods in your online store. Over the next three months, you set up a website to do this, experimenting with page layout, pricing, marketing, fulfillment alternatives, customer service, etc. The goal isn't to strike it rich, but to determine the combination of ideas that will result in a winning combination—and to educate yourself about a business that may be your future. If all systems are go, then you can feel more confident with a bigger investment in time and dollars. If things didn't work out the way you expected, then the test-drive will have saved you from making an expensive mistake.

Building an Entire Business Operation

Building a business is very much like learning to swim. There are two ways to learn: either jump into the deep end and figure it out, or start in the shallow end and take it slowly. Making money in your spare time is the shallow end; it's lower risk because you are still getting a salary. In the tips below, we explore building an entire business operation by jumping right in.

Give It Your Full Attention

How much time does it take to build an entire business? It depends on the scale of the business that you are interested in starting. Most entrepreneurs will describe the start-up phase as long days, work-at-desk lunches, weekend work, and a stunted social life. This may seem unappealing, but consider what you are doing: this may be the biggest gamble of your life. You are investing your time, money, and reputation; calling in all of your favors; and using every corner of your network. If you are successful you will have complete control over your time, financial freedom, and perhaps a few bragging rights. If you are not successful, putting food on your table may be tough. What's a few extra hours if they can improve your chances of success?

The challenge that many people have when making the transition from employee to entrepreneur is that they don't give the process their full attention. Here are some tips that might help:

- Set expectations with your family and friends. You need their support when times are tough, but you also need their understanding for your long hours.

- Use a time planner to manage your time. Microsoft Outlook, Google Calendar, or an old-style paper calendar all can do the job.
- Bring a notebook with you to capture ideas while waiting in line, transit, etc.
- Be intentional with your nonwork time: schedule in exercise, family time, professional development, and community leadership.
- Use technology to help. A smartphone and a tablet can help you be more responsive. More importantly, they can help you monitor your online business wherever—and whenever—you choose.
- Choose to spend your time on the highest value activities. Before starting a particular activity, ask yourself if there is a higher value activity that you really should be doing. If you do this before you sit down in front of the TV, you would probably watch a lot less of it.

Keeping just a few of these things in mind during your transition can reduce your stress—and increase your chance of success.

Consider the Entire Business Cycle

Every business follows a cycle, and online businesses are no different. There is a specific value chain from the availability of a product or service, to the ultimate delivery to a customer. Your value chain should include the following:

- Ensure availability of your product or service (by manufacturing it, buying it from someone else, or having service hours available)
- Marketing (finding your customers)
- Sales (getting customers to complete transactions, and collecting the money from them)
- Delivering the product or service

Underneath these steps are accounting and finance, human resources, and technology.

Each of these items—which also will appear in your business plan—needs to be set up. If you design a wonderful website to sell a wonderful product, you won't be successful unless you think about how to drive people to the site—marketing. And if you forget to ask people what they want (marketing again), you might not even be selling the right products! At the beginning, if you're not sure what to do, spend some time brainstorming with friends and family. Later chapters will fill in many of the blanks if you're still not sure.

Take Alternative Approaches

How many routes are there between your home and your favorite store? Likely quite a few. Some are faster, others are more picturesque, and yet others avoid major streets. No one is better than the other; the appropriateness of a route depends on you. Likewise, there is more than one way to build a business online, each with its pros and cons:

Start-up: A pure start-up is very much like a completely blank page. As the founder, you can draw on that page whatever you like. You choose the products, market, channels, and marketing approach. You provide the initial financing, the website design, even the name of the company. You can do it by yourself, or if you prefer, do it with a partner. Pros? You have complete control over everything. Cons? Complete control might be overwhelming, and even riskier if you don't have a wide background.

Franchise: There are a number of companies that have a template for an online business that you need only purchase rights to, and they will provide you with a manual and training on their processes. Typically, they will have a ready-built website where they simply slot in your information; they will do the online advertising, e-commerce, and product delivery.

ESSENTIAL

A franchise business is a significant investment, and should be looked at as such. Take the term sheet/franchise agreement to an attorney who is experienced in franchise law for a review.

Seek out others who are in the system, and ask about their experience and their financial success (or lack of it). Again you have pros: a ready-built, proven business, where you need only slot in your time and energy to be successful. And you have cons: you are constrained by what is in the agreement, and cannot go beyond it. For example, you may not be able to do separate online advertising or use the logo offline, without explicit permission.

Purchase: Sometimes it is easier to get into a business that is already running than to start one from scratch. There are two types of purchases: financial purchases, and strategic ones. Financial purchases are relatively simple: the value that you add is purely financial. A strategic purchase can add something else: for example, connections into another market, functional expertise, better technology, a flow of web traffic, or low cost products. Strategic purchasers will always pay more than financial ones, as they see synergistic value in the business. This suggests a key purchase criteria for you: what kind of online business can take advantage of your special strengths? Or said another way, how can you be a strategic purchaser?

One of the biggest challenges to buying an online business is the price. To get around this, you may consider purchasing an online business that is failing—then do a turnaround, or use the assets to kick-start a completely new business. Pros? No start-up pain—you can focus on accelerating an already-functioning business, instead of starting from scratch. Cons? Price, and the risk of unknown legal skeletons in the closet.

Hybrid Offline-Online Businesses

The best example of an offline-online business may be in the world of retail. Amazon.com is 100 percent online-based, and uses this setup to drive a price advantage. A hybrid strategy is one where you take your offline business and add an online component. Both Barnes & Noble and Best Buy also have an online channel—but they use their bricks-and-mortar advantage to let customers pick up their purchases in store.

Adding a Sales Channel

People come to your real-world store, so why not provide an online storefront as well? Companies purchase your products from your salespeople, so why shouldn't you also offer a direct purchase experience over the web? Many business owners know that it makes sense to broaden their sales channels, but sometimes forget about the effort required in doing so. For example, if your customer's purchase experience requires some consultation with a salesperson, this aspect of the sale needs to be duplicated online. Sometimes it can be automated using technology, and sometimes it requires people (and time) on an ongoing basis.

Adding a Delivery Channel

Many businesses are strapped for money because of the high cost of maintaining inventory. If you sell a digital product, you might be able to deliver it online at practically no cost. When was the last time you purchased a CD or rented a DVD? Once sold only through specialized stores, many people now purchase their music and movies through iTunes.com or Netflix.com. Books are now also going digital, through the Kindle, Kobo, Nook, and iBookstore. Beyond the savings to your business in dollars (reduced inventories, etc.), digital delivery can save valuable time and there are no time-consuming logistics to consider.

What Got You There Will Not Get You Here

Particularly for existing businesses, there needs to be a recognition that online truly adds another dimension to the business. What was successful offline may not work over the web. Some differences, adapted from the author's "Make It Happen Tipsheet" at *www.budurl.com/randallcraigtips* include:

- Online customer expectations are very high, especially for problem resolution. Twitter has added an expectation of immediacy.
- Customer service agents need to be as connected online as they are over the phone. This means adding both technology and training.
- The geography for sales may be far wider. Your online business, including your customer service, may need to cater to customers in several languages and across several time zones.
- Social media means that word travels fast—for the good or for the bad. Connecting with prospects and customers beyond your site—and monitoring their conversations—is the only way to influence the buzz.
- Advertising is often performance based: pay-per-click does not exist offline. To take advantage of this add-on requires time both for planning and for monitoring.

One way to triangulate on the differences between online and offline customer service is to ask your current customers.

Not everyone already has an offline business they can build online, so where might an idea for a new business come from? Sometimes the business possibilities walk in the front door, surprising you. Other times you find entrepreneurial success only after you have been walked out the door because of a layoff. And sometimes a change in the economy breeds new business ideas. In the next chapter, we will explore more options—and opportunities—for finding the right path.

CHAPTER 3

When Opportunity Knocks

Sometimes a business opportunity thunders into your life when you're not expecting it. A corporate downsizing that leaves you jobless may place you in the position to consider starting a business. Or perhaps you have created a unique product and want to find a way to bring it to market. Maybe a close friend or colleague taps you on the shoulder and asks you to join her in a business endeavor. Sometimes all the planning in the world yields nothing, and then when you least expect it, opportunity knocks. This chapter reviews your options: what are the different opportunities that might come your way?

The Upside to Downsizing

Young people entering the work force today can expect a career that takes them through many different phases and employers. This experience is in sharp contrast to their grandparents, who may have had the stability of joining a firm right out of school and retiring from the same place with a tidy pension forty years later.

Many companies have come to recognize that the only way to compete is to specialize—to stick to their knitting. Anything that isn't core to their business is either minimized or outsourced. You might be surprised by what is being outsourced: mailroom services; payroll processing and other human resource (HR) functions, including coaching; technical support; IT operations and development; customer service; even sales. While these changes have meant layoffs that were personally hurtful and economically disruptive, the entrepreneur smells opportunity. Think about it. Is there a way that you can approach other businesses to offer an online version of a service they no longer wish to "own" internally? (The answer is . . . of course!)

FACT

One thing's for sure, there is no shame in being laid off due to a corporate downsizing or merger. So many people have gone through this mill that it is commonly accepted as not being a poor reflection on you or your performance. Sometimes it is just bad luck.

So what to do if you are one of the thousands of people who find themselves the star of an unplanned farewell party? There are two broad answers to this question: keep doing what you were doing, or do something new.

Option One: Stick with It

After being laid off, you will probably consider looking for another job in your field. But to get something at the same level or better may require relocating. If you are not currently burdened with real estate, kids in school, or other major commitments, this may be just the excuse you have needed to see another part of the country—or the world, for that matter.

Perhaps you want to continue in your field but cannot, or do not want to, make a major move to a different area. This could be a great time to review your skills and experiences and transform yourself into an independent provider of services. You may even be able to get hired as a subcontractor by the very firm that turned you out. While these are not "online business" options, you should consider them if you are not yet ready to take the leap into the entrepreneurial pool.

Most likely you would start off by offering your own services. Say you were a marketing manager for a consumer products company. Throughout your tenure you were building relationships with advertising agencies, members of the media, printers, convention centers, travel agents, and hotels. So, without missing a beat, you have a full contact list of talented and reliable vendors you can put to work immediately for your own customers. It may even make sense to join forces with some of these vendors and create a new, more compelling marketing firm. Once you have that business figured out, the next step would be to determine if part of the services, or part of the marketing, should be delivered online.

Option Two: Radical Change

Have you ever found yourself driving in the country on a beautiful fall day thinking, wouldn't it be great to chuck it all and run a charming bed and breakfast? Or maybe the secret chemist side of you has been watching the aging baby boomers drop serious money on youth-restoring creams and you are thinking, "I could do that." Or maybe you had an idea for a special website: the next YouTube or Twitter. Well, that pink slip has now freed you to get started on what has only been a niggling idea until now.

ESSENTIAL

If you're planning to make a radical shift with your new venture into a new area for you, fear not. In our information-rich world, you will be able to get whatever background you need to start your new undertaking and make it flourish. Doing some market research and going on a test-drive can help.

Making a big change is scary, especially when you didn't plan the change. However, you may be ready to stop working sixty hours a week for someone else and do it for yourself. When you are the boss you only need to look in the mirror to see if it is okay to leave for a few hours to go watch your child's performance.

Your Idea, Someone Else's Know-How

If you perform a specialized task day in and day out, whether it's kidney surgery or installing copper gutters, you are naturally going to find ways to improve your efficiency. You may even have designed a special device that improves your work and could help others carry out the task as well. If you are a medical professional or a contractor, you may not have the time or resources to organize all the steps necessary to convert your idea to a marketable product. However, there are folks out there who are seeking ideas to bring to market.

Your widget may seem like a small miracle to you, but will it sell? Some market analysis will determine whether enough customers would buy it to make commercialization worthwhile. Or, you may find a company related to your field that will purchase your design and pay you a royalty for it.

It's great to have a service idea that can relieve a business owner of part of the administration duties of running a company. Getting another group to help sell your idea is better. Say you have a payroll service that small businesses can use instead of hiring a full-time bookkeeper. Marketing directly to the 50,000 or so small businesses in America is a great idea. But what if you created a website that automates part of the process, and licensed a branded version of the site to accounting firms?

Taking the Family Business Reins

It's possible that your future career was settled before you were born. However, not all children of business owners can expect to take over a multibillion-dollar enterprise. Some folks will have to look hard at taking over the local gas station that has been in the same family for three generations or joining a law practice with one or both parents. Consider some of the advantages of running the family business:

- It is an established business.
- It has an established clientele.
- It is known and valued in the community.
- There can be tax advantages as opposed to selling and distributing proceeds.
- Family members should be more naturally vested in the success of the business.
- It is possible to learn all aspects of the business before committing to take over.

The goal of passing a business on to the next generation is to preserve wealth, and possibly to provide employment for family members. An estate planner, an accountant, and an attorney all need to be involved in the planning.

ALERT

You never want to make big life decisions in the throes of a crisis. The choice to take over a family business should be unhurried and dispassionate, rather than in the immediate aftermath of a death.

Before deciding to join a family business, ask the following questions:

- How will equity be determined?
- Will family members who work in the business have the same stake as those who do not?
- To what degree, if any, will the older generation remain involved?
- When and how will the transition take place?
- Is there an escape clause if a sibling wants to sell shares?
- Are in-laws factored into shares of the business—how about after divorce?
- What will the decision-making process be as the company goes forward?

One idea that may appeal to you is to run an online offshoot of the business: sales, online partnerships, or customer service. If the online business route hasn't been done yet, growing and managing this new offshoot will not upset the traditional hierarchy (or family dynamics). In addition, your success will build respect and credibility for you in the eyes of your family and colleagues.

Business Brokers Shop for You

Although there are professional business brokers, a banker, attorney, or other party can just as easily put buyers and sellers together informally. Being involved with your local chamber of commerce can help you gently get the word to prospective sellers that you are interested in making a purchase.

Beyond business brokers, investment banks are hired to facilitate sales of larger, usually publicly traded firms. They command correspondingly gargantuan fees. No matter who you use, be prepared to provide some form of compensation to them.

Know What's Hot

Many web entrepreneurs want to bring the newest ideas to market—whether it's a nifty real-world gadget or a unique web service. The difference between the long-term winners and losers has less to do with what is hot at the moment than what will serve a continuing need in the marketplace.

You know your business—have you noticed any new or growing segments of your audience? Are customers asking for something new? Or something old, delivered in a new way? Check out the competition to see what new services or products they're offering. Read industry blogs, magazines, and trending Twitter topics. Identifying an emerging trend that has staying power can be your best bet for a new business in a crowded field.

How Green Can You Be?

One trend that seems to be here for the long term is sensitivity to the environment. Being green is smart on many levels. As you consider your new business, going green will color decisions from the type of light bulbs you use, to the kind of car you drive, to where your products are manufactured. It will determine how "virtual" your business is, to whether your web hosting company is powered by renewable energy. From a marketing perspective you will want to assure your prospects and customers about your commitment to sustainability. For now, this will be a differentiating factor for your company. While the example of "green" was used to showcase a hot trend, you can substitute any concept or set of concepts that you think may have current traction: cloud computing and Voice over Internet Protocol (VoIP) are but two other examples.

Looking outside at the business environment is one way to come up with a business idea. But for many people, looking inside—at their personal experience—is more effective. After all, if you are the expert, surely there is a way to sell your knowledge or services online?

why build my own business instead of selling my ideas?

CHAPTER 4

Meet the Expert: You

How credentialed do you need to be to prove you can do the job? Perhaps you only need to be a graduate of the "university of hard knocks," where your life experiences give you the knowledge you need. Yet, if a person is going to do business with you, there cannot be a shred of doubt that you can deliver the goods.

There are many, many examples of tech leaders who may not have lots of letters after their names, but have many numbers in their bank accounts: Michael Dell, Bill Gates, and the late Steve Jobs are but just a few. Bringing your experience, energy, and drive to your new endeavor will move you toward your goal, but you may also need degrees or certifications to demonstrate your expertise. Whether or not you have a degree, you do need to find a way to amplify your experience and knowledge out to the market. This chapter suggests a number of ways to do this; yes, with degrees and certifications, but also through article marketing, blogging, and speaking.

Highlight Your Track Record

If you are starting a business that is a direct offshoot of an industry you have worked in for some time, you will be strengthened by the experience you gained talking the talk and walking the walk in that field. No matter what level of responsibility you had, you will have been exposed to the issues of your particular company in the context of that industry. All of that experience is logged in your brain, ready for you to tap into with your new business.

Begin an organized inventory of your experience. As you make an honest assessment of what you know, you need to acknowledge your weak spots, and then begin the task of filling in the gaps. Engage someone who has a bit more experience in your field as a mentor. Any number of folks can furnish you with different perspectives, and many of them will also offer a more extensive knowledge base.

ESSENTIAL

When looking for a mentor, try to find a person who is not only knowledgeable in his field but who also knows you. This person should be able to give you credible feedback on your plans and your suitability to undertake the business you've chosen.

As you have identified your experience, it's important to start building your reputation online—LinkedIn is a great place to start—so that when other people check you out, they will be satisfied that you are more than just a person with ideas.

The key to success is to not hold back. Stop dreaming, and get going with the preparations that will launch your entrepreneurial career. The knowledge, expertise, and experience that you bring to the table as an individual business owner is the yeast in the dough. If you do not already have these traits, you will gain them through hard work, education, and using the experience around you.

Licenses and Certifications

Various types of professionals—from doctors and lawyers to electricians and plumbers—are regulated by their own professions, as well as by the government and municipalities. If you are in one of these professions, you absolutely must have the licenses required. An advantage to licenses and certifications is that they often require you to uphold certain ethical standards; this may be a selling point for you relative to the competition.

Before committing to investing in special licenses or certifications, research what these credentials will do for you. In some cases you may want to complete a training program or earn a college or advanced degree for your own self-esteem. This is great, and it very often does the trick. But take a look at the cold, hard facts to see if a few more years of work in the field will achieve the same economic impact just as easily.

FACT

If you are a development professional for nonprofit organizations, there are specialized MBA programs that target this field. If you are planning to become an independent development professional, you may decide this is an important credential to support your expertise. Similarly, other industry-specific programs abound. Check them out.

Advanced Degrees

Since you are preparing to start a business you may have considered getting a master's degree in business administration (MBA), if you do not already have one. Once considered a most distinctive and career-advancing degree, the almighty MBA has become somewhat ubiquitous. Nevertheless, it may be an important step to improving your standing as an expert in your field, giving you an edge over your competition. Shop around to find a program best suited to you.

One of the advantages of working toward an MBA is that most programs require you to do projects in each course on a real (or planned) business. By doing the projects on your own soon-to-be business, you get an easy double-dip: you need to do the legwork anyway, so why not get a degree at the same time.

Whatever industry you choose to set your stake in, know the landscape. Even though you are not looking for a job because you plan to be self-employed, it is useful to know the industry norms. You can also do this by looking at your competitors: what degrees, certifications, and licenses do their managers (or owners) have?

Many community and junior colleges offer programs in everything from interior design to running a funeral home. There is no fluff here, only the concrete, specific topics needed to get you going. Plus, many colleges can assist you in getting internships in your field of choice, which may lead you to clients over time. The financial investment at a community college will be a lot easier to swallow than at an elite Ivy League school. It is up to you to weigh the relative advantages of any educational option.

How Many Letters Do You Need after Your Name?

There are a number of reasons to consider pursuing individual certification or industry accreditation. At the very minimum, it is a reflection of your willingness to make the effort to prepare for and be tested on your industry's objective standards for competency. Certification usually requires a combination of having worked in an industry for a minimum number of years, taking several courses, and passing an exam.

QUESTION

What is the difference between certification and accreditation?
Certification applies to individuals. Accreditation applies to organizations. You can be certified in your field, while your company can be accredited. Certification validates you as holding the threshold of experience and knowledge to perform competently. Your company is measured for its structural competencies in how it delivers goods and services to the market.

There are many advantages to being accredited or certified. When weighing whether to pursue these credentials or not, consider the following things that these qualifications will allow you to do:

- Create a competitive marketing advantage by differentiating yourself or your company from competitors.
- Deliver services more efficiently and profitably to your customers.
- Increase your professionalism within the industry.
- Stay current with industry trends and requirements.
- Evaluate your own core competencies against nationally recognized standards and best practices.
- Enhance and motivate individual performance.
- Participate in extensive peer-level communication and networking opportunities. These conversations happen at member-only events, and member-access-only web forums. Your "letters" are your ticket in.

Many people haven't taken formal education for many years so earning a qualification can get your mind back in gear. And earning a few extra letters after your name certainly helps boost your ego.

Be sure that the certifying or accrediting organization is credible. Especially online, there are many fraudsters who have dreamed up their own certifications, and are making money by duping unsuspecting registrants.

Get on the Speaker Circuit

It can be intimidating, if not downright scary, to stand before a sea of faces—even a very small sea of ten to fifteen of your colleagues—and hope that what comes out of your mouth is coherent. It may be worth getting over this anxiety: when you can address a group about a topic in which you have extensive knowledge, you join that all-important group of people known as experts.

The fact that you are talking to a group does not make you smarter; it makes them smarter. And the smarter they get about what you know, the more valuable you become. Some people actually morph into paid professional speakers in their area of expertise. If that is the case with you, then selling your expertise online (books, videos, coaching, etc.) as an adjunct to the paid presentation can significantly improve your bottom line. And what you sell online reinforces your reputation as someone who should be hired to speak.

FACT

Public speaking is a skill that can be acquired through practice. Organizations such as Toastmasters International specialize in training on the basics; if you are interested in the business of being a paid professional speaker, connect with the Global Speakers Federation and your local chapter of the National Speakers Association. Both groups also provide training opportunities.

It is not enough to have a solid knowledge base. You have to be able to get information across in an appealing way. Unfortunately, not everyone was standing in the charisma line when gifts were being doled out through DNA. That doesn't mean you can't be a credible presenter with a bit of training and a lot of practice, however. The more folks see and hear you, the more your business reputation will be enhanced, and at the end of the day, this should bring you more customers.

Perhaps speaking publicly is your aspiration, or perhaps it may evolve for you. Until that day, opportunities to speak about what you know should be looked at as another way of solidifying your credentials as an expert.

Blog Your Way to the Head of the Pack

Today, millions of people are reading and writing opinions using blogs or video logs (vlogs). While some are low-value rants, others are well-written, make coherent points, and bring a perspective others are eager to read. This may be an excellent way for you to make a name for yourself in your field, and implicitly drive business to your online venture. There are even websites that show you how to establish your own blog. Here is a six-step, no-cost course delivered through e-mail: *www.budurl.com/strategicblogging.*

If you write about your observations of trends in your field, you will get people thinking. While viewers are thinking about your observations, they will become familiar with your name and your business. You will have established yourself as an authority in your field. This can only help draw customers. It can also give you something tangible to offer when you are pitching new business.

Submit Unsolicited Articles

Every imaginable activity, profession, or endeavor has an association that nurtures the interests of that group. Within all of these special interests will be newsletters, less frequently in traditional ink and paper, more commonly online. Many have regular writers, but there is always an interest in editorials, or even guest columnist submissions. Whether you are launching a jewelry line on the Internet or selling online coaching, you have something to say about it.

It might seem like a distraction from your core mission to begin writing articles that may or may not be accepted, but consider the possibilities. If a publication thinks enough of your point of view to publish or post it, then certainly a prospective customer will too.

One thing that you should be wary of are so-called engines that will submit your article to hundreds of online article directories. While it is true that someone might see it when they are looking through a particular directory, Google frowns on duplicate content (they think it may be web spam), and they penalize the search engine rankings for those who do it.

CHAPTER 5

Finding That Killer Idea

Business dreams come in all shapes and sizes, and making one come true is an experience that can take many forms. You might be stepping into your family's firm, buying a franchise, launching a web storefront, or selling your time online. In any case, you'll need to understand what you are in for.

All You Need Is One Great Idea

Starting up a business requires some levelheaded thinking about risks and rewards, in addition to a lot of careful planning. Many individuals feel drawn to starting a business because they see a problem that needs a solution. For just a moment, put aside all the research that you'll need to do to determine whether your business venture appears worthwhile. Dream about a perfect world in which your business is sure to be a success. Ask yourself the following questions:

- What is it that you really enjoy doing?
- What would give you a sense of satisfaction?
- What type of business would make you proud?
- Did you want to do it with partners, or all by yourself?
- What type of business could you immerse yourself in for fifty, sixty, or seventy hours a week?
- Do you want to run a full-time business or a sideline, part-time business?
- Do you see yourself in an office? Online only? In a storefront location? Working from home?

Once you've painted a mental picture of your perfect world, the next step is to start applying it to real market conditions and your personal situation. Questions to ask yourself at this stage include:

- What would you enjoy doing every day that could be profitable?
- Will people pay for this service or the products you want to sell?
- How much financial backing do you think you can get?
- What is your risk tolerance level?
- How much of your money can you afford to invest?
- What resources can you gather to run a business?

Design the perfect business scenario for yourself. If, after three to four years, you find yourself in a situation that's close to what you pictured, then you've done very well indeed. After all, since we aren't living in a perfect world, you can't expect the scenario to play out precisely as you envisioned.

For some people, the right business is centered around a practical skill, such as sewing, carpentry, or cooking, while for others it is based on knowledge or expertise in a technical area. If you are thinking about starting a business based on your skills, surround yourself with people, articles, books, blogs, magazines, and anything else you can find to support you in areas where your skills don't reach. Take classes. Join an organization or association. The idea is to get yourself immersed in this area of interest and determine whether it is a hobby or something you really want to pour your heart, soul, and money into: the concept of a test-drive is particularly valuable.

ALERT

People who've become successful in business often forget to look back at their initial dream and realize how close they are. They focus on the 30 percent they haven't accomplished and neglect to see the 70 percent they have. Always remember that most successful big businesses grow step by step.

An interesting way to find a business idea is to look at businesses in other states and countries. Are there any concepts that you can bring to your local area? Is there something being done in a non-English speaking country that, with a few tweaks and some translation, can form the basis of your new enterprise?

Meanwhile, you also need to be looking at the marketplace. You may love to do something that is either too narrow in scope to make money at, or so popular that other people with the same ideas have already dominated the market.

Make Sure Your Idea Can Be Profitable

The sad truth is that your dream venture may in fact not be financially viable. Before going too far down the primrose path, you need to answer some hard questions to determine whether your idea will actually work. Find out how big the market is for the product or service you are envisioning. Be sure to look at comparable products and try to learn all you can about the costs for producing, promoting, and delivering them to the marketplace. Try to learn what kind of net profit margins exist in that industry. Take the time to write a business plan. (More on business plans later.)

When you are determining if your undertaking can be profitable, you will want to figure out your overall strategy. Will you be competing on price? On selling a unique product or service? Or perhaps competing on another dimension, such as responsiveness, quality, or after-sales service? The challenge of an online business is that it is easy to make comparisons on some dimensions (price), but hard to compare on others. Your strategy—and your brand—need to convey clearly what differentiates you. Then you will need to research the market carefully to ensure that the strategy really can generate a profit.

Buy a Proven Winner

Sometimes the fastest way to get going in business is to buy a business that is already profitable. However, you will need to do some due diligence before signing on the dotted line. As you weigh this option, consider the following pros and cons:

PROS

- No start-up phase
- Possibly big savings in start-up costs
- Existing client base
- Technology in place
- Going concern in marketplace
- Goodwill already established
- Management and staff already hired
- Supplier and other vendor relationships already in place
- May be able to purchase only the assets you want and not assume liabilities
- Immediate cash flow
- Easier financing opportunities as an existing business

CONS

- Why are they selling? There may be hidden skeletons in the closet that the current owners are running away from
- Old receivables may be hard to collect

- Customers may not be loyal to business
- Business may be in a dying industry
- Technology may need to be replaced
- May be locked into bad long-term contracts
- May be more costly than starting from scratch
- Takes time and money to research opportunities of good value
- Relocation may be necessary for you and your family
- May be difficult to change established reputation—good or bad—in the market

The process of due diligence is critical if you are thinking of buying, and you shouldn't do it alone. Your team should include your accountant and your attorney, so they can address accounting and legal risks. Team members should include an experienced technology architect, who can examine the company's technology. A marketing expert can objectively examine the proven winner's marketing strategy, and an HR expert can evaluate the quality of the team. Finally, you will want to have someone who is experienced in transactions, who can guide you through the process. While this sounds quite complicated, it need not be. The amount of due diligence that is done depends on the size of the transaction. Smaller transactions are usually smaller risk, and therefore may not need the same level of review.

One of the more difficult questions in the online business world is what defines a proven winner? Is it cash flow, the number of transactions per month, or the number of eyeballs? Twitter, for example, has almost no revenue, but generates a significant amount of traffic that eventually will be monetized. Wikipedia is a not-for-profit organization, but has tens of millions content pages. Or maybe buying a proven winner is not the best option at all. What about buying a dying business cheaply, turning it around (because of your special skills or connections), and then selling it at a profit? Connecting what you want to do with why you want to buy is critical.

One way to answer many of the questions addressed in this chapter is to talk to other people. They may be experts in the industry, functional gurus, or people who are connected with a sector of interest. At the same time, spending time networking with others is a great way to get the word out about your new enterprise. But where can you meet these people, both in the real world and online?

CHAPTER 6

Networking

There is no point in having a business if you're not letting the world know about it. Besides the usual promotions, ads, signs, direct mail, online newsletters, Tweets, Facebook posts, and blog entries, you have a very important secret weapon to ensure your success—you! Make the effort to participate in as many industry and business organizations as time permits and you will unlock the door to learning more in your field and drawing more customers to your business.

Join Your Tribe

Eagles fly with eagles. Fish swim with fish. What tribe are you part of? Do you spend time with people who do similar things to you? Maybe you have a knack for coordinating paint colors and fabrics. Friends have admired your clever touch and have sought your advice for years. Friendly inquiries are beginning to evolve into referrals to people you don't even know. Now you are on the brink of becoming a professional interior designer. Your talent is certain. You have ferreted out great resources for fabric and trim, but you could use some advice on finding the best workrooms to produce your designs.

You won't get that question answered in the yellow pages. But if you look into the relevant national professional group, in this case the American Society of Interior Designers (ASID), you will garner all kinds of helpful information about the industry you are entering. All fields have these vertical groups. Many have requirements for membership that you may need time and experience to gain. Even if you are ineligible to join, you may be able to attend their monthly meetings and annual conventions as a guest. And if they have an "open" LinkedIn group, you may even be able to participate in their online conversations.

ESSENTIAL

If you can't find a local membership group in your field, start one! There may be a national organization already in place and you could be the initiator to launch a local chapter. The national group can provide guidance for standards to be met for membership, how to establish bylaws, and other helpful information to make a go of it.

Also remember there's no limit to the number of professional organizations or societies you can join. As long as you can handle the membership dues and time commitments, join away! Having your name appear in more places—and developing relationships and reputation—can only help you get exposure for your business.

Join Organizations with Your Prospective Customers and Suppliers

While joining organizations with your peers is great for professional support, joining groups that have your prospective customers can be even more powerful. Here is where they will talk about the challenges and problems that they are having. You can use this information either to guide your own product development, or if you have a product or service already developed, as a source of business leads.

Joining groups that contain potential suppliers also has benefits: learning about upcoming trends and new products can help reduce your cost of delivery. Suppliers also will get business leads: if they know you and trust you, they will pass these leads to you.

Civic Organizations

If your business is serving your local community, you need to be known locally. Besides listing your number in the yellow pages, registering your business address with Google and Bing and running ads in local media, you need to be visible as a person beyond the doors of your establishment. A great way to accomplish this is by joining a local civic organization such as Rotary, Lions, or the chamber of commerce. Coming to know your fellow business owners will provide a type of camaraderie that is just not available with your employees. You can share ideas about business operations or local market conditions. And you can find out about upcoming legislation and regulatory change, sometimes even before it happens.

FACT

The biggest advantage to belonging to a local civic organization may be the chance to collaborate with others in promoting your individual businesses. Maybe you can join together in a series of online advertisements focused on a local event in your neighborhood. Maybe, as a group you can organize an online contest that requires purchases (or visits) at each business's website.

Typically these groups meet monthly, and feature a speaker on a topic of general interest to the group. These meetings may also give you the inside track on what is happening with your competitors. Another retailer may be about to launch a major new website; or a national chain might be moving into your area with a major marketing push, driving people from your online business to theirs. Knowledge is power, and sometimes the local grapevine is the quickest way to get the information you need.

Associations and Organizations

In addition to trade groups, you will likely be able to find a society or association for virtually any profession or interest group whose goal is to support its members with some or all of the following:

- Industry updates
- Continuing education
- Certification programs
- Government relations—or lobbying—on your industry's behalf
- Group purchasing discounts
- Customer leads
- Marketing support
- Online discussion forums
- Leadership programs

There is even an association of associations, called the American Society of Association Executives, which can provide you with information on local and national associations for your field. Visit their website at *www .asaenet.org*. If you are in Canada, the Canadian Society of Association Executives provides similar information, at *www.csae.com*.

Industry Awards

One way to stand out from the crowd in your field is to be designated a star by winning an industry award. The Academy of Motion Picture Arts and Sciences has the Oscar. Broadway has the Tony. Your field likely has a means to recognize excellence as well. Often, these awards are established by the professional association or society for a particular industry. Categories such as best practices, marketing, advertising, and more are established, criteria are set, and deadlines imposed for submission. Judging is done by a group of experts in the field. In some cases awards are earned after meeting certain criteria—without any competition.

Just starting out in a new business, you may not be able to go for an industry award right away. Yet, you may be able to bring past glories along with you. If you earned "the President's Award" for three straight years while working for your former employer, there is no reason you cannot toot your own horn and feature these awards in your ads and promotions. These awards differentiate you: who wouldn't want an award-winner instead of Mr. Average?

It will take some research to learn how awards are given in your field and by whom. Once you know the categories, guidelines, and submission requirements, don't hesitate to get your business compliant and ready to apply. If you need to be nominated, find out how to go about it. There is no reason to be shy about letting the world know you have been recognized as the top salesperson, most accurate analyst, or source for the city's best chocolate turtles. One caveat: make sure that the awarding organization is legitimate. In the early web days just about every site sported a logo proclaiming that it was the "best of the web."

Everyone loves a winner, and many local newspapers and magazines run readers' choice contests in just about every category of business imaginable. These truly are popularity contests and are not based on any industry standards. Often several levels of awards are issued—gold, silver, bronze, etc.—thus many businesses wind up with bragging rights. Really aggressive businesses will ask their patrons to vote for the business rather than sit back and hope it makes it on its great products and services alone. There is nothing wrong with asking for votes, as long as you don't try to "buy" them.

Professional Networking Groups

A professional networking group is structured to help members generate leads. To make it worthwhile to join, the group may restrict membership to only one person per field. If you own a printing company you would be happy to meet with owners of many other businesses, from caterers to sales trainers, because they are all going to need printed materials: menus, manuals, or, at a minimum, business cards. You wouldn't like it if your networking group included other printers who would be going after the same business.

Here are a few places to find a local networking group: *www.bni.com*, *www.letip.com*, and *www.LeadsClub.com*. Before committing to one of these, ask to attend as a visitor to make sure that the types of attendees, and the local chapter's "culture," fits with your needs. And be aware of the fine print: some networking groups require that you attend a minimum number of sessions, or you lose your membership.

There is no limit to networking groups—should one be closed to your particular niche, another can certainly be found. You might even seek one in a locale you are contemplating expanding into as a way of gaining some entrées. And, just as with local chapters of national professional organizations and societies, if you can't find a professional networking group in your area, start one!

Volunteering as a Strategy to Meet New Customers

When you join a professional society, a civic organization, or a professional networking group, you are looking to gain knowledge or new business in your field. If you become active in one of these organizations, you may join one or more committees and offer your services as a volunteer for the advancement of the group.

There are also plenty of other volunteer opportunities that may draw customers to your business as a result of your visibility in these nonprofessional groups. A few examples might be:

- Hospitals
- Youth groups
- Disease/health charities such as the American Cancer Society
- Disaster/relief groups such as the American Red Cross
- Houses of worship
- Cultural institutions
- Schools
- Alumni organizations
- Public affairs groups, such as the League of Women Voters or the Democratic or Republican Party
- Amateur sporting events

Some groups require membership to participate in their volunteer opportunities, but most are just happy to have willing people help out. In either case you may be able to help the organization by contributing "in kind," meaning that you would contribute goods or services from your business instead of money. Whatever method you choose, volunteering will serve to expand your knowledge and experience, as well as get your name on the map.

Social Networking Sites

The greatest benefit of the Internet is that it can wire people and ideas together, regardless of where they are physically located. No longer must networking take place in specific physical locations, or even at specific times. Social networking can be used for games, photos, and family correspondence, but if you are looking to start an online business, social networking sites such as the following should also be used for networking.

LinkedIn Groups

LinkedIn is the best-known professional networking site in the world, with over 160 million people participating, and with over 1.3 million groups. These groups have been created by associations, alumni groups, special interest groups, companies, and individuals. If there is something that you are interested in, it is likely that a group exists on the subject. Some of the groups require you to be approved before being let in—approval might be dependent on being a member in a real-world organization. Others are open for anyone to join.

To find out which groups might be relevant to you, think about what you are hoping to use the LinkedIn group to do. Connect with peers? Learn from prospective customers what their needs are, or maybe for competitive research? Then, within LinkedIn, search for groups that match. You'll be presented with a few pages of search results—it's just a matter of reading the summaries, and then applying to be a member of the relevant ones. You can be a member of up to fifty different groups.

One important note for whenever you join a new group: each is a bit different, with its own etiquette, culture, and rules. Spend some time figuring this out by reading posts and comments before contributing to the conversation yourself. In some groups, for example, if you are commercial and self-promotional, they will ban you from the group altogether.

Beyond the groups, LinkedIn is a powerful one-on-one networking tool. It allows you to catalog your connections, and see theirs. If your online business is service-based, and if it primarily revolves around you, then Linked-In is also an important way for others to find out about you. Fill in your profile, add your website, and start collecting endorsements.

Finally, don't forget to create a company profile in LinkedIn. It is free, and creates yet another touch point for prospective customers.

Twitter

It seems that this social networking site has coined an entirely new language: tweeting, twitterverse, hashtags, direct messages, followers, and @usernames. Don't stress about the jargon—or what Twitter is supposed to give you. The most important thing to know is that people are having short (140 character) conversations with others, and you can too. Here's how, in five easy steps:

1. **Sign up at Twitter.com, choose your Twitter name, and fill out your profile.** If you see a name that starts with the @ symbol, that indicates that it is a Twitter name. (For example, @RandallCraig.)
2. **Search for topics that interest you.** If you are interested in financing or marketing, search for those terms. You will see a number of conversations with those terms in them, as well as a number of Twitter users (often called "tweeple" or "tweeps") who have that term in their profile.
3. **Follow people who you are interested in networking with.** They will often follow you back, which allows both of you to send private Direct Messages to each other. A Direct Message is a Tweet that goes privately to a specific person, in contrast to a regular Tweet, that is open for everyone to see.
4. **Identify conversations that are relevant.** If you've noticed words with the "#" in front of them, these are called hashtags. The thinking is that if everyone who is having a conversation about a particular topic used the same hashtag, then it would be easy to follow the conversation just by searching for that hashtag. An example would be #ProspeakingTV.
5. **Grow your followers.** As you participate, and others see the value that you add to the conversation, they will begin to follow you. As more do, Twitter can be used not just to network, but also to reach out to prospective prospects, clients, and partners.

There are many different strategies for getting the most from your Twitter time. Check out *www.budurl.com/7twitterstrategies* for a number of them.

Facebook

Facebook is the biggest social networking site going, with more than a billion users from all around the world. Like LinkedIn, there are two primary activities that you will want to do: build up your profile and begin the networking conversation with others.

One of the more confusing parts of Facebook for newcomers is the difference between a personal profile and a fan page. When you sign up, by default you get a personal profile. You can choose who sees it, and what goes on it. Once you have the profile, you can create a Facebook fan page, which is for the "corporate you." Even if no one is yet your fan, developing a fan page means that people have a place to check out your business. When they "like" the fan page (e.g., become a fan), everyone in their network will then be exposed to you. What this suggests is that to attract fans, you need to give them something of value. It can be a discount, more immediate customer support, a way to interact with you, or even funny product pictures.

Beyond creating your own community around your fan page, search for the fan pages from your customers, competitors, and places where your prospects spend their time. Participation will improve the awareness of your business—and your reputation.

Industry Forums and Discussion Groups

Beyond the main public social networks, there are a number of websites and discussion forums that have become today's de facto water coolers where everything in a particular industry is discussed. Searching for discussion groups on any particular topic is not difficult: just go to Google. Selling to frequent travelers? Go to *www.flyertalk.com* and learn about what is important to them. Selling to Volkswagen car enthusiasts? Go to *forums.vwvortex .com*. These are just two examples: each has many millions of posts, and thousands of users. Network away!

While you are networking, you will learn a significant amount about the industry, functional area, and competition. You will also begin to formulate a few key questions that need to be answered in order for you to be successful. Is there a market for my product or service? How do prospective customers make their purchase decision? What name would work best? This is where market research comes in.

CHAPTER 7

Researching the Market

Without a market for your service or product, your idea—and your business—will be dead in the water. Before going too far with your new venture, a little reality checking to make sure there will be clients for your new business is critical. In this chapter, you'll learn about basic market research, how to look critically at an industry, trends, and the impact of competition. Doing this will help you define your niche. This chapter also addresses two key questions: what should the business's name be, and how to determine the domain name for the website.

Conducting Market Research

How many people would be willing to purchase your widget? If you had unlimited time and money, you could ask everyone in the country. Since this is clearly not possible, market research techniques have evolved to answer this for you. Instead of asking the entire universe of potential purchasers, you can ask a small sample of people. If the sample is representative of your market, then the percentage of purchasers in the entire market can be estimated. This is not an exact science, but it can give you a far clearer idea of your prospects. (Political pollsters always account for the error by saying "the results are accurate plus-or-minus five percent, nineteen times out of twenty.")

How do you begin to do the research you need? A competitive market analysis by an expert would be terrific. However, you may not want to spend that kind of money to start a small business, although it wouldn't hurt to get quotes from a few market research firms. Naturally, the larger and more comprehensive the analysis, the more money you'll need to spend on it.

If you can't afford professional market research, an interesting alternative is the local business school. Many MBA programs require students to work on real-life projects with real-life businesses. Having the students do a market research project on your behalf means that you'll get an independent view of the feasibility of your project—at a price that is very right: zero. A second bonus: most MBA students are very tech savvy, and would likely find a project involving an online business more interesting than a traditional one.

You can also do your own market research. Some information sources include:

- Your local library, or any good business library, where there are numerous research volumes that will provide you with up-to-date data on companies, demographics, and market research.
- Business periodicals including *Forbes*, the *Wall Street Journal*, and numerous others.
- Trade publications and industry newsletters, so you can learn exactly what is going on in the industry before you jump in.
- Your local chamber of commerce or city hall records office or bureau, which can provide you with data on competitive businesses.
- Annual reports from other companies, which help you get an idea of what your own expenditures, income, and overall cash flow might

look like. If a company similar to your proposed venture has recently gone public, their prospectus or offering memorandum will have significant market data.

- The Internet, where you can get your hands on numerous facts and figures.
- Individual company websites, where you can find out what's going on with similar businesses.
- The Small Business Administration (SBA) at *www.sba.gov*. This site will give you tips on a range of topics from writing a business plan to securing low-interest loans.
- Other business owners, who can tell you what it's like as an entrepreneur.
- Associations with members in the same industry.

Some people assume that their business concept has to be completely original in order to be successful. Not true. How many pizza parlors are in your town? How many auto dealers? And if you search on Google for just about any business concept, you will probably find thousands.

If you are going to take on an existing business concept, you will need to differentiate your business to entice customers. Hotmail was the first e-mail provider that offered e-mail for free. Amazon offered free delivery if you spent a certain minimum. And WordPress.com offered free blogs. "Different" need not always mean free, but it is one way to stand out from your competition.

Assessing Your Potential Market

One of the first things to do is get an idea of the size of your potential market. Will you be catering to a specific market by selling a specialized product like booties for dogs, or will you be reaching a mass audience with a product like sun hats?

It's important to gauge the overall industry and where it's headed. Opening a business in an industry that's headed for a fall is an invitation to disaster. Conversely, you may find the hottest growing industry. Can you tailor your skills and passion to fit into an up-and-coming industry?

You also want to assess your competition. How many similar businesses are there? What companies are capturing the lion's share of the market? Is the field oversaturated? Can you carve a niche market from a larger one? What can you do to differentiate yourself from the competition? Study how well your potential competitors are already doing in the marketplace. Can you catch them napping and entice some of their customers to switch? Is there a way to learn from their mistakes—or successes?

As you conduct your research, look for substantial information that supports your idea and your business plan. If you do, then full steam ahead. But if all signs are negative, you may have just saved yourself from disaster.

Industry Trends

Besides looking at the dollar figures and competition within a certain industry, you should look at the trends. One way to do this is to use the PEST framework. PEST stands for Political/Economic/Social/Technological.

An economic trend, for example would be if you found that there have been a great number of layoffs from major nearby companies. There may be a greater need for outsourcing, because these companies still have tasks that need to get done. You might open a placement service for freelancers and contractors. You could also open up a resume-writing service or even start career coaching for people who are having interviews.

A social trend, for example, would be if more people in your neighborhood own dogs than ever before, there may be a need for pet care or pet accessories. If people are also traveling more frequently, then there may be a need for a kennel featuring doggie vacations. This might suggest starting your own doggie vacation website with some amenities that dog owners would find appealing for their pets.

Given that you are reading this book, you likely know about the trend toward online business. A specific technological trend would be the use of social media. Maybe you might open a business blogging for other businesses? Or reviewing products and selling advertisements on your review site? Or perhaps providing remote customer service through social media for large corporations?

If you look at the trends taking place around you, locally and nationally, you can start to think about specific market needs. Trends may illustrate needs in specific areas and point to voids that you might fill. The next step is to determine if the need is great enough that a business could profit by filling that void.

Also look at the overall economic climate to determine if the time is right for your business. A town experiencing layoffs and going through hard times will not be the best place for selling luxury items or extravagant services. Timing is everything.

ESSENTIAL

Be aware of the present, but focus on the future. It's to your advantage to be able to foresee demographic shifts and changes in the economic climate. If you can continue to structure and restructure your business in accordance with events in the world around you, you'll be able to stay on the cutting edge—or at least keep pace with the competition.

You can also use your own awareness as a consumer to find voids in the marketplace. If you're unhappy about having to drive ten miles to find a stationery store, then perhaps other people in your area are experiencing the same need for greeting cards and paper products. Conduct your own survey. Hand out 100 short questionnaires asking people where they buy greeting cards, stationery, and other such products, and whether they would shop at a store in their community if one opened. If 60 percent say they would, then you know there's a need for such a store. However, if 60 percent indicate they order cards and stationery goods online, then there may not be sufficient demand for a new bricks-and-mortar store. But there may be need for a better online one.

If you feel comfortable with technology, use a free or low-cost service like *www.SurveyMonkey.com* or *www.Zoomerang.com* to put together an online survey. Then send the survey link to your e-mail list and post on your social media profiles.

Here are some key questions to ask yourself:

- Who is your target market group?
- What does your research indicate that this group needs?
- How much will people pay for these goods or services?
- Will there be enough profit to make for a successful business venture?
- What trend or trends will be prevalent in the near future?
- What impact will these trends have on your target market group?
- Who is your competition and what are they offering or not offering?

- Based on current needs, upcoming trends, and the competition, what can you do to gain a competitive edge in the marketplace?

Trends reveal more than industry developments. They also represent changes in society. Are there more single-parent families that may need your services? Are more seniors buying certain health and vitamin products? Are more teens able to travel abroad than ever before?

Scout Out the Competition

To be competitive in the marketplace, you need to know exactly what the competition is doing. Therefore, if you're going to have the best craft website, you'd better see what the most popular sites are offering and figure out what you can offer to draw customers to your site. Gaining a competitive advantage can mean changing a particular style, image, packaging, or service; adding new products or functionality; changing the pricing structure; or trying a whole new look. Whatever the competition isn't doing well to draw customers is what you need to implement.

ALERT

Change for the sake of change doesn't work, so research what you think is a viable plan of action. When Coca Cola switched to New Coke, Pepsi did not respond with New Pepsi. They waited to see what the effect would be on Coke's business. It wasn't very good and New Coke disappeared. You may need to wait to see if your competition's bright idea is a hit or a dud.

Find Your Niche

Filling the right void in an industry can make you an industry giant. FedEx saw a need that either wasn't being addressed or aggressively marketed by another company: prompt overnight delivery. They stepped in, promoted overnight shipping, and eventually became industry giants. Naturally, you have to make good on your claims, but finding new ways to do something, make something, or sell something can put you in an advantageous position.

Once you find a competitive advantage or fill a void, you need to make sure to promote that fact. FedEx made it clear from the start that overnight shipping was its specialty.

FACT

Customer service can be the difference between beating the competition and lagging behind. Provide service that makes people want to return to your site and do business again. Not surprisingly, surveys show that customer service is a key competitive differentiator. It can be as simple as responding to e-mails within twenty-four hours (or four hours).

You might be able to corner an industry by becoming a specialist. City Bicycles NYC, for example, is one of a few small bike shops in Manhattan. Other stores may sell bikes, but this store is the definitive place to go for them, because it has expertise in that one area and a wider selection. While such a store might not succeed where only 3 percent of the population cares about bikes, 3 percent of New York City is a huge market. Add to that the fact that biking is a great way to stay fit and the owners have a successful business.

A typical mistake of many entrepreneurs is not to define their niche narrowly enough. Challenge yourself by asking this question: Can I focus even more than I currently do? For example, if you sell crafts online, perhaps you can focus yourself by saying that you sell sewing crafts online. Or sewing crafts online to women. Or sewing crafts online to young women. Or sewing crafts online to young women who are African American. The power of the niche is incredible: it means that you can focus on fewer products, a tighter prospect base, and more highly tuned advertising.

While it's always advantageous to beat the competition's prices, you may not be able to do so and still turn a profit. Instead, see if you can add value in other ways:

- Warranties or service plans
- Free repairs
- Gift-wrapping
- Free shipping
- Private sales for loyal customers
- Overnight delivery

- In-store pick-up for web orders
- Personalized attention
- Twenty-four-hour service
- A secure payment system online
- An affiliate program to pay customers for their referrals
- Product customization (engraving, color choice, etc.)

As your business grows, determine what you can do to improve service and customer relations. Keep track of what the competition is doing so that you don't miss anything that it's doing to innovate. It's no coincidence that every time one fast food chain has a movie tie-in promotion, its competition ties in with another hot movie. You need not go so far as to attack the competition, but always be ready to think of your next move. Remember, competition is like a chess match. Company A makes a move, then Company B needs to make a countermove, and so forth.

Name Your Business

Finding a name for your business isn't always as easy as it sounds. The right name can make the difference between success and mediocrity. Most importantly, a name helps clients find you! It's important that your name be:

- Short
- Easy to remember
- Easy to spell
- Easy to pronounce
- Original
- Defining

The first five entries on the list are self-explanatory, but the last one—defining—is the important quality that indicates what your business is all about. The names of Aunt Peggy's Bakery or Mrs. Field's Cookies not only tell you who makes the product, but more importantly, what is in the package. A website named "www.JustRedKites.com" not only tells you what it sells but what it doesn't (namely, anything else). However, "www.Jakes Corner.com" tells you absolutely nothing.

You can include a lot of information in a name, even a concise one. "Ace Overnight Delivery" clearly describes a delivery company that provides overnight service. If possible, it's advantageous to include a feature of your products or services in the name to give potential customers a heads-up on what you offer.

FACT

> Of course, many companies have simply used a common name, such as Wendy's or Uncle Ben's. If you can heavily promote a person's name that's easy to remember, you can also grab attention. People relate to the personal feeling that a name exudes.

More often than not, the best business name is something that sounds right to you. You'll probably consider numerous possibilities before coming up with the one you like best. Perhaps you'll include your own name, as Arthur Murray's Dance Studios does. For a law firm, it's customary to be more formal and use last names of the partners, such as "Steinman & Harris, Attorneys-at-Law," which sounds more professional than "Mark and Ted, Attorneys-at-Law," or "The Little Shop of Law." Keep in mind who your target audience is. Fun, trendy names may attract a young audience, while more formal names may be better suited for a conservative industry.

Sometimes using the name of your town or location draws attention and puts you one step ahead of your competitors. Yorktown Deli sounds like the official deli of the town, though it isn't. However, when looking for a deli in Yorktown, you may think of it first—and Google certainly does. Another tactic is to use the name associated with the town or city in which you're doing business. New York City, the Big Apple, is home to the Big Apple Circus, and you will likely find a Big Apple Cleaners or Big Apple Diner. New York is also known as the Empire State. So you'll find business names there that include the word "Empire," just as you'll find Washington, DC, businesses with "Capitol" in their names, or businesses in Texas using the words "Lone Star." The name you choose needs to be meaningful to your audience, but it also has to be meaningful for Google; being found on the web is critical for any web business.

Bounce names off other people and get their reactions. If the name is throwing them off, then it may be misleading. The name "Monsterdaata.com," for example, may confuse people who focus on whether or not the word data is misspelled, rather than on the services of the website. Also, if the name has people thinking of another, similar business, the similarity will be counterproductive as you try to drive customers to your business. Furthermore, a name similar to someone else's may get you in trademark hot water. Run the name by your lawyer and ask her to double check before you commit.

There are numerous ways to derive a name, so take your time, research the market, and in the end find one that makes you feel good. Like a comfortable shoe, the name should fit just right.

Domain Names

A domain name is the name of your website, and is the name that connects what you type into the browser with the physical computer that houses the website's files. Having your own domain name also lets you have a customized e-mail address. Examples of domain names are Amazon.com, Facebook.com, Google.com, or eBay.com. The first word is the domain you own, while the second word (.com, .net, .org, .us, .ca, .co.uk, etc.) is the domain suffix, or top level domain. For example, Google.com, Google.ca, and Google .co.uk are actually different domains, although they are all owned by Google.

Choosing a Domain Name

Choosing a domain name is becoming harder and harder, as so many names are already taken. You'll want to start with your company's name, and then test to see whether it is taken by someone with a similar name. You may also find that a person (a "squatter") has purchased the domain for speculative purposes: they buy it, hold it, and then hopefully sell it to a company who wants it very badly. If this is the case with you, then either decide to purchase it or move on to another name. For some big companies, the value of the domain name is so high, that they will pay anything to get it from one of these squatters: Facebook reportedly paid $4.5 million for fb.com.

To choose a domain name, go to an Internet service provider (ISP) website: *www.godaddy.com* and *www.ipower.com* are two of the largest small business-oriented providers. Look for a link that says "Register Your Domain," or just "Domains," usually under a product drop-down menu. Type in your prospective domain name, and see what comes up. You will likely see that the .com version of your name is taken. If this is the case, then you have five options:

1. Change the domain name slightly by adding something more descriptive to it. For example, instead of hair.com, try hairbrushes.com, betterhair

.com, or thehairplace.com. Sometimes simply adding the word "the" in front of your name can solve the problem.

2. Change the domain name to one that speaks to the benefits of your product or service, or one that makes an emotional connection. For example, try greatlooking.com, ImWorthIt.com, etc.

3. Choose to use a different domain suffix. Instead of hair.com, use hair .net, hair.org, or hair.us, if they are available.

4. Purchase the domain name from the current holder.

5. Change your business name. (Since you are just going through the naming process, this isn't as bad as it sounds!)

Once the name is chosen, then register it. You can ask your webmaster to do this for you, but it really is quite simple, and most people can do it themselves. The cost is usually under $15/year. On top of this is the cost of web hosting, and e-mail, which shouldn't cost more than $10 a month.

Pre-emptive Strategies

Once you have your name chosen, you will want to make sure that you also register similar names. Can you imagine what would happen if a competitor registered a name very similar to yours, and pointed this domain to its website? It's far easier to do this registration pre-emptively, instead of dealing with a problem later on. Think of it as a cheap insurance policy. Here's a list:

- Register your domain with the most common domain suffixes, as well as .com. This means registering the name as .net, .org, .us, .biz, .ca, .co.uk.
- If there are words in the domain that can be spelled differently but sound the same, register all variations. A name like fx4business.com should also be registered as fxforbusiness.com, fxfourbusiness.com, fxforebusiness.com, effects4business.com, affects4business.com, effectsforbusiness.com, and so on.
- Add the most common prefixes and suffixes, to prevent others from doing so. "The," "A," "Best," "Better," are examples.
- If there are so many variations that the cost and ongoing management seems onerous, go back to square one and try a different domain.

Thinking through your choice early can mean less market confusion later.

Not-So-Popular Domain Suffixes

You may have chosen the perfect name—The Best Pet Store, but the .com version of the domain name was already chosen. Instead, you register the domain name TheBestPetStore.net. While you were lucky that the .net version was available, what happens if someone remembers your name, but wrongly assumes that you are .com? Or what happens if the company that owns the .com version has trademarked their company name—and later demands that you release the .net domain? (They can do this!)

In your search for a unique domain name, it is tempting to find even more obscure domain name suffixes—but it is generally not a good idea for the reasons cited earlier. On the other hand, there may be a case for using a not-so-popular one:

- Your target customers might be in another country. Every country has a two-letter domain suffix: .ca is for Canada, .cn is for China, .uk is for the United Kingdom, etc. For them, a non-.com local domain suffix is just as comfortable as .com might be for you. The entire list of every code is available at *www.iana.org/domains/root/db*.
- Some of the country domains are very convenient two-letter abbreviations. If your business has to do with video, for example, a domain that ends in .TV might be appropriate. If you have an online cottage rental site, you might create a domain with the .ge suffix (e.g., cotta.ge). Other interesting suffixes include .no, .me, and .do.
- Some newer domain suffixes are designed for special purposes, and it might be more important for you to be connected with that special purpose. For example, the .xxx domain is meant for adult content websites, while the .jobs domain is designed for companies posting jobs.

If you are hoping to drive as many people to your website as possible, a domain name that is tightly tied to your company name is the best course of action. If it isn't available, then you may want to reconsider your choice of name.

The business name (and the domain name) that you ultimately choose must mean something to your prospective customers, should be meaningful to you personally, and should provide a clue as to the nature of the online business itself.

CHAPTER 8

Online Businesses

There are many types of businesses online, some discussed in Chapter 2. At this time, we want to delve into the topic a bit more deeply: partly to help focus your plan beyond your market research, and partly to expose you to the broad number of variations that you might consider.

Business Acronyms

There is no shortage of acronyms in the world of online business. Three of the more common ones refer to your target market: Business-to-Business (B2B), Business-to-Consumer (B2C), and Business-to-Employees (B2E). There are some broad commonalities to online businesses of each category. Here are some of them:

B2B

Often the value of B2B products and services is higher, so more pre-sales support may be necessary. One of the B2B challenges is whether to sell direct to end-consumers (and thus undercut your own customers), or funnel consumer-sales leads directly to them (and thus miss the opportunity to capture "retail" margin). B2B sites might also require off-web account registration and setup.

B2C

The potential volume of customers is fairly large, so online support is important. Getting customers into the online storefront is usually accomplished through pay-per-click advertising. As B2C sites are often highly transactional, a site design that is simple will sell more than one that is complex.

B2E

There are a number of products and services that companies may want their employees to access (and purchase). There is also a fair amount of internal corporate information that needs to be disseminated. A B2E site—often called an employee portal or intranet site—is designed to meet these needs. Sometimes it includes access to services provided by external partners—here is your online business opportunity—and sometimes it only includes internal corporate information.

Online Product Sales

In the olden days, people would wait for the latest Sears, Roebuck catalog to be delivered. They would pour over each page, ordering products that would be delivered to the post office. Urbanization, the automobile, and rising catalog delivery costs changed this model and the world wide web changed the model once again: books, crafts, office supplies, shoes, hats, photographs, artwork, furniture—the list of what can be purchased online is endless. Google has become the de facto largest shopping mall in the world, and there is no reason why your business shouldn't have a storefront there as well.

One of the challenges of online product sales, and particularly for physical items, is the cost and hassle of packaging the product for delivery. Before you go headlong into this area, spend some time considering how to make this part of the business more efficient. For example, if you are considering selling a book that you've written, will reducing the book's thickness or weight also reduce your shipping costs? Can you find a fulfillment company that will inventory your products and ship your orders, so you can concentrate exclusively on marketing and sales?

Online Services Sales

Online services are similar to product sales, except that there is no offline fulfillment: you are selling your (or others') time. This might be appealing if you are a life coach or management consultant, and are looking to have new clients find you online, and possibly schedule and pay you over the web as well.

ALERT

Make sure that your new clients understand what they are buying—and that you know what you are selling. If you charge for an hour of your time, and they are dissatisfied, they may dispute the transaction with their credit card company, costing you the sale—and even more time.

Information Marketing

The problem with selling your time is that there is only so much of it. If you capture your knowledge into a document, you can then sell it over and over again. There are two challenges with this: first, there are many free resources that are easily available through a quick web search; second, once a person has your information, it is too easy for them to share it.

This second problem—digital rights—is a big one. If a purchaser posts your information online, then it is easily findable through a web search . . . which leads you back to the first problem. There are ways to mitigate this risk, but the methods are all not without their faults. If you password-protect the document, expect a flood of support requests asking for the password. If you use a proprietary format, then it might not be readable on different platforms (e.g., PC, Mac, Android, iPhone, iPad, Kindle, etc.). The remaining online business concepts have all come into existence, partly as a response to the digital-rights issue.

E-Mail Course Delivery

Instead of providing access generically to a document, e-mail-based information marketing divides the content into bite-sized chunks and sends them out over a period of time. The idea is that customers can only consume so much at a time, and like a live course, would value instruction that is delivered over a "term." From a digital rights perspective, it is tougher for all of your content to be posted on a website, as it requires stitching each e-mail together, stripping out custom messaging, and stripping out the recipient's name. Of course, each individual e-mail can be forwarded—nothing can be done about that.

There are a number of products that can do the payment processing and automatically start the e-mail course: check out *www.budurl.com/every thing1sc* (1ShoppingCart) and *www.budurl.com/CRMautomate* (Infusionsoft).

An example of a no-cost six-segment course on blogging can be found at *www.budurl.com/strategicblogging*.

Online App Sales

An app, short for Application, is a program that delivers functionality to the user. The app can live on the web—i.e., it is a website—or it can be a downloadable program for your smartphone. If it is on the web, it does a specific thing: for example, it converts a Microsoft Word document into a PDF file, or compiles all of your uploaded photos into a printed photo book. If you develop a web app, then you are responsible for all of the payment infrastructure, programming of the app, and customer service.

Web apps can also live within Facebook and certain other social networks. For example, Farmville and Mafia Wars are apps in Facebook; using them is free, but you can upgrade to a paid membership, and you are exposed to advertising along the way. Apps that live within a particular social media site are usually required to use the host platform's payment mechanism. In the case of Mafia Wars, for example, a VIP membership is sold through Facebook, thereby ensuring that Facebook also gets its cut.

Mobile apps are sold in Apple's App Store, and are designed to deliver specific functionality on any of their i-devices. Android, Windows, and BlackBerry all have similar app stores for their respective devices. One of the benefits of developing a mobile app is that while there are about 7 billion web pages, there are only a million or so mobile apps. The theory, anyway, is that with less competition, there will be more sales.

Of course, developing any type of app requires a knowledge of programming well beyond what most people have. That doesn't mean, though, that you should ignore the possibility. If you have a great idea, and market research shows that there is a demand, then why not investigate the possibility of having someone else do the programming and design for you?

From a digital rights perspective, a web or mobile app is exceptionally safe; it's just about impossible to transfer a mobile app from one device to a friend's. And web apps hide their functionality behind a secure paywall.

Membership Sites

If you have enough intellectual property, and you are focused on a very narrow niche, a membership site might just be the choice for you. Picture this: a resource site and community that contains web pages, videos, discussion forums, chat, and more, that is only accessible to those who pay a monthly fee. Members could even purchase additional products and e-mail courses while in the site; customers' credit cards are kept on file within the site for this purpose. A side benefit is that members are far less likely to share their log-in credentials: site access gives credit card access.

In a certain sense, membership sites are the Holy Grail of online businesses because they are an annuity: each month, the access fees keep rolling in. The marketing challenge is that the membership site must show a high enough value—with more being added every month—or your customers will quit.

Technically these sites have some complexity. They require a secure place on the web for the content, along with an e-commerce capability that controls access to each individual piece of content. Check out Customer-Hub, *www.budurl.com/everythingCustHub* as an example.

Online Service Marketplaces

In towns of old, there was always a place where merchants and customers would meet to buy the latest goods, haggle over prices, and transact their business. It shouldn't be a surprise that this is also true in the online world. There are literally dozens of these online marketplaces that exist—maybe your online business is really as simple as setting up shop in a service marketplace.

One of the most popular sites is *www.elance.com*. More than 1.3 million service providers are registered on the site—everything from accountants to marketers to programmers to administrators. And consider *www.oDesk.com*, which also claims to be the biggest contractor portal, serving more than 350,000 businesses. If you are a specialist, then there probably is a marketplace site for your area of expertise. Another example is *www.99designs.com*. On this site, graphic designers compete for work on logos, postcards, icons, websites, and other design tasks.

How They Work

You are either a buyer or a seller. If you are a seller, you list your expertise, products, and services. Buyers do one of two things:

- They search for what they are looking for, and contact you through the website to consummate the sale.
- They post their requirements on the site, while you (and possibly hundreds of others) post a bid to do the work. The winner is notified, and the sale is locked in.

Normally, the product or service is paid for through the online marketplace, using a credit card or PayPal. The site then deducts its fee and passes on the balance to the seller.

Finally, the buyer will provide a rating and comments on his experience with you. The better your rating, the better you'll do attracting more clients.

Define Your Expertise: Focus

What kind of doctor would you like to perform your heart surgery: a specialist in heart surgery, or a just-graduated general surgeon? The answer for most people is obvious: the heart surgeon. Likewise, customers rightly know that the deeper and more specialized your expertise, the more likely that you'll know how to fix their problems quickly.

Even if you do have wide-ranging experience, it is important to portray yourself honestly as a specialist in a few key areas. Here is what strategists call the "virtuous circle":

- It is easier to market yourself to a more targeted audience.
- More sales in this area will give you even deeper knowledge. Your greater knowledge will also improve your reputation amongst all potential customers in your niche.
- This deeper knowledge will differentiate you from your competitors. Over time, specialization will become an unassailable strategic advantage.
- The cycle continues: Specializing will make it easier to market yourself to your targeted audience.

The more focus you have, and the more that your market knows about it, the more successful you will become. The virtuous cycle gives you this.

Set Yourself Up for Success

What does success look like in the online services market? Surprisingly, not so different from any other business: a steady stream of work that (hopefully) pays well. Getting there, though, requires hard work:

- Research the going price for your services: too high, and you won't be chosen. Too low, and you'll be flooded with work . . . but will not be able to pay your bills.
- Set up your profile appropriately. Your prospects may search for your expertise using any number of keywords, so using these terms within your profile increases the chances of your being found. Two tips: check out your competitors for ideas, and don't forget to include

similar terms within your profile. (E.g., if you provide social media advice, use both that term and social networking.)

- Focus on quality delivery. The ratings are critical to future purchase decisions, so do great work, and provide great customer service. Bonus benefits: repeat business and referrals. An average or poor rating is very difficult to recover from.
- Divide your time appropriately between business development and business delivery. Many people get themselves into trouble because they forget this. Consider this: if you spend all of your time on a big project and don't do any business development, you will find yourself with zero on your plate when the project ends. Conversely, if you spend all of your time doing business development, when will you find time to do the actual work? Balancing the two is the only way to build a sustainable business—and reduce your financial stress.

While these points seem like they are common sense, with all of the many things on an entrepreneur's to-do list, they are often forgotten.

Bidding/Pricing

Figuring out how to price your services seems more like an art than science, but it really isn't that hard, if you know three basics.

1. What is the most that the prospective customer will pay? The amount that a customer chooses to pay has a direct connection to the severity of the problem that you will solve, and the value that you add. The amount that he can pay is also influenced by the state of his business, his budget, and his impression of the quality of your (future) work. If your solution will save the customer thousands each week—or help him grow his sales by thousands each week, then he is likely to pay more than if the number were just in the hundreds.
2. What are competitors charging? If you are charging more for the same service, you will attract very few, if any, new customers. If you charge just slightly less, then your price advantage will be a strong attractor factor.
3. What is the minimum that you are able to charge? This minimum can be defined in many ways. What is your cost of production? What is the

minimum that you need in order to support your desired lifestyle? And are there alternative activities that you can be doing that actually pay more?

Hitting the pricing sweet spot may take some trial-and-error. The key is to learn from every transaction: what would have happened if the price was set just a bit higher, or just a bit lower?

Other "Time" Sales

Beyond Elance, oDesk, 99designs, and other marketplaces, there are a number of other sites that list tasks—with a budget. These include:

- Amazon Mechanical Turk, *www.mturk.com*: Sign yourself in, and then earn by completing quick low-value tasks that can't be automated.
- *www.fiverr.com*: What will you do for $5? Post it and wait for your customers to find you.
- *www.done.com*, *www.agentanything.com*, and *www.TaskRabbit.com*: List your availability to do errands for people in specific cities.

Might you base your new business on one of these sites? That's the beauty of being an entrepreneur: it's completely up to you.

Client Service

Why slog it out, competing with others for new clients when you already have earned the trust of existing ones? The key to repeat business is doing great work: delivering quality on time and on budget, being friendly, and having a great attitude. And if your customer is dissatisfied, make sure you address her concern in a professional, yet empathetic way.

At one time, retailers believed in the mantra "the customer is always right." While this is usually true, it is generally not a great policy to adopt. What if the customers make unreasonable demands? What if they change their requirements, after you have agreed on the price and the deliverables? What if they just don't want to pay?

The best time to address these types of problems is beforehand. Make sure that both you and your prospective customer have a crystal clear agreement on specifically what you are going to deliver and when. If the work is fairly complex, provide documentation that she will approve before you begin. If the work is expected to take a very long time to complete, use the concept of a milestone. Break the job into bite-sized portions that can be completed, approved, and paid for along the way.

Depending on the size of the engagement, you can close the loop by asking your client several questions:

- "Can you please put a positive rating and comments on the market-place site?" (This is to help you attract other clients.)
- "Are there any other projects that you might want to use me on?" (This is to help you get more work from them.)
- "Are there any other people or companies that you can pass my name on to for my kind of work?" (This is to generate referrals by tapping into their network.)
- "I'm always interested in improving my service: Can you share what was the best part of working with me, and what is the one thing that you think I can do better?" (This is to both confirm your strengths and improve your weaknesses.)

Notice that each of these questions are open-ended and can't be answered with a simple yes/no response. Asking in this way will yield far better insights into your client's experience with you.

Create a New Marketplace

Why work in a shop when you can own it? If you have detailed knowledge of a specific industry or niche, and you see a service or product gap, then there may be an opportunity for you to plug that gap by creating your own marketplace. This is exceptionally difficult, as most ground has already been covered. That being said, the savvy entrepreneur sees a gap where others don't, and profits as a result.

The business model for these types of sites is simple: by matching a service provider with a customer, you can skim a certain percentage of the fee paid. In addition, you can earn money by selling advertising on the site, and offering "premium" placement and upgrades to service providers.

The growth of the Internet has also meant an explosion in the number of businesses that support other Internet businesses. In the next chapter we explore some of these, what they are, and how to be successful running them.

CHAPTER 9

Working "in" the Web Machine

With billions of pages, millions of companies, and millions of eyeballs, you might consider creating a business where you are actually doing something on the web itself. Companies need people to design their pages, do the programming, create and edit the content, and get their site found. In this chapter, we explore what it might be like to serve clients doing these types of activities.

Web Design

What makes a website beautiful? What makes it a realistic extension of the company's real-world brand and visual identity? What makes the site easy to use, both to increase sales and reduce support costs? Great web design makes all of this happen.

Skills Required

Typically, web designers have a college diploma in the field, and have spent the early part of their careers working at an ad agency, creative house, or doing design under the mentorship of a creative director. Designers have an intimate understanding of color, fonts, layout, and all of the other "levers" at their disposal. They understand technology enough to know whether or not their designs can be implemented, but they are usually not programmers.

It is possible to learn design without going to art school, and there are a number of courses that can start you on that path. What is most important is having a design aesthetic: an innate understanding of what works and what doesn't.

Software

Most designers swear by the Adobe Creative Suite: Illustrator for line drawings, Photoshop for image manipulation, and InDesign for page layout. The software is quite expensive, but can now be purchased on a monthly subscription basis. If you are a student, you may qualify for the fully functional—but significantly cheaper—student versions. Alternatively, there are other far cheaper graphics programs that can do quite a bit of what Photoshop can do that you might want to try first. Check out Pixelmator on a Mac and Paint.net on a PC. If you are thinking about becoming a web designer, learn how to use the software properly; it will have a direct impact on both your productivity and profitability.

How to Sell Your Services

The most important thing that a web designer needs—besides talent—is a website that showcases his or her talent. Specifically, put together a site that includes your background, a portfolio of your design work, your process, and contact information. If people like the way your site looks, they will assume that you can do similar work for them.

The challenge is that you may not have a portfolio to show when you start. Some budding designers will spend time working for someone else to build their personal portfolio. Others will do pro bono (free) work for friends and family to build their references. Whichever path you choose, you will need to be proactive in your search for clients. Upgrade your social media profiles to include details about your new business, then share what you are doing with your network. Find businesses with tired websites and pitch them a design upgrade. Look for requests for proposals, or RFPs, that you might be able to win.

Probably the most important thing to realize, however, is that design is only half of the battle. Once the design is complete, you will need to find a programmer to develop it. Instead of waiting until you have a client, consider pitching yourself to programmers who are looking for a designer.

Competition

Competition among designers is fierce. At the top end, there are the agencies. They have the bandwidth and experience to do just about anything. Because of this, however, their cost base is much higher, and they may not be able to match your (lower) rates.

The next step down are the freelancers. These are individuals who have a steady stream of web design business coming in; sometimes they work by themselves, sometimes with a partner. Freelancers can have more than twenty-five years of experience, or they can be completely new. The majority of designers have been freelancers at one point or another in their career.

Next are the design students. This group needs to pay for school, and figures that it makes more sense doing web design part-time than working in the local 7-Eleven. They see that doing web design part-time helps build their portfolio, even before they graduate.

Finally, there are the marketplace sites, such as 99designs, where each design project is put out to tender. Here, designers do the work on spec (free), until the project originator chooses a design by making a payment. Except for the winner, no one else gets paid for his work.

Each of these competitors works at a different price point; before you start, you'll want to survey who precisely is your competition—and what category they are in.

Web Development

Each web page is made from a number of different languages and standards: HTML, CSS, and JavaScript. Functionality on the server is likewise built using certain technologies: PHP, .NET, Java, and more. A web developer takes the user interface created by the web designer, marries this with the required functionality defined by the client, and makes it work on a specific technical platform. In a certain sense, a great web developer is like a plumber who works behind the scenes to bring the website to life.

Skills Required

If designers are the creative ones, then developers are the analysts. Developers typically fall into two categories: some specialize in taking the mock-ups from designers, slicing the graphics, and then using HTML, CSS, and JavaScript to create the pages. Other developers focus on connecting the page to an underlying database, developing functionality back at the web server, security, and networking.

Many developers can learn HTML, CSS, and JavaScript on their own, using web-based tutorials and a bit of experimentation. The more sophisticated programming back at the server is usually taught in college courses. That being said, if you have some experience in programming, there are many web tutorials that can bring you up to date on the more modern web programming platforms.

One skill that many web developers forget about is work effort estimation. How long will it take to actually do the required programming? While web development has a certain romance to it, it is, after all, a business. Estimate too low and you'll be losing money. Estimate too high and people will think you are inefficient . . . and won't hire you.

Software and Hardware

Websites are built with HTML, but the back end tends to use one of three main platforms: Java (Oracle), .NET (Microsoft), or PHP (Open Source). Depending on what platform you are using, there may be a development environment that will help you be more efficient. If you are developing for mobile, then you will likely use either the Apple development tools or the Android development tools. Microsoft and RIM have tools for their mobile platforms as well.

What is probably more important is the ability to test your programs. This may mean setting up a testing server and testing PCs, Macs, and different mobile devices. There is nothing more frustrating to clients than a program that is filled with bugs because it hasn't been adequately tested.

How to Sell Your Services

Much like web designers, developers have a number of options for selling their services. Here are the two most common strategies:

1. Remember that development generally happens after design. If you develop strong relationships with designers, you can develop a strong referral network for work.
2. Start knocking on doors—the real, as well as the virtual ones—looking for contract work.

In the world of IT, there are a number of different certifications; consider spending the time to qualify. When clients look at you, they will see someone who meets a certain minimum standard of capability; you will instantly separate yourself from any of your noncredentialed competitors.

Finally, you will need to create a website that not only highlights your accomplishments, but one that demonstrates your ability to use the technology appropriately.

Competition

Looking at the listings at online web marketplaces such as oDesk and Elance, the first question through your mind might be how your competitors can offer their services at such a low price? One of the major reasons is that many people on these systems are from countries with a different standard of living, different purchasing price standards, and different expectations. In other words, a dollar might go very far indeed overseas, so why price the services at high American rates?

Competition comes from two other sources as well: students, who are keen to do bargain-basement coding to help pay their tuition, and internal corporate developers who would rather do it themselves than outsourcing it to a person like you.

Content/Writing/Blogging/Tweeting

Can you make a living as a writer? If you ask journalists, they will say that it is tough. The number of full-time (and freelance) journalism jobs are fast diminishing as blogs are becoming the de facto source of news for many people. If you ask traditional book authors (or publishers), they will say that free content seems to be squeezing any margins left in their business. Yet when one door closes, another opens: if blogging (or tweeting) is so popular, can you make a business of it? The answer is yes . . . if you are good, work hard, and are a little bit lucky.

This business of writing on the web has picked up a name: content development. The world seems to have an insatiable demand for it—but perhaps not in the exact formats that existed in the 1950s. Here are several of the business models that have evolved:

- **Freelance writer:** You approach a company and pitch your ideas for an article. If they agree, then you are paid for your writing, usually on a fee-per-word basis.
- **Contract blogger/tweeter/poster:** Working on behalf of a company (or an agency), you are responsible for keeping a community alive—or kick-starting one—by continually adding content in your client's area of interest. For some organizations, this type of writing has a bit of customer service responsibility as well; in the purest form, you are a reporter, writing "advertorial" content.
- **Ad-supported (or sponsored) blogger:** This is a more entrepreneurial model, where your writing has attracted a significant following. The more highly targeted your followers are, the more that they are of interest to an advertiser. Revenue comes from banner ads, Google Adwords, and behind-the-scenes sponsorships.

ALERT

If you are compensated in any way to write about a product, you are required to clearly disclose this to your readers. It's not just the ethical thing to do; it's also the law.

If you are handy with a video camera and know how to edit video, these same models also work: freelance videographer, contract video blogger ("vlogger"), and ad-supported video blogger.

Skills Required

If your online business is all about writing, then you will need to learn how to write. It is true that most people have been writing since second grade, but they haven't been doing the same type of writing, each and every day. They haven't honed their craft to a professional level. Writers and editors will often say that it takes years for a writer to "find his voice": a style and perspective that is all his own. Whether you choose to take some courses or not, the best way to become a great writer is . . . to write.

Beyond the writing process, you will need to determine what you will be writing about, and for whom. You will need to find it in yourself to sit down in front of a blank computer screen, and create something, literally from nothing. Creativity, analytical skills, and a passion for your subject matter are all important. Here's a free resource on blogging that can help: *www .budurl.com/everythingBlog*.

Software and Process

What you need to know will depend on what you are hoping to accomplish.

- If you are writing a blog, then learn how to use WordPress. This is free blogging software and is available at *www.wordpress.com* (if you want them to host your blog), or *www.wordpress.org* (if you would rather host your blog yourself).
- If you are tweeting, then learn how to use *www.Hootsuite.com* (or *www.tweetdeck.com*). These programs—both do the same thing— help manage your Twitter communications and relationships far more efficiently than Twitter by itself. The free versions of these will do 99 percent of what you will need.
- If you are doing a video blog, or are creating a video channel on YouTube, then you will need to learn a bit more. Purchase a tripod, video camera, microphone, lighting, and a backdrop, then begin experimenting. Slightly better lighting—and a decent lapel microphone—will go a

long way to making you look like a pro. After the filming comes editing. For most people, the free iMovie (Mac) or Movie Maker (Windows) will do. If you want to move up a notch, look at Final Cut Pro X (Mac) or Adobe Premiere Elements (PC). Once the video is created and edited, you will need to master the (relatively easy) upload process to YouTube.

All of these programs have great help and support resources, and are relatively easy to learn.

How to Sell Your Services

If you are hoping to do freelance writing, then the first step is to find out who your buyer might be. Most websites for trade magazines, for example, have a page about submissions. In it, the sites will describe their audience, the type of content they are looking for, and the process and contact points for you to begin. The page will usually also state whether they will pay or not. When you are starting, you may wish to do a number of free articles, just to build your portfolio. (The challenge is that when you already have the portfolio, you will be competing with "free.")

The concept of portfolio-building is equally as important if you are hoping to blog or tweet on behalf of a company. Selling your services to an agency or corporate buyer is far easier if there is a ready record of your writing style. To develop a portfolio here, either start your own blog or approach a local community group and offer to do it for them.

If you are hoping to support yourself through advertising or sponsorship, your income will depend completely on two factors: the number of readers, and your ability to sell ads. At the beginning, you will need to do both yourself; this may be a challenge, as the skill of selling is vastly different than the skill of writing. Once you have grown the number of followers though, you can delegate the sales effort to one of a number of ad networks that do this full time. Or you can take on a partner—you write, and your partner sells.

Competition

Sadly, there is competition from everywhere: former journalists and freelancers, public relations agencies, stay-at-home moms, students, business executives, and other entrepreneurs like you. The supply of content (and content creators) is going through the roof. But consumers' demand for quality content is also going through the roof. The laws of supply and demand work on the Internet as well: if there is more supply than demand, then the price—your compensation—will plummet. If there is more demand—and people are willing to pay for it—then your compensation will skyrocket.

For these reasons, the Holy Grail for many content creators is to own their own content and be the master of their own blog. Yes, it is challenging to build your followers to a high enough level to attract advertisers, but at least you aren't competing against other writers for fewer and fewer well-paying contracts.

ESSENTIAL

It's okay to start with one model, then move to another—so long as you do it strategically. For example, start your online writing business as a contract blogger, developing your skills and a portfolio. From time to time, pitch freelance assignments on subjects that interest you. Meanwhile, start your own blog with the intention that as it becomes economically feasible, you will quit your day job to blog full time.

Getting Started

There is no other way to say it: if your online business is all about writing, then write. If you are not sure if this is what your online business will be, you can still test-drive it before you leave the security of your day job. Set yourself a daily quota: each evening, write a blog post, then tweet about it. Before long, your topic focus—and your efficiency—will improve.

Search Engine Optimization and Search Engine Marketing

Search engine optimization, or SEO, is all about finding clever ways to ensure that a client's site appears near the top of the organic Google (or other) search engine results. Some of the work is ensuring the website is properly coded, while some of the work is ensuring the content includes the proper keywords. Part of the work is ensuring that other sites link to your client's, and a final part of the work is ensuring that there is enough social buzz about the site.

Search engine marketing, or SEM, is all about finding ways to have your client's advertising appear alongside relevant search queries, and then writing a relevant call to action, so that users will click on the ad and go to your client's site. Both of these are important, and will be explored in greater detail in Chapter 19.

Skills Required

Both of these fields are in a constant state of flux. The search engines are constantly changing their algorithms. Your clients' needs are constantly changing. Your clients' competitors are becoming increasingly sophisticated. And users are increasingly fickle. This means that you will need to be constantly monitoring what is happening for changes—and potential opportunities for your clients. Because everything is measurable—impressions, clicks, and transactions—if you stop working for a second, it will show in the results, and you might lose the client. On the other hand, great results mean great client retention.

To be successful as an SEO or SEM professional, you also need to know enough about the technical underpinnings of the web—and specifically HTML—to optimize the code. You need to be a great copywriter—to capture the imagination of the users and get them to click. And you need to be a great salesperson yourself—to connect with and sign new clients of your own.

Software

Almost every SEO or SEM provider uses software to manage all of the ads that they have placed, to assess the effectiveness of their SEO efforts, and to brainstorm new keywords or test new ideas. There are hundreds of programs out there that can do this, from ones that expect you to be managing a minimum of $10,000 of ads monthly, *www.acquisio.com*, *www.kenshoo.com*, and *www.omniture.com*, to quick-and-dirty free websites that help test keywords, including Google's keyword tool, (*www.budurl.com/keywordtoolgoogle.*

Search Google for SEO or SEM software, and you'll have pages of software along the entire spectrum.

How to Sell Your Services

There are three main ways to sell your services: The most obvious is to look for businesses that are in need of SEO and SEM and make your pitch. This will involve writing a proposal, outlining specifically what you will do, when, and at what fee. The business will be keen on knowing what they can expect with respect to results, and why you should be the one delivering the services.

The second way is to sell your services to smaller ad agencies, working on a subcontract basis. They may be more interested in the creative, and may not have the interest (or skills) to do SEO or SEM. They may wish to hire you as a subcontractor, or they may wish to have a percentage of your fees for any client they refer. The sales strategy in this case is to network in places where agencies spend their time: association meetings and conventions.

The third way to grow an SEO or SEM business is to partner with a web designer or web developer. Again, they know their business, but they also know that to deliver a complete solution, they also need to have a web marketing component. They may also look at you as a source of new business: your clients may ask for additional web work, and you need to refer them somewhere . . .

Competition

Competition comes from the usual sources: agencies that do it themselves, offshore sweatshops that have rooms filled with people selling (and doing) SEO and SEM work, and freelancers who are selling their services through the various online marketplaces. Competition also comes from prospective clients themselves who think that they can do it on their own. To a certain extent this is true, but the risk is that, if the clients use the latest SEO "trick" from today, they might be seriously penalized tomorrow. If the prospective clients aren't on top of the market, then they may find themselves sideswiped.

Getting Started

Begin reading everything that you can about SEO and SEM online, then apply this to your own company's website. Once you have demonstrated that you can do this service for yourself, then it becomes easier for you to show how you can do it for others.

Training

With so much innovation on the Internet, and so much business dependent on it, there is an insatiable demand for people who can answer the question "how." How to update their website? How to use social media? How to do basic SEO or basic SEM? How to do customer service over the web? For some clients, it is as basic as how to use a web browser.

There are many different modes of training. It can be delivered in person in front of a group. It can be in person, one-on-one. It can happen via webinar for a group of people, or via Skype with screen sharing, one-on-one. It can also be "virtual" training, without you even being present, in an e-learning environment.

Skills Required

There are several things that you need to have locked down if you are to be successful in a training business:

- **Subject matter expertise:** You must be an expert in the area. For you to retain credibility, you will need to have the background to answer tough questions beyond the formal curriculum.
- **Training know-how:** This means understanding how to design the training regimen—sometimes called instructional design—so that the learning objectives are met.
- **Strong communication skills:** Being an expert doesn't make you a great teacher. Being able to keep the learners engaged does. You will need to do this through your examples, interactive activities, speaking skills (in the case of a live or recorded presentation), or writing skills (in the case of text-based training).
- **Technology:** If you are delivering your training live, then you will need to feel comfortable with the technology, including PowerPoint and remote presentation software. Even the best training can be wasted if technology gets in the way. And your credibility as an expert depends on it.

Even though these factors are critically important, you don't have to be "perfect" right from the start. At the outset, consider taking on some low-risk training engagements (friends and family) to improve your skills.

Software

The software you use will depend on the nature of your training business. For example, if you are primarily going to do one-on-one, in-person training, then you may not need any special software at all. But if you are training remotely, then using remote presentation and control software (either *www.webex.com*, *www.gotomeeting.com*, or *www.adobeconnect.com*) are critical. You will also probably use PowerPoint (PC and Mac) or Keynote (Mac only).

If you are looking to compile your training into a website, then sell access to it afterwards, this approach will require a significantly greater investment. Look into membership-site software such as CustomerHub, *www.budurl.com/everythingHUB* or WishList Member, *www.budurl.com/everythingWishlist*. Or, craft a custom solution that is more tightly branded to the name of your organization. These latter options will require more technical effort, and likely cost.

How to Sell Your Services

Once again, the importance of alliances and partnerships is critical. Since training always occurs at the back end of the web design/web development process, allying with a web developer makes a lot of sense. At the same time as they are selling the actual website build, they can also sell your training services. Of course, the developer will earn a handsome fee for this privilege.

If you believe that people would be looking online for your services, then consider using pay-per-click advertising on Google, Bing, LinkedIn, or Facebook. A quick way to test this out is to search for the type of training that you offer, and see if your competitors' ads appear. If they do, then there is likely at least some demand.

One of the more important ways to demonstrate your expertise is to make it freely available. While this sounds like it is in fundamental conflict with the idea of growing a business, it really isn't. Giving people a taste of your expertise—and having it indexed by Google—is a powerful way to draw people into your website. And starting a blog or newsletter is probably something that you'll want to do anyway.

Finally, even though you have an online business, you are physically located in a specific geography. Get out and network with the business community and other local leaders. Make sure that your business is listed in the various local online directories. And consider whether offline ads might make sense: many people prefer to buy local when they are buying online.

Competition

There are very few barriers to entry into the training business: anyone can call themselves a trainer. For this reason, the competition is fierce: traditional training companies expanding into the online world, solopreneurs who have a special skill that they are hoping to sell, and technology companies that see training as an add-on to their other products or services. In addition, there is the seemingly unlimited amount of free training that is available merely by searching on Google.

To be successful against this backdrop, you must find a way to differentiate your training business: is it because you have a special skill, a local presence, or a well-known client list? Or perhaps a few key testimonials, better technology, a lower price, or more pervasive advertising? Competition is tough, but a better offering marketed more effectively will make you even tougher!

Getting Started

Start with market research to determine who would be interested in your training services. Then start on the instructional design: what are your courses and what modules are in each course? Then write the training script, and translate it into PowerPoint, graphics, and text. If you know of a business that needs the training but might not be able to pay your full rates, consider asking them to be a "beta partner," someone who helps you shake out the kinks, in exchange for a lower rate. Not only will you test-drive your training, but you can get a testimonial at the same time.

Setting Fees

When it comes to the perks of being an entrepreneur, tied for first place with the lifestyle has to be the chance to make a lot of money, but how exactly to price your services is a matter of some debate. Basically, there are three approaches:

- Hourly rate
- Per diem, also known as a day rate
- Value-based fee

As you weigh the best approach for you, be sure to include all expenses associated with being a "gun for hire." When you are an employee, space and equipment are provided. So are paid holidays, vacations, and perhaps a good portion of your health insurance premium and more. When calculating your fees, you must consider your needs beyond what you had perhaps seen in a paycheck.

ALERT

Many businesses choose their fee levels based on gut, not based on analysis of costs. If you don't set your fees above your costs, by the end of the year you will have lost money, guaranteed. If it is impossible to build a profit into your business model, then you should either change the business's direction or close it.

The challenge of setting your fees is half art and half science. You will need to determine what the market rate is for your type of business—the Internet can help with that. Consider the midpoint of the range, then move the price slightly up or down, based on what you can justify in your market (and at your experience level).

Hourly Rate

The least attractive compensation plan, from the clients' perspective, is being charged an hourly rate. It terrifies them to think that if they have a question the meter will start running. Hourly rates force them to prequalify the level of urgency to speak with you. They may say to themselves, "Is this really a $250 question, which could turn into a $750 answer?"

It is also the most confining way for you. No matter what your hourly rate may be, your ultimate income is limited by the number of hours in the day and week. It would be highly unlikely that you could get away with charging for 100 hours of work in any given week—even if you actually put the time in! A client would certainly raise an eyebrow at such an invoice, perhaps wondering about your ethics and whether you might be padding the bill. The only way to grow your business when you are charging by the hour is to hire more people . . . to increase the inventory of hours that are available for sale.

ALERT

The most common financial stumbling block for service providers is underbidding a job. Nobody wins when you work twice the amount of time as what you have contracted for. Your pay gets cut in half, and the client does not have a true appreciation of what it takes to meet her objective. You can never get back the hours you have expended.

Per Diem

First cousin to the hourly rate is a per diem rate, a flat rate per day. Although you are calculating a bigger chunk of time for a higher rate, you are still limited to the number of available days. A savvy customer knows the going rates and you will be confined to market norms, particularly for services where a number of competitors might be considered. If you choose this method for pricing, you will need to make philosophical choices about where you want to fall within the ranges the market will bear. For example, if there is an expectation that a company will pay $2,000 to $5,000 for your SEO services, you will need to decide if you are the "deal" at the low end of the range, or if you believe your track record warrants asking for the higher end.

Value-Based Fee

As a consultant, your overarching goal will be to build a long-term relationship with a client, based on trust. The client needs to believe that you have his best interests at heart. The "value" part of the relationship comes from the client believing that you bring something extra to the table—and that your fees are commensurate with the value you add. By working with you, the client is acknowledging his in-house staff cannot perform the role or achieve the results you can on his behalf.

CHAPTER 10

Caution—Online on the Edge

Get rich quick! Sign up for the hidden profit system! Grow hair on your palms with this quick and easy ointment! There is no shortage of frauds, come-ons, and shady claims littering the Internet. And sadly, there is no shortage of would-be entrepreneurs thinking that these are a shortcut to wealth and financial independence. It takes hard work to build a real business—don't fall into the trap of thinking that there is "free" money to be made. After all, if these various systems actually worked, the promoters would be using the system themselves—not trying to sell it to others. At the same time, there are a number of completely legal ways to make money online, but you may feel uncomfortable walking on the moral fence. Just because you can do something online, doesn't necessarily mean that it is right to, or that you should. In this chapter, we'll review an inventory of dubious business practices and online activities that you might choose not to start.

Fraud

Fraud is illegal in just about every jurisdiction around the world, yet it exists both offline and online. As you investigate different online options, look out for shady operators who are preying on the needy. There are a number of indicators that might clue you in to something that doesn't look right.

Police are getting better at spotting—and prosecuting—fraudsters. Don't get hooked into using the Internet for shady activities yourself— if it's against the law in the real world, it's just as illegal online.

Spoofing Legitimate Sites

Sometimes fraudsters will create a website that looks exactly like a legitimate business, but will host the site with a domain that is a bit off. The following domains, all made up, are spoofs of *www.microsoft.com*:

www.nicrosoft.com
www.microsotf.com
www.microsoft.com.exceloffice25.com
www.microsoft.com.341today.com

The last two may have Microsoft.com in their name, but the real domains are exceloffice25.com and 341today.com. When the user clicks any of these links, and sees a site they expect to see, they may subscribe, transact, or open themselves up in some other way. The fraudster can then use the information collected for some nefarious purpose.

Spoofing E-mail Addresses

Think of the last time you've received an e-mail from one of your friends: how do you know that it really was they who sent it? Sadly, the Internet's e-mail system is inherently insecure. With some simple technical wizardry, any hacker can change the "Sender" of an e-mail to whatever he wants. Sadly, there are many hackers sending e-mails attempting to defraud unsuspecting recipients.

The golden rule is this: if you receive an e-mail from a friend or family that contains a strange link, or a strange writing style, don't act on it. Pick up the phone and call the person at his regular phone number.

Drive-By-Downloads

When someone asks you about viruses, do you think of the last time you were sick, or the last time your computer was sick? Drive-by-downloads happen when you go to a website, and unbeknownst to you, a file is downloaded to your computer. Or you click on what seems like a legitimate pop-up window, and a file is downloaded in the background.

Many fraudsters hope to infect your computer with something that allows them to make money (steal money?) from you over time. The download might cause browser windows to open with ads from time-to-time. Or it might log keystrokes when you go to a particular banking site, then send those keystrokes to the fraudster, who proceeds to empty your bank account. Or maybe it gives you additional functionality, but it tracks personal information as you use your computer.

Yes, there is money to be made this way, but it isn't a particularly proud way of starting an online enterprise. And it might land you in jail. The general rule is for you to always use a virus and adware checker—and watch out for websites that want you to click to download a file, speed up your computer, or some other come-on.

Stock Touting

In the olden days, penny stock promoters would have rooms filled with people making cold phone calls to people, convincing them to purchase a stock. When the stock price began appreciating, they would dump theirs, make a ton of money, then begin promoting another. Many of these same promoters have realized—like you—that there is money to be made online. Their tools are social media, e-mail, and bogus posts on investment discussion forums.

Be careful when you receive investment advice from people you don't know, even if they sound knowledgeable. And be careful about unwittingly passing this information along to your friends. There is no substitute for spending time with a licensed investment advisor who knows your goals and risk tolerances. If you are so sure about the merits of a particular investment you hear about online, take the recommendation to your real-world advisor, and get their opinion first.

Health Cures

A close relative of the stock scams are those related to health. Whether it be cures for terrible diseases, or cures for the problems of aging, there is always a ready market for being healthier. Scammers who promise the world with their lotions, potions, and systems find it easy to sell their wares to a willing (and sometimes desperate) clientele. If you are considering investigating this as a business for yourself, do some detailed due diligence to ensure that the company and its products are legitimate and effective. If the product is only available over the Internet, then it likely isn't a generally accepted cure. Asking your medical doctor for her professional opinion first is a good start.

Multi-level Marketing

Sometimes known as MLM, multi-level marketing is a clever sales system that recognizes that most people find it easy to sell to their friends and family. Here's how it works:

- You join the system by signing up, and often purchasing a starter bundle of products. The system may also give you a custom website page as well.
- You sell your products to your friends, either in person, or by driving them to your website. Your profit is the difference between the cost of the products and the selling price.
- To make "real" money, convince your friends and family to start selling the product. When they sign up and purchase any products for sale, you get a commission.
- If you convince them to sign people up, you also earn commission on sales for two levels: those you sign up, as well as their signed-up people.
- As long as you have people downstream who continue to sign new salespeople up, you can make a ton of money.

Many MLM schemes are legitimate ways for companies to skip the retailers and grow their market share by direct selling. Unfortunately some are not legitimate, and some have business terms that are onerous and unreasonable. If you are interested in MLM, read the fine print very, very carefully.

Spam

The Hormel company probably could never have imagined that the name of their luncheon meat would be transformed to represent unwanted junk mail. Depending on where you look—or what laws you are reading—spam is defined as unsolicited commercial e-mail. The reader hasn't requested the solicitation, but must wade through it anyway.

From the sender's perspective though, e-mail marketing might be an important part of their sales process: if they send 100,000 messages, and 0.3 percent respond with a purchase, then they have 300 sales. The more targeted the list, the higher the response rate. The problem is that many e-mail marketers purchase (or steal, or harvest) e-mails that are completely irrelevant. They send 100,000 e-mails out, and manage to annoy 99,700 people in the process; savvy marketers realize that this is the exact opposite of the reaction that they want.

What's worse are those operators whose spam touts dubious products—the health cures and financial scams. Every few years, the laws develop even stronger teeth, with ever-growing penalties. Depending on your jurisdiction, there are laws that specifically forbid sending commercial e-mails to people who have not requested the information. Spam at your peril!

Spammers work by sending messages to e-mail lists that they've acquired. Yet how different is this from a legitimate business reaching out to it's prospects? Given the volume of spam that exists, an entire industry of list providers and e-mail service providers have sprung up, on both sides of the ethical fence.

Purchasing Lists: Legitimate or Not Legitimate

It is possible to purchase e-mail lists, but your e-mail service provider may have a policy against your actually using them, unless they are lists that are certified as being "double opt-in." This means that after a person has signed up, they validate their desire to be contacted, by clicking on a link in a special e-mail that the system sends to them.

A far more productive—and legitimate—strategy is to partner with people who already have a double-opt-in list, and offer your products and services by "advertising" in their e-mail. Since the sender is trusted, the reader is more likely to open the e-mail. When they read your call to action, they will be reading it with the implicit endorsement of the list owner. And it is more likely that they will transact as a result. Generally speaking, if you find someone whose list sounds interesting to you, riding along with them will either cost you cash or a share of all profits—sometimes as much as 50 percent.

E-mail Service Providers: Acceptable Use Policies

There are a number of Internet-based organizations that blacklist e-mail service providers who supposedly send spam. E-mail service providers are paranoid that the actions of one or two of their bad apple customers will result in their entire company, and all of their customers, being blacklisted. For this reason, most e-mail service providers have explicit acceptable use policies, and the technology to monitor compliance. If you do not comply, you run the risk of being cut off completely.

Before you sign up with an e-mail service provider, familiarize yourself with the restrictions and protections they have in their policies. Some restrictions are to protect their customers (and themselves) against being blacklisted; others restrict the types of businesses they will host. It's better to find out about your provider's policies early than to wait until later when they may surprise you by shutting you down.

Unethical Practices

Would you take a job at any company, or are there certain industries or certain jobs that you would not consider under any circumstance. Because you are opening your own business, you can decide for yourself what kind of business you wish to run. Sometimes, though, there is a fine line between an acceptable business practice and what some would consider unethical. Most people would consider the following practices on the wrong side of the ethical line—do you? The first few may be due to a legitimate issue of timing, but the last few are beyond the pale.

- **Spam:** Sending unsolicited e-mail. Yet sometimes a legitimate e-mail to a customer is flagged by the customer herself as junk, because she can't remember you. Or she can't remember giving you permission to send her e-mail.
- **Bait and switch:** When a different product is offered because the advertised one is no longer available. Sometimes this can happen by mistake: your shopping cart automatically suggests alternative products, which your customer chooses because the one she was interested in wasn't available in her color.
- **Charging credit cards before shipping product:** Unless the customer explicitly agrees to prepaying for a product or service, a credit charge should be made only when the product ships. But what happens if there was a shipping delay of a few days, but the card was already charged?
- **Selling e-mails/names/addresses:** This is a huge privacy no-no, unless the customer has explicitly agreed to it. But what if the customer did agree to it, and they forgot?
- **Preying on children:** There are longstanding regulations regarding selling to minors, in addition to specific Internet regulations about the same. But how do you know that it wasn't a child who took his father's credit card to make the purchase?
- **Selling hacked software:** Software that provides free functionality, yet has hidden functionality that invades the privacy of the user, or adds obtrusive pop-up advertising. This type of software is one step away from being a computer virus.
- **Selling "stolen" movies, music, or books:** There is an incorrect notion that intellectual property should be free for the taking over the Internet, through media sharing sites. (How would you like someone taking your service or product, and then making it available for free to the world?) People who run these "businesses" claim they are only operating a directory service, and are not personally involved with stolen digital merchandise. The courts don't buy this argument.
- **Nigerian money scams:** These are the e-mails and social media posts asking for your help to liberate a huge pile of money; just provide your credit card (or cash) and the owners of the site will take it from there. (And they will take you as well.) This scam uses a technique called

social engineering, which preys on basic human nature to cause gullible people to do their bidding.

- **Questionable medical "cures":** The Internet is fast becoming a global compendium of health knowledge on just about every ailment and condition. Unfortunately, there are many snake-oil salesmen looking to take advantage of a sick person's desperation. These companies likely don't offer any money-back guarantees—or guarantees of product safety, either.

- **Raising money for not-for-profits (or fake not-for-profits) and skimming:** Here a fraudster represents himself as a bona fide charity, doing the tough work of fundraising. This is about as low as you can get. You have some compassion, so you make a donation. They either keep the entire amount, or keep a gargantuan commission before donating the remainder to a real charity.

Will you become a shady operator, using the Internet for not-so-upright—or even illegal—gains? Probably not. But other people have gone this route, so you need to be careful out there.

Know Your Moral Compass

While the previous group of businesses ranged from a bit unethical to just plain illegal, there are businesses that are legitimate, but may be distasteful to you. Just like in the real world, there are some businesses that you likely avoid. Yet they exist, so someone must be paying them.

Two of the biggest Internet businesses are online gambling and online pornography—but do you see yourself as a purveyor of either of these products? There are other businesses such as those catering to smokers that nonsmokers would ignore. Vegans may not be interested in an online business selling meat. How about medical tourism? And so on. Know your moral compass, and let that guide your online business choice and how you operate it.

When you do finally choose your business—one that you are comfortable with—what will it look like? And how will it be structured from a legal and tax perspective? In the next chapter, we'll look at the nuts and bolts of this last question.

CHAPTER 11

Structuring Your Business

Once you've gotten over the hump of choosing an industry and focus for your business, it's time to work on the structure of the venture. You also need to decide what type of operation you prefer. Do you work better as a lone ranger, or with a buddy? These and other considerations will drive your decisions on how to organize your business.

Perhaps the most serious aspect of launching your new business will be planning for the tax and legal structure of your entity. The people involved in establishing and later running your business will be a factor in deciding your legal structure. It is important to consider what liability protections are needed, and for whom. You need to weigh the tax consequences of your actions, from establishing your business, to operating it, and ultimately to ending it through a sale, dissolution, or even death. The following information is intended solely to give you a rough overview of the various organizational structures. Only a professional accountant and attorney can give you the best understanding of the consequences of various options and guide you in the decision-making process. In fact, some of these details can vary quite markedly by state. You can find cookie-cutter legal documents, as well as government rules, on the Internet, but you will be doing yourself a disservice if you forgo the experience and wisdom of professionals in this important area of planning.

Partnerships

Once they were Sears, Roebuck and Company, now they're just Sears. Whatever happened to Roebuck? Comics ponder this question, while business partners often wonder which one of them will be Sears and which will be Roebuck. Will you be the next Ben and Jerry? Will you be together for many years?

A partnership exists whenever two or more people work together in a single business and have not formed a legal entity, such as a corporation, under state law. You can find business partners who have been in stride for twenty-five years, and others who split up shortly after the sign on the front door was put into place. It's all in how you approach the business and whether or not you have common goals and compatibility. If one person sees the business as a friendly, local mom-and-pop operation, and the other is thinking about new locations, franchises, and four catalogs a year, the pairing may not be right.

People who team up to go into business need to be on the same page. It is usually a good idea for prospective partners to spend some time together, developing a common vision, mission, values, strategy, tactics, and overall game plan for a new business before jumping headlong into getting the new business off the ground. They also need to:

- Recognize each other's strengths and weaknesses.
- Accept that one partner may put in more hours while the other may be highly visible and get name recognition.
- Divide up tasks fairly, based on their respective strengths.
- Have an open line of communication.
- Learn how to resolve conflicts and differences of opinion.
- Decide percentage of ownership and control of the business. A fifty/fifty split is never good. Someone needs to have the final say.

It's imperative that everything be spelled out on paper, especially among close friends, who may need that written agreement as a legal document at some point in their business future.

General Partnerships

All types of business structures have certain legal implications. In a general partnership, each of the partners is jointly and severally liable for the debts and liabilities of the business. That means that both partners' personal assets are on the line for all of the business's liabilities. Between themselves, the partners can share the profits and losses any way they like. But to the outside world, they are both responsible for the business. Unless there is a written or oral agreement that can be proved, partners will share profits and losses equally. Partners can and should determine in advance who is responsible for which aspects of the business.

FACT

From a tax standpoint, a partnership is not treated as a business. Instead, the partners may be taxed individually. Each partner pays personal income tax. An IRS form (Form 1065) shows the pass-through of income and loss to each partner. Even if you run a business with someone without filing or creating an agreement as a partnership, you will likely be considered a partnership for legal purposes.

A general partnership can be advantageous because it allows you to pool resources and often makes it easier to gather funding. Partnerships enjoy a greater compendium of knowledge and skills. If partners share common goals and visions for the company, they can often complement one another by focusing on different functions. Any liabilities incurred, however, are shared among all the partners. This can be a disadvantage if one partner is clearly at fault or causes the business to go into debt. Each partner in a general partnership is responsible for the actions (and sometimes for the inactions or omissions) of the others, and for the overall business. So if your partner sends the company into debt and takes off for Rio, you are still held responsible.

Limited Liability Partnerships

Limited liability partnerships are another option that can be advantageous. A limited partner, unlike a general partner, takes on limited risk and is only liable for her investment and not for the entire business. If, however, the limited partner is a manager, she can be liable for debt. Even in a limited partnership, a general partner is necessary to take on the overall company liabilities. However, the general partner can be a corporation so that no individual is personally liable for the business. Also, limited partners can be replaced, or leave the business, without having to dissolve the partnership, which reduces legal entanglements. To form a limited partnership you must file with your state and pay a filing fee and annual fees.

Sole Proprietorships

If you choose to go it alone, without incorporating or otherwise establishing a business entity, you are a sole proprietor. This is the easiest form of business to start because you don't need to draft partnership agreements or register to incorporate. You may need to obtain proper licensing in your state, county, town, or city to conduct your type of business, and you will need to file a "doing business as" (DBA) form.

Being a sole proprietor means that you are the boss, the head honcho, the big cheese, whose name will appear on greeting cards and other congratulatory notes when you announce that you are officially open for business.

As a sole proprietor, you'll be the one lonely soul reviewing the profit-and-loss statements. You'll be the one with the tough decisions to make, and no matter how much you delegate responsibilities, the overall accountability of the business will fall on your shoulders, for better or worse. On the plus side, if and when the business takes off, you'll be the one reaping the rewards.

ALERT

One of the problems of being a sole proprietor is that you are responsible as an individual—so if your business goes into debt, even if you shut the doors and take down the sign, you can still be held liable. You can take out product insurance, insure your equipment, and put your house in your spouse's name, but it may not be enough to protect you completely.

As a sole proprietor, you don't need approval to make changes and implement new ways of running the business. In fact, others need your approval. You don't have to worry about a partner being in agreement with your decisions. Even taxation is a simple process, as you pay taxes based on your income.

At the same time, it can be psychologically difficult to go it alone in business. Just as you don't have anyone to answer to, you also don't have anyone else to do half the work, raise half the money, and solve half the problems as you do when you have a partner. If you're confident in your abilities and can handle a wide range of responsibilities, calling in the right people at the right times for help, then this might be the best structure for your business.

Corporations

A corporation is a legal entity unto itself. In a corporation, you may have less liability exposure than as a sole proprietor, though it's not as simple as just teaming up with a few partners. Instead, a corporation is a legally formed entity with laws, rules, and guidelines to follow.

Once you begin the process of incorporating, you will also need to determine if there is another business in your state with the name that you planned to use. You may need to change your name slightly. Conversely, you may think of several variations on the name you like and incorporate under a few of them to keep other companies from having similar names. However, remember the general trademark rule: If you don't use it you will lose it.

The process of incorporating is done in accordance with state laws and can be completed by filing the proper paperwork and paying certain fees. You'll need an attorney to assist you in the process and to review the state requirements. You will pay a fee to the state for incorporating, file corporate certificates annually, and possibly pay annual franchise taxes. Subsequently you may need to register as a "foreign" corporation in other states in which you plan to conduct business. For guidelines you can generally contact the secretary of state in the state where you are planning to incorporate or do business. It is also advisable to get a corporate seal in case documents require it.

The most significant advantage of incorporating is that it allows your business and personal responsibilities to be handled separately. Therefore, you are protected to a much greater degree. Your corporation can be held responsible without your being held personally liable. This is very significant in the event of a lawsuit, because you can protect your personal assets. You can also leave a corporation without having to dissolve the business, since you and the corporation are separate entities.

It can also be easier to obtain funding as a corporation than as a sole proprietor or partnership. As corporations grow, they may sell shares in the business to stockholders who are not involved in the day-to-day activities of the corporation, but have a vote in its policies and share in the profits.

Corporate tax rates are different than those imposed on personal income taxes. It's a good idea to look at the comparative rates when deciding whether to incorporate. For a smaller business in the $50,000 to $75,000 range, the tax rates for incorporating may also look slightly more favorable (25 percent as opposed to 28 percent). However, you'll be paying fees to incorporate, as well as legal fees and accounting and tax preparation fees, so you may not be benefiting after all—especially when you take into consideration the additional paperwork.

Self-employment tax is, as the name would imply, for people who are self-employed. When you work for someone else, your employer is responsible for paying half of the combined Social Security and Medicare payments for you as an employee (as of 2013, 7.65 percent of your salary). The other half is withheld from your earnings. In this case, however, since you are both employer and employee, you pay both halves of the 7.65 percent for Social Security and for Medicare, or a total of 15.3 percent of your salary and wages. This is in addition to your income tax payments.

ESSENTIAL

Do everything possible to demonstrate that your corporation is not a sham by separating your personal world from your business world. Keep personal records separate from corporate records. If you need money from the business to pay a personal bill, do not pay it with a company check. Withdraw the money as salary or dividends, paying the appropriate taxes.

Once you incorporate, you pay yourself a salary or other compensation from the corporation. You also pay corporate taxes, as well as your own income taxes based on how much salary you receive. Unlike a sole proprietor, whose profits land on top of his taxable income, a corporation pays tax separately.

C and S Corporations

From a tax perspective, there are different types of corporations. The most common is the C corporation (it has just been described and is taxed as a separate entity at corporate level tax rates). There is also an S corporation, which is a small business corporation. By definition, an S corporation is a company that cannot have more than 100 shareholders, and it can only have one class of stock. An S corporation still provides personal liability protection. However, the profits from the S corporation are not federally taxed but are passed through to your own personal income and taxed accordingly—just like a partnership. Generally, losses are not allowed to flow through to personal taxes. Check with your tax professional before making this or any tax-related decision.

Often, someone running a small business does not incorporate until the company is seeing significant profits because:

- There may be franchise fees and attorney fees to pay.
- It will be necessary to file both corporate and personal tax returns, which can be time-consuming and costly.

On the other hand, you may choose to incorporate if:

- You want to keep your business and personal assets separate to guard against lawsuits or paying higher personal income taxes.
- You suddenly see significant profits as a sole proprietor.

These are general rules of thumb; speak to your accountant about when you should incorporate—every person (and business) is different.

Limited Liability Company

You can also form a limited liability company (LLC). This type of entity provides the limited personal liability benefits of a corporation and the tax treatment of a partnership. Profits are passed through to you and taxes are paid as part of your personal income tax. An LLC can, when you reach that point, have unlimited stockholders and corporate stockholders, like a C corporation. An S corporation, on the other hand, is limited in number of owners, and you cannot have entities as stockholders in most cases.

Making the Choice

accountant for the startup
lawyer for the establishment

You should weigh the pros and cons of incorporating, discuss the options with an accountant, and hire an attorney to guide you through the process. There is no set rule dictating who does and does not need to incorporate. It's a personal decision based on the size, structure, and type of business as well as your personal assets, tax status, and potential for liability.

ESSENTIAL

If there are other individuals involved in helping you start up your new business or investing in it, you may find the process of selecting and establishing a business entity to be helpful as you consider such issues as defining who has control over the new business, how you will raise capital, and others.

If you choose to incorporate, you will need to select a state in which to file. Generally it is the state in which you will have physical facilities. You can, however, select another state and qualify to do business as a foreign corporation in your own state. Corporate laws, costs of incorporating, and the state's tax structure will usually be deciding factors, especially for online businesses. Doing business in any state, whether or not you are incorporated or a foreign corporation, makes you subject to that state's tax laws.

Joint Ventures

Beyond the legal structures for your business, you might have heard of another common term: the joint venture. A joint venture isn't a legal entity in the same sense as the other forms, but rather is a general term for an agreement between two entities who want to work together.

Each joint venture partner brings a special skill to the table, and typically is looking to get something special in return. For example, imagine an Internet sales company and a delivery service. On one hand, the Internet sales company might simply sign a contract with the delivery service to deliver their sales. A joint venture takes it one step further:

- The two agree that the joint venture or "JV" agreement will be for a set number of years—say five.
- The delivery company will provide employees to act as customer service agents for the JV.
- The Internet sales company will pay for the development of mobile delivery tracking functionality.

In this example the delivery company is providing people, while the Internet company is providing expertise.

Before entering into any marriage, it is important that you know what you want out of it: companionship, financial security, children, or some other aspect. This is no different with a JV; if you know what you want out of it, the who-does-what-question will be easily answered.

Get Tax Advice Now!

When talking with your tax professional, ask for the particulars of how income is taxed in the various legal structures. In general, income can be taxed twice in a C corporation. The corporation's earnings are subject to federal income tax, and then the shareholders will be taxed on any after-tax income that is distributed to them as dividends. Taxes are collected from corporations on a sliding scale. There are ways to avoid the double taxation in a C corporation, such as:

- Retaining earnings and not distributing them to shareholders.
- Structuring payments in a deductible form such as interest, rent, or royalties.
- Compensating shareholder-employees with payroll, reducing earnings subject to tax.

S corporations and partnerships are not subject to federal tax. These structures allow profits and losses to be passed through to individuals.

It is possible to change your election and move from one legal structure to another, but there are restrictions and consequences for doing so. Again, seek the advice of professionals when considering a change.

FACT

Certain personal service businesses are not eligible for graduated income tax on earnings. A personal service business is defined as one in which an employee-owner performs the principal activity; examples include hairstyling, housecleaning, or private chef services. These businesses are subject to a flat 35 percent tax rate (as of 2012). Check with your attorney to see if your service falls into this category.

Deductibility of Losses

The way a loss is treated depends on how a business is organized. In general, with sole proprietorships, and some partnerships, the loss passes through to the individual. With a C corporation, there are many more variables and much more flexibility in applying the loss backward and forward to different tax years. An S corporation does not have the flexibility of these forward or backward losses. Your tax advisor will be able to counsel you on your options based on the particular circumstances of a particular year.

Taxable Year

You will need to decide when you want your taxable year to start. You do not need to have your business taxable year be the calendar year in most instances. If you can demonstrate an accounting period in which you regularly wrap up your books and determine your annual profit and loss, you can use that time frame for your taxable year. In a partnership it can be a little tricky, but the decision would be determined by the taxable year of the one or more partners whose aggregate interest exceeds 50 percent. Most businesses follow a calendar year, but you may find reasons to organize your taxable year otherwise.

Choose an Accounting Method

Before settling on your business structure, you will want to weigh the pros and cons of various accounting methods. The primary consideration is whether you would benefit from operating on a cash basis or an accrual basis. With a sole proprietorship, S corporation, or partnership you may make this choice. With most types of C corporations, you are prohibited from using a cash basis. Check with your accountant.

Exiting the Business

As exciting as it is to start something new, it is necessary to keep a level head with a view toward the ultimate wrap-up of your venture. No one has a crystal ball to see exactly what shape the end will take. Nevertheless, you can think about the ultimate tax responsibilities associated with each business structure option and make an informed choice in the early stages. Selling the assets or shares of a company triggers either capital gain or ordinary income and its attendant tax liabilities. The details of how this would apply to your undertaking should be thoroughly reviewed with your tax professional. The rules are different for each option, and are further complicated by choices made along the way, such as opting for a different form of organization. The tax consequences of liquidating or dissolving your business has tax consequences dependent on how you are set up, but generally a gain realized by selling off assets winds up passing through to you as the owner.

Believe it or not, there are cases where your entity may suffer an inadvertent termination. An S corporation's election is revoked when it exceeds 100 shareholders, has more than one class of stock, or in a few other cases. If a partnership is no longer operating, or sells more than 50 percent of its interest, a termination of the partnership may be instigated.

Retirement or Death

The death of a sole proprietor does not generate any immediate business-related tax responsibilities. If a shareholder of a corporation passes away, the corporation may want to buy back the shareholder's stock. Most likely, the heirs or estate will want to redeem the stock. There are myriad rules surrounding the execution of such a redemption and the corresponding tax fallout. Partnerships have quite a bit of flexibility in planning for the death or retirement of a partner, including everything from considering such an event to be the dissolution of the partnership to selling the partner's share to a third party.

Offering Employee Benefits

Generally speaking, tax code permits favorable tax treatment for benefits to employees only. The key here is that persons who are self-employed are not considered, in this tax view, as employees. A sole proprietor is usually treated as a self-employed person. Shareholders in S corporations as well as partners in a partnership are considered self-employed individuals and not employees. Shareholders who work for their own C corporation, however, may be treated as employees. The benefits people expect, such as health and accident insurance, pension plans, life insurance, and employer-paid meals or lodging may be a significant factor in deciding how to structure your business.

At this point, you may have chosen your business, and figured out the right tax and legal structure. Next comes your chance to tell the world about it: putting together your business plan.

CHAPTER 12

Crafting a Business Plan

There's an old saying, "If you don't know where you're going, any road will get you there." But you do have an idea where you are going with your business concept. Now it is time to get that plan down on paper so you'll know how to make the concept real. Business plans are dynamic and you will want to revisit yours frequently as your business grows and changes shape. It may seem daunting at first, but think of it as a chance to demonstrate the validity of your concept.

How to Know If You Need a Business Plan

In an ideal world, an entrepreneur would have all the planning for her business sorted out and neatly presented in a document worthy of review by investors before opening the door for business. Some businesses start slowly and organically, growing out of a hobby. Examples include a baseball card collector who starts to sell via eBay or Etsy, or someone whose expertise in a particular field gets tapped informally and he decides to set up shop as a consultant. In these instances, a business may be going before a plan is put in place. Even so, the value of a business plan cannot be underestimated. If you get too caught up in the excitement of starting something new, and a year or so into it realize you have not planned for cash flow properly, instead of growing your business you may find yourself bailing out a sinking ship.

More than just a proposal to draw interest from investors, a business plan sets the foundation from which you will build your business. You will use your proposal as an outline to guide you and help you make sure each area is covered and each goal is met. The plan will help you make sure you stay on track and don't lose your focus.

ESSENTIAL

There are many reasons to write a business plan, from defining a business at the outset to providing a chart for future growth. Your outline can also be used to set a valuation on your business when you are getting ready to sell. The most common use, though, will be to support your application for a loan.

While business plans will vary depending on the structure and the type of business, many of the principles remain the same. The basic elements in a business plan are:

- Executive summary
- Description of the company
- Goals and objectives
- An overview of the industry
- Market analysis
- Products and services

7 • Marketing plans and strategies
8 • Financial plan
9 • Overview of key personnel

Business plans include additional information as necessary to tell the overall story of how the business will be formed and evolve into a profitable entity. Furthermore, the business plan will demonstrate how your business will move forward once you have opened your doors. You may begin with a fairly simple plan if your initial financial needs are not extensive. Over time, you may need to obtain more money and will have to show how it will be used for your expansion ideas. Projected sales figures, cash flow, and anticipated profit and loss for the first three years will help you illustrate the anticipated results of your plan.

Getting Ready

Writing a business plan may appear intimidating at first. However, if you take it step by step, you won't be defeated by the thought of creating this important document. You should realize before you begin that you will have to revise the plan as you incorporate new ideas. As you're developing the plan, be sure to show portions of it to other people for feedback, to assess what's missing or unclear. Then return to the plan and make the needed revisions. Don't sweat over every word you put on paper—numerous changes will be made down the road.

→ monday.com

FACT

The best business plans are concrete. They define specific goals and decide who will be responsible for meeting them and when they will be met. For a plan to work, it must be practical, with more emphasis on implementation than on lofty strategies. Interim dates for review and course correction should be part of the plan from the beginning.

Since thousands, if not millions, of business plans have preceded yours, you don't need to reinvent the wheel. Look on the web for sample business plans to get a general idea of how they have been put together. Remember, the best plan is not the one with the most jargon, most pages, or most superlatives and keywords. The strongest business plan is one that clearly paints the picture of your business and <u>demonstrates how and why it will be successful</u>. Remember though, that the business plan that you eventually write must be your plan for your business, not a copy-paste from someone else's.

Neatness also counts. While it probably won't make or break a business deal, it is certainly to your advantage to have a professional-looking business plan, complete with cover page and binding. Make sure you have proofread and edited the document. Graphs, charts, illustrations, and photos can enhance a presentation if you're looking for backers. If you choose to develop the plan in a PowerPoint presentation format, you may also be able to use video. Use these extras, however, only if they significantly help make the case for your plan.

ESSENTIAL

If you are looking to be different, consider putting your business plan on a password-protected website. As you are building an online business, this might demonstrate your fluency with the channel, more so than a traditional plan.

Organize the format so that a reader can skim through the proposal and see the highlights before studying it. If you don't need to get investors, and the plan is for yourself and your partners, you may be less formal. Either way, don't cut corners. Include all the pertinent information. You'll be glad you did when you refer back to the plan.

A Step-by-Step Guide

The process of writing a business plan is easier if you take it one step at a time. In the following sections, you'll find all the information you need to write a plan that convincingly explains what your business is about and why it will succeed.

Title or Cover Page

Include all contact information for yourself and your partners, if any, on the cover page. This page doesn't need to contain much, but keep in mind that first impressions say a lot. You might use an elegant typeface for a more upscale business or a cutting-edge logo for a company appealing to a young audience. A one-or-two sentence descriptive summary is useful.

Table of Contents

A table of contents (TOC) provides an easy way to find key information. In the TOC, you present an itemized overview of what's included within the business plan. The table lets readers go back and find each subject without having to flip through the entire plan again and again.

Executive Summary

The executive summary is the single most important section of the business plan.

express your confidence

In one or two pages, your executive summary should include a description of the products or services offered and the features that make your business distinctive. It's important that you present your target audience, costs, objectives, marketing plans, and financial projections. Your summary should express your confidence in the future success of the business and make potential investors want to read more. Don't hesitate to rewrite as many times as necessary to polish this important section.

until you are satisfied

ESSENTIAL

Things to work on:
1. *business description*
2. *marketing plan*
3. *operations*
4. *financial plan*
5. *management overview*

Although a business plan is structured in a particular order beginning with an executive summary, the executive summary is the last piece you should write. First, work on the business description, marketing plan, operations, financial plan, and management overview. When you have all these components completed it will be easy to extract the highlights for the executive summary.

Establish a foundation for your business. Point out the current climate and explain what it is that you will offer. For example, you could say, "Last year, mobile phones had the highest penetration in New York: 1.5 times the national average," or "According to statistics from XYZ Source, the demand for frozen, healthy prepared foods will rise 10 percent per year for the coming decade."

Then explain how this fact or figure opens the door for your business to step in and solve a problem, provide a service, or simply make life simpler for these individuals, your target audience. For example, "Momfood will be available in two metropolitan markets in the coming year, rising to fifteen in ten years."

Include your strongest selling point. You may have some nifty Internet technology. You may be the first to do something, or the first to do it in a specific way. Whatever aspect you choose to highlight, be concise. Finally, if you are seeking financing, be clear about how much you need, what you will use it for, and when the investor might expect his money back.

Business Overview

This section of your business plan is also known as the business description, company overview, company plan, or company summary. This is the place where you can elaborate with a comprehensive description of your plans, being sure to stay within a few pages. Start off with the goals of the business. Explain the legal structure (sole proprietorship, partnership, corporation, etc.) and the status of the business. Is it a start-up or is it an expansion?

FACT

Each business has its own systems that govern its operation. Guide the reader through the process, from ordering the inventory to updating the website to client checkout. Will customers be billed immediately for their purchase, or can they pay in three auto-billed installments? Perhaps you will offer both options for different levels of service. This is the place to explain your plan thoroughly, but simply.

If it is an existing business, describe its history to this point. List the existing and proposed services and products. Next, include the resources needed to run the business, the location, and the anticipated time until you will be open for customers. If you are planning a new concern, also include methods of record keeping and how the business will operate. Most importantly, you need to explain why the business will be successful.

A popular term today is "business model." While it sounds a bit mysterious, all the term means is a description of how the business will make money. Will it sell advertisements and give away services, or will it charge for services and not have any ads? Will it be a trading business, buying merchandise cheaply and selling it for profit, or will it be a marketplace, taking a slice from each transaction along the way? There are numerous business models that are possible—explaining yours right up front will help readers understand the basis for your ideas—and why they might invest.

Business Operations

As part of your business overview, it is necessary to explain exactly how your products or services will be produced and sold. Explain your product in succinct, easy-to-understand language. This is not a place to dazzle the reader with high-tech or industry jargon. Writing this section is very good practice for marketing the product or service. If you can explain it clearly in your business plan, you'll have a prototype for future marketing literature. And, lastly, include all of your requirements for facilities, equipment, and personnel, as well as the supplies that will be needed, and the sources of these supplies.

Management Team

Here you will list the key players, with short bios and the value that each team member brings to the table. For businesses seeking capital, this information is significant, since the potential investors want to know the recipient of their investment capital. They will be particularly interested in knowing if your key people have the goods to take the business to the next level.

One or two paragraphs should be sufficient to sum up the qualifications and overall background of each key person involved. Don't get into philosophies or include extraneous material. Include pictures if you like, and links to each person's LinkedIn profile. You might also mention your board of directors or advisors and include their names and backgrounds.

Market Analysis

A major part of your business plan will address the market you are entering. The number one priority of this section is to provide evidence that there is enough of a market to support your business. Start by pinning down the unique characteristics of your product or service, or at least define the particular niche you will serve. If you sell office supplies online, as an example, there may be three major competitors, but none of them uses local sources, which you do.

To show how your distinctive features matter, you will need to show the characteristics of your target market. Using the office supplies example, you might be able to show that 35 percent of your prospective buyers care about local sourcing, and are willing to pay a 15 percent premium. These statistics can be used to reinforce the validity of your key differentiator, and guide your later pricing and marketing strategy.

You will need to understand overall trends in the industry, look at your competition, do a market analysis, research prospective technologies and websites, and ultimately come up with a solid, but perhaps flexible, marketing strategy. Even in advance of concrete market research, you will have a gut feeling about the market and how your endeavor will fill a need. Try sketching out a rough outline of where your customers will come from. Put some percentages on each segment based on where you believe you will get the best response.

Industry Analysis

In this section, you take a step back and look at the big picture: the industry as it currently stands and projected future developments. You will need to do your share of research before putting this part of the plan together. It is key to note the size and growth rate of the industry as a whole. For example, if your business will be part of a $10 billion industry that in the next ten years is expected to grow to more than $50 billion, then include that information. Of course, you need to define your industry very carefully. What is the scope: global, national, or regional? The industry issues and trends may be very different, depending on what you choose.

ESSENTIAL

Use charts, graphs, or simple text to explain the sales and profit trends culled from your research. Present changes in the industry and share news that will provide your business with an entry point into the market. Also, clearly delineate the market in your area or region. Then show the response of your business to the marketing demands and trends.

The end result of the industry analysis should be a demonstration of why your business will be able to grab a piece of the pie. It is important for you as a future entrepreneur to see this very clearly in order to advocate for your proposed enterprise. If you don't have a potential market share, no matter how great your idea may be, you'll have trouble convincing others that your company will be successful.

Marketing Strategy

In this section, you need to explain who your target market is. Describe this market and why they would pay for your product or services. The main components of your marketing strategy should include:

- Pricing
- Advertising and profile building
- Networking
- Promotion
- Sales strategies
- Partnerships
- Sales tracking

Readers of your business plan will want to know how you came up with your pricing. If you are selling a product online, did you factor in the cost of customer service, and web hosting as well as the product itself? Did you account for the need to discount a certain percentage?

Most successful businesses are geared to reach a specific market. The size of the market will depend on the nature of the product. Explaining how you will reach your market is a very important part of supporting your business plan. Keep in mind that if you try to reach too large an audience, you may be unable to serve the customers you attract. If your website can't handle a big influx of customer queries, these prospects will become frustrated and go elsewhere. Likewise, you should also be careful about having such a specific, narrow target group that you don't have enough potential customers to make your business profitable.

There are a number of advertising and promotional avenues to consider. You will need to spell out which you are choosing and why. Most importantly for online businesses, however, is to think about the websites where your prospects can be found, then negotiate (or purchase) links from that site to yours. List these sites in your plan.

However you expect to do it, you will need to explain how you intend to capture a portion of the market. Detail the methods and media you will utilize to promote your business. Beyond the Internet, will you use direct mail? A radio and television advertising campaign? Are you seeking subscribers? Membership? You then need to spell out how much money you will spend on publicity and advertising. It's very important to justify your marketing strategy to show others (and remind yourself) you aren't throwing your money away.

If you have contacts or relationships with publicists or others who can help get your name in the media or give you discounts on advertising, this is the place to let that fact be known. Perhaps you have some barter opportunities that will preserve cash at the outset. Highlight these. If you have ideas, including any special promotional events, giveaways, special combination pricing, or free delivery, contests, or anything else that will hype your business, include those plans here.

The Internet is filled with examples of partnerships; an investor might be interested in knowing who might be elements of yours. Partners can be used to funnel leads to your online business, or they can be used to help deliver it. For example, an online party supply store might be able to provide leads to party planners, caterers, entertainers, and others. A fulfillment company might be able to carry your inventory, package it, then ship it to your customers.

Show how you expect to be perceived in the marketplace, whether you will be competing on price, or attacking the luxury end of the market with a high-service offering and luxury merchandise.

Competitive Analysis

Rather than a negative, your competition may be one of the best supporting arguments for the success of your business. First, if there are already other companies doing what you plan to do, it proves there is a demand for it. Naturally, you have ideas to serve this market better, with innovations, better quality, more competitive pricing, or all of the above. Prove it. You'll need to do some investigative research so that you can adequately describe your competitors. You want to present an overview of their business operations, their location, products, share of the market, and anything else you think is pertinent—all in a concise form. You may need to visit competitors' sites and possibly go through a few transactions to get a better idea of the customer experience. Or you may have had discussions with clients of your competitors.

Your next step is to make comparisons to your business and explain how you will improve upon the products and services offered by your competitors. Study what the market wants and show how you can do better. If you can show that you will draw customers based on what you're offering (whether it's service, products, location, or anything else), then you can gain the upper hand.

You aren't trying to denigrate other businesses; you're simply trying to separate what you intend to do from what's being done by others. Let those who are reviewing your business plan know that you're prepared to carve out your own segment of the market and how you propose to do so.

Financial Plan

Everything in your business plan so far is a setup for the main event, which is the numbers. Be clear about your total projected financial needs and how the funds will be used. This section demonstrates how your business will become profitable. It follows a logical trend and tells your financial story, just as the rest of your plan provides a compelling background for the numbers. There's nothing wrong with asking your accountant or any qualified financial expert to help you put this part of the plan together.

You'll want to show clearly how much money you're seeking and then explain exactly how you plan to spend it. Product acquisition and inventory? Marketing? Sales commissions? Technology? Make sure it's all spelled out. All expenditures need to be justified, beginning with your start-up costs and continuing with your ongoing operations costs.

ALERT

You will probably finance your new business from a variety of sources. Don't hesitate to be forthcoming with the mix of resources as you write your business plan. Most importantly, you will want to show how much of your own money you are putting into the venture. Other investors won't write a check unless they see that you've done so first.

You then need to explain where your profits will come from. Be conservative to a fault. Don't fantasize. Include the next three years in a projected profit-and-loss income statement. Break the statement up by months at first to show how you plan to build the business, and then break it up by years. Include your:

how do I get to this point?

- Break-even analysis
- Projected balance sheet
- Projected income statement
- Projected cash flow (you need to illustrate that you will not run out of cash)

Just as you want to show your projected expenses, assets, and liabilities when starting a new business, you should include financial statements from the previous three years if the plan is for an existing business. No matter how brilliant your idea is, if the numbers don't add up, your business will not succeed. The bottom line is just that—the bottom line.

Reviewing and Tweaking Your Plan

Now that you have all of the key ingredients included in your plan, it's time to step back and look at it with fresh eyes. Can it work? If you are satisfied that your idea deserves to be funded, you will want to check over your document carefully. Make sure you've included all key points, the business plan flows clearly, all spelling and grammar has been checked and edited, all graphs and charts are easy to read. Print the plan on high-quality paper and bind it: you want it to have a professional appearance.

One of the more powerful things to do is to test-drive your plan with a few trusted people. If you have anyone in your family or personal circle with a business mindset, getting their feedback can be invaluable. Even more important, send a copy to your accountant and attorney, and get their feedback as well. These professionals are (or will be) part of your team moving forward. If they see any red flags, it's better to find out earlier than later. And they may know of an investor that is interested in your type of online business.

A business plan usually runs from twenty to thirty pages in length. Lines should be double-spaced and there should be enough white space around the margins so that words don't look too dense. Make sure pages are numbered, and double-check your table of contents.

Attach any supporting documents that you have in an appendix. This could include any research material, articles, detailed resumes, graphics, product illustrations, or other data you think are relevant. Keep these supporting documents to a few pages.

ESSENTIAL

Once you have filled in the rough business plan, start shaping it as you think through and plan out each dimension of your business. Remember, the business plan needs to be a realistic portrait of your business. If the pieces don't fit together or the numbers don't add up, not only will the plan fail, so will the business.

Business plans vary in their style and manner. Some have subsections throughout the plan, while others paint broader strokes. There are numerous variations on the main theme, but the business plan should include, in some form, the elements discussed in this chapter. Don't worry about the writing at first—just do your best to express your ideas and explain your business.

This chapter has focused on preparing a plan for a start-up business, but planning doesn't stop there. You may want to generate internal plans as you proceed in your business. Less formal than plans for funding proposals, these internal documents can be used for managers to set and measure goals. If you review them annually, you can assess your progress.

Once your plan is complete, continue to think of it as a living document. Revisit it, updating pertinent information and goals over time. The plan will help keep you on track and offer a benchmark against which to measure your progress. When you have a proven track record of setting and meeting goals you become more attractive to future investors.

CHAPTER 13

Get Your Capital Act Together

Businesses can do one of three things financially: make money, break even, or lose money. Often at the very beginning, it is necessary to operate in a deficit. At some point, however, you will want to have something in the bank to show for all your hard work. Making money is a goal. Finding and using money to get you to that point is another story.

Finance Basics

No matter how terrific your idea is or how ready the market is to buy it, nothing is going to happen without funds to get the plan moving. You may have some general ideas on how to build your business, but now is when you need to face reality and look at the cold hard numbers. Some would counsel you to have enough funds set aside to carry your day-to-day expenses for at least six months to a year. Knowing you don't have to worry about your personal expenses, you will be free to give your idea your full attention.

6 months
7500.00

12 months
15000.00

In the simplest terms, money for your business will come from one of two sources: you, or you and others. If yours is a service business, you may be able to comfortably fund your start-up costs yourself. But no business starts with zero cash infusion needs. In most cases you will need to find funding beyond your own capabilities. Many entrepreneurs seek additional capital from private sources such as family and friends. Your start-up funds could also come as an equity investment giving the party an ownership stake in your business. Relatively smaller and shorter-term funding comes from banks, savings and loans, or credit unions.

Be aware, bank loans will not provide your first dollars. Banks want to be sure others are taking a risk on you—including you. Angel investors are usually wealthy individuals who are willing to stake you some seed money. Venture capitalists are firms that would be taking a share of your company in exchange for the money they give you.

FACT

Venture capitalists are sources that should not be tapped until you are ready for significant and rapid growth and contemplate selling within the next few years. Most venture capitalists are not interested in keeping their money locked up in your business for the long haul.

Before you embark on the quest for dollars, take the time to do a thorough analysis of why you need money now. Here are some points the Small Business Administration suggests you consider:

- Are you able to work with your current cash flow?
- Are you looking for a cushion or funds to expand?

- How urgent is your need? Anticipate cash needs rather than trying to borrow under pressure.
- How much are you willing to risk?
- At what stage of development is your business?
- How will borrowed capital be used? Lenders will want to know.
- Overall, what is the state of your industry? Is it depressed, stable, or growing? Each situation drives different money sources and needs. Flourishing businesses in a growing economy will get better terms.
- Is your business seasonal or cyclical? Retailers often sell most of their products in the period leading up to Christmas, and require loans to survive low-sales periods.
- How strong is your management team? Be ready to prove their capabilities.
- How does your financing request dovetail with your business plan? If you don't have a business plan, writing one has to become a top priority.

There may be some other factors as well; the point is to consider these before you meet potential investors.

How to Get Start-Up Cash

When you are seeking money from outside sources, you have two broad paths to pursue: debt financing and equity. Debt financing is money you borrow (usually) from a financial institution such as a bank, and (sometimes) from friends and family. These borrowed funds must be repaid over a period of time with interest. When you seek a business loan, the lending institution will ask how much of your own money you are staking to the business. Additionally, you can be asked to submit assets you have as collateral for the loan. Assets that could be used to collateralize a loan include investments you have in real estate, stocks or bonds, or some other fairly liquid form.

There are formulas that apply to particular types of loans, but you should plan on demonstrating your ability to front anywhere from 10 to 30 percent of the equity in a start-up business. If that isn't scary enough, the bank is going to tell you next that you will have to personally guarantee the loan. This means that if the business fails, the debt obligation remains, and you will be personally making those payments. Once the business has become viable with a track record of profits, or can prove profits are in the near future, different terms can be negotiated.

A new source of government-backed funding through the Small Business Association (SBA) is called the Early Stage Innovation Fund, which provides seed money for fast growing start-ups. The rules can be a bit complex but the Fund might be another resource that fits with your business strategy.

ALERT

Keep in mind the premise that the asset you use as collateral will be sold if you default and do not repay the loan. The antique train sets you have lovingly restored may be worth something on eBay, but they are not going to carry the day with an ultraserious loan officer.

Venture Capital—Know All Your Options

Banks earn interest on loans. It is their obligation to be conservative in selecting how they write loans to keep the banks' shareholders' risk of loss to a minimum. Other funding sources might be willing to take more risk, but want more in exchange. Venture capitalists can be a good source of start-up funds: most venture capitalists are people who made a killing with their great idea or product. Now that they have cashed out they want to use the capital (money) they created as a tool for creating even more wealth. Venture capitalists are always on the hunt for the next great idea. It could be yours. Unlike a bank that gets paid back on a predictable schedule, investors do not realize any profit—or loss—until your business is sold.

Venture capitalists come in many sizes and shapes and sport many personalities. They often reflect a greater interest in business ideas from the industries where they were successful. Just like dating, you'll meet people who aren't interested in what you have to offer and others with whom you don't feel comfortable entering into an agreement. One of the biggest mistakes you can make is jumping at the first offer of money that comes along. On closer inspection, you may find other strings attached, such as control issues.

It's very important that both sides feel comfortable when entering this kind of business relationship. When you meet with investors, they're sizing you up, too. Are you someone they want to put their money behind? Does your plan sound feasible, and can you make it happen? Their evaluation of the investment often turns not on the idea, but of the person sitting before them. Many people can come up with good ideas, but few can actually make them work. That's why so many businesses fail in the first few years.

Investors are looking for:

- A sound idea
- A good, comprehensive business plan
- Someone with the drive, determination, and skills to make that plan happen

You're looking for:

- Someone who understands your idea or shares the same vision
- Someone who will let you maintain control of your business
- An individual, or individuals, with the funding to help you make your idea happen

It's also important to distinguish between venture capitalists who are only interested in a financial relationship, and those who are interested in being more active in the business. This second group—strategic investors—may connect you to potential clients, suppliers, and other partners; these connections and their advice ultimately may be more valuable than their financial investment.

Before you start raising money, it's worth mentioning that financing is often tied closely to control issues. If you get a loan, then you need to pay back the money with interest, no ifs, ands, or buts. If you take on an investor, you may be giving up some degree of control over your business as well as a percentage of your profits. A venture capital company will definitely require an equity position in your company. Therefore, determine specifically what people want for their investment. Are they seeking profits, control, or both? And make sure you know how to get out of a deal before you consummate getting into it.

ESSENTIAL

At the very beginning you might need to rely on your training or past industry or entrepreneurial experience to demonstrate your readiness to head this new venture. As the business grows, you may need to bring in talented folks in specialized areas: sales and marketing, finance, inventory management, technology, and more. Investing in this talent will offer proof of your commitment to success and to strategic planning for the continued growth of your business.

Another interesting alternative to consider is "crowdfunding," where you put your business plan online, and various individuals—the so-called crowd—pony up money. Check out *www.Kickstarter.com*, *www.indiegogo.com*, *www.rockethub.com*, *www.wefunder.com*, and *www.peerbackers.com*.

Silent (or Not-So-Silent) Partners

The best way to find angel investors is to get out there and network. There may even be investment networking groups in your area you can join or that can help you circulate your proposal. Angel investors are particularly attractive because they can be the source of equity funding you will need in the early days. They can provide as little as a couple of thousand dollars to amounts in the high seven figures.

Venture capitalists tend to be deluged with plans for many times the number of companies in which they can invest, so referrals may help your plan get a serious read. This crowd is looking for very high returns on their investment so they are constantly combing proposals for opportunities that offer them a chance to get in on something that has an excellent chance of growing quickly.

Venture capitalists will likely have a behind-the-scenes influence on the day-to-day management of the company, but can intensify their involvement if they sense management is making decisions that will hurt rather than improve their profit prospects. Keep in mind that they will expect to have certain milestones met and will want reports on your progress toward meeting them.

Because equity investors will literally have a stake in your business, they will be scrutinizing your proposal for a number of factors. Plan to answer the following questions:

- Are you opening a new market that has tremendous growth?
- How rapidly will your business reach market dominance?
- Where will your profits be generated?
- Can high profit margins be sustained as competition comes after you?
- Do you have a plan and a timeline to sell?
- Can it be protected from imitators with patents or proprietary technology?
- What obstacles do you foresee and how will you overcome them?
- What industry experience do you and your team have?

Probably the most important question that equity investors will want answered is simple: when—and how—will they get their money back.

FACT

Know the impact of debt versus equity financing. With debt financing, you retain control of all aspects of your business, but pay interest along the way. With equity financing, your investors can exert some control in your decisions, even to the point of making you sell the company. If family or friends are equity investors, it could change your personal relationships, not necessarily for the better.

In all cases, you will need to make a solid presentation that shows how the money will be used, the risks, and the return. Showing your passion for your undertaking will go a long way, too, in convincing any investor of your seriousness. The real litmus test for the viability of your idea may be how soon your profits exceed your expenses.

Opening Funding Doors in Any Economy

If you are thinking of starting a new business in a down economy, it only means you must be that much more diligent in assessing the potential market for your goods or services. Likewise you may have to widen your search for funding. Perhaps you will need to scale your idea to what you can personally invest. Just remember, investors are always looking for a good bet. If you can prove your online business is one, you can grab the brass ring and get launched.

Some tips:

- Make sure your business plan addresses every possible concern your investors may have.
- Create the strongest market analysis possible supporting demand for your idea.
- Look for a few early customers. Real contracts will demonstrate to investors that your assumptions are realistic.
- Try and put together a few early investors that will impress larger prospective investors.
- Make a case for how you will prevail where others may have failed.

You will likely meet a number of potential investors before you have a deal. Remember that each time you meet someone and make your pitch, there is something to learn.

Personal Credit Scores Matter

You are not going to convince a bank to part with its money based on your good looks. You should have a personal financial record that is squeaky clean and demonstrates prudent judgment and reliability. Even if you are incorporated, the bank will be reviewing your personal financial track record when you go for a loan. First and foremost, they want to be sure that you and your business, if it has been operating for a while, have a solid credit history. Top credit scores can be the make-or-break difference for your getting a loan approval. If you have a good history of meeting your personal loans—and this includes every credit card, school loan, mortgage, auto loan, or other loan you currently have or have paid off—you may be viewed as creditworthy.

Sometimes even with a sterling track record your application can be turned down. Don't despair—keep shopping for institutions that are looking for customers like you. Likewise, if the business can prove it has consistently met its obligations for lease payments and the like, a record of dependability will have been established. You can order a credit report for a nominal fee from Equifax, Experian, or another credit bureau to see what your credit record looks like. If you find any irregularities, such as credit cards you thought were closed but remain open, you can clear them up. Or if there is a one-time blip in life that caused you to miss a payment, such as a medical emergency, it can and will need to be explained.

ESSENTIAL

Did you know that even if you have unused credit on credit cards, a lending institution will view that as debt obligation? That's because you could access or use that credit at any moment. If you did, you could exceed your loan capacity. If you do not use or need a particular credit card, even a store card, close the account now.

If you filed for bankruptcy within the past seven years, you may not be able to secure a loan. Likewise, if you have a pattern of slow payments or collections against you, most lenders will not be eager to support your loan request. Lastly, banks and governments are closely tied, especially when the government is backing loans. A strong record of meeting all tax obligations is very important in establishing your creditworthiness. Even when taxes are not owed it is imperative to have a record of filing returns on time, for both state and federal income taxes. All of these factors paint the picture of your creditworthiness.

Prove Your Business to Be Loan Worthy

When you approach a lender you are making the ultimate sales pitch for your company. You will need to be prepared with a fully developed loan proposal—which is a variation of your business plan. If you do a sloppy job, there may not be another chance. A bank will look at a poorly prepared loan proposal and may decide it reflects on your professionalism. Remember, they are in the business of loaning money to make money. They want to be very sure you will be responsible in repaying the loan.

You want to show not only that you fully understand your business but also that you know why your business is viable. A loan officer will want to read a succinct summary first. This will introduce you, including your business background, the nature of your company, what the money will be used for, and how it will benefit the business. You should spell out how much money you are looking for, the terms you desire, and when you will be able to repay the loan.

When you make your pitch, keep in mind that the person reading the application is a banker or other financial lender and may or may not be familiar with the ins and outs of your business and industry. They may be jaded against online businesses, and they may not feel comfortable with technology. Be sure to include a brief overview that includes not only the genesis of your individual endeavor, but a view of the market and how you see your company relative to the competition. Describe the type of organization you have or want to have and the proposed future operation you envision. List your products, services, customers, and suppliers. Include resumes of all the key players, including all the owners, managers, and any specialists who will add to the credibility of the business.

Good Documents Are Gold

Important documents that you should include with your funding proposal are copies of any licenses you hold, contracts, leases, franchise or partnership agreements, letters of reference, articles of incorporation, and plans and specifications. In other words, furnish every possible piece of paper that gives the loan officer or investor a full understanding of your business's legal standing and obligations.

The financial statements you actually supply need to be recent, no more than ninety days old. In addition to the balance sheet, the bank will want to see profit-and-loss statements, and accounts-receivable aging (how much your customers owe you, and for how long). If your business is just starting, the challenge will be to demonstrate how businesses similar to yours perform in your industry. You would certainly be striving to at least meet, if not exceed, the industry norm. As a start-up, it will be very important to provide a pro forma balance sheet to demonstrate how soon you will become profitable so the bank can see how and when you will repay the loan. This document would include anticipated earnings, expenses, and your forecast for profit-and-loss performance. Provide clear explanations to support any of your assumptions, especially if they don't line up with industry trends. You may have knowledge of some new technology or change in legislation that will make your projections achievable when your industry's history might suggest otherwise.

FACT

It's not good to overborrow. In the same way banks will frown upon too much debt in your personal credit history, they will not like to see too much business debt. If too much of your cash flow is used to repay loans, it may not be available to accrue in a meaningful way to help you grow or improve your business operations and services.

If you have loans from any of your shareholders, and these can be put in a second position (meaning the bank would get its money first), the value of the shareholder loans could be considered as equity. This could improve the net worth of the business on paper, moving it from a negative to a positive position, and making your business a more attractive risk for the lender as discussed in the following chapter.

CHAPTER 14

Put a Financing Plan in Place

Once you have done a thorough financial self-examination, determined how much money you will need to borrow, and established the facts to support your creditworthiness, it is time to review what types of loans will best suit your needs. You may discover that you need a combination of types and sources. Expect the approval process to take at least two to three weeks to a few months, assuming no complicating factors arise in the loan review process.

Traditional Loan Offerings

Loans are structured in a couple of different ways. A term loan has a set period of time in which to repay, and usually a fixed interest rate. The entire amount is available for you to use for the reasons you have proposed to your lender. Typically, a business will use these funds to cover expenses such as equipment purchases, property, furnishings, and other items that over time would be amortized. The repayment period for a real estate loan is usually twenty-five years. Loans for equipment might mature in five or ten years.

You can also borrow by establishing a line of credit. This reserves funds for your use to cover expenses in peak times before income is generated. If your business will have seasonal fluctuations, a line of credit will help smooth out the peaks and valleys of income and expense. In many cases, the line of credit terms require you to repay the money quicker than with a term loan, or the credit line will be available only for a fixed period of time. You can always renegotiate the terms. As your business grows, you may need a bigger line of credit to work with; or as interest rates fluctuate you may want more favorable terms.

ESSENTIAL

Lenders will look for collateral from your business to back loans. Your accounts receivable, contracts with customers, inventory, and equipment, may be considered of value in securing your loan. These assets would be converted to cash in case the loan was not repaid according to its terms.

Special Loan Programs

If your proposal to borrow money does not fit into the standard parameters of the lending institution, you may be eligible for special loan programs. The Small Business Administration, a federal agency that backs most small business loans anyway, guarantees specialized loans. Many state and local municipalities also have programs to back bank loans. Instances where these "outside the box" loans come into play include cases where an owner cannot come up with a required down payment, or perhaps does not have enough assets to offer as collateral to back a loan. Another reason for a special loan may be because the business is just getting off the ground and doesn't have a credit history.

Loan Sources Other Than Banks

Surprisingly, insurance companies are willing to offer debt instruments that can provide you with capital. They are not set up to provide short-term revolving debt, but can write loans with a seven- to fifteen-year term. The interest charged to borrow in this manner is tied to the current treasury rate. The insurance company would add some percentage points to that rate to cover its risk and generate a return.

Commercial finance companies can offer you short-term revolving debt in the form of a credit line. They use your receivables or inventory to back this type of loan. It is far more expensive, with interest rates running one to four points above a bank rate. However, you have the flexibility to pay down the loan the minute you collect your receivable. In this way you are only paying on the money actually used.

Interest rates are an important factor in the overhead costs of your business. Some lenders will offer you a lower rate if you are willing to ride the tides with fluctuating interest rates in the market. Although it may be tempting to shave off a bit in initial interest rates, it may be more prudent to accept a slightly higher, but predictable, rate for the life of the loan—especially during your start-up period.

Vendors

Obviously you will pay for everything you buy for your business. You pay for things like postage stamps on the spot, but a great many of your other expenses can be negotiated for extended payment of thirty or more days. By extending generous payment terms, your suppliers become quasi-lenders. Needless to say, it is imperative to honor the terms and pay when expected. Once you have a track record as a reliable payer it will be easier to approach your suppliers if you get into a crunch.

ESSENTIAL

If you start a business by "bootstrapping," you forego any outside financial assistance and restrict your needs to the most basic. A fancy office? Forget it—how does your basement sound? Maybe you don't need a sign right away. Begin with used equipment, maybe even another's cast-offs. Conserve your cash for the basics.

How Soon to Profitability?

The most important question for both you and your lenders or investors is when you will become profitable. Even in advance of writing a full-blown business plan, it is extremely useful to get a break-even analysis down on paper.

The idea behind this exercise is to determine the sales revenue you will need to cover your costs and begin making a profit. You can use the exercise to test different price points or to calculate how long you will need capital to carry the business before it generates enough cash to sustain itself. By testing out your pricing and profit margins, you might discover that you actually cannot make a profit. Hopefully you have discovered this before becoming overly invested in what you have proven will be a losing proposition.

To construct a break-even analysis for your business, follow these steps:

- **Figure out your fixed costs.** These are expenses that do not fluctuate from month to month. They include rent, equipment leases, insurance, phone, electricity, marketing, management salaries, monthly hosting costs for your website, and any other predictable obligations. For your test calculation, pad the fixed cost estimate just to be sure you have a conservative projection.
- **Determine the cost ("variable cost") for each unit that you will sell.** Note that a unit can be a product or a service. The cost of a product, whether it is a book or a craft, is easy enough to determine. The cost of a unit of someone's time is based on the salary and benefit costs.
- **Determine the gross profit per unit.** The gross profit (contribution) is the difference between your selling price and your cost to buy or provide it.
- **Calculate your breakeven.** To do this, divide your annual fixed cost by the gross profit per unit and you will see how many units you will need to sell just to cover your costs. That just gets you to breakeven: more

sales will push you into profitability. Using a spreadsheet is a great way to make this calculation, and also do some what-if scenarios.

If you are unable to break even with your expected costs and revenue, make adjustments to your plan. Reduce or delay some overhead expenses. Find cheaper workspace, or hold off on hiring until you have the established revenue stream to support staff. Negotiate for better rates from your suppliers. Raise your prices.

Using the following example, you can see how a break-even analysis works. The following chart shows how to plot where an imaginary online umbrella store turns from losing money to making money. The fixed costs will include rent, insurance, marketing, payroll, hosting costs, telephone and Internet access, and equipment leases. Variable costs are for the purchase of umbrellas wholesale. A simple breakdown of costs, pricing, and sales helps pinpoint the target sales goal to move into profitability.

Description	Amount
Fixed Cost	$800.00 per month
Selling Price	$15.00 per umbrella
Variable Cost	$6.00 per umbrella
Gross Profit	$9.00 per umbrella
Breakeven	$800.00/$9.00 = 90 per month (approximately)

The following table shows profits on sales of 0 to 225 umbrellas. Sales under ninety umbrellas result in a net loss. After selling ninety, profits begin to climb.

Umbrellas	Fixed Cost	Fixed + Variable Cost	Sales Revenue	Profit
0	$800.00	$800.00	$0.00	-$800.00
10	$800.00	$860.00	$150.00	-$710.00
20	$800.00	$920.00	$300.00	-$620.00
30	$800.00	$980.00	$450.00	-$530.00
40	$800.00	$1,040.00	$600.00	-$440.00
60	$800.00	$1,160.00	$900.00	-$260.00
80	$800.00	$1,280.00	$1,200.00	-$80.00
90	$800.00	$1,340.00	$1,350.00	$10.00
100	$800.00	$1,400.00	$1,500.00	$100.00
120	$800.00	$1,520.00	$1,800.00	$280.00
140	$800.00	$1,640.00	$2,100.00	$460.00

Umbrellas	Fixed Cost	Fixed + Variable Cost	Sales Revenue	Profit
160	$800.00	$1,760.00	$2,400.00	$640.00
180	$800.00	$1,880.00	$2,700.00	$820.00
200	$800.00	$2,000.00	$3,000.00	$1,000.00
225	$800.00	$2,150.00	$3,375.00	$1,225.00

Balancing your pricing can be a bit tricky. There are the hard factors you have to consider, such as the cost of the goods and your overhead. Then there is the dynamic of the market. Is yours a product or service that has lots of competition that could force you to keep pricing low to attract customers? The overall economy can affect what you can charge. If the stock market is doing well, people feel a little freer with their cash, even if they are not big investors themselves. If general business reports are glum, folks tend to keep their hands in their pockets. Some businesses are more seasonal, making the products difficult to sell during the off-season. In all cases, the goal is to sell at a profit. You may need to prepare more than one model for your break-even analysis, using different pricing assumptions. You will discover soon enough what pricing levels work in the real world.

When You Have the Money in Hand

Once you have your initial capital, the race begins to the day your sales revenues generate positive cash. There is cash and there is cash flow. Cash is what you have in the bank. It is liquid and it is available to meet your obligations immediately. Cash flow is the movement of money in and out of your business. Cash flow occurs even if you are not making a profit. During periods when you are not bringing in more revenue than you are spending, you have negative cash flow. When your cash receipts exceed your expenses, you have positive cash flow.

In the early days when the business is getting going, you may have negative cash flow as you spend some of the funding you have secured. It is an extremely good idea to include cash-flow projections with your other business plans to make sure you don't get to the end of your reserves before positive cash flow kicks in. As a business owner, it is critical that you understand your cash needs. You will need to have ready access to additional cash if you need it: Keep lines of communication open with all of your lenders, investors, and creditors.

One other group that you need to keep in the loop are the various government agencies, regulators, and others. Your business must satisfy a number of their requirements in order to operate successfully.

CHAPTER 15

Regulations and Legal Matters

Once you have figured out a basic plan for your business, there will be some regulatory and legal matters to attend to as discussed in this chapter. Though the processes may seem tedious, it's very important that you operate legally to protect your investment in the business. Although there are plenty of resources to access on your own, using the professional services of an attorney to guide you through this process will be money well spent.

Licensing and Regulations

Financial brokers, insurance brokers, doctors, dentists, veterinarians, attorneys, pharmacists, and certified public accountants are among the many professionals who are required to have a license. Likewise, many companies must be licensed in order to conduct their business. It's up to you to contact either the town hall, the records bureau, the secretary of state, the Department of Consumer Affairs, or other governing body to determine which licenses you need to conduct your business. The SBA can also help. Go to *www.sba.gov/content/5-steps-registering-your-business* and *www.sba.gov/content/business-licenses-and-permits* for basic licensing information. Many cities now provide this kind of licensing information online as well.

FACT

Trade associations and professional associations are useful resources for licensing and compliance information. These affiliations consist of members who are all in the same business so they are used to answering typical questions from individuals starting out in that line of business. Trade associations may also provide training for compliance with various regulations.

In most cases, business licenses are not costly, but they can make the difference between staying in business or being shut down—and even a temporary shutdown can cost you a lot in revenues. Certain cities make it clear that you must have a business license in order to operate. For example, any business of any type in the city of Chicago will need a business license. There are nearly 200 different types of business licenses in Chicago, and your business will certainly fall under one heading, if not several. So if you're starting up a business in Chicago, make a visit to city hall.

Some businesses need to adhere to federal regulations. Radio stations, for example, must follow Federal Communications Commission (FCC) rules. Internet-based businesses present many gray areas in regard to application of standard regulations set forth by governing bodies such as the FCC and Food and Drug Administration (FDA). Thus far, it has been difficult to impose restrictions on the Internet because websites can be based out of, and accessed from, anywhere.

Most business licenses have expiration dates. Don't forget to make note of the date your license expires and what the renewal process entails. That way you won't be scrambling around at the last minute trying to find what you need to get your license renewed.

It's in your best interests to be aware of all regulations and licenses necessary for your profession, your business, and your community. Here's a to-do list for licensing:

- Obtain any and all required federal, state, and local licensing.
- Familiarize yourself with all zoning ordinances and local regulations, if your online business also has a real-world presence.
- Establish a system to periodically check the expiration dates of all licenses.
- Post all licenses that require posting, and put all others in a safe place.

Licenses are critically important to your business. Consider taking a photocopy of each of them, and keeping the copies offsite.

Inspections

The fire department and health department are among several agencies that can inspect your business. Code violations can result in a fine the first time around, and the fine can become increasingly steep for repeat offenders. If you will be renovating space or an entire building, you will need a building inspection—and in some areas, a building permit—before you can even begin work. Check with your city hall first.

Zoning Ordinances

It's no coincidence that all the fast food chains are in one area of town and none are situated among a row of private homes on the lake. There's more to this than just preventing a lovely view from being ruined. Communities enact zoning laws to maintain the structure, property values, and way of life in neighborhoods. Zoning laws are primarily designed to separate commercial and residential areas.

Beyond the ordinances regulating which kind of business may be operated in a certain area, there may be other restrictions. For example, signage may be limited to a certain size or advertisements may require approval.

ESSENTIAL

Some towns can provide you with a color-coded map showing the various zoning districts. Having this visual may be helpful as you plan your location, if you are having a real-world presence. Some towns also have mixed zoning, which may be good to know about. Contact your local city, town, or county clerk's office for maps and other information.

Be aware that zoning requirements may have an impact on your online business. If you operate from your home, and have a steady flow of clients or suppliers dropping by, your neighbors may have a surprise for you in the form of a zoning restriction. The county clerk, community planning board, and city hall are places to go for more information.

Leases

Once you find a location that suits you, you'll need to have your lawyer carefully review the lease. An online business may prefer to lease an office (instead of purchasing it) so that capital can be used to fund growth elsewhere within the business. You need to know exactly what is expected of you and what you're entitled to expect in return from your landlord. A multi-year lease can represent a significant financial commitment. Make sure it fits in with your business plans and financial resources.

Just because someone offers you a lease doesn't mean you can run your type of business from that location. Check the zoning restrictions first. Conversely, just because the zoning allows for certain types of business in an area doesn't mean the landlord wants you running that business in her building. Landlords don't want businesses that will cause them headaches.

When looking at a lease, find out if you can sublease the space. This way, if business doesn't grow as quickly as you anticipate, you can fill those empty offices temporarily.

Other points to clarify in your lease are the cost of various services, and who pays for them—you or your landlord:

- Utilities—lights, heat, air conditioning
- Garbage removal
- Parking—number of spaces
- Signs in the lobby or on the building
- Snow removal
- Elevator access
- Internet connection

Cover all your bases so you aren't left with any surprise monthly charges.

Fictitious Name Forms

If you choose to run your business under any name other than your own, you will have to file a fictitious name form or "doing business as" (DBA) certificate in the county where the business is being conducted. This form indicates that your business is being run under a specific name. Do a name search to make sure the name isn't already being used by another business. The wider the scope of the business, the broader the name search will have to be and the costlier it may become. A local business named Silver Star Virtual Assistants may not need to worry about finding another Silver Star Virtual Assistants three states away. But if you're doing business under that name online and it is likely that customers will be from other states, the name may be problematic.

Keep in mind that operating under a DBA does not protect you from personal liability for the debts of the business. Only a corporation, a limited partnership, or a limited liability company can shield you.

Trademarks, Patents, and Copyrights

Incorporating in your state will protect you against another company incorporating under the same business name, but not across state lines. Also, this protection only works if you started using the name first. But what about your brilliant invention or original work? If it's your business, your creation, or your original idea, you'll want to protect it from being used by another business. The three most common forms of protection for entrepreneurs are trademarks, patents, and copyrights.

Trademarks

A trademark can be a name (one word or several), logo, symbol, design, slogan, series of words, or combination thereof that makes your product or service distinguishable from others. Companies use trademarks to help protect the image and brand-name presence that they are trying to establish. For example, the name "Pepsi" is a trademark name, and the phrase "You deserve a break today" is also registered.

You can apply for a trademark with the United States Patent and Trademark Office (USPTO) as long as you use the trademark for commerce regulated by the U.S. Congress, or have a bona fide intention to do so. You can obtain an application from, and file it with, the USPTO (*www.uspto.gov* or 703-308-9000). You can also perform a trademark search at the USPTO website to see if others have already registered the name or trademark you want to use.

ALERT

After holding a trademark for five years, you will be required to file an affidavit to keep the trademark active. Don't neglect this or you could lose control of the trademark. Not only will you have to go through the entire filing process again, someone else may grab the trademark before you do.

Many businesses will use the services of an attorney who specializes in intellectual property—sometimes called a patent attorney—to do the filings. While it is possible to do the work yourself, if it comes to a dispute over the name, you certainly don't want the opposition to win because of a silly mistake that you made on the initial application.

Patents

If you create or invent an original product, you might want to patent it. A patent protects the invention you've created from being pirated and created or sold by someone else. You'll need to conduct a patent search to know if your original invention has already been invented and patented elsewhere.

You can conduct a patent search at the USPTO in Washington, DC, or at one of the nation's patent and trademark depository libraries located in cities all across the country, or online at *www.uspto.gov*. It may be in your best interest to have a patent attorney file the application on your behalf.

Copyrights

While trademarks protect a name and your image, and patents protect tangible products (not ideas), you can protect creative works such as artwork, music, books, brochures, advertisements, and computer software programs with a copyright. These are handled by the U.S. Library of Congress. For a small fee you can obtain a copyright by filing the proper application. Go to *www.copyright.gov* for more information and application forms. Copyrights are good for up to fifty years after the death of the person who has registered.

Screenwriters and even authors can also obtain protection from the Writers Guild of America, East or Writers Guild of America, West by following their submission guidelines. You do not have to be a member to register a property with the guild. Go to *www.wgaeast.org* or *www.wga.org*. The guild dates and seals a copy of the work in an envelope, which you sign for, and then locks it away in their files.

Even if you don't file the document you create, you may benefit from simply noting on the document your name, the word "Copyright," and the year you first published or used the document in business.

Agencies, Agreements, and Regulations

The U.S. government's official website for small business, *www.business.USA .gov*, has a laws and regulations section with links to sixty different federal organizations that are designed to assist you with such business needs and concerns. Business.USA.gov is sponsored by the SBA, the U.S. government's Small Business Administration.

Many companies do work for or with government agencies. To work with the government you will need to register your business at *www.sam.gov.*

The agencies you may need to be involved with while running your business include:

- Environmental Protection Agency (*www.epa.gov*)
- Federal Aviation Administration (*www.faa.gov*)
- Federal Railroad Administration (*www.fra.dot.gov*)
- Federal Trade Commission (*www.ftc.gov*)
- Federal Transit Administration (*www.fta.dot.gov*)
- International Trade Administration (*www.trade.gov*)
- Maritime Administration (*www.marad.dot.gov*)
- U.S. Citizenship and Immigration Services (*www.uscis.gov*) (formerly Immigration and Naturalization Service)
- U.S. Consumer Product Safety Commission (*www.cpsc.gov*)
- U.S. Customs and Border Protection (*www.cbp.gov*)
- U.S. Department of Commerce (*www.commerce.gov*)
- U.S. Food and Drug Administration (*www.fda.gov*)
- U.S. Department of Labor (*www.dol.gov*)
- U.S. Patent and Trademark Office (*www.uspto.gov*)

It is worthwhile to do some networking with other businesses in your area and industry, if only to ask which government agencies they have been involved with.

Privacy, Age Restrictions, and Digital Rights

Regulations and laws are always changing—no matter your online business, there are three areas that you will need to be aware of: young users, digital rights, and privacy.

Young Users

If your online business is aimed at children, then there are additional regulations that you should be aware of. The Children's Online Privacy Protection Act (COPPA) applies to all websites that collect information from children under thirteen years old. The FTC, which enforces the act, has detailed information on compliance, at *www.budurl.com/everythingCOPPA*.

Digital Rights

Unfortunately, there are many websites that post not-paid-for movies, music, books, and other digital goods. It's tempting to download these products, but just because data is available online, doesn't mean that you have the right to use it. Starting an online business yourself, you should be highly sensitive to this: What if someone started using your products, and didn't pay for them? The strong arm of the law is just as powerful online as off: stealing is stealing.

If your business sells digital products, there are some ways to protect yourself, often using technology. The question you will need to answer is whether or not the costs—both for implementation and for customer service—are worth it.

Privacy Policies

A privacy policy tells site users in very clear language, what you are going to do with their information. It lets them know how often you might contact them, the purpose of your contact, and whether your information will be shared with others. It lets users know how you are protecting their data, and often the country in which the data resides. It lets users know whom to contact if they have any questions or concerns. To generate a privacy policy, check out the online privacy policy generator, at *www.budurl .com/everythingPRIVACY.*

Beyond creating the policy though, you have to live it: if you say that you aren't going to share each contact's name, then you can't trade it to another business. You must put processes in place so that your policy is actually followed.

Each town, state, and country has it's own laws and regulations. Especially because you are starting an online business, you may have the flexibility to choose a location that is more business-friendly than where you are now.

CHAPTER 16

Locating Your Business

While many online businesses may never have a physical presence for their customers, you may need a location for deliveries, or you may want your staff to work together in one location. The Internet certainly opens doors, but for some customers, often an old-fashioned door is the only one they want to pass through. Access in both the real and virtual worlds may be the way to go. Assuming you do require a physical location, this chapter will help you figure out where and how to situate your business venture.

The Right Space

You probably have a mental picture of where your business should be located. Your budget may determine how much space you can afford initially. Even though you want to be conservative, with hard work, your business will grow. So you may also want to consider how you'll obtain more space than you will presently require. Can you find and afford a space slightly larger than you need at present? Or can you find a space with the option for expansion later without taking on the unnecessary overhead right out of the gate? Another option is to sublet extra space to another business, but then you have to worry about being a landlord while you are getting your own business launched.

ALERT

When searching for a place in which to do business, you may find your options are limited and you have to make the space fit your needs. Remember, you can add paint, put in new windows, and have the wiring inspected or redone, but you cannot perform miracles. You'll have to say no to certain marginally acceptable locations, even if it means continuing your location search a little longer.

Commercial realtors, advertisements in local media, and word of mouth are three key ways in which you can find a space for your business. However, before checking out an office or retail space, review a checklist of the needs of your business. Among the questions to ask yourself are:

- How much space does my business require?
- What equipment will I need in my space?
- Can I start out working from home or share space somewhere?
- Do I need to be in the heart of town or can I be in a low-traffic area?
- How much of a commute am I willing to make?
- Do I need to travel by public transportation?
- Will suppliers, vendors, distributors, or customers be able to reach this location easily?
- How much can I afford?
- How much fixing up or renovating am I willing to have done?

All of the work required to get your physical space ready is time taken away from actually running the business. Don't forget to schedule this time for yourself—or hire someone to do it for you.

Storefront Businesses

A retail store has special needs, the most important of which is high visibility. The store needs to be designed to sell to existing customers—but also drive users to your online venture. And your online presence should be designed to drive people to your real-world location.

The best retail location is the one that people can find easily, draws walk-in customers, and is easily accessible by car or public transportation (depending on whether you're in a rural or urban area). It's a location where your business can grow thanks to a supportive business community, little direct competition, and a strong demographic base for your products. It's also an area where you feel safe and can attract a high level of experienced personnel. And it will also have a reliable, high-speed Internet connection.

Office Space

Unlike a retail business where drive-by and walk-in customers are essential, an office does not usually need to worry about high visibility. Yet many of the other concerns about finding a space for your business remain the same. You still need to consider utilities, security, rental costs, and commuting distance from your home to the office. Parking is still an issue, although not as consequential, unless you anticipate a big staff or a large number of visitors right off the bat. And indoor appearance will generally be more important than outdoor appearance, unless your clients visit often.

Many business owners look for the right tone and atmosphere that will enhance their employees' productivity. Most want to know that restaurants are nearby. The more a facility or area can offer to employees, the more appealing it will be to the highly skilled individuals you are looking to attract.

ESSENTIAL

If you're going to spend most of your waking hours at the office, choose a place that is functional and makes you feel good about yourself and your business. If you are squeezed into space that is laid out awkwardly, communication and efficient traffic flow may be difficult. An office should have some character and represent the image you're trying to project with your company.

For a more temporary environment in which to grow, you might lease short-term space from another company that is perhaps slightly larger than your business and has some unused room to spare. This can prove advantageous if they provide some essential services, such as security for the whole office space, a common eating area, and even some technical assistance. It may even be a complementary business to yours, where client referrals may occur easily back and forth. You may, however, be asked to chip in on repairs or maintenance expenses or other aspects of the overall space. Cover all the details when you sit down and meet with the owners of the space, including how to get out of the sublease.

Manufacturing and Warehouse Space

If you need to set up a full-fledged factory, you'll need plenty of space for manufacturing and storage, as well as a location that can accommodate extensive shipping.

ESSENTIAL

There may be occasions when customers will visit your facility, so you should have at least a small waiting area with clean, comfortable furnishings. Commercial printers often have customers come to approve press proofs. An area in your factory with properly lighted tables is the kind of customer amenity that may distinguish you from your competitors.

Most online businesses are not manufacturers, but rather traders of products or services. If your business is in this second category, then you will still need space to warehouse the inventory before it is shipped. On the other hand, many online businesses make the sale first, then arrange for the product to be drop-shipped directly from their suppliers to the customer. This cuts inventory investment, and removes the need for a warehouse.

Watch the zoning restrictions carefully. If you plan to be noisy or use hazardous materials, you will need to seek out industrial areas, since other neighborhoods will likely not want your business.

Home-Based Businesses

Many online businesses start from and remain in the home. The success of a home-based business centers on you and your ability to self-motivate and remain committed to your work. One person working from home can remain focused and motivate himself to put in a productive forty-five-hour work week, while another will stray over to the television set, check out friends on Facebook, and end up cheating on the enormous task of being an entrepreneur.

Setting up your home office means finding a location in the home where you feel comfortable working. If you have a spare bedroom that can be converted to an office, everything can be contained behind a closed door. If you need to use a computer that is shared with other family members, you should seriously consider purchasing another.

You need a place without distractions. You also need a place near electrical outlets for your computer, printer, and any other equipment. Include filing cabinets, your phone system, and any other necessities, and lay out the space in a manner that puts everything within easy reach. Keep your work area as clean and efficient as possible.

Advantages of working at home include:

- Maximum flexibility for organizing your own time
- Significant time and money saved by not commuting
- Home comforts, including your own kitchen and bathroom
- More time around the family

- Some equipment already on hand
- A low-cost starting point

Disadvantages of working at home include:

- **Losing focus.** It can be easy to get distracted by housekeeping, errands, television, or neighbors stopping by.
- **Family intrusions.** Your family may assume that because you are at home, that you aren't doing work, and therefore are available to cook, clean, and shop. At the same time, your family needs to respect your boundaries: if you're in your home office, you're at work and not to be disturbed.
- **Working too much.** When you work at home, you're always at work.
- Loneliness. Working at home can become lonely, as you find yourself missing the companionship and camaraderie found working with others outside the home.
- **Inconvenience of meeting with clients.** When an important client is sitting in your living room and Baby Lizzie starts wailing, you may consider having an office away from home.
- **Limited expansion potential.** If you suddenly find that you can't handle the workload of the business yourself, you may want to bring in an assistant or hire other employees; often there isn't the physical space to do this in a home-based office.
- **Increased liability insurance.** You may need to pay higher insurance in case a client falls on your doorstep and sues you.

You can run an online business from your home or from an office. Since it's operating in cyberspace, no one will really know the difference. In fact, much of the work on websites is outsourced and involves people working from numerous locations.

Shared Services

An option for a home-based business is paying for an office identity. Companies that provide these shared services can give you a more professional appearance without assuming long leases or other expensive overhead.

When you purchase an identity package, all you are paying for is a professional address and telephone service. Someone will answer the phone with your company name. Your mail can be sent to and from an address that isn't 14 Mulberry Lane.

For someone starting out who needs a professional appearance, this can be a short-to-medium-term solution. A very limited office area can usually be rented on a month-to-month basis. It may be fairly easy to add space as you grow. Common areas, such as a professionally appointed lobby with a receptionist, add to your solid appearance. Often, conference rooms can be rented on an as-needed basis. Services such as photocopying, mail sorting, faxing, etc., can be purchased on a fee basis.

Shared services are certainly not the least expensive way to get yourself set up, but may fill the bill while you get going. Once you have more reliable cash flow, it may make sense to negotiate your own office space and take on equipment leases yourself.

CHAPTER 17

Furnishings and Equipment

Whether operating in the real world, online, or both, your business will occupy physical space somewhere. Planning a budget for your investment is the nuts and bolts of your business, and sticking to it can be a make-or-break difference for the feasibility of your venture, especially in the early days. Once you determine the total of everything you will ultimately need in your physical place of business, take a hard look at what your absolute minimum needs are to get started.

Assessing Your Needs

Before you rush to your local office supply store or cruise through the many online options, take a hard look at your bare-bones start-up needs. Once you have an idea of the items necessary to get the job done, weigh the advantages of traditional and more creative resources. Anyone can buy retail. But what about tracking down someone else's cast-offs? Check local ads for gently used desks, chairs, conference tables, storage units, and the like. You may be able to work with just about any mish-mash collection as long as it is serviceable. While it is cool to have cool digs for your online business, clients will interact with you on your website—so spending extra money on real-world furnishings makes even less sense.

That being said, one of your first steps should be to decide what equipment you consider absolutely necessary. Typical major equipment includes:

Google Voice

- A communications system, including telephones and voice mail
- Computers and/or tablets
- Computer software
- External hard drives for backup
- ★ Printers/scanners/fax machines (Fax machines are less important as most people scan to e-mail instead.)
- ★ Filing cabinets
- ★ Storage units or shelving
- ★ Desks or workstations
- Shipping supplies
- Various chairs (computer chairs, conference room chairs, and so on)

If your business has a real-world retail presence, don't forget cash registers, display cases, shopping baskets, and much more. Security systems will also be necessary for all types of businesses.

Will Clients Be Visiting Often?

The more often you plan to be meeting with clients in your location, the more important it will be to project the right image and decorate accordingly. Whether it's trendy (if you're doing web design or other high-tech work) or more traditional (for a legal or accounting office), you'll need to look for furnishings that make the desired impression. On the other hand, if your office is just for you and your employees, think of ways to create a comfortable work atmosphere while cutting some corners.

How Much Space Do You Have to Work With?

Just guessing at square footage requirements without planning for the actual usage can be a waste of time. A long skinny space may not be nearly as efficient as a square space with the same area. Block out space for equipment, desks, hallways, and storage. And don't forget fire regulations.

Comfort and Layout

Assess the space and the number of people who will be occupying the premises during the workday. People need a degree of personal space and, with that in mind, you can fit only a certain number of people into an office without overcrowding and creating an unproductive—and even unhealthy—work environment.

An open environment often creates a better team atmosphere than you might find in traditional offices with closed doors. However, the personal space and privacy issues need to be addressed. If you're going to set up cubicles, make sure they're roomy, comfortable, and allow for individuals to add their own personal touch.

ESSENTIAL

Keep in mind that certain tasks can be outsourced, while others can be performed by telecommuting employees. In some instances, you can have more than one person sharing a desk, if each person is only working from the office one or two days a week.

Many online businesses hire employees who are expected to work from home. If this is what you are planning, you might think that comfort and layout are not something that you need to worry about. Think again—these two items are important: there is a direct connection to employee productivity. If you are hiring remote workers, ask a few questions about their home office environment during the interview process.

Telephone Systems

Along with computers, your telephone system will generally be your most important technological need. If you're working from home, you should consider a separate line—or a cell phone—for business calls. When you set up an office, you'll need to consider setting up a phone system that's adaptable as your business grows. When evaluating your phone needs, consider the price, the service support, and the features of the system.

FACT

When determining the number of phone units you will need, begin with one for every workstation or desk. Next, identify places it would be convenient to use a phone, such as your reception area, meeting rooms, and common workspaces.

You might want to explore VoIP options (voice over Internet). Many VoIP providers—RingCentral (*www.budurl.com/everythingPhone*) is one example—supply hybrid systems that provide all of the features, including long distance, 1-800 service, and fax, at an exceptionally low cost. As an even lower cost alternative, consider looking into Skype (with their Skype online number service), and Google Voice. The entire telecommunications industry is in such a state of rapid change it is worth spending time to search for the best deals.

ESSENTIAL

When shopping for communications services look for a package that bundles landlines, Internet connection, and cell support for your employees' smartphones. Communications services are competitive and rapidly evolving. Make sure to do your homework.

Cell Phones at the Office

According to the International Telecommunications Union, there were more than 6 billion cell phones in use worldwide as of the end of 2011, illustrating that mobile phones are the preferred way of communicating for nearly every man, woman, and child on the planet. You'll need to assess whether it is better to provide your employees with cell phones restricted to business use or to develop a policy to help subsidize their personal phones that are used partially to conduct your business. You may also want to consider only using cell phones, and skipping landlines altogether.

Cost-Effective Decisions

Look at how each equipment purchase serves the best interests of the business as a whole. Even a television for the lounge can be a productivity booster if your business needs to have updates on a 24/7 cycle. Keep in mind you generally don't need to buy top-of-the-line products—you can fool most of the people most of the time with near-top-quality furnishings.

Green Choices May Equal Greenbacks

Many smart business owners are taking a second look at the ways they are outfitting their offices with an eye toward helping the environment and the bottom line. Certainly using second-hand furniture is a green choice. So is using a water filter instead of paying for costly water in plastic bottles.

Leasing Is Worth a Close Look

As you take a look at the cost-effectiveness of your office equipment, consider whether to buy or lease. Leasing or renting smaller items like paper shredders is not cost-effective. However, you may want to lease some of your larger equipment, including copiers, furnishings, and computers. If you're starting out and don't want to make large purchases, or can't afford to, this may be a way for you to meet your equipment needs without a major cash layout up front. However, over the course of a one- or two-year lease, you may end up spending as much as or more than you would if you had purchased the item to begin with. Do a thorough cost-benefit analysis before deciding which route to pursue.

Here are some advantages to leasing:

- While you may be required to put down a deposit up front, your initial expenditure is not as great as it is to purchase items.
- You can get better equipment for your money.
- You aren't stuck with obsolete office equipment after a couple of years.

Here are some of the disadvantages to leasing:

- You may spend more on the item, over time, by leasing than if you purchased it.
- Leasing may use some of your credit capacity, preventing you from getting a much-needed loan for another area of your business.
- For items that don't depreciate greatly, such as furniture, you don't have any resale possibilities and can't claim the items as assets because you don't own them.
- Leases are very difficult to break.
- You're responsible for someone else's property, which means if you damage leased equipment, you may find yourself paying additional money.

There are a number of downsides to leasing; here are two. The application is very intrusive—very much like a bank loan application, with no guarantees of approval. More importantly, at the end of the lease, you don't actually own the asset; payments never end.

Cost-Cutting Ideas

You have a wide range of options for furnishing and equipping your office. Besides your local Office Depot, Staples, or office furniture store, you can also check in with the folks at eBay, *www.ebay.com*, *www.kijiji.com,* and Craigslist, *www.craigslist.org.*

Should I look into bartering for office equipment?
You may be able to trade your product or service for equipment. How about developing a website for the desks you spied at your local consignment shop? Try to think of creative ways to find what you need.

Used, remodeled, refurbished, or recycled furniture, as well as office equipment, can help you save significantly. In the case of equipment, you might be able to take over the original warranty. Some other places to look for used furniture or equipment include auctions, estate sales, and businesses that are relocating (or going under).

Keep supplies well stocked and put someone in charge of them so they don't walk off in great quantities. Ask whoever is in charge to make sure to order new supplies before the old ones completely run out. But don't over order. This is one of those "profit-leak" places you will want to watch closely.

Technology—Get Up to Speed

When it comes to technology, you need to be a good shopper. This includes comparing prices, looking for first-rate service policies and tech support, and checking to see what's covered under warranties. Of course, as a future online entrepreneur, you may have a head start on what (and where) to look.

Make an initial list of how you anticipate using your computers and how many people on staff you'll have working on them. You will have to decide whether you need to have specialized servers for your online business, or if you are going to host your site on a shared server. Most start-up online businesses will rent server space—one less thing to worry about.

It's not hard to find computers. Every major office supply company has plenty of models, and all the popular manufacturers have websites and plenty of advertisements touting brand-new products and special deals. Quite often, the second or third model down from a manufacturer is better. These models may be easier to obtain, and you may find them at a good price. Don't pay for a host of computer features that you do not need. Shop for your specific needs.

Speed is a relative factor that often fools computer buyers into spending more than they need to. Don't get overly concerned about comparing speed between models. The speed is a function of your personal speed and your Internet connection—not just your hardware.

Shopping for a Computer

Whether you plan to buy in a local store or online, spend some time browsing computers in person to get a feel for the latest models. Consumer Reports has detailed comparisons of major computer brands for service, quality, and other factors; their reports are available online and in their magazines.

Probably the most useful concept when it comes to comparing computers is that of total cost of ownership (TCO). This is calculated by adding up the cost of the hardware and warranty, along with the cost of tech support (including support workers' salaries), divided by the number of useful years you can be expected to use the machine. Often, the cheapest computer turns out to be the most expensive.

Shopping Online

You'll probably get the best prices if you go directly to one of the manufacturers' sites, such as *www.dell.com, www.apple.com,* or *www.hp.com.* You can also do well with online computer e-commerce sites, such as *www.tigerdirect.com, www.NewEgg.com,* or *www.buy.com.* You'll also find websites selling reconditioned or discontinued models, but always make sure you shop on reputable sites. Search carefully, take your time, and check out policies on warranties, customer service, and shipping.

Computer Stores

Often, you'll pay a little more at a computer store, but you should get better service. (The operative word is "should.") Best Buy is known for launching the cleverly named Geek Squad, which will make onsite tech repair calls. The Apple store has the Genius Bar. A poorly run computer store tries to push whatever they have in stock, provides insufficient answers to your questions, and is often motivated by commissions. Pay attention to the kind of service you're getting, and move on if it doesn't meet your needs.

Office Supply Stores

Generally, you'll find a more limited selection at office supply stores simply because they do not specialize in computer sales. However, you may stumble upon a good deal, often on older models, which they need to move out to make room for newer merchandise.

Software Options

The current market has a wide range of products available, for both the PC and Mac. Being an astute shopper means reading up on the various offerings in each category and reviewing their features. Although options are continually upgraded, some of the software to look for includes the following:

- **Accounting:** QuickBooks Pro, Sage 50, etc.
- **Planning and contact management:** Google, Day-Timer Organizer, Franklin Planner, Sage ACT!, Google Docs, and Microsoft Outlook
- **Office suites:** Microsoft Office, OpenOffice, iWork (for Mac only), and Google Docs
- **Business presentations:** Microsoft PowerPoint, Apple Keynote, OpenOffice Impress, and SlideRocket
- **Spreadsheets:** Microsoft Excel, Microsoft Works, Apple Numbers, OpenOffice Calc, and Google Docs
- **Word processing:** Microsoft Word, Apple Pages, OpenOffice Writer, Corel WordPerfect, and Google Docs
- **Project management:** Microsoft Project, Primavera P6, Teamwork Project Manager, and Zoho
- **Graphics:** Adobe Illustrator, Adobe Photoshop, Pixelmator (Mac), Paint.net (PC), and Adobe InDesign

You can purchase software from many online retailers, or you can go to the manufacturers' websites and buy directly. When shopping online, make sure you check the in-stock availability of the item, look for product features, compare prices and return policies, and take note of shipping charges.

Computer Networks

Businesses that use multiple computers often set up a computer network. The network allows them to share and exchange information. For example, you can have common files that several people can access and work on with relative ease (although not at the same time). In a business where people are frequently interacting and collaborating on a project, a network can be very valuable. The whole area of cloud computing (see below for an explanation) has exploded over the last few years—the question of storing files on a local network versus in the Internet cloud has changed the way we think of the local network server.

FACT

While networks can be very helpful, there are also associated problems. If the network is down, it slows everyone down, not just one person working on a file. It's also important that sensitive materials, which aren't for everyone's eyes, don't end up on the network without proper security measures.

Get Online

The key to an online business is actually getting yourself online. There are numerous Internet service providers (ISPs) to choose from. For the most part, you will want as fast a connection as you can afford. Your phone company will sell a service called digital subscriber line or DSL, while your cable company will attach a special cable modem and deliver an Internet signal that way. While cable is generally faster, it tends to slow down when numerous people—such as your neighbors—are all using the system simultaneously.

In addition to these technologies, there are two other ones that you might hear about. Fiber, in which case the providers run a fiber optic "wire" either to the junction box down the street or directly to your office; this is usually the fastest of all of the technologies. The second is long term evolution technology or LTE; this is a cell phone wireless standard that is so fast that it may replace the "wire" that comes into your office completely.

Within your office, wireless networking, known as Wi-Fi, can give you the freedom to work virtually anywhere. You can install a wireless router to your existing Internet connection to work from anywhere in your home or office.

Computer Policies

Just as it's important to buy your hardware, install your software, and train your employees on how it all works from a technical standpoint, it's important to establish acceptable-use policies. Set up your guidelines from the outset. Computers in the workplace are not for solitaire, personal e-mails, or getting a jumpstart on holiday shopping. Setting up policies and even blocking access to tempting (but irrelevant) websites may be necessary. On the other hand, many managers realize that blocking content is fruitless: if someone wants to waste time on Facebook, they need only pick up their smartphone to skirt the corporate firewall.

While you don't want to become Big Brother, you also need to let it be known that you do monitor what sites are being visited. If you encounter suspicious activity, monitor usage more closely and have employees change their passwords.

ALERT

A worldwide crisis of computer viruses has put businesses on the defensive. Many invest in software to provide "firewalls" against these menaces. Having a strict policy for your employees on the types of sites they cannot visit, and warning them never to open suspicious e-mails can help deflect some of these crippling invaders.

Cloud Computing

One of the wonderful things about the world of online business is the colorful terminology. Cloud computing sounds far sexier than outsourced centralized datacenter. The term itself came from the world of computer engineers, who would draw diagrams showing two local computer networks connected through the Internet. The Internet was represented by an illustration of a cloud.

Today, cloud computing means several things: instead of installing a program on your computer and running it locally, the functionality is sitting on a server on the Internet, and you access the program, usually through your browser. Cloud computing can also refer to having data stored remotely on the Internet. Several of the best-known consumer cloud products include Google Drive and Apple's iTunes.

ADVANTAGES:

- Software as a service: you pay a monthly fee for the functionality; usually this means you are paying less than if you owned the software outright.
- No need to worry about compatibility: it runs through a browser.
- Because all of the heavy processing is being done by the computers in the center of the cloud, you may not need to buy the fanciest computers on the shelf.
- As a small business, cloud computing might give you a "big company" look.
- Backups are no longer on your personal to-do list; the data is safely stored on the cloud. In fact, if there is a catastrophe that destroys your premises, what you moved to the cloud will remain safe—and instantly available.
- No need to pay for and install upgrades on each machine, as the functionality is centrally managed.
- As you add more users to your company, it is easy to give them access to identical functionality.

DISADVANTAGES:

- You are delegating information security responsibility to another company; if they get hacked then your data might be at risk.
- The cost is a forever monthly cost; purchasing (or developing) functionality yourself means that it might be cheaper in the long run to give cloud computing a pass. You won't see the constant exodus of dollars from your bank account if you're not renting space on the cloud.
- Sometimes it is difficult to migrate away from the cloud services provider.
- The speed of access is often slower than local network access speed.
- Your industry may have restrictions on where the data can be housed; out-of-country storage may be verboten. (German for forbidden.)

Should you use the cloud or not? There is a certain symmetry to using the cloud in your business: after all, that is where your online business is actually located.

Getting your business's hardware and software systems up and running is one thing, but these are only the start. For anything online, the website is the doorway from cyberspace into the business.

CHAPTER 18

Building Your Online Presence

Online business is fast-paced; developments and opportunities are constantly exploding. It is an exciting place, yet one where missteps can hurt. Whether you plan to use a website to supplement your offline business or will operate solely in the virtual world, there are a number of questions you need to ask and steps you will need to take to be successful.

What Is Your Site's Purpose?

Not all websites are the same, nor are they intended to be. You may need your site for e-commerce, actually making sales online. Or you may use it as another marketing tool, such as an online brochure, to promote your real-world business. Keeping printed material up-to-date and in the hands of your potential customers can be slow and costly. Having a website is important for all businesses, but critical for online ones. So, you will want to put your best foot forward with your site, making it as attractive and useful as possible.

ESSENTIAL

One of the exciting aspects of operating in the virtual world is that, by definition, everyone is "thinking outside the box." This may be a chance to broaden your services. Say you want to sell vintage linens. You might find customers starting to ask for antique serving pieces and table accessories. Presto—you now know about what new products to offer.

Think seriously about the purpose of your site. Do you envision it as a functional place where you will actually conduct business? Will it establish you as a credible presence in your industry? Do you want your business mission to be presented here as another key marketing tool? Will the site improve customer service? Will you want to collect data from those who come to your site so you can stay in touch with them?

Next consider what your customers will expect from your site. How easy can you make it for them to find your site? Once there, you will want them to understand the objective of the site. If it is an information-only site, you won't want viewers to be frustrated trying to find a way to interact with it. At a minimum, you will want to furnish contact information for customers to reach you, either via e-mail, social media, or other conventional means.

As you get ready to create a site, do an assessment of what you already have that you can use, such as marketing brochure copy, photos, or graphics. If you have been listing your products with other larger sites, like Amazon or eBay, consider whether you can transfer any material easily to your own site.

When you are dreaming of what the site will be, think about how a user will move around in it. Imagine your homepage as the road map, then sort out each section of the site and its utility to the user. Can you, or should you, use rollover buttons or animation to jazz it up? How about embedding short videos from YouTube, or comments from your Twitter feed? As you develop criteria for your website, cruise the web and see what other businesses have done—especially your competitors. You will undoubtedly find sites you like and those you don't. This knowledge will be a big help as you envision the big picture for your site, and even more so as you get into the specific design and operation details.

Building a Website

The good news is that there is a range of options when creating your website. Whatever route you take, treat the site like any other business expense. Set aside dollars to create, set up, market, and maintain it. Once you make the commitment to create a website, remember it will be as much a reflection of your business as the sign on your door, the look of your premises, the level of customer service, and of course the quality of your product or service. Be sure it shows the same degree of professionalism you bring to every other aspect of your endeavor.

FACT

If you're not sure what colors to use, check out *www.colorschemer.com*. You can use this site to find the best colors to use in your web design. It can allow you to match colors you have in images or get creative by adding new colors into your design.

If you are really watching your dollars, you may want to take advantage of one of the do-it-yourself website-building programs that most Internet service providers offer. These programs offer templates; you only need to enter your copy and add pictures, and voila, you have a website. The downside to using a template is that you are limited in your creative options, and it is possible another business's site could look startlingly similar to yours.

If you want to get a little more creative and come up with a truly unique site design you might try one of the "what you see is what you get" (WYSIWYG) programs such Adobe's Dreamweaver, which is available on both the Mac and PC. A little more skill is needed, but you will end up creating a custom site. If you are really ambitious you can always take a class to master hypertext mark-up language (HTML), which is the computer code that brings you what you see on your computer.

AllBusiness.com offers the following recommendations as design resources:

- Usability.gov, *www.usability.gov*: This is a website hosted by the Department of Health and Human Services. It offers help with design basics and usability statistics, and provides best-practice guidelines.
- Useit.com, *www.useit.com*: This site is run by Jakob Nielsen, a noted usability expert, who offers the ultimate in guidance on his site.
- The "Web Content Accessibility Guidelines," *www.w3.org/TR/WCAG20*: This is a resource from the World Wide Web Consortium specifically written for tailoring website usability for people with disabilities. These standards can be used broadly to make your site useful for any visitor and thus are definitely worth following.

Remember that these resources are designed for professionals in the field of usability, not laymen. Nevertheless, reviewing them will help you work more effectively with web designers and developers.

Hiring a Professional Web Designer

Professional web designers have the skills and the creative talent to transform your ideas into reality using the medium of the web. They will have far more knowledge than you of the latest features available, what is working well for other companies, and where the challenges lie. If web design is not a particular strength of yours, it might make good sense to lean on a professional for this key aspect of your business.

From the very outset it will be important to have a clear understanding of what your goals are and how the designer can help you meet them. If you find a designer who already has knowledge of your industry, it may make things go smoother and faster. Of course, you will have to pay for this talent and experience.

You will need to consider the big issues, of course, such as driving more customers to your business, but you will also need to get down into the nitty-gritty details. If you do not have a logo, this is something your web designer can help create. If you need your designer to help with writing text, you will want to negotiate how that approval process will work. You may also prefer to have a professional writer do the writing, but have the designer coordinate it all for you. It is always a good idea to set reasonable response times for both sides so the project doesn't languish because either you or the designer is awaiting another round of drafts.

Think about what you want for an overall look. The visuals will set the tone. You may just need straightforward product visuals and shopping cart functions. Or you may need to have images conveying solid dependability. Your credibility may be enhanced by listing any licenses you hold, as well as client testimonials.

Getting Referrals

Be forthright in asking to see examples of a designer's work and requesting client references. Don't just ask for them; you actually need to take the time to call the references. Of course you will want to know how the project worked out overall, but probe into some of the particulars. How much discrepancy was there between the approved bid and the final invoice, and what were the factors? Was the designer able to furnish detailed invoices? Ask how the interaction went throughout the web development process. Was the designer able to hear the client's wishes and take the web concept to another level, or did she do exactly what the client envisioned and no more? This may be the most important answer to consider, especially if a strict budget is in force. How is the site working? Has the client had many user complaints? Has it met its business objectives?

ESSENTIAL

To prevent any confusion once you are live on the web, take the time to test your site on each of the major browsers, including Internet Explorer, Firefox, Safari. Test it on several mobile platforms as well: iPhones and iPads, Android phones and tablets, and Windows phones and tablets. Subtle differences in their respective protocols can affect how your site appears. For more help visit *www.Browsershots.org.*

One key measure is the reliability of the site. It may be the best-looking site on the planet, but if it is down or not performing the intended functions, you might as well be closed for business. Perhaps the best test of a designer, or any vendor, is how she responds when there is a problem. Seek details on how quickly and competently the designer handled problems along the way.

The boundaries of the contract are another key point. It is important to be clear how much support can be expected following the initial setup of the site. There will always be kinks to be worked out in the development stage. Ask the referral whether they plan to maintain the site themselves or continue on a contractual basis. The bottom line is you need a web designer who has the talent, skills, and experience necessary, and is someone with whom you can communicate.

Web Designer Fees

Be sure to have the fee structure clearly negotiated before any work begins. For example, if you contract with the designer to complete the work by a specified date, and that deadline is missed, will she be able to continue to charge you her hourly rate until the work is finished? You might want to know how your project fits into the designer's schedule. Discuss ahead of time what kinds of issues could disrupt the project schedule. Will you be her major focus or will you be fighting for attention with other simultaneous projects? She should be able to give you an idea of how long your project should take, setting up reasonable expectations for both of you.

ALERT

One of the technologies that you might hear about is Flash. It was used for interactive animations and "Flashy" graphics. Unfortunately, it doesn't work on iPads or iPhones, so if you want your site visible on these platforms, stay away. And if your website designer tells you that it doesn't matter, you probably want to stay away from her as well.

The Fine Points

In addition to getting yourself a great-looking website, your designer should have the goods—or the colleagues—to build one with all the appropriate technical features needed. Find out which web standards her designs will follow. Be sure to have her test your design with multiple browsers. Find out if she knows how to add back-end functions. For example, if you want to have images rotate through your homepage, does the designer know how to do this? Ask who will host your site, and if she gets a commission from the hosting service. You may want to update your site after it is initially designed—find out how you would do this. Be clear about who owns the rights to the copy, or to any images, video, or animation on the site. Clearly it needs to be you. Don't make any assumptions and risk a nasty surprise later.

Ten Tips for a Site That Sells

Over the next few chapters you will learn more about constructing your site, bringing people to it and transacting. Before that, however, there is the big picture: what are the top ten tips for a site that sells? Broadly speaking, the tips fall into two categories: bringing people to the site and converting the browser into a buyer.

BRINGING PEOPLE TO THE SITE

1. **Provide offline offers and links:** Drive people to your site from advertisements, links on brochures, business cards, billboards, or anywhere people might see you or your products.
2. **Use Search Engine Marketing:** Drive users to your website by advertising online. Pay-per-click advertising is available from Google, Bing (Microsoft), Yahoo!, and others. If someone is searching for your type of product, why not drive them to your website?
3. **Use Search Engine Optimization (SEO):** What makes some websites rank higher than others? The search engines are always changing their algorithms, so nobody really knows for sure. That being said, many people have made educated guesses, based on clues that Google and others make. Key amongst them is making sure that each page embeds relevant keywords, is up-to-date, and has many inbound links from popular sites.
4. **Take advantage of social media:** Most people are influenced on what to buy (and where to buy it) from their friends. Getting people to recommend (like and share) your products and services in the social media world can also provide a steady flow of prospects to your site. Of course, getting people to do things with you on social media means you first must be actively using social media yourself.

1. **Create landing pages for ads:** Every advertisement triggers a question or a need. When the user clicks the ad, he should be directed to a page that addresses the specific need. A typical mistake that new online business owners make is that they have the ad link to the homepage.
2. **Put sales items on your homepage:** If your goal is to sell, don't make people hunt and peck looking for your merchandise. Bring as much as you can right up front.
3. **Implement one-click purchase:** Every time you force a user to click, they are likely to leave your site. The fewer the clicks, the more sales you will have.
4. **Deploy on a secure site:** Most people are comfortable with online transactions, and most people know what a secure page looks like (there is a tiny lock icon, and the website address starts with https://). If your site isn't secure, you may scare away customers halfway through the transaction. More importantly, if the site isn't secure, you may be liable for any fraud.
5. **Use good pictures, descriptions, and testimonials:** People generally don't transact unless they are certain that the product or service will meet their needs. Great photography, well-written descriptions, and testimonials (written and video) all increase the buyers' confidence—and the likelihood they will buy.
6. **Implement a lead capture system:** Not everyone who comes to your website will purchase right then and there. Asking for their names and e-mail addresses means that you can reach out to them later on, when they might indeed be ready to buy.

Web Hosting

For small businesses that want the impact of a web presence without a Fortune 500 level of investment, choosing a web-hosting company is the way to go. You simply hire one of these firms to provide the infrastructure and data management you need to get you on the web. There are literally thousands of web-hosting companies and related services. As you consider using one, think about what features you need for your site. Two of the most popular are e-mail access for customer contact and a shopping cart for e-commerce. Some companies offer tools for site construction as well.

FACT

There are nearly 10,000 web-hosting services to choose from. Larger host companies have larger servers that can manage more data, and may be more reliable. However, they may provide a lower level of service and support. Try to get the cancellation rate for any company you may consider. It may give you an insight to their customer satisfaction: the more cancellations, the less satisfied their customers likely are.

Finding a Web Host

Most web-hosting companies are geared toward either small businesses, such as IPower, *www.ipower.com* or HostGator, *www.hostgator.com*. Believe it or not, 50 percent of web-host customers find their site of choice through word of mouth. The rest may see ads that run in the major technology trade publications such as *Wired* or *PC Magazine*, or through a simple Google search.

Subscription Choices

In most cases when you use a web-hosting site you will contract for a subscription rate for a set period of time. Depending on the company, you may be able to sign on for a monthly, quarterly, semiannual, or annual rate. Costs range from a few dollars to more than $100 per month. The perception may be that if you pay more you get more, but that is not necessarily true. It is difficult to comparison shop—some say it's similar to buying a mattress. Look for and take advantage of money-back guarantees or free trial periods.

Domain Names—Again

The Internet Corporation for Assigned Names and Numbers (ICANN) is a nonprofit worldwide organization whose responsibilities include tracking every domain name to be sure it is unique. By going to their site, *www.icann .org*, you can research names. However, you may need to secure a name through a reseller who has blocked a group of names. To determine if the name is already taken, log on to Whois, *www.whois.com*, or go to your web-hosting company's website and search for the domain that you might want. Chapter 7 reviews the mechanics of choosing a domain name.

Your domain name is key to your business identity and the ease with which customers will be able to find you; therefore, it's not something to take lightly. Some web-hosting packages may include a free domain name for the first year. Otherwise expect to pay a nominal fee ($10 to $35) annually to register your domain name.

ALERT

A popular activity of spammers is to troll through domain registration listings, harvesting names and e-mail addresses for later marketing. If you don't want your name open for all to see, then look for a privacy option when you register your domain. For a nominal extra charge, the domain registrar will hide your name from public viewing.

Preparing to Launch Your Site

Once you have gone through the rigors of setting goals for your website, and then designing it, you will want to run through a few final steps before going live. First, review your initial goals for the site. If it was meant to be informational, have you included the information so that visitors can find it easily? If you wanted a tool to make sales, is it organized to work efficiently?

ESSENTIAL

When creating the individual pages of information for your site, brevity rules. There is nothing more aggravating than plodding through layers of a site trying to find something. Make sure you have done a good job of organizing your information in logical groupings.

Beginning with your homepage, make sure the icons are obvious and are easy to use and understand. Check to be certain you have succeeded in getting all the pertinent data presented in an attractive and easy-to-understand manner. If you have a search function for your site, make sure it works in a user-friendly way. Test to confirm whether your links make the connections intended. Make sure a visitor to your site will be able to tell which items are links and which are not.

Test how easily a user can move around on your site. Have you built in effective shortcuts to find any page? The user should be able to figure out how to find the information he's seeking.

Visuals Are Key

Everything from the font size to graphics and animation should improve the user experience. Make sure the visuals don't compete: the background shouldn't fight with the message, or make it difficult to read the copy. Make sure that the font is big enough for those over fifty to read. As you look over the final creation, see if you have included extraneous components that do not add to the usefulness of the site. Sometimes, too many clever elements get thrown in during development that in the end are really unnecessary. Keep your target audience in mind. Potential customers may not want to perform too many tasks, or watch a ninety-second video, before they get to the objective of their visit to your site. Likewise, you can keep your site from getting bogged down by using product images that have small file sizes. No one likes waiting for a site to upload.

Navigation

Think of the construction of your website as if it were a salad. Separately, the components are a bunch of vegetables. Together they make a splendid lunch. Your navigation tools should make it as easy to find a page on your site as it is to identify the radish in the bowl. Give each main category on your site its own tab or button.

The navigation of every page should follow the same format. Consistency is king. And information should be organized from the perspective of your end users. What may seem perfectly logical to you may not speak to the goals the users want to achieve at your site. Study other sites, including your competitors', and see what navigation methods you can adapt for your own.

Spyware, Adware, and Virus Trouble

Nothing is more discouraging when using the web than to discover that your system has been infected with an adware or spyware invasion. The first clue may be that your computer is processing at a snail's pace, especially when trying to perform tasks online. Your homepage may have changed without your input. New icons may appear on your desktop. Annoying pop-up ads may be proliferating. Any or all of these may be telling you that some insidious application has latched onto your system and may be stealing data. This can be dangerous because your personal information can be captured and broadcast without your knowledge.

By using a combination of software and fastidious work habits, you can minimize invasion of these applications. First and foremost, avoid opening strange e-mail attachments. Consider running virus-filtering software on your e-mail server. Next, stay away from free download offers that include adware in their software. Make sure your employees, or any contractors who may have access to your computers, conform to your policies for protecting the system from these threats. Should you find you are plagued with any of these applications, run a program to purge them from your computer. For PCs, you can get either Spybot Search and Destroy or Ad-Aware programs for free directly from *www.download.com.*

Perhaps even more important for you, is that you don't want your online business's website to be infecting the computers of your prospects and customers. Speak to your web developer about "hardening" your server against infiltration, and adding code that notifies you when someone attempts to hack in.

Wrapping It Up

In order to access the Internet, you first need an Internet service provider (ISP). Next, you need a web host, which is where your site will reside. As discussed earlier, your evaluation of a particular host should include the services they provide and, perhaps more importantly, the amount of server capacity they offer. Lastly, you need a file transfer protocol (FTP) program, which is the software that actually places your files on the web host server. If you use any of the WYSIWYG programs (such as Dreamweaver), FTP access is generally included. If you are building your site using a host-based content management system (WordPress is an example), FTP is useful, but you will be doing 99 percent of your work directly from within the program's control panel.

Building a website is important, but it is unreasonable to think that people will magically find your online business, unless you proactively make this happen. That's the next step.

CHAPTER 19

The Laws of Website Attraction

The most brilliant business idea in the world—with all the necessary funding, equipment, and employees—will go nowhere without a solid marketing plan. To muscle into the market you need to be able to show a good reason to draw customers away from competitors. This chapter will get you started with market research, help you identify your target market, and introduce you to the laws of website attraction: how to get buyers in the front door.

Start with Market Research

If you plan to sell to a particular market, it's important to know all about that market. Research means finding out what customers want, don't want, and why. Surveys, questionnaires, and focus groups are a few ways to find out the needs and desires of your potential customers. You may also be able to tell a lot about your customers by observing them and taking note of who they are and what they're interested in when they're at your site. Get some basic information from your server logs using a free tool like Google Analytics. When customers make a purchase or any kind of inquiry, you can ask them where they heard about your business. Have you ever been asked for your zip code when you are checking out at a chain store? They capture this information to learn where their customers are coming from.

There are many factors that will impact your marketing plan, including:

- Your budget
- The type of products or services you're offering
- The amount of volume you can handle
- Your methods of distribution
- The amount of personal service you are able to provide
- How quickly you expect your business to grow

Consider the unique attributes of your business while designing questionnaires, surveys, or any other type of research-gathering materials. For example, if you're planning to do business worldwide—or to different language groups locally—be prepared to conduct surveys in other languages and be aware of cultural nuances that may affect how your product is perceived.

Market research can tell you many things. You can learn about the pricing, trends, and competition in your industry. You can gain a greater understanding of the actual value of what you're selling in the market, meaning what people are willing to pay. You may also uncover trends in the marketplace that can be advantageous. For example, if surveys indicate that free shipping is more highly valued than an extended warranty, then your marketing can focus on free shipping. Your approach need not ignore the extended warranty, but recognize that free shipping is more likely to result in a sale.

What is the difference between primary and secondary research? In primary research, you gather information from your surveys, questionnaires, tests, focus groups, and other direct means. Secondary research draws on work that other people have done, such as the census, books, magazines, data services, or websites. Primary research is more precise because it is tailored to the exact questions you want answered. Secondary research is faster and cheaper. Ideally, you will use both.

Look at trade publications and reports from organizations and groups in your field to get the latest industry news. Libraries, websites, company reports (annual or quarterly reports from public companies), and the local chamber of commerce are just a few places to look for local business information.

Surveys

Keep surveys short (ten to twelve questions maximum), whether they're given online, in person, or by telephone. Phrase questions in a straightforward (nonjudgmental) manner, with neutral language, and keep questions one sentence long. Get the age, gender, and approximate income level (provide ranges to select from) of participants. For a low cost online survey instrument, look at both *www.SurveyMonkey.com* and *www.Zoomerang.com*; they are both easy to set up and have become so common folks tend to take them willingly.

Focus Groups

Focus groups are wonderful ways to get insightful answers to questions and opinions about your product. You will want to have a neutral group in a neutral location with a neutral host and provide a pleasant atmosphere. Often focus groups are watched through a one-way window or mirror or taped for future evaluation. Keep the session to an hour and a half or two hours at the most; longer than this and the attendees will lose interest.

During the time of the session you want to get the most meaningful feedback possible. The facilitator conducting the focus group should press the participants to give specific feedback.

Know your product, know (or learn) your market group, and then test the product on the right group. For example, if you're testing your new wedding planning website, test it with engaged couples—not with a room filled with 50 percent divorced men who may have no immediate interest in planning another wedding.

Tracking

Keeping close tabs on who buys what product or service is a way of gathering information. Are all your credit card receipts from the same zip code? Do customers always seem to visit the same pages on your website? Google Analytics can provide sophisticated information by tracking the page views, sources of traffic and many other attributes. This can help you define your target audience; or it might point out that who you are targeting is not who you want to target. You might simply notice in the e-mails that you receive that most of the last three-months' customers were female. Pay attention and you can gather inexpensive marketing data.

Identifying Your Target Market

Just as children's games say clearly on the box what ages the game is geared toward, nearly every product or service has some demographic group that will be most interested in spending money to own, use, or rent. The number of businesses that have failed because the owners haven't taken the time to determine their target audience is staggering; know your target market. Some questions to ask yourself when outlining your target market include:

- What is the age range of the customers who want my product or service?
- What is their income level?
- What level of education do they have?
- What is their marital or family status?

- Is this a product or service they need, or a luxury item?
- How will they use this product or service?
- What will draw them to my product or service?
- Which gender will be buying my product or service more often?
- What special features or attention are they looking for?
- What do they like or dislike about the product or service in general?
- Is this an impulse buy or something they are saving up for?
- Where do they gather their decision-making information?
- What do they usually purchase just before your product or service? And what at the same time?
- Who do they usually turn to for advice prior to making the purchase decision? What social media or shopping sites do they spend time at?
- Is this something that will become a repeat purchase?

These are just a few of numerous categories into which you can break down your target market. You don't want to make a marketing plan that is ultimately so narrow that it limits your sales to a few perfect customers. On the other hand, if you think your product or service is perfect for everybody, you have not defined what makes it special, and for whom.

Reaching Your Market

Let's say you've established that your ideal customer is a single woman between the ages of twenty-five and forty-two, with an income in the $35,000 to $55,000 range, who resides in the suburbs of a large city, drinks diet soda, watches soap operas on television, speaks to her mom twice a week, dates men three to five years older than herself, and has a cat. Well, perhaps you didn't get that specific (you generally don't need to), but the point is, once you've established who your audience is, it is far easier to figure out how to reach them: your primary tools for doing this are pricing and promotion.

Pricing

Before venturing into the methods of getting your name out there, consider your pricing strategies. In a new business, you may need to establish your reputation and brand name with potential customers by keeping your product or services below average market prices. (Or provide special services or incentives that your competition cannot provide.) If a new product and an established brand-name product are priced the same, the established brand will most often be the winner.

You might also use time-factored pricing as a promotion point. For example, you can promote a lower price if customers buy before a particular date. Be careful not to lower your prices below cost or make prices so low that customers don't return when you're selling at your regular prices.

ALERT

Note that just as you are watching your competitors' pricing, they are watching yours. Be prepared to trigger a response matching a competitor's pricing offer. During the holidays many online sellers may use free shipping as a lure to get customers to make purchases on their sites. Once a few of the big guys try it, soon everyone needs to offer it to remain competitive.

Pricing is also linked to perceived value. If someone is expecting to pay a certain amount for a product or service, he won't question that amount. If you're able to cut costs, you can lower the price. However, it is not necessary. For example, if you're selling notepaper at $10 per box and buying it in mass quantity at $6 each, you're making $4 per package sold. If everyone is used to paying $10 for notepaper in your area, then no one will think about the price. If, however, you can suddenly get notepaper at $3.50 from a different distributor, it doesn't mean you have to lower your price to $9.50. If you stay at $10 per box you're staying at the market price, which means more profits for you. If, however, you want more volume because there aren't enough orders to allow you to take advantage of the lower costs, you might lower your price—and promote the new price through online discount incentives such as search engine marketing (pay-per-click ads), Groupon, fliers, signage, and other advertising. Keep in mind, though, that people can become used to lower prices, and may eventually see the lower price as the new "regular" price, which can hurt your business.

Promotion and Advertising

If you have a product or service and you want to make money from it, you'll need to promote it. Promotion includes selling, sales promotion, and advertising. Selling can include talking with customers, making sales calls, or sending e-mails. Sales promotion can include anything from how you arrange your products on your shopping cart homepage, to the specific offers you send out via e-mail or social media.

There are numerous ways to get your name out there, and once you've done your market research and established who your target audience is, you'll need to put together your promotional budget.

Promotions can be seasonal, such as offering a free Christmas ornament to customers who spend over $50 in your online boutique during November. Promotions can be tied to events, such as when you become a sponsor of a road race to support a local charity, or underwrite a Little League baseball team. Promotions can be tie-ins with other events. Think of all the children's meals at fast food chains themed to the newest movie release.

As you'll learn, posting bills and fliers is advertising, so is direct mail; these can be less expensive methods than major newspaper or magazine ads. And they pale in comparison to the cost of a TV advertising campaign. Depending on the nature of your business, you'll need to evaluate the types of media available. If you're planning and promoting an annual one-month festival to be held every October, then you'll use your ad money to advertise in a big way in August and September. However, if you're selling products or services year-round, you'll want to spread the budget throughout the year.

Direct Mail

With the ease and low cost of e-mail, marketers sometimes forget about traditional mail. Direct mail is often referred to as "junk mail" by its recipients, but can yield a greater response if you target the consumer for your product or service correctly. Magazines seeking subscribers have long relied primarily on direct mail, and today numerous products and services also seek significant returns from direct-mail marketing. Direct mail differs from a mail campaign to your regular customers because it involves buying or compiling a specific list that best suits your target market or demographic needs. Certainly, many people will toss what you send into the garbage. However, if you send out 100 direct-mail pieces at a cost of $100, and make six sales of $60 each, you're ahead by $260. You've also put your name in front of the other ninety-four people, four or five of whom may remember you at a later date or have a friend who needs whatever it is that you're selling. The key is to drive the reader to your website to transact: pricing offers, testimonials, and quick-response (QR) codes can all help to accomplish this.

ESSENTIAL

An offer should be included in every direct marketing piece. The offer can vary depending on the importance of the target recipient. With direct mail, your goal is to make at least enough profit to cover the cost of the mailing, including printing, postage, the price of the list, and so on.

Timing is everything when it comes to direct mail. Plan your mailing for opportune times. For example, you won't want your direct-mailing piece to get caught up in the holiday postal overload—or at the height of the summer vacation season. Make your piece stand out. Use color, a photo, or a clever quote. Postcards can be effective direct-mail pieces. They're cheaper than letters and grab attention immediately.

Avoid mixed or confusing messages. Use a tone that reflects the demographics of your readers. If your piece has too much to read, people will toss it. Don't insult or put down your audience. Rather, share how you can improve upon its way of doing things.

E-Mail Marketing

E-mail marketing is a very effective way of reaching a worldwide audience. Internet users hate spam, or the electronic version of junk mail that comes when companies buy lists of unwilling participants. Most savvy folks have spam-filter software on their computers to rebuff the avalanche of unwanted messages bombarding them daily. The same people might not mind junk mail in their real-world mailbox—in fact, they're used to it—but e-mail is considered more intrusive. Even if your message does get through, the delete button is easy to hit before it is ever looked at.

To make the most of e-mail communications, you need to have good lists of existing or prospective customers who will accept your solicitations. It's to your advantage to market yourself clearly on your website or even on another website of a similar nature. You want people to sign up for e-mails from you, or agree to receive them. Blind e-mails from massive lists generally annoy people, and don't work if they are blocked.

FACT

Direct mail should grab the attention of the recipient and prompt him to take action. With digital printing technology it is possible to customize a message for your targeted recipient. Creative (or some would say deceptive) packaging, such as a mailing piece that looks like a check is enclosed, will improve the odds of your piece getting opened.

If you do plan to use e-mail, keep the message concise and make sure people can get off the list if they want. Constantcontact.com is an example of an e-mail service provider that can help you set up basic e-mail marketing programs. In Chapter 22 you will learn about more sophisticated e-mail marketing, from the context of customer relationship management.

Signage

What does signage have to do with online business? Depending on the nature of the business, it may be critical, or it may be completely irrelevant. The idea is to drive people both to your real-world business, but also to your electronic storefront. Put the website's address clearly in the sign, and potentially add a QR code as well.

Signs draw people into an establishment and keep the company name highly visible to new and old customers alike. The lettering, the colors, a logo, and anything else that makes your sign stand out are significant. Passersby are only glancing at your sign as they drive or walk past. A simple three- or four-word sign is easier to comprehend than one containing two sentences.

Along with your actual signs, you can take advantage of inexpensive but effective advertising with posters and fliers. In major cities, there are numerous construction sites and other such areas that have advertisements posted all over them. As long as the posting of bills is allowed, this is an inexpensive way to be seen by numerous people. The traffic that passes by in a major city is tremendous. College campuses are also great places to post fliers.

Handouts can also be an effective way of letting people know about your hottest products or specialized services. Instruct those handing out such materials to be courteous and to avoid sticking them in people's faces.

Be clever. Anywhere you think people who are prospective customers might see your company name is where you want to have it placed. Just abide by laws, rules, and regulations—or you could be fined.

Newspapers

Newspapers provide a means for reaching a particular region (or the nation, if it's a paper with a wide circulation, such as *USA Today* or the *New York Times*). You can time your ads to run when you choose, and reach a large audience. Keep the ads simple and make sure they provide a means by which customers can reach you—web address, social media profiles, e-mail, and phone number. Remember to place your ad in the section best suited for your product or service, such as Sports or Lifestyle. You can also include incentives like coupons. Be forewarned, however, that photos and artwork don't always look good in newspapers.

Look at the ad rates carefully and measure the size of ads that you might want to buy. Generally you will need to run your advertisement several times so people become familiar with your ad. Sunday papers can be good because people save them. *PennySaver*, free commuter papers, and similar publications might also be good for small inexpensive ads, depending on your product.

Magazines

Magazines allow you to reach a more targeted audience. Also, your ad will have a longer shelf life than it will in a daily paper, which gets tossed or put in the birdcage. Trade magazines can be beneficial for business-to-business sales or industry recognition. Select magazines that are best suited for your product or services, and remember that they usually have a long lead time. Get a calendar showing when ads are needed at the magazine. Magazines allow for marvelous artwork, so you can be colorful and creative.

Radio

Radio is an excellent way to reach a locally targeted market, since different demographic groups listen to different stations. Radio allows you to be creative with sound effects—and you will spend a lot less money than you would by advertising on television. Be concise and conversational in tone, get to the point quickly, don't be obnoxious, and try to be entertaining and snappy—whether the copy is produced or is read by on-air talent. Make sure the location of your store or website is clearly stated and the web address is repeated. High-traffic times like morning or evening drive times will get the biggest audience.

ESSENTIAL

When looking into radio advertising, consider easy listening stations or light music stations, which are played in establishments like restaurants or even over telephone lines when people are put on hold. The listening audience for such stations is often larger than the ratings reveal because of all these secondary listeners.

Television

Be creative when it comes to television. For example, if a local talk show needs lodgings for their guests, you might provide rooms at your hotel free of charge in exchange for a promotional announcement. If you run a limousine service, provide free transportation for all guests in exchange for a daily mention of your company on their show. Such deals are worked out all the time. And then there are infomercials. They're expensive, but they can be very effective for certain products.

ALERT

Get recommendations before signing up with an ad agency or consultant. Also, make sure to monitor your ads to be certain that they run when they're supposed to and look—or sound—as you wish. If the ad didn't run properly, or at all, you must make sure the media source knows it.

Outdoor Advertising

Billboards are a great way to put your brand name in front of the public. Be imaginative and keep it simple. Remember, people are driving by and have no time to read five lines of copy at sixty miles per hour. A new curious place for advertising is a small sign attached to the gasoline pumping hose, in public washrooms, on taxi roofs—literally everywhere. Do your research or perhaps hire a media buyer who is an expert on the many options available for outdoor and other forms of advertising.

Trade Shows

Trade shows are another great way to be seen. Design a booth that grabs people's attention and displays your products or services. Have plenty of literature and friendly, knowledgeable personnel on hand. Nothing beats that face-to-face contact, even if it is a brief encounter in a hectic trade-show environment. A more in-depth conversation can be had afterward. If you can't afford to have a booth at a trade show, show up anyway, just for the networking.

Other Creative Options

Other forms of advertising are all around you. You can promote yourself with T-shirts, sweatshirts, pens, notepads, or baseball caps. Newsletters (online or offline) can also spread the word about what you're up to and what you offer potential customers. Getting in front of the public—preferably your target market—is your goal. Advertising can be one method of doing so, but there are other means of getting publicity.

Some other ways to get exposure:

- Trading links with other sites.
- Registering with Google local and Bing local.
- Using specific keywords to increase the likelihood of your company name coming up during a search.
- Swapping ads with other sites.
- Joining trade organizations and being written up in newsletters and on their sites.
- Mentioning your company name on newsgroups, in chat rooms, or in forums. (If you do this, though, be careful to understand the "netiquette": if you are too commercial in some online communities, you will hurt your reputation more than help it.)
- Running so called "wrap around" e-mail campaigns that remind recipients about other forms of advertising you are using such as direct mail, TV, or outdoor.

Many of these options cost little or no money: it's just a question of creativity to expand this list further. The underlying question for any marketing activity is simple: where can you put your message so that your prospects can see it. In other words, fish where the fish are.

Publicity

You need not always go out and spend top dollar on advertising and promotional ideas to get your name before the public. Stories about your business in newspapers, magazines, on the Internet, or as part of radio or television newscasts can be remarkably successful ways of increasing business. Unlike advertising, you don't pay for these directly, but you may pay for a publicist or public relations agency to help put you in the limelight, or at least in a few key stories.

ALERT

One of the biggest reasons for the downfall of several major web-based businesses was the overextension of their advertising beyond the value or profitability of their product. This can be the downfall of any business. If you're spending an average of $10 to promote a $7 item, you're in trouble. Publicity can dramatically reduce the cost of promotion.

When you're starting out, you can do some of this work yourself through writing and sending (or e-mailing) media releases to anyone and everyone who you think might be interested in a story about what your business is doing. Send information about new products, upcoming events, new technology or inventions, interesting news, mergers, or anything else that could potentially become a story. Look for a clever attention-grabbing hook. Think up an eye-catching title and include the who, what, where, when, and why of the proposed story. Double-space your press release, keep it to one page (two maximum), and make sure you include specific contact information.

Press kits are important and should include a collection of recent press releases, clips from stories that were written about you or your company, and an overview of what the company is all about, plus bios of the key players. If you have them, include papers or speeches you have authored. A professional-looking press kit is a very important business tool, but most entrepreneurs have realized that the immediacy of the web has meant that the press kit itself should be in a special media section of your website.

Public relations (PR) involves more than trying to place your name in front of the media. A good PR firm can help you maintain a positive image on those occasions when things go wrong. This includes cleaning up negative publicity that may result from incidents, activities, or accidents involving your business. If one of your products was recalled, you'll need to spend time working with your PR professional to reassure the public your company has addressed and dealt with the problem. Your reputation and how it plays in the media are very important.

ESSENTIAL

You can position yourself for good media coverage in stories related to your industry by establishing yourself as a recognized authority in your field. Getting yourself published in trade publications makes you an expert when general media is doing a piece related to your industry. Always make yourself available for background information even if you are not going to be quoted.

Search Engine Marketing: Bidding for Keywords and Clicks

Drawing the right buyers for your items is managed in the virtual world with its own set of tools. A uniquely media-specific tool is pay-per-click (PPC) advertising. The most important PPC sites are Google, Facebook, and to a lesser extent, LinkedIn. You can buy keyword ads that match words your prospective buyer enters in a search engine. Say you are going to sell a gentleman's Seiko steel tank watch. You will get a far more targeted response if you buy the words "Seiko steel tank watch" rather than just the generic "watch."

The price for keywords can be bid up depending on the demand. You submit a per-click price you are willing to pay for the word or phrase you want to use to drive traffic to your site. You also commit to a budget amount you are willing to spend in total. Using our watch example, say you bid seventy-five cents per click and set a budget amount of $150 a month. If yours is the highest bid for your keywords, your ad will pop up at or near the top of the list when someone searches for those words. Your "kitty" of $150 will not be touched if someone reads your ad, only when someone actually clicks on it. For $150 at seventy-five cents per click, two hundred shoppers could click on you. If your bid was seventy-five cents but someone else bid ninety cents, your listing would appear further down the list. More obscure words are less in demand and thus less expensive to reserve. You may have a number of different keywords reserved at any given time for whatever you are selling.

If one set of words is not effective, try to massage the copy. In fact, most PPC advertisers use several different versions of the ad, and see which ones are most effective. They drop the poorer performer, make some other minor changes, and start the assessment process all over again. Try to direct those who respond to your keyword triggers to the specific page on your website that has the product being offered—a landing page. By saving them the step of moving from your homepage to the innards of your site, you'll convert more browsers into buyers.

SEO: Search Engine Optimization

The real secret to the success of your site is the element you do not see: the search engine. It cannot be overstated how important it is that search engines—and Google in particular—can actually find what users want.

One way to test how many of your site's pages are being picked up is to log on to Google and enter your site name in the search box. This should turn up any URL history of the site. If it does, one option offered is to "find web pages from the site yourdomain.com." Click on this link and make sure the number of pages the engine finds matches the number you have on your site. If the engine finds fewer than there should be, it means that the engine robots cannot find all of your pages. The robots use links as they traverse the web. You may have pages that are not linked, or some pages may be dead-ended.

The best way to ensure that you are fully linked is to make certain all of your site's pages have internal links, which link them to each other internally. External links connect you with other sites and will help a search engine find your site. An excellent way to help robots to find your site, as well as to help users navigate the site, is to have an up-to-date site map.

Search engines are programmed to weight the ranking of a search result based on a secret and always changing algorithm. Reportedly, there are 100+ factors that determine your site's ranking, each one being of different importance. Generally speaking, if you try aggressive tricks to fool the search engine, your ranking can actually be reduced. Google suggests that if you create a site that makes sense for people, then your page will be ranked appropriately. That being said, here are some suggestions on how to manage your ranking:

- **Increase the number of "natural" inbound links:** The search engine rightfully assumes that the more sites—and the more authoritative these sites are—that link to yours, the more likely that yours is the "authoritative" source on the subject in question. This means that having fifty links from your friends and family is better than having five. But having fifty links from CNN.com, usatoday.com, and other major sites will have an even bigger impact.

- **Don't increase the number of links unnaturally:** There are some companies that sell links from a series of computer generated pages, just to increase your inbound link count. Google, for example, will severely penalize you (e.g., drop your listing to close to the bottom) if it senses you are doing this.

- **Embed keywords within the body of your site and the title of each page:** Having the right keywords in the title or descriptive copy may take some trial and error. There are companies who, for a fee, can massage your keywords to increase not only visitors to your site but also increase the number of visits.

- **Don't play games with the keywords:** Google takes a dim view of people trying to cheat the system. Don't use white keyword text against a white background, or lists of keywords "stuffed" onto the page.

- **Use Meta tags:** There are several HTML tags that contain information that search engines use, but cannot be seen by users unless they examine the underlying HTML. The Meta description tag contains a few sentences describing the page. The Meta keywords tag contains a list of keywords that describe the page content. If you are paying someone to build your site, make sure that the creation and writing of the Meta tags is included.

- **Skip Flash:** Flash technology is not particularly search-engine friendly, as the text within the Flash file is not well-indexed. It also has the downside of not being viewable on iPads and iPhones. Instead, ask your web designer to use a technology called HTML5.

- **Keep your content fresh:** Another key indicator of relevance is the freshness of your page. The more often you change the page, the more up-to-date the page appears to the search engine. More importantly, the fresher your content, the more often users will return to the site to see what's new.

ALERT

Second only to making a site user friendly is making it search-engine friendly. Incorporate keywords into site content descriptions. Web-monkey.com at *www.webmonkey.com/tutorials* offers beginner resources. Google provides their keyword tool at *www.budurl.com/ keywordtoolgoogle.*

Social Media Marketing: Power and Pitfalls

Sometimes it feels like the only way people are communicating is through social media channels on smartphones or tablets. It's true—there is tremendous potential for exposure and massive information sharing through social media, but it can also be a huge distraction. To get the most from social media you need to understand how it applies to amplifying a business. Both the messaging and the tools are different in a business context than personal use.

Social Networking

Social networking sites like Facebook, Twitter, and YouTube are no longer the sole reserve of teenagers. Businesses are setting up Facebook pages to stay in touch with clients who check in regularly to see what is new in their world. You want to become part of their regular search as a favorite vendor, or source for what is happening right now. Updating a Facebook page regularly ensures that your company name will be visible to your target audience every day—and it's free!

One of the key differences, however, is that traditional media is one way: broadcast. Social media is all about the conversation, and the community. It requires a different mindset—one that is open to criticism, and opportunity. As traditional media such as print advertising contracts, social media is gaining in impact. Some businesses are using Twitter to stimulate customer loyalty by promising information that will be found exclusively through this media. Many restaurants, for example, will tweet their daily specials midmorning.

You should assess who you are trying to reach. Build your fan or follower list by linking your Facebook and Twitter pages to your website and e-mail signature. If you have an e-mail list, send out a message announcing your social media presence and invite your contacts to follow you. You can send updates to customers about new products, special sales, and other events. Post photos or videos that will interest your customer base. Invite fans and followers to a private sale or an anniversary celebration. Hold contests and invite feedback. The possibilities are endless!

ESSENTIAL

A common rookie mistake for a young business is using the same content on all social media channels. Anyone following your business and seeing the exact same copy or links to videos will think you are lazy or not savvy, and perhaps worse—you look unimaginative and boring.

Where to Start

The five most widely known social media resources are Facebook, Twitter, LinkedIn, YouTube, and Google+. Each has personal applications and each has business applications. If you want to check out a larger view of what is going on in social media, go to the social media enthusiast site *www .mashable.com*. If Facebook is a target channel, remember that businesses have "fan pages," while individuals have personal profiles. But to start a Facebook page for your business, you must first create a personal profile (which gives you a personal page), and only then create your business page.

Yelp is a neutral social media platform that can be a great place to introduce your business via social media. You may put your business on it and then ask clients to comment about you—favorably of course. Be aware that Yelp is a forum for folks to vent what they like, and perhaps too often get fired up to broadcast what they didn't like about an experience they had with a business. Most often the complaints have to do with a poor customer service experience. On the plus side, you can use it to promote events to draw more customers or raise awareness about your kind of product or service.

Should You Be LinkedIn?

LinkedIn is the world's foremost professional networking site. The tone of conversation is more mature, and often focused on professional advancement, getting a job, and discussions within the unlimited number of groups that exist. Like Facebook, there is a concept of personal profiles and company pages. Most businesses don't realize that the company pages are free, and have room for descriptions about products and more. This content—all of which is free—gives you credentials in the real world, and helps Google find you quickly online.

QUESTION

Can I use my personal Facebook page to promote my business?
You can, but it is better to separate your personal and business pages. Just as you don't want to comingle your personal checking and your business checking accounts, you want to keep social media separate. You can use your personal Facebook to follow your business. It is even more important to keep personal and business separate on Twitter. By its nature, brevity can be perilous for misinterpretation.

Is YouTube Right for You?

YouTube has made the entire world into microfilm producers. For a business, YouTube can be used to tell a story as part of your marketing. You can embed a video on your website. Even better, a YouTube video can be used for a "how-to." If you own a yarn shop, a series of short video instructions on knitting techniques can be a great reinforcement of your expertise, and by extension, a terrific resource for knitting tools.

Even better is to use YouTube for user-generated content. Have a contest and invite your customers (and others) to make a video showing how your product is used. Then have people vote on which one they think should win. If done correctly, this grassroots effort will reach out to the videographers as the videos are created. Then later, they will actively promote the video to their network (and the wider market), looking for votes.

Pinterest

This site is modeled after a pin board: whenever you see an interesting graphic on the web, you click on a button, and the graphic is magically posted on your virtual corkboard. People can "Like" the pin, they can repin it, and they can comment on it. One possible use of Pinterest is to create a photo gallery of your products, or a gallery of customers' products. Or a gallery of customers.

Blogs

Web logs, commonly known as blogs, have taken over the role of newsletters for many companies and organizations. By nature, blogs are intended to be quick reads focused on one topic. If you are considering starting a blog it is a good idea to spend time reading lots and lots of other blogs. See what style others are using that might be good for your undertaking. Take note of the worst ones as well as the stars. Blogs are their own beast and need to be hosted. Some of the top blog hosts are *www.wordpress.com, www.tumblr.com, www.livejournal.com,* and *www.blogger.com.* More powerful is if you set up a blog as your website. Ask your web developer to set up WordPress (from *www.wordpress.org*) for you.

When writing a blog try to keep it "skim-able," meaning a reader should be able to read it quickly and get your salient points. The best blogs use photos, graphics, and video to break up the text. Also try to keep a designer's eye on how the page looks. Make sure there is good contrast between the type and the background for easy readability. Above all, remember that what you write has to be valuable to the readers—otherwise they won't bother reading it! Here is a free six segment course on Blogging: *www.budurl.com/everythingBlog.*

One strategy for getting your word out is to be a guest blogger. The idea is that if you write on others' blogs, their readers will become familiar with you, and eventually follow you back to your blog and website. To be a guest blogger, first identify the blogs where your customers spend their time. Read the blog entries to understand each blog's style, target audience, and the type of content that gets posted. Comment on posts where you can add value, both on the blog and also within your own blog. After doing this for a period of time, you will have earned the right to reach out to the blog owner, and ask if he is open to your being a guest blogger. The first thing that he will do is search for you on his blog, then search for himself on yours. The second thing that he will likely do is open the door to a conversation. When you have his attention, you're pretty much there.

Social Media Pitfalls

Social media can be a great asset to your business, but it does require time. If not yours, someone else's. As you get started using different channels you may find some fit better than others with the nature of your business. Whether you are considering using a Facebook page, Twitter, or writing a blog, someone has to have the responsibility to do it. Writing a blog can be time consuming. To keep it fresh, and your followers interested, it needs to be updated frequently. Who is going to do it?

Don't confuse blogging with keeping up your website. The website reflects the totality of your business. A blog is more like an editorial, or an infomercial. It is very specific in its focus and perspective.

Link Exchanges

Simply put, a link exchange is where you and another website owner agree to link to each other's website. They are important for two key reasons: it helps direct readers from one site to yours, and it helps Google discover (and better rank) your site. Reach out to sites where your prospective customers might spend time, and pop the question to the site owner: would we both win if we traded links? If you have a blog and you approach another blogger, the question is whether you would both win if you were listed on each other's blogrolls. (A blogroll is a list of blogs that appear on one of your blog's pages.) The answer, if you have properly selected partner sites, will usually be yes.

The challenge in doing this is when you approach websites whose reach is far greater than your own. They may even sell advertising, and see your link-for-link request as a way to circumvent payment. Best to start with sites that are approximately the same size as your own. If you do want to approach larger sites, ask them if you could contribute an article. They likely won't pay you, but they will allow you to put a few lines at the bottom of the article saying who you are . . . and a link to your site.

ALERT

Nofollow is not your friend. There is an HTML code (Nofollow) that controls whether Google gives "credit" for the link back to your site. If you make a deal to exchange links, make sure that you specify that the link cannot be nofollowed.

QR Codes

Look carefully at labels, advertisements, posters, and just about everywhere, and you'll see a stamp-sized square with a "bar code," called a QR code.

QR codes contain data that when scanned by a smartphone, usually open a web page. Creating a QR code is easy: *www.goqr.me* is a free online tool to create one.

While not everyone has a QR code reader on their smartphone, it is becoming more and more popular. To read a QR code, download an app from your smartphone's app store. Check out ScanLife, which works on the iPhone, Android, BlackBerry, and Windows.

FACT

Did you ever wonder what QR actually stands for? It is an abbreviation for Quick Response.

The power of the QR code is that it bridges the real world with your online world. Instead of expecting your prospects to memorize long website addresses in your ads, a QR code can provide direct access to your website. Or picture a QR code on your retail shelf, that when scanned, might show a product usage video, or a testimonial.

To use QR codes most effectively, remember that the user will be scanning the code from their small-screen smartphones. "Aim" the QR code at a mobile-optimized page, instead of your regular nonmobile website—your users will thank you. And they will be more likely to transact.

Posting in Forums and Groups

Well before social media, and in fact, well before there was a web, there were discussion forums. Today, just about every subject under the sun has at least a few discussion forums, where aficionados meet online to discuss the latest and greatest in their area of interest. Some of these are on Facebook, others on LinkedIn, while others are managed directly through various websites.

If you want to find out what is happening in your geographical, functional area, or industry, you probably want to connect with your peers online. Doing so reduces your business risks, and also connects you to professional development and professional support. To find your crowd, search within LinkedIn groups, Facebook, and Google. And if you are a member of a real-world professional association, you may wish to start there first.

From a marketing perspective, you will want to look at forums and groups a bit differently: where do your prospects spend their time? They may be asking questions about your products that only you are best positioned to answer. They may be discussing their needs—and you happen to offer a product or service that can help. Or they may be discussing their strategies—and offering clues on how you might fit in.

As a guest on their forums, be careful not to be unwelcome. Overt sales pitches are a no-no. But offering value-added information, with a link to your site under your name, would be fine. Notifications about your latest pricing is a no-no. But asking questions to understand their issues is fine. Over time, you will develop a reputation online that is either positive or negative, and will translate into sales—or make you a pariah.

Offline Marketing

With an online business, it is tempting to consider marketing only online. But marketing in the real world exists—and so do your competitors who live there. Look around at how they are doing their marketing. Do any of their ideas make sense for you?

So how can you drive users to your site? Well, there are literally hundreds of ways to drive users to your site, but the items on this short list—in no particular order—might spark some ideas that you hadn't considered before:

- Put your website on everything that you print. While you're at it, add a QR code everywhere too.
- Attend a trade show. Don't forget to have a laptop where you can demonstrate your website—and sign people up on the spot.
- Advertise in the newspaper, magazines, and anywhere else where your target market lives. This last point is critical: spending dollars advertising where your prospects are not doesn't make any sense.
- Generate media attention for your business. Tie your service or products to a newsworthy item, and send a press release about it.

- Pick up the phone to let your existing customers know about a special deal online. But better make sure that it is a deal that is only for them, and only for a limited time.
- Send coupons, direct mail pieces, or a brochure via old-style snail mail to prospects. The key to doing this successfully is to ensure that the list is targeted to the real decision makers.
- Attend monthly trade association or chamber of commerce meetings to develop relationships with people who might want to use your services.
- Speak at events where your prospects spend their time. As a speaker, you develop instant credibility as an expert, and are able to direct attention to your online business.
- Develop partnerships with companies that also supply products or services to your prospects. To sweeten the pot, consider paying a fee for each prospect referred.
- Provide an incentive for current customers to refer new ones. Since current customers are usually proud of their purchases, they are likely to share this with their network, if asked (or incentivized) to do so. This might mean additional discounts, early notification of new products, or some other benefit.

All of these ideas do a great job developing awareness for your online business, but that is not enough to be successful. You need to sell.

CHAPTER 20

Selling Online

Once you have worked all the bugs out of your site, it is time to put out the virtual "Open for Business" sign and start selling. The Internet has created an expectation of immediacy in communications so be sure to stay alert to the activity on your site. If your web business is a supplement to a real-world business, you may find yourself pulled in different directions. Be ready to adjust. It may become necessary to add staff to respond to online orders and inquiries. Your competition may force you to be creative in your promotions to retain customers. Flexibility is the name of the game. In this chapter learn about the options you have for actually selling your products or services . . . and getting paid.

Service Business

A product business sells products: books, crafts, or music downloads. A service business sells a person's time to complete a task: gardening, accounting, or computer repair are a few examples. While the Internet has truly opened up world markets to the entire spectrum of businesses, when it comes to service businesses, it is the person—not the product—that is most often being sold. Some services lend themselves just fine to the online world. Travel specialists, for example, can help a client in Boston or Brisbane from a base in Boise. However, if a service business involves house calls, it is limited to time and space. For a service business, the bare minimum online presence should be a basic site that credentializes your expertise or the effectiveness of your service. Unlike your landline, which would be listed in a big fat yellow book produced by the carrier in your area, your website could be listed on many online yellow pages sites. People seem to have their favorite online directories. Check out these:

- *www.anywho.com*
- *www.superpages.com*
- *www.switchboard.com*
- *www.yellowbook.com*
- *www.yellowpages.com*

ESSENTIAL

Providing immediate contact between a buyer and seller of very expensive items, such as real estate or high-end jewelry, is a popular trend in online selling. Some online services are offering a way to connect with a live person with the necessary expertise, not just a call center on some remote continent, to gather further information beyond what is posted on a site.

As with your telephone listing, you pay for an Internet yellow-page listing. As these markets grow and converge, it is increasingly possible to make combined purchases for listings in local yellow pages and online directories. Talk to your local sales rep for details. Online marketing agencies are another source from which you can purchase placement. There are a number of online leads services, most of which are specific to an industry such as real estate or insurance. Take a peek at Leads.com at *www.leads.com* or Elite MLM Leads, *www.elitemlmleads.com*. Market research shows that a significant portion of those who go to online yellow pages are ready to buy and this is the most compelling reason to get into these directories.

On the other hand, the sales pitch to spend significant dollars getting enhanced placement and bigger paper directory listings may be the best thinking of yesterday. These enhancements may be for some, but many believe that the best "yellow book" in the world is spelled G-O-O-G-L-E, and that you should spend your hard-earned money on a better website, social media marketing, or search engine marketing.

Retail Sales

Successful selling online, just as in the material world, is a combination of the troika of famous virtues: quality, service, and price. If you have progressed to the point of having a product to offer, you have undoubtedly gone through all the steps to assure its quality. Whether you are offering car parts or handmade quilts, to ensure customer satisfaction in this consumer-conscious society you are going to have to stand behind your product. Selling online may seem easier, but the same standards apply, and in fact it may be more challenging to deal with returns, repairs, or other quality-related complaints.

FACT

Business-to-business transactions also take place online. As with retailers, in some cases the online sites are a supplement to a brick-and-mortar location. Some online entrepreneurs are using the web for industrial sales—and doing it only online.

If you find that online sales are more profitable, you may want to follow in the steps of other smart marketers and find ways to drive traffic to your site. The giant discount shoe retailer Designer Shoes Warehouse, or DSW, often offers discounts and promotions that are only available online—not in its stores. Any size business can consider having a weekly online special good for a limited window of time.

Get Linked with Compatible Sites

Shoppers cruise around online with almost wild abandon. Your challenge is getting visitors with attention spans of nanoseconds to your site and keeping them there. One strategy growing in popularity is getting your business linked on compatible sites. In order to have those businesses link to yours, you will likely have to link to theirs. For example, if you are a florist, it would be great to be linked on local photographer, bakery, and function-hall sites. In turn, by having links for these businesses on your site, party planners can enjoy the efficiency of "one-stop shopping." Each of you will be giving validation to the other in this reciprocal promotion. Furthermore, Google uses the number of inbound links as one indicator of your site's relevance and ranking.

This exchange of links doesn't need to be restricted to local businesses. If you have a particular product you are selling online, such as passport covers, it might make sense to find similar online retailers who are selling travel services and have cross-links.

Auction Sales

Is there a person on the planet who has not heard of eBay and dreamed of turning those Pez dispensers in shoeboxes at the back of the closet into hard cash? Online auctions have exploded far beyond a virtual marketplace for exchange of trinkets and trash. Serious business is conducted and the rules of engagement are rapidly evolving. If you have a traditional retail business, why not also sell through eBay (or other online auction sites) as well? It's just another sales channel.

Here are some tips and truths to keep in mind as you contemplate online auction selling:

ESSENTIAL

There are a tremendous number of resources for advice on how to use online auction selling successfully. There are scores of books and websites, such as *www.ecommercebytes.com*, devoted specifically to industry issues surrounding online selling, particularly on eBay. You might even try training classes to sharpen your skills.

- Start small. Test the market by selling a few things before investing in a big inventory.
- As with any business endeavor, create a business plan that includes financial goals, legal structure of the company, inventory acquisition and management, and target growth.
- If it is a business, run it like a business. Keep records of all transactions, file tax returns, etc.
- Sales tax rules can be tricky for online sales. Make sure you are compliant.
- Research and take advantage of special software programs that can enhance your sales. There are tools available that can guide you in understanding timing patterns of bidding, track your auctions, and give you important data about your customers.
- Title words are the bait for your buyers. After experimenting on your own, look into services that can hone your descriptive language and drive more sales.
- Most major sites have ratings for buyers and sellers. Watch for comments about your buyers.
- It is perfectly acceptable to wait for payment to clear before shipping your goods.
- If you amass a truly large inventory, one way to keep it fresh is to operate multiple online stores. Pull items off if they are not selling and relist them at another time.
- Look over your shoulders at competitors: What are they selling? How are they describing their items? What pricing strategy are they using?
- Stay up-to-date with your technology investments, both hardware and software. If you are down you are out.

As you plan or expand your business, weigh how online auction selling fits into your overall strategy. Initially, you may need the vast reach of these sites to get your products out there in the market. Over time, it might make sense to use the auction sites to drive buyers to your own website, where the sale of the same product will net you more income. In all likelihood you will operate with a combination of the two. Established customers can be enticed to buy directly from your site. The auction sites can continue to attract new customers. You will need to keep a balance between the expensive auction sites with their tremendous customer base, and your more narrowly focused but less expensive proprietary website.

Payment Options

If there is one dimension to your online selling that you do not want to have a problem with, it is getting paid. There are a number of payment choices that can increase the security of transactions between you as seller and your buyer. Nothing is foolproof, however, and you will need to weigh the risks and benefits for your individual business. One of the available options is to use third-party payers who can facilitate your buyers' paying you with certified checks. At the other end of the continuum is the strategy of establishing merchant accounts with banks that can process credit card payments. Perhaps the best-known payment system, thanks to the phenomenon of eBay, is PayPal, which is used for buying and selling transactions on that site, and many more. You should also research getting a merchant account established through your bank or another commercial institution. Regardless of which payment system you select, there is a risk of not getting paid. In the normal course of processing payment transactions there can be glitches with too many or too few funds going in or out of your account, which will require follow-up to resolve.

Naturally there is some cost associated with using a third party to collect payment for you. These are expenses that fall to your bottom line. It is worth investigating which merchant account providers are out there and which one best matches your particular needs. See if there is any flexibility in the fees and discount rate. Feel free to ask to see a sample monthly statement. You definitely want a highly competent and respected service for this function. Even the best of the best seems to be a target for hackers, however, so be sure to review the agreements to determine the protection that is included. It will be important to reassure visitors and prospective customers on your site that their credit card information will be protected.

If you have sales going through a third party such as Amazon, you can expect to pay listing fees. These may be per-item fees or, if you have enough volume to warrant it, you can register as a pro merchant for a flat monthly fee. The real knife in the heart is facing a steep commission of 15 percent per sale plus a bit of the shipping charge they collect. However, when you are signed up with a seller account, the minute that sale is made, you are paid. Some sites such as Half.com, *www.half.ebay.com*, which is owned by eBay, do not charge a listing fee. In that case a fee is assessed once a sale has been made.

ALERT

Look out for red flags when trading online. A major no-no for anyone is wiring money. Never, ever, wire money anywhere if it is required as part of an online transaction. Any online vendor worthy of doing business with will use a secure payment plan. As a seller, have your payment system and your shipping linked—don't release merchandise until you are sure you have payment.

When reviewing merchant payment systems be sure to consider other charges, such as set-up, monthly, gateway, and transaction fees. Inquire whether there are any fees associated with fraud protection or enhanced reporting. Your buyers' identities and personal information have to be secure in whichever system you select. Probe to discover how this is assured. Once you have the facts, you will certainly want to research the reputation and reliability of the company. The worst time for you to discover you cannot penetrate a phone tree to get to a real person to resolve a dispute is when you are in the middle of one.

You will not be able to sustain your business if your money-handling processes are not in order. Money is still real in the virtual world. This is one area you absolutely have to get right in order to succeed. The details of how e-commerce actually works can be filled with technical jargon far more confusing than it need be. The remaining parts of this chapter will give you a better idea of how the parts of technology fit together; after all, if you are going to be successful online, it makes sense to look under the hood and know what's going on.

Shopping Cart Concepts

How actually does an e-commerce system work? It's actually quite simple. On your site you will have a shopping cart that is responsible for organizing your products. If you have ever purchased a book on Amazon, the shopping cart is the primary way buyers look at the products, choose them, and then start the payment process.

Once the person decides to check out, the shopping cart will add the appropriate shipping charges, taxes, and ask the buyer to type in his credit card and other details. At the point the buyer clicks "Submit," the shopping cart bundles all of that information, and passes it to a credit card gateway.

The gateway is the link between your shopping cart and the credit card company. It transfers the purchase details (credit card total, name, address) to the credit card company for validation, and if it is approved, it will tell the shopping cart to display a page that says so. Meanwhile, in the background, it sends the transaction amount, less fees, to your bank account. Depending on the gateway company you use, they likely will provide Internet Visa/Mastercard/Amex/Discover merchant numbers for you. Again, to summarize: you will need to select a shopping cart, select a gateway, then connect them together to be able to sell from your site.

What makes it a bit confusing is that some companies sell shopping carts that you can then add on to your website. Others host the cart on their site. Others make the assumption that if you need a shopping cart, you likely need a gateway as well—and sell them both together. And some gateways have developed rudimentary shopping carts themselves. Comparing apples with apples is not easy, which is why most would-be online entrepreneurs ask their local web guru for assistance.

Building Your Online Shop

You will need to define each product within the system. This means for each product you'll need to load in a price, description, categories, a picture, whether it is taxable, shipping information, and more. Once the products are defined, the system will usually create a standard-looking product page.

Once the products are set up, you can define optional payment plans: must they pay all at once, or can they spread payments over several months? Finally, you will want to "merchandise" the store. Can you show some specials on the home page? Can you upsell and cross-sell related products? Of course, before you go live, you should test the store to make sure that it does precisely what you want it to do. Does "Add to Cart" actually add to the cart? Does the system calculate taxes and shipping properly? Does the money actually make it into your account?

Shopping Cart Options

How should you choose which of the hundreds of shopping carts that are available? Here are some selection criteria:

- Easy to set up
- No per-transaction fees
- Well-known, with quality customer support
- Supports many different credit card gateways
- Free customer support
- Supports digital products (if applicable)
- Supports an affiliate program
- One common database for both e-commerce transactions and e-mail newsletters

There are some shopping carts that are "Open Source" (free), that you merely ask your web developer to install and configure on your server. Examples include Agora, osCommerce, and Zen Cart. Other shopping carts are centrally hosted, and integrate in with your website, sometimes with premium features and on-call support. Examples of these include 1shoppingcart (*www.budurl.com/everything1sc*) and Infusionsoft (*www .budurl.com/CRMautomate*). Both of these products also include e-mail capabilities.

Credit Card Gateways

The rules for accepting credit cards are becoming as arcane as the terminology needed to understand how they work. Here are a few definitions that can help:

- **Discount Rates:** This is the percentage fee that the gateway deducts from each transaction to pay for its overhead. Generally speaking, whenever someone uses either an out-of-country card or a premium card (Gold, Platinum, etc.), the discount rate spikes up a percentage.
- **Transaction Fees:** In addition to the discount rate, you will also pay a per-transaction fee, usually about ten cents.

- **Other fees:** These can range from statement fees, to reporting fees, to anything that the gateway thinks it can get away with. Before you commit, review and compare at least two gateways.
- **Holdbacks:** At one time, a certain percentage of each transaction was held for a period of time—usually about six months—just in case there were transaction disputes. Holdbacks are less common (and for a lesser amount) today than in the past, but are important to know about. Between the discount rate, transaction fees, and holdbacks, your cash in hand will always be smaller than the value of all of your sales.
- **Chargebacks:** When a customer disputes a charge, you have to prove that the transaction took place. If you are not able to, then your account is charged back the amount of the sale plus a penalty, and your customer has the full amount credited. If there are too many chargebacks, the gateway may charge either higher fees, or drop you altogether.
- **CVV codes:** This is the three digit code on the back of the card; when the customer uses this code during the transaction, it is an extra level of verification.
- **Verification:** Credit card companies use many different types of anti-fraud measures. The foremost is to compare the credit card owner's mailing address with what the card holder enters in the shopping cart. They also verify the card number, expiry, number (and physical place) of recent transactions.
- **eTerminal:** Normally every transaction gets entered through the shopping cart, but if the gateway has an "eTerminal," you can manually enter transaction amounts directly in the gateway web page.

The most important criteria for choosing a gateway is that it fully works with your shopping cart. In fact, most carts provide a list stating what is compatible and what isn't. After compatibility are ease of use, rates, and how often you will get paid.

Setting up your website is a major milestone. But since the early 1990s a lot has been learned, most importantly how to increase the percentage of users who eventually transact.

CHAPTER 21

Advanced Concepts: Converting Browsers to Buyers

If you have a retail store, there are many things that you can do to increase sales. The reason for storing milk at the back of the store is to force the shopper to walk by everything else, and possibly pick something up. The reason for "facing" labels to the front is so that the packaging might catch a shopper's eye. The reason for displaying magazines and chewing gum near the cash register is to capture last minute impulse purchases. Likewise, the online world has a language—and techniques—all of its own. In this chapter, we review many of the most important ways that you can work to convert browsers to buyers in your own online business.

Conversion

The measure of your success in converting visitors to consumers on your site is known as the conversion rate. Simply, it is the calculation of how many sales (or sign-ups, or whatever action you want the site visitor to take) that occur in relation to the total number of visits to the site.

ESSENTIAL

The easiest way to find out about your users is to install the free Google Analytics at *www.budurl.com/everythingAnalytics* program on your website. It will tell you how many visitors came to your website, which pages they went to, where they came from, and dozens of other interesting nuggets of information.

There are a number of ways to improve the conversion rate, including:

- Make sure that your web page is clean and easy to understand, with very little extraneous information.
- Be clear about what you want people to do when they get to the page.
- Offer an incentive for acting.
- Use the tactic of scarcity: only two items left.
- Use the tactic of time: on sale until midnight tonight.
- Use tasteful (and unobtrusive) video.
- Add click-to-chat and real-time assistance (see later in this chapter).
- Add a pop-up window at some point in the transaction. The window can point to a sale item, ask if help is needed, or ask if they wish to subscribe to a newsletter.
- Make sure that your transaction technology is secure. (The web URL should start with https://.)
- Use testimonials to improve the buyer confidence.
- Allow purchasers to rate and comment on your product or service; third-party endorsement is very powerful.
- Provide open access to customer support pages, once again to improve buyer confidence.

One of the more powerful conversion strategies is to understand why people are not purchasing. There are three primary ways of doing this: usability testing, interviews, and Google Analytics.

Usability Testing

This is something that you can do even before your online business is officially "live." Assemble a small group of people, each with a computer, and get them to go through a few scenarios on your website: find an item, add it to the shopping cart, find another, make a purchase, etc. Observe them while they do this, watching for hesitation and confusion. Then afterwards, ask the group about their experience. Based on what you find, you should have a list of potential changes to your site.

Interviews

While not particularly scientific, interviews can expose some qualitative perspective on the purchasing experience. Using a pop-up box on your website, a survey, or even a link within an e-mail, ask for volunteers who would be interested in participating. You will likely need to provide an incentive for them to do so, but make sure that it is very small. It is better to have interviewees who want to help because they want to help, than interviewees who are just doing it for the incentive. The interview can be either over the phone or in person. E-mail interviews (e.g., surveys) sometimes don't expose the emotional nuance around people's answers, so they are less effective.

Ask the interviewees questions about their experience with your site: why they went there, what they were looking for, and what they were expecting. Ask if they were disappointed by their experience, or if there was anything confusing. Then ask if they had any ideas that would make the experience easier. If you have a potential revised design, or new graphics, you can also ask them for their opinion. Finally, ask about your competitors: are there any features or ideas on other sites that you should implement on your own.

Google Analytics

It is easy to be befuddled by all of the available information within Google Analytics (*www.budurl.com/everythingAnalytics*). When trying to understand and improve conversion, there are a couple of key statistics that you will want to review.

Site Content

Click on the "Content" menu in the left column of Google Analytics to get into this area, and you'll see an overview of the number of page views over a specified time period. Once there, click on the submenu for "Landing Pages." This shows you the most popular pages, how much time people spend on your site and other fascinating statistics. Notice that the vast number of people land on the homepage, but how very few (as a percentage) click through? Either they landed on your site by mistake, or they were looking for something but didn't find it.

The exit pages are the last page that a particular user went to on your site, before she left. The top exit pages are a great indicator that the users didn't find what they were looking for. Fix this by having more descriptive links so everyone knows what to expect, and better content on the landing page so users can easily find what they are looking for.

Traffic Sources

In this area you can see the percentage of users that came from search engines (e.g., clicked from a search results page), referrals (clicked from another site), or direct traffic (typed in the web address directly, or used a bookmark). You can also see, for search engines, the keyword used to find your site.

One of the most fascinating graphics is the Visitors Flow view. It shows you the drop-off by page. You can visually trace how visitors interact with your site.

Google Analytics gives you a robust way to understand user behavior on your site—but more importantly, it will help you figure out where you might focus your attention.

Landing Pages

Look on your business card. What website address is listed? Likely, it is the homepage. Look at your brochures, advertisements, and even links from partner websites. The link that is used is also most likely the homepage.

While the homepage is good for a person who randomly gets to your website, it is not purpose-built to address the specific needs of the user coming from a specific place. For example, if you have a poster advertising a specific product, why not have a link that goes directly to that product page? Or even better, why not have a link that goes to a purpose-built page that continues the conversation started in the ad? The page might use the same imagery and headlines. It might continue the design theme of the ad campaign, providing a way for users to sign up for a special bonus. And it might have special product pricing that is not available in the rest of the website. This type of page is called a landing page.

Because the landing page has a unique web address, it is picked up in Google Analytics. This gives you the opportunity to assess the effectiveness of the initiative, make mid-course corrections, and try again.

If you are using pay-per-click (PPC) advertising, landing pages are mandatory. The text in your ad is designed to pique the interest of the prospect; the landing page is designed to provide a satisfying response. If the PPC ad dumps the user onto a generic homepage, it is unlikely that he will find what he is looking for. Or he may be distracted by content meant for different types of users. The following are eight key attributes of a landing page, from my Make It Happen Tipsheet at *www.budurl.com/everythingLanding*:

- It is paired with a very specific advertisement.
- The page should go through multiple rounds of A/B testing. (Two identical ads point to two different versions of the landing page; the one that converts fewer buyers should discontinued, the other should be revised for a new test, etc.)
- Very little navigation to the main site; the goal is for them to read/consider/act—not to meander off.
- Simplified messaging, all designed to expose the problem and share the solution.
- Simplified design and graphics: because there is far less content (and links) than a traditional web page, the eye will naturally focus on the remaining important information.
- Multiple calls to action (e.g., Subscribe, Purchase, etc.).

- Multiple content delivery modes—but identical message: video, descriptive text, testimonials, "trial" subscriptions, etc. Different people respond to different stimulus.
- Consistent design beyond the landing page. Since the site is designed to convert, a vastly different look-and-feel beyond the landing page (e.g., the next page in a sequence) can cause user uncertainty, and possibly abandonment.

Copywriting Tips

Writing copy for ads, web pages, and other promotional material is a skill that takes years to master—even though you learned the basics in grade school. More so than traditional writing, copywriting is designed to achieve a specific purpose: to persuade, to get a user to sign up, to get a user to click "Buy Now." Here are ten tips that can help take your regular-person writing skills and start you on your way to being a copywriting superhero:

1. **Clearly define the purpose of your writing.** What do you want the users to learn or to do? What state of mind are they in before they get to your page? Do you need to educate them first, or do they already know enough to make a purchase decision?
2. **Write with the audience in mind.** If you know whom you are writing for, you have a stronger chance of meeting their needs. Think about how different your writing style and word choice would be if you were writing for older teenagers compared to retirees. Take a guess—identify the two audiences with the following two sentences: "With an ambience of Tahiti, let us pamper you with our South Pacific delights." "Bam! South Pacific Happy Hour every day at 6 P.M." Hint: the first sentence is aimed at an older demographic. Writing with the audience in mind is the most important part of copywriting. They don't care about you, they only care about how you (or your product) can solve their problem. Therefore you need to make sure that what you write is relevant—or they won't be reading anything further.

3. **Use words and phrases that connect, but don't overdo it.** Even if you are focused on one group, you don't want to turn off secondary targets that find your page.

4. **Use a headline that intrigues.** Speak to the value of your product or service. What would make the user want to read on? What would make them stop and think? What would make them say "Yes, I think it is worth my time reading further."

5. **Write a killer first paragraph.** The first sentence of the first paragraph needs to set up the challenge. The remainder of the paragraph needs to provide the solution. Or if you are writing a number of paragraphs, the remainder of the first paragraph can amplify the problem, while the following paragraphs provide the solution. Consider the copywriting section of this chapter. The first sentence sets up the problem: copywriting is a skill that takes years to master. The remainder of the paragraph (and this entire section) then provides the solution.

6. **Focus on benefits, not the features.** A feature is an attribute of a product: "the receiver has a 200-watt amplifier." A benefit answers the "so-what" question in the context of the importance to a reader. "The amplifier is powerful enough to fill an auditorium" is a better benefit statement. But what about "You will always be heard with our powerful amplifier—even in the biggest of auditoriums." This last benefit statement emotionally connects the purpose of the 200-watt amplifier with a presenter's need to be heard.

7. **Use a variety of formatting techniques.** Use subheads, bullets, bold, italic, sidebars, graphics, and video. This makes it easier for the reader to scan.

8. **Identify the obstacles to action.** For example, if total cost is a barrier, speak to the cost per day, the savings compared to other products, the ROI (Return On Investment), and the fact that better workmanship means that the product will last longer. Neutralizing obstacles clears the way to a purchase.

9. **Use statistics to justify your position, and increase your credibility.** These statistics can help the prospect justify her purchase, both to herself and to others.

10. **Have multiple calls to action.** A great salesperson always remembers to ask for business—you should too.

It takes time to write great copy—and for key pages on your website you need to take the time. After you have written the copy, print it out and proof-read it. Are there any typos or grammatical mistakes? Does the text sound either too sophisticated, or a bit patronizing? Is there too much fluff in your writing, or does it get right to the point? Finally, for a few key pages, show your copy to another person for their review and comments.

ESSENTIAL

Testing different versions of copy is a great way to find out which is most effective. You can do this manually, or use code from Google Webmasters Tools at *www.google.com/webmasters/* to automate the process.

Squeeze Pages

A squeeze page is a marketing technique where you offer a valuable item (a how-to white paper, a coupon, or some other item) in exchange for a prospect's name and e-mail address. There are pros and cons of using the technique. On the pro side, why shouldn't you get something of value in trade? If a user is not willing to offer up her name and e-mail, then perhaps she is not really a prospect after all? On the con side is user fear of getting bombarded with spam. If you do use this technique, here are some suggestions to make it more effective:

- Consider whether you really need to collect the information. If your goal is to get your information in front of as many eyeballs as possible, registration will be a barrier for many.
- Only collect the information that you absolutely need. The more you ask for, the less likely someone will fill it all in.
- Be exceptionally clear about what they will receive: a forty-two page report that outlines how to solve problem X. A subscription to our monthly tip sheet with the latest findings on solving problem X.
- Have a clearly stated privacy policy, shown up-front: "Your contact information will not be shared with or sold to anyone."
- Consider showing a sample of the value-add.
- Use video and/or testimonials to develop confidence in your offer.

Finally, once the users have entered their information, have them land on a page with a very obvious link to the product. At the same time, send them the product link via e-mail.

Pop-Ups

A pop-up window will ask the user a question: to fill out a survey, to inquire as to whether they really want to leave the site, or to provide access to a special deal as they are leaving a page. Because it interrupts the user's thinking process, it is important that the pop-up actually contains value to him. If not, it will just be an annoyance.

ESSENTIAL

Make sure that when a user returns to a page where there is a pop-up, that it doesn't pop-up again. Some systems remember a user's "no thank you" preferences, while others don't.

Pop-ups can be implemented using many different technologies. Make sure that you test the system that you implement, as some types of pop-ups are blocked by the browser.

Chat

Just as a retailer trains a clerk to ask if you need any help, chat functionality does this on the website. Research shows that there is a different conversion rate when chat is available.

Passive chat is a button on your website that may say "Click to Talk to a Live Agent." When the user clicks this button, a chat box opens on the screen with the name of an agent. Back at your office, an agent is notified that someone wants to chat, and the agent accepts the chat call on her screen. The agent can manage a number of simultaneous conversations with users, depending on her skill and the software that is being used. When there is no agent available, then the on-screen button says "No Agent Is Available; Click to Leave a Message."

Active chat may have a button, but it doesn't rely on the user to click to ask for help. Instead, at a particular point in time, a small box will pop open introducing an agent, and asking if help is needed. By clicking on this proactive query, the user initiates the chat session.

Does it make sense to implement chat? It's a great idea, but first things first: set up your business, set up the online website, set up your supply chain and your marketing. Then set up advanced functionality like Chat, Pop-ups, and Squeeze pages.

Cross-Selling and Up-Selling

The master at cross-selling and up-selling in the real world is McDonalds. When you go into their restaurants, after you order your hamburger, they ask two questions: "Would you like fries with that?" and "Would you like a large for twenty-five cents more?" Fries are a complementary product that "go" with a hamburger: this is cross-selling. Offering a large instead of small is up-selling.

The master at this in the online world is Amazon. When you go through the transaction process, there are a number of different times when you are presented with interesting suggestions. People who bought this book also bought that book. Based on your previous purchases, here are some additional suggestions. Here is book two in the series—add to cart? If someone is already committed to making a purchase, why not offer them a complementary product? Cross-selling and up-selling can easily double your sales.

While this technique may seem a bit underhanded, it may very well be that a person won't commit to the sale at all unless they can also purchase the complementary product. For example, if you were purchasing a Kindle from Amazon you might be concerned enough about damage that you wouldn't buy it unless you were offered a range of different protective cases at the same time.

There are two steps to implementing a cross-selling or up-selling process. The first is to pair all of your products with cross-sell/up-sell products. The second step is to embed this in your shopping cart technology, so that the additional products are offered automatically when the user commits to the purchase.

Converting browsers to buyers is critical to a successful online business. But even more important is how to handle browsers who don't immediately transact. Read on, and learn about how Customer Relationship Software can help.

CHAPTER 22

Customer Relationship Management

Managing prospective and current customers is one of the most important things an entrepreneur needs to do. Online businesses, however, have a particular problem. Because buyers can come from anywhere, the number of them can quickly exceed your ability to remember them all.

Big businesses have used customer relationship management (CRM) computer programs for decades, but only now is it becoming cheap enough for smaller businesses to use them. Example CRM systems for small business include Infusionsoft, *www.budurl.com/everythingCRM*, and SugarCRM, *www.budurl.com/everythingSUGAR*). Even if you don't use CRM technology, the underlying concepts can make the difference between success and failure. In this chapter, you will learn how to capture the contact information of users who may not be ready to purchase, and then eventually convert them into buyers.

Capturing Nonbuyers

With all of the time and money that you spend getting people to your website, the prospect can choose to do one of two things: leave or buy. In the real world of retail, this happens all of the time: a prospect comes in looking to purchase a small appliance, doesn't see what he likes, and leaves. Smart retailers use their salespeople to ask the prospect if he needs any help. If the answer is no, or if the help isn't actually helpful, the prospect leaves.

On the web, there is a third option between leave or buy. If there were a way to collect the basic information—even just the name and e-mail address—then the CRM system can reach out to the prospect at a later time with more information that might result in a sale. Or, the extra contact might result in the prospect telling his friends about the website. Or, if the e-mail is perceived as a low-value communication (e.g., spam), it will result in the prospect never going back.

From an online business's perspective, the challenge is figuring out what will cause a prospect to want to provide her name and e-mail. The trade must have value, and it must be relevant. Here are some ideas:

- A PDF how-to guide on choosing a product from that category
- A coupon for a product discount
- Attendance at a special event, or a promise to send a "preview" invitation for certain sales
- A webinar with a celebrity or senior executive
- A product or service upgrade
- Access to product usage videos

Whenever someone comes to your website, he has a particular need that needs fulfilling. It may be that the prospective customer is not ready to purchase when you are ready to sell. Keeping in contact with him keeps your name and the value that you add front and center. When he is indeed ready to purchase, he'll remember you and make the purchase. And if someone asks for a recommendation, he may refer others to you as well.

E-Mail Marketing

Do you enjoy receiving spam? If not, why would you think that your prospective customers would? No one likes junk mail, precisely because it is junk.

The trick to e-mail marketing is to be specific in your communications, and ensure that each e-mail is filled with value. You are not trying to "sell," but rather you are helping a prospect develop greater confidence—and a stronger relationship—with you and your online business. You are building trust, and helping him buy. Doing this is harder than you might think. If you trade a name and e-mail for access to product usage videos, where is the permission to send marketing e-mails? If you do send customers e-mails after this trade, are you losing trust, as you haven't asked for permission to do so? (Hint: Whenever you ask for an e-mail address, you need to tell the customer precisely what it is for. It isn't just a trust-building exercise, it is the law.)

There are two main types of e-mail marketing communications:

Broadcast E-Mails

There are two types of broadcast e-mails: blasts that are one-time-only announcements, and regular newsletters. Single announcements need to be important enough to catch the attention of the reader and can't happen too often, or else they will be lost in the noise; their specialness will be lost. Regular newsletters can be scheduled daily, weekly, or monthly. Most online businesses don't do daily newsletters, because the amount of time required to write and edit them is huge. Weekly newsletters tend to be short—three-to-five paragraphs—and focused on a single topic. Monthly newsletters tend to have several articles, including some that are regular columns each month.

How often you send something out depends on what you've promised upon sign-up. The more frequent, the higher the recall, but if it isn't valuable, the more likely your e-mail will annoy. The less frequent, the lower the recall, but the lower the time investment. If you promised an e-mail with the weekly "deals," your customers will unsubscribe if you suddenly send it out each day. They will unsubscribe if you suddenly start including political commentary or other irrelevant (to them) content. You will disappoint them if you start sending it out every month. Meeting and exceeding their expectations starts well before the first sale. A large number of unsubscribes means that you have let them down—and lost the future sale. A growing list means that eventually, you will capture the sale—even if it wasn't on the first visit to your online business.

One of the things that many online businesses will do is recognize that their audiences want to receive the same information, but perhaps in different ways. Once a newsletter is written, it may make sense to repurpose the content onto a blog. Or to summarize it into 140 characters for a Tweet. Or to compile a number of newsletter articles into a PDF guidebook. Here is a list of the many different ways that you can repurpose your content: *www .budurl.com/everythingRE.*

Autoresponders

While broadcasts go to everyone at the same time, autoresponders (sometimes called "sequences") go to one person when they request it. Picture this: you've just purchased a fancy flat-screen television for your home. You would like to set up a complete home theater system, but the manual seems impossible to understand. You go to the retailer's website, and see that they offer several e-mail courses that seem helpful:

- Choosing a new TV in three steps
- Four fabulous features of your new TV: one weekly for one month
- Setting up a home theater: five lessons in five days

The third course looks interesting. Each of these are set up so that when a user gives his name and e-mail address, the CRM system will send out an e-mail to him, in the case of the home theater option, daily for five days. Each e-mail might have specific instructions on doing part of the setup. It may have embedded links to how-to videos. At the bottom of the e-mail (or in a sidebar), there might be links to products that the user might need (cables, adapters, etc.). At the end of the fifth e-mail, there would be no other communication, since the user had not agreed to receive anything else.

Marketing Automation

An important CRM concept is "tags." A tag is a descriptive word that you can apply to a contact: youth, senior, book purchaser, Christmas card, newsletter subscriber. When you set up a CRM, you can decide on all of the different tags that are relevant. Then slowly but surely, you can tag each contact with as many tags as are relevant. Much of this tagging can happen automatically. For example, when a person signs up for your e-mail newsletter, the CRM will add them to the database, and then tag that person as a newsletter subscriber.

Beyond a name and e-mail address, you are able to learn a lot from users who choose to receive your communications. In the home theater example, the users have self-identified as owning (or being interested in) home theaters. When they sign up for the five lesson autoresponder, they can be tagged as autoresponder subscribers, and as customers having an interest in home theater. Later, you might choose to send out a slightly different newsletter to people tagged as "home theater."

Marketing automation can even be added to autoresponders. One week after the last e-mail lesson, you could program an e-mail to be sent from the manager, asking if the home theater lessons were helpful, and pointing out some additional resources. Or ask them to fill out a survey. Or even better, offer them a free in-store lesson on a more complex aspect of setting up a system. These additional offers are relevant to the prospects and they add value: they are less about "selling," and more about increasing their trust in you. When they are ready to buy, they will. And they will remember you.

Another powerful way to use marketing automation within a CRM is to embed automation links within your e-mail communications. A CRM knows who clicks each link; if a link said "Click Here to Receive Our Latest Sale Prices," this would indicate a hot prospect—a prospect that was getting ready to purchase. The user could be tagged as a hot prospect, and instead of a general e-mail newsletter, he could receive one with specific offers. If the link said "Click Here to Have a Support Representative Answer Your

Questions Personally," then the CRM could tag the prospect, then forward a request for a sales or support person to contact the prospect right away.

Opportunity Management

Any professional in the world of sales knows one thing: People go through a process when they are deciding to purchase. They find out about your offering, they check you out, and they eventually purchase. From the company's perspective, there are suspects (people who you don't know much about, but may be interested), prospects (people who have expressed an interest), and customers (people who have purchased). Depending on your business, there may be additional categories (for example, suspects, prospects, proposals outstanding, customers), but the basic model—the sales funnel—is the same in every business.

Typically it makes sense to track users as they go through each stage, so that you might better understand how your business is doing—a CRM makes this possible. For example, if the number of suspects suddenly takes a drop, then you know that eventually you will have fewer prospects, and fewer sales. Depending on how your sales funnel looks, you might choose to take a different approach to your marketing. Fewer suspects might mean you should increase your pay-per-click advertising. Fewer prospects might mean that you need better information on each product on your site. Fewer customers might mean you should improve your pricing, provide a better user experience on your site, or perhaps use a more robust CRM program.

One of the fundamental differences between a mailing-list program and a CRM is that a mailing list program is focused on the list—users join the list—while a CRM program has the user at the center. "Attached" to the user are tags, e-commerce orders, autoresponder subscriptions, opportunity stages, and all of her contact information. Instead of multiple databases—e-mail, e-commerce, opportunities, demographics, etc., there is only one.

Play Fair When Getting Your Online Customers

Your online world needs to be tied to your real world using all the tools you can. E-mail marketing is certainly appealing, but there is a downside: spam.

The uprising against the tsunami of unwanted, and in many cases offensive e-mails, has triggered the CAN-SPAM Act, which spells out very specific restrictions for using this channel. Some of the regulations:

- **Opt out:** A recipient must be given the opportunity to ask to be removed from your list. You then have ten days to honor this request.
- **Play in your own backyard:** The government frowns on harvesting e-mail addresses from other sources or creating ad hoc lists.
- **Closed door:** If someone opts out of your list you may not share her address with anyone else.
- **It may be an ad:** You have to call an e-mail an advertisement if the recipient did not ask to receive it. You are exempted from this requirement for those folks who have opted in to receive your e-mails.
- **Truthful:** A big no-no is trying to trick the recipient. Don't be clever with the sender info and the subject line content. You definitely can't use technical trickery to make the e-mail appear from someone else.
- **No P.O.:** Somewhere in the e-mail you must include your company's brick-and-mortar address. P. O. box numbers are not allowed.

ESSENTIAL

You can build your customer base with a quality e-mail newsletter, and a blog that is easy to read, timely, and useful. Once recipients become accustomed to your high-quality effort, they will look forward to opening and reading it rather than trashing it—or labeling it as spam.

One thing is for certain: legislation (such as CAN-SPAM) is not going away, and in some jurisdictions, it is becoming even more strict. Following the rules isn't just a question of complying with the law—it actually is a good business practice.

Selling your product is one thing, but what if you run out of inventory? The entire question of purchasing, inventory, and delivery is just as important to your business as sales: it impacts sales, margins, and customer service.

CHAPTER 23

Product and Services Management

Whether you are selling Limoges china or lion-taming equipment, you will want to find sources with the best prices and reliability. Having enough product on hand to meet demand without having too much money tied up in inventory can be a tricky balancing act. In this chapter, you will learn about the supply chain: purchasing, inventory, and fulfillment, as well as how to price your products or services so they will sell.

Nimble Inventory Management

The first priority is making sure you have the quality products (or services) your customers are looking for available for sale, when they want them. Points to cover when planning your supply strategy, either for finished goods or materials you will convert into items for sale, include:

- Where to order
- How much to order
- Which goods to order and which ones to avoid
- When to reorder
- How much to have in inventory at a given time
- What to do if the merchandise you receive is unsatisfactory

When starting an online business, buying will be your job, along with anticipating upcoming trends and knowing what to buy and what to avoid.

One of the ways companies have been able to marry customer service with positive cash flow is by shortening the time between making a product and selling it. It takes time to make each unit. An expensive inventory sitting in a warehouse (or basement) waiting for a customer means valuable cash is tied up.

Product Procurement

You're opening an online store, but where do you find the merchandise to sell? You have a few options. One is to attend trade shows, which is one of the most significant opportunities for retailers to see live product demonstrations, meet representatives from major manufacturers, and establish a relationship. Nearly every industry has trade shows, nationally, regionally, or even locally, if you're in a major metropolitan area. You can also contact manufacturers directly. Find out who the sales representative is for your region, or if the company sells through a distributor or a wholesaler. Research the trade publications for your industry and read them thoroughly. You'll find listings, ads, and articles about manufacturers. Finally, there are general directories for suppliers, manufacturers, and distributors, as well as industry-specific directories. Look for them at business libraries and online.

When you buy items wholesale you need to consider:

- What are the sales terms?
- Is there a minimum order?
- Can you return items that don't sell?
- What is the method of shipping and are there additional charges?
- How long must you wait to receive the items?
- How quickly can you restock?
- What do you do if the items show up damaged?
- What happens if the shipment never arrives at all?
- Can you buy on credit, and if so, what are the terms?

Your relationship with sales representatives and vendors is very important. If you establish a good working relationship, you can then trust each other and work together for many years. The bottom line is, you need each other. Vendors make money if you continue to buy from them and you make money if their products sell to your customers.

ALERT

Be wary of distributors who are too aggressive in trying to sell you a line of products not familiar to you. Know the brand and the products before buying—do your homework. And if you take item X, don't get suckered into taking items Y and Z, too. Pawning off poor merchandise with the good merchandise is an old trick.

Keep the Inventory Fresh

From web pages to catalog layout to the design and layout of your store, how well you present the goods you're selling will impact heavily on their sales. Study the layout of other online stores to get an idea of how you want yours to be set up. Then work hard on a logical traffic flow that will create an easy-to-navigate store and allow customers to see the merchandise.

ESSENTIAL

In department stores, you usually have to wander through the maze of fragrance counters to find the basics department. This is no accident. The more tempting (and highly profitable) products such as fragrances and cosmetics seduce the shopper on the way to the necessary purchases. Use this same concept with your online store.

Zero Inventory Strategy

If inventory is so costly, why not have an online store with none of it? Yes, your store could have product descriptions, pictures, and even customer reviews. But no product. This is possible if you struck a deal with either the manufacturer or with your distributor. Whenever you send either of them a fulfillment order, they deliver it to your customer, and only then charge you for the product. With an online storefront you can change merchandise as much as you like, so long as you have a supplier willing to direct-ship the purchase for you.

Buying

When you start out, you won't be making many deals. You'll be writing checks and buying merchandise C.O.D. As you build your business and establish relationships with vendors and sales reps, you will have greater negotiating power. Over time, you'll go from looking for goods to stock to turning products away. Practically everyone who publishes a book, creates a software program, or develops a toy or game contacts an e-tailer like Amazon. It can accommodate many of these items because the online service doesn't need to stock the shelves. Amazon can order just a few copies of a book and wait to see how it sells before ordering more.

When deciding which items to buy, consider the cost per item and determine the markup. Is it worth your while to buy the item? Read up on the latest trends and newest products in your industry, and stay ahead of, or at least keep pace with, your competitors. Every time your competitor has a new product available and you don't, you're losing a sale and signaling to customers that you aren't as up-to-the-minute as you should be.

Soak Up Information Everywhere You Can

You can learn a lot from others who have run their online businesses for many years. Successful retailers love to talk about how they built up their empires, and as a future empire builder, you need to soak up as much of that collective wisdom as possible. Join associations or the local chamber of commerce. Look at trade journals and gather as much information about retailing as you can.

FACT

STORES magazine, at *www.stores.org*, has a wealth of retail information plus an industry buying guide that will help you put your store together, from the sign in front to the bags customers carry out when they leave. You'll also find links to numerous retail-based sites at *www.retailindustry.about.com*.

Pricing Your Goods and Services

Your pricing decisions will affect your sales volume, profits, image, inventory, ordering decisions, and more. Prices that are too high can alienate customers, while prices that are too low can hurt your profits and ultimately your cash flow.

Keep good records of the cost for each product. This means that if you order from different distributors, you should know the various costs and can come up with a cost average. For example, if you purchased a brand of T-shirts for $3.00 each from one distributor, $2.88 from another, and then found someone else selling them for $2.75 in bulk, then your profit could be an extra $0.25 per unit, just because of your astute purchasing. While this may not appear to be much, over an entire year, it adds up. It can make the difference between profit and loss.

In an online business, you're concerned with the cost of the products or services and the price at which you can sell the product. The difference between these two amounts is your markup. Therefore, if you're buying items at a cost of $2 per item, and selling them for $6 each, your markup is $4 each. There are numerous factors that come into play when you're pricing goods and services. However, the strongest driving factors are:

- Suggested retail price by the manufacturer
- Your cost base
- Competitive prices

Consider the costs of running your business. You need to pay your employees, your rent, and other bills. If your expenses add up to $10,000 per month, and you expect to sell 5,000 units a month, then you need an average markup of $2 each on whatever it is you sell to cover these fixed costs.

Consider the popularity of the item. Is this a hot-selling item that will move off the shelves just as quickly at $20 as it would at $17?

Consider your customer base. Do your customers look for high quality? Are they looking for unique selection and a lifetime guarantee? If so, they won't mind spending more. If, however, they are looking for bargains when they come to your site, then you need prices that match or beat the competition. Particularly because of the various price comparison websites, higher prices will mean fewer customers—unless you differentiate beyond price.

Pricing to Draw More Business

If a lower price will draw more customers and increase overall traffic, then you might price an item at close to cost, which will result in less profit per item but more overall sales plus more store traffic.

Think of accessories or add-ons. If someone is purchasing an electronic gizmo from you, might he need batteries or an extra charger? Or perhaps an extended warranty? If you have any type of item that offers numerous accessories, you can take a lower markup on the main item. A dollhouse itself can sell at close to cost. Then you can get a higher markup on the furniture and other accessories needed. You can program your shopping cart so that if a customer buys item A, they get a percentage off items B, C, and D if they buy the entire set.

Think volume. Consider whether the item is one that you expect to sell in large quantities, producing a good overall return, or if it's a rare item that will only sell a few units, meaning you'll have to turn a profit on each one to make it worth your while.

Be mindful of trends. If you're dealing with clothing or other items that will change in style within a few months, then be ready to mark down the item so that you'll be able to move it out as the trend fades.

Determine what added benefits you can offer. If you charge more but throw in gift-wrapping or other services, you may attract customers for the added perks. While you're spending money on wrapping paper, you're also building an image and satisfied customer base with each purchase made. Build customer loyalty with frequent buyer incentives. Another benefit of loyalty programs is the ability to collect e-mail addresses for later marketing.

Think partnerships. Technology exists to track the source of any prospective customers to your website. For companies that wish to affiliate with you, consider paying them a commission, either for leads or sales.

Keep in mind that pricing is an ever-evolving process, and will change with new products, changing costs, more or less competition, and the economic picture. Unless you're selling a very specialized product or service, you probably will have a range of markups for different items.

Services

One of the biggest pitfalls for selling services is setting prices too low by not factoring in all of the costs of running the business. Don't forget overhead costs, including rent, legal fees, marketing, accounting, bookkeeping, and so on. Then the specific service must be competitively priced. This can be tricky because service providers offer different specialties, different reputations, and different backgrounds.

Create an hourly rate. Even if you quote a flat fee, determine it by calculating how many hours the job will take and how much you can bill per hour. Always estimate that a job will take a certain percent longer than your initial calculation.

Make sure you will be reimbursed for out-of-pocket expenses. If you need to make an out-of-town trip on behalf of your client, be clear about who is responsible for associated expenses.

Whether you're running a web design service, life coaching, or financial planning company, you need to evaluate what the market will pay. Then do your break-even analysis and be ready to change your prices when necessary.

ESSENTIAL

Consider selling a subscription. If you are selling a service, offer a different price if the prospective customer commits to purchasing your services each and every month. Because many shopping carts can automate the monthly payment process, you not only lock in the revenue, but you save on the administrative work along the way.

Automated Fulfillment and Supply Chain

One of the more powerful business concepts is the supply chain: At the highest level, materials flow from suppliers to you, then out to your customers. Drilling down exposes more detail. First you order, then arrange for delivery; then you inventory the goods, possibly adding value by changing them in some way. Then you sell them—marketing—collect payment, and then ship. In the excitement of setting up your business, this last step—fulfillment—is often forgotten. The logistics of this can mean the difference between profit and loss. And it can mean the difference between working through the night packing orders, or having some time for yourself.

There are four main ways to deliver; depending on your business, you may use one, two, or all of them.

- **Do it yourself:** This is the simplest alternative, and the most time-consuming. When an order comes in, you print a packing slip, take a product from the inventory, package it up, print a mailing label, determine the cost of shipping, get the right number of stamps (or fill out the courier form), and then go to the post office (or call the courier). Then you send an e-mail to the customer saying that their order has shipped. When the next order comes in, you repeat the process, all over again.

ESSENTIAL

A useful concept is "highest and best use." It states that each person should be used for the highest value work that he is capable of. As the president of your new online business, does it make sense for you to be taking parcels to the post office? Not really. But at the beginning you may have no staff, so you are the only one who can do it. Or you may be in a cash crunch, and while you don't want to do it yourself, doing the work means zero cash outlay.

- **Partner:** If your supplier is set up to ship directly to any address of your choice, you can avoid carrying inventory altogether—and avoid paying staff to pack and ship the product. Most shopping carts have the ability to automatically send fulfillment information to an e-mail address of your choice, while at the same time sending you payment confirmation. While you may pay slightly more for having your suppliers do the shipping, it will save you considerable time.
- **Outsource to a third party:** If a supplier partner won't handle the fulfillment, there are hundreds of other companies that will. If you do decide to outsource to a fulfillment house, make sure that you check their references and do a few test transactions first. Most importantly, ask about all of the fees. Surprises are always unpleasant—and can turn a profitable sale into a disappointing loss.
- **Digital delivery:** The beauty of digital products is that the cost of producing each item, after the initial product creation, is zero. Many shopping carts can handle the delivery of digital products. The customer purchases the product, and the download link shows on the purchase success screen. The link also goes to the purchaser with his receipt. One of the anti-fraud benefits of many of these systems is that the link is encrypted so that it can only be clicked once, and then expires after a predetermined amount of time.

Whichever you choose, monitor it carefully, as it has a direct impact on your customer service—and your profitability.

It's not a bad idea to review your product or service management decisions and strategy after the first six months. Product and service management are sometimes neglected, but together with your employees, they are the underlying core of the business.

CHAPTER 24

Employees: Choose Well, Manage Well

As soon as you reach the stage where you literally cannot do it all, it is time to bring in the troops. Hiring employees, even if some are unpaid, brings your online business to a new level by incorporating new skills, new perspectives, and better customer service. There are both traditional and creative ways to bring in people to get the job done. Being clear about the task at hand and the level of skill needed will help tremendously in deciding how to meet your growing staffing needs. In this chapter, learn about the different ways to find, hire, and manage the people who work for you.

Prepping Before Hiring

Prior to hiring anyone, you need to prepare, and preparation means focusing on a number of details. If you're going to have employees, you'll need to be ready to do the following:

- Get a federal ID number as an employer
- Recruit qualified individuals, review their skills, and contact their references
- Train and supervise others
- Adjust to various personalities
- Delegate responsibilities
- Recognize that some things may be done successfully in a manner different from yours
- Make sure you're a good communicator and listener
- Know the going rate for wages and how much you can afford to pay
- Pay employees on a regular basis no matter how business is going
- Establish rules and guidelines so that your employees know your expectations and don't take advantage of you
- Pay unemployment taxes, Social Security, and Medicare when due
- Have desks, phones, computer terminals, and other supplies ready
- Know how to lay people off or fire them

Are you prepared to do all of this? Can you handle conflict between employees? Can you motivate employees to work at peak levels? As an employer, you'll have to set the tone and lead by example. You'll need to determine your own style and be consistent and fair to all employees. Hone your leadership skills in advance. Learning as you go can result in poor business practices and even lawsuits. You want to project an image of professionalism.

Crafting a Job Posting

A job posting will help you hire a person for a specific job. It also serves as a blueprint for the tasks associated with that job. Here are the key elements of a job posting:

- Date of posting
- Name of company

- Brief description of company
- Job summary, with the primary functions described
- Compensation (you may or may not share this in the posting, but you need to be clear what the job will pay)
- Necessary background and skills for doing the job
- Benefits
- Contact information

In order to get applicants who closely resemble your ideal candidate, you must offer specific, clear information about the job. If your posting is vague or misleading, you may end up with a bunch of applicants who are completely unqualified for the job. If this happens, it will be your fault—not theirs.

Once you have completed writing the job posting, look at it one final time. What are your screening criteria? If you have 100 applicants, what can you do to quickly weed these down to the top ten? The screening criteria need to be quantitative, and clear to the applicant. Here are some examples:

- Must have five years experience
- Must have a college degree
- Must be bilingual Spanish and English
- Must provide salary expectations in the cover letter

If someone applies with three years experience, or without a college degree, or doesn't specify that they are bilingual, or doesn't provide salary expectations, then they will not make the short list. And you will save a ton of time.

Where to Find Your Staff

They say good help is hard to find, but it's not impossible. It's all a matter of clearly defining what your needs are and screening the applicants accordingly. The better you know what you're looking for, the more likely you'll be able to find someone with those skills. Your next step is to translate these requirements into a job posting, and then placing that posting where applicants can find it.

Craigslist and Kijiji

If you're hiring locally, place ads on these two sites. Also consider classified ads in trade publications. Keep the ad brief and make the job description (and list of requirements) clear. Include any technical know-how that a person should have and exactly what you want to see: a resume, work samples, and cover letter.

ESSENTIAL

Some metropolitan area newspapers feature greatly expanded job-listing sections once or twice a year. If the timing works out, this is a great time to include your listing because the paper aggressively markets the section, drawing the attention of a large pool of job seekers.

Job Boards

You can post a job opportunity on your own website or on any of the many employment websites. Career Builder.com at *www.CareerBuilder.com*, Monster.com, *www.monster.com*, and Simply Hired, *www.simplyhired.com* are among the many places where individuals look for work—which makes them excellent places to post.

Employment Agencies and Headhunters

Employment agencies generally sign up far more applicants than they can find jobs for, so they may have someone to place in your business. They will charge you a fee for their match-making services, so unless you are looking for a very unique individual, recruiters are generally not your first stop.

ALERT

Make sure your job-posting requirements are commensurate with the salary or wages you are offering. If your budget doesn't match your grand wish list for credentials, education, and experience, you will be frustrated when you only hear from candidates who expect to earn more than you do.

Friends and Family: Your Social Network

The business world is largely based on the "who you know" principle. Consider those people you know and trust—but remember, when friends work for friends, trouble can ensue. Establish a business relationship in the office that is separate from your personal relationship.

More importantly, use LinkedIn, Facebook, and Twitter to let your social network know that you are looking to hire. LinkedIn specifically has a mechanism (much like the job boards) where you can post a job for a fee, then look through the profiles—and the connections—of each of the applicants. If you are involved in any LinkedIn groups, don't forget to post what you're looking for within the group itself.

Staff Alternatives: Contractors, Freelancers, and Interns

There are many online listings where you can post positions for freelancers or contractors. And there are an equal number of freelancers and contractors who have posted their qualifications on the Internet. It's important to check their references, the work quality, and background of such independent workers.

The benefit of using these folks is that you pay only for what you require. Here are some things you need to determine, before giving them a contract:

- How soon can this person commit to the project?
- Can she meet your deadline?
- What are her hourly rates?
- How many hours does she anticipate the job taking?
- Does she work on-site or off-site?
- How does this person expect to be paid?
- Does she mind signing a confidentiality agreement?

Research rates for the same job to make sure the candidate's rates are in line with others in the field. Writing, graphic arts, and most other professions have associations, unions, or websites where you can find compensation information.

Once you've established the boundaries and guidelines for the job and how your company works, write up a basic contract agreement. From the contractor or freelancer, you want sufficient notice if he can't finish the project, and make sure it's clear that he will only be paid for the work he's done. If, however, you need to end the project at a certain time or cancel, you should also give notice and pay the person for the work he's done to that point.

ESSENTIAL

While contractors and freelancers are not employees and do not get the benefits of staff, you should still treat them in a proper, professional manner. Contractors and others who are self-employed do a lot of networking, and inappropriate practices can give you a bad reputation.

Internship programs through local high schools or colleges are great places to find energetic young talent willing to learn in exchange for course credits or a name on their resumes. It is a great way to try out a young person who may be a rising star in a few years. Some internships are paid, while others are unpaid. If you are not paying your interns in dollars, then you will need to find other ways to compensate them: closer mentoring, better projects, a great reference letter, and perhaps a few perks. It is a small world, and their experience (and your reputation) will be shared widely long after the internship is over.

Interviewing Candidates

After you decide on your methods of searching, you will then decide who you want to call in for interviews. If you are flooded with resumes, it might be worth your money to hire someone to read through them and narrow down the field to the best candidates.

FACT

If you get a crush of responses to your job posting it might be worthwhile to do the first round of screening interviews by phone. From this group you can winnow down those who came across with enough knowledge and polish to warrant a face-to-face interview.

Many people think that it's easier to be the interviewer than the interviewee. However, because you're the one representing your business, there is a lot of pressure on you to act in a professional manner and in a way that adheres to proper protocol. Remember, there are some questions you can ask prospective employees, and others you can't. For example, you can ask all about past jobs, past responsibilities, favorite tasks or work-related activities, and why they left their last jobs. You cannot ask if they're married, have kids, or about their sexual orientation. You can ask about goals, dreams, special skills, strengths and weaknesses, long-term plans, and preferred work style (team, individual, and so on). You can't ask about a person's religious beliefs, age, political affiliations, or disabilities. In short, personal questions are out and work-related questions are fine.

ESSENTIAL

Reread the candidate's resume just before you start the interview so you can focus on her qualifications. The resume may trigger an interesting talking point revealing how she would fit into your organization. The candidate will relax a bit knowing you took the time at least to read the resume, a small courtesy to her and required preparation for you.

When interviewing, stick to the subject (the job), explain the company, make no judgments, and use common courtesy. It's often advantageous to ask someone how he would handle a certain responsibility or how he would act in a specific situation. The answers to questions like these may prove more valuable than the standard "Where do you see yourself in three years?" Get an idea of how an individual solves problems. You can—and should—request references, and have the person's resume in front of you as a guide during the interview. Take good notes when interviewing someone so that you can go back and compare candidates later.

Depending on your needs, you might also consider asking the final candidates to do some (paid) consulting work, so you can evaluate what it is like to work with them—and the quality of their output. When you do decide to hire someone, establish a start date. Provide each employee with the W-4 form for the IRS, any benefits information, the I-9 form from the U.S. Citizenship and Immigration Services, and an employee handbook if you have one.

Running Background Checks

You don't have to check up on everything, but a little research can't hurt. People sometimes make gross exaggerations, and research could prevent you from hiring a dishonest person. Get the applicant's permission to call previous employers. Then check on the previous jobs, dates, salaries, and skills. Depending on the position requirements, verify any degrees or licenses the candidate has included in her resume. Specific references given to you by the candidate are also fine to call, but they're obviously always people who will say good things about the person.

ALERT

Depending on the particular position for which you are hiring, you may also want to run a criminal background check. You certainly do not want to learn the bookkeeper you are about to hire has a felony record for embezzlement.

You should also check the Internet, but since many people share the same name (sometimes even in the same city!) make sure that you don't make any judgments that are a case of mistaken identity. Here are a few things to check:

- Do the person's LinkedIn profile and resume match? Or are there omissions?
- Who knows both you and the candidate in common, within LinkedIn and Facebook? These people might also be worthwhile references.
- Do a Facebook and Twitter search on their name. Verify that there is nothing that is in conflict with your organization or business.
- Do a Google search on the person's name, along with one or two keywords (e.g., city, skills, former employer, etc.), and see if anything problematic comes up.

If the factual information the applicant provides is incorrect, be suspicious. Make sure, however, that if you call a company to ask about someone who worked there six years ago, that you're talking to an individual who can look back in the files (assuming the company keeps files that far back). Just because someone working there at that moment never heard of the person doesn't mean she didn't work there in the past.

ALERT

Just as you cannot ask questions regarding the person's private life, you cannot disqualify him based on his religion, political beliefs, sexual orientation, etc. If the candidate believes that you did this after looking at his social media profiles, then he might take you to court.

Outsourcing

What is the secret to many big companies' success? Management consultants and CEOs will often point to two factors: people and focus. People means making sure that you have the very best folks on your team: smart, creative, analytical, hardworking, and easy to get along with. Focus means doing one thing exceptionally well—and not being distracted by things that are not core to the business. This is where outsourcing comes in.

What Can Be Outsourced?

In short, almost everything. And because of this, it is possible to grow and scale an online business with a very small central staff—maybe even just you. Here are some of what can be outsourced:

- Graphic design and branding
- Technology, both development and management
- Sales
- Manufacturing
- Inventory warehousing, logistics, and fulfillment
- Customer service
- Human resources
- Bookkeeping and accounting

How do you figure out what stays and what goes? Generally, the criteria is that the strategic "core" of your business should stay inside, but everything else should go. For example, if you are selling custom artwork, then the creation of the artwork (and possibly the marketing) would be done by you, but the web design, development, bookkeeping, and other aspects of the business you might send externally. There is a cost to outsourcing, but because you do not need to worry about these externally provided services, you can remain that much more focused on your direct responsibilities.

Reasons to Keep a Function Internal

Traditionally, businesses have all of their functions delivered by employees within the organization by the way of HR, IT, sales, and more. Now that there is a choice, why might you prefer doing it this way?

- **It's strategic:** If doing something internally is what makes the end product different from your competitor's, then doing it inside probably makes sense. If you use a secret process during the product or service creation or delivery, then sending it outside risks sharing that secret.
- **You'll have better control over quality or scheduling:** When you promise that something will be delivered by a certain date, or that it will be of a certain quality, the only way to be 100 percent certain about meeting these commitments is to do the job yourself. If you outsource, you will need to set standards, then make sure that you monitor your outsource partners for compliance.
- **Patriotism:** Some outsourcing is done offshore; keeping the work in the country—or even in your community—means that the value that you create stays where you are.
- **Ethical concerns:** When the outsourcing supplier is on the other side of the world, that supplier may have different business practices. Does it use child labor? What are the working conditions for its staff? Is the supplier environmentally sound? Does it work in a country that has a poor human rights record? Knowing that your business is operating by your moral compass means that you can sleep at night.

Beyond the above reasons, many entrepreneurs just prefer to see the work being done with their own eyes.

Reasons to Outsource

In the past, the reason to outsource was simple: it was cheaper. Some companies, however, recognized that outsourcing might provide them a strategic advantage. Here are some of the reasons that typically justify sending work outside:

- **Improved focus:** Keep your staff focused on the core strategic business activities, and let someone else do everything else. And since the "everything else" is what they are best at, they will do it better than you.
- **No internal skills:** If you have a need to get something done, either you or staff can learn how, or get a specialist to jump on that problem immediately. Since there is a cost to the learning curve, it is often cheaper to find specialist skills externally than growing them inside.
- **Lower overall cost:** Some tasks can be done far cheaper by going to a person (or company) based in a part of the world with a lower cost of living. There is a risk, however, that as the exchange rates change, you may end up being locked into a contract costing you significantly more.
- **Keep costs variable:** If you experience seasonal peaks, or have a special project that needs completion, outsourcing the work matches the costs with the needs. You only pay for labor when you need it.
- **Greater management flexibility:** Outsourcing means no HR hassles, no furniture or equipment costs, and no rental of space to house full-time staff. It also means that you can scale up or down, as your needs change.

Whether you choose to outsource or keep the work inside, it is not a bad idea to review your options each year as you grow. Decisions that you make at start-up might be different a year or two down the road.

Virtual Assistants

Back in the 1930s, most managers had a secretary. She (and it was almost always a female) would take dictation, type letters, answer the phone, set up meetings, get coffee, and do just about everything else that needed doing. Over the years, this role changed to include responsibility for all administrative aspects of a manager's job, and the title also morphed to executive assistant. The role included event management, some tech support, correspondence, customer service, financial analysis, and much more. As the economy tightened—and computers automated many of the administrative tasks—companies hired fewer and fewer administrative assistants. But the need to do this work didn't go away. In big companies, managers often had to shoulder the work. In smaller companies (and start-ups), the need was met another way: enter the virtual assistant.

What Is a VA?

A virtual assistant is a specialist in administrative duties, and is hired to do either a special project, or specific tasks on a recurring basis. The International Virtual Assistants Association has a list of 101 ways to use a VA that you can find at *www.budurl.com/everythingVA*. Here are a few examples of what a VA might do for you:

- Bookkeeping
- Data processing
- Electronic newsletters
- Event planning
- Marketing support, e-mails
- Internet marketing
- Purchasing
- Research
- Secretarial and phone support
- Transcription
- Writing, editing, and proofreading

Like every person that you might hire, each VA has his or her own strengths and weaknesses. Understand what your core requirements are, and match the VA with the task. There is nothing wrong with hiring two completely different VAs to do two completely separate tasks.

There is another benefit of hiring VAs over an employee: the cost of their professional training, their computers, and their rent are embedded into their rates. You don't need to budget for these separately.

How to Find One

Probably the best way to find any employee is to ask those around you—finding a great VA is no different. Beyond this, advertise on Craigslist and Kijiji, search through Elance and oDesk, or check out the membership directory at *www.ivaa.org*. While you can use offline ads, as an online entrepreneur you probably want someone who already is familiar with working in an online environment.

Questions to Ask

On one hand, VAs are no different from any other contractor—so ask them the same types of questions. On the other hand, they are different. Because they can be so involved in the business—admin does cut across all lines—a great working relationship is critical, as is the ability to work without supervision. Because you will often be telling the VA what to do, but not always how to do it, there is an opportunity for the VA to bring process efficiency—and new ideas—to your new company. Finally, a VA is different from contractors in one other way. They often become part of the ongoing operation. How will you handle vacations? Does the VA have a partnership with another VA so they can cover each other's away time?

When to Move On

Even the best relationships come to an end. Perhaps you require someone on-site. Perhaps you are using them so much, that it is cheaper to hire someone full-time. Whatever the reason, it is important to change the arrangement in a professional manner. You might choose to use them again, to cover a peak in workload. You might need to use them to train their replacement. And for certain, you don't want them speaking negatively of you to their virtual—but very real—community. The best time to talk about the process for disengaging is at the beginning, when you are considering hiring them. That way, when you do separate, both parties know what is expected of them: notice period, return of company property, deletion of company files, etc.

Attracting and Keeping Great Employees

Significant turnover in a business can slow down productivity, curb your profits, and squelch morale. The more time spent on training new people, the less productive work is getting done, by you and by them. Besides additional compensation (which isn't always possible) there are other ways to attract and hang on to talented people, including:

- Allow for flexible working hours
- Allow work-from-home arrangements

- Provide top-of-the-line computers and high-speed connections
- Encourage employee suggestions and feedback—and pay attention to it
- Help with child care
- Encourage and set up social outings
- Offer fitness activities, such as a lunch-hour yoga class or a fitness room
- Be understanding in the case of emergencies and extenuating circumstances, and allow for a limited paid leave in certain situations
- Set up an ergonomic office or business
- Consider job-sharing situations, where two people do one job by dividing up the tasks and splitting the schedule
- Pay for professional development seminars or courses
- Recognize and celebrate achievement and excellence in your team

While you can attempt to create an environment that will both attract and retain good workers, you can't be a social welfare provider. You are treating employees as responsible adults and enabling them to make choices about their work habits. No matter how generous you are, they owe you the highest level of productivity in supplying top-quality products or services to your customers.

Establishing Rules and Policies

Whether your business has an official handbook outlining the rules and procedures of the company or simply a list of policies, it's important that you establish basic rules and guidelines that people are expected to follow. More and more employees are jumping at the chance to sue their former employer. Don't make it easier for them to do so. Spell everything out. Put rules and regulations in writing in case someone ever questions company policies. This helps set the ground rules for everyone and, if you have managers, rules and policies help them manage. More importantly, rules and policies help ensure that everyone is treated consistently and fairly. Your policies should include information on:

- Vacations
- Pensions and retirement benefits

- Holiday pay
- Safety regulations (including those imposed by outside agencies)
- Sick leave and disability
- Reviews and raises
- Specific grounds for termination
- Incentives and bonuses (if you offer any)
- Sexual harassment
- Drug use, drug testing, and smoking
- Hours and work schedule
- Theft or misuse of company property, equipment, or funds
- Defined work status (full-time, part-time)
- Inappropriate use of the computer and/or Internet (or other technological equipment)
- Discounts on merchandise or services

If you have more than twenty people working for your business, you should consider putting all this information into a booklet or private website for when an individual is hired.

Show Them the Money—and Benefits

You'll have to do some research to find out what the average salary is in the geographic region for the type of job you're offering. Pay rates vary in different parts of the country; with an online business, you may pay quite differently if your employee is in New York or Grand Forks, North Dakota. If you pay too low, then your keen new employee can be easily lured somewhere else.

ESSENTIAL

Working with a professional employee organization (PEO) gives you the opportunity to share the HR responsibilities with a third-party company. Your employees are leased to the PEO, which provides a range of services, including payroll management, better pricing on group health insurance, and advice on how to handle employee issues such as terminations. A PEO can also provide background checks for new hires and offer legal advice related to HR issues.

If you can't match the going pay rates, make up for it in other ways, such as telecommuting possibilities, additional vacation time, and so on. Someone making $50,000 with three weeks of vacation and two days a week of working from home may be happier than someone else making $60,000 with two weeks of vacation and a five-day-a-week commute to and from the office.

You should also set up some system of raises, benefits, and additional incentives. Be consistent, though. Employees often find out what other employees are offered and are resentful if they haven't been offered similar perks. Be very clear with all offers that you make, and put it in writing.

FACT

Benefits that might attract top talent include tuition payments for job-related education, a relocation package, additional health benefits such as prenatal care or CPR training, adoption assistance, child care, and benefit plans that cover life partners who are not married.

Letting People Go—Know the Law

It's not easy to let people go, especially if termination is not a result of their actions but simply a matter of funding (or lack thereof). Nonetheless, you must handle the situation professionally.

There are a number of reasons for letting someone go. If you're firing someone because of his actions, you must let him know the grounds on which you're dismissing him. Your reasoning should be supported by company policy (which should be in writing), if not by local or federal law. If, however, the person is simply not working up to the capacity that you had hoped for, you may need to give the individual notice in writing so he has a chance to correct problems. It is no longer acceptable to simply let him know that the situation is not working out.

People react to being fired in many ways. Have someone else alerted to what's going on so that the individual's access to the computer and or company files can be shut down when necessary. Have a witness to the severance conversation to avoid "he said/she said" later on. Let him talk, and answer his questions to the best of your abilities. Arguing will get you nowhere.

In most situations, the employee will want to know what he's getting to cushion the blow. Almost every company provides its employees with some type of severance pay. This can be higher or lower depending on the specifics of the termination agreement and where you are located, but they should get something unless they've broken company policies or the law. Speak to an attorney who specializes in labor law to understand your legal obligations.

There's another reason you must be careful. Today, the moment someone is told that he's being let go, the thing that likely enters his mind is not "severance package" but "lawsuit." This may mean you need to review your own termination practices over months or even years.

Try to fire or terminate everyone in the same manner. If you act in one way with one employee and in another manner with another employee, it can come back to haunt you. If you have proof that the person has violated company policy, broken the law, committed fraud, or acted in a violent manner, then you have just and legal cause in your favor.

ALERT

Every state has its own laws and regulations regarding employee termination. One concept that you may have heard about is employment at will. This means that the employee and employer can individually decide to sever the relationship without any further obligation. Do not rely on employment at will laws to reduce the cost of firing an employee, as a number of court cases have awarded significant severance payments nonetheless. Check with an attorney experienced in labor law first.

It's important that you handle the situation of laying off employees as professionally as possible. You want to protect yourself and your company but also let others know that you're human and have a heart. Don't forget that those employees who aren't being laid off will be watching your every move. You'll need to boost their morale or they're likely to update their resumes and start looking, out of fear that they'll be the next to go.

Keeping personnel records is important, as this will help as you manage your team. Keeping purchasing records is important, as this will help you determine profitability. And so on. The only way to manage your business is to ensure that as you build it, you are also building your record keeping systems.

CHAPTER 25

Bookkeeping, Record Keeping, and Administrative Tasks

While your great idea gets the juices going and creates the energy to bring you success, nothing will undermine you quicker than sloppy business records. You need well-kept records for tax obligations and to show how the business is doing and help plan for its growth. This chapter offers information about what to keep track of, as well as tips on administrative duties and outsourcing.

Good Records Keep Things Going Smoothly

Good bookkeeping and record keeping are essential to operating a successful online business. When you start your own business, you need to know why these daily chores are important, so you'll be motivated to keep up with them.

- **To monitor or track the performance of your business:** Good records will allow you to gauge which items or services are selling and which ones aren't. You'll also get a firm understanding of which expenses are necessary and which ones may be higher than you'd like them to be.
- **To calculate tax return figures and pay taxes:** When you're working from a set of accurate financial records, it's far easier to comply with the various tax and filing requirements.
- **To pay yourself and others:** You can't pay yourself or distribute profits if you don't know what those profits are.

ESSENTIAL

If you're looking for investors or you want to secure a loan from the bank, you'll need to show accurate financial statements. The IRS and other regulatory agencies require accurate financial statements from you, too. You can only furnish accurate statements with reliable bookkeeping.

- **To sell the business:** If you want to sell your business someday, the buyer will want to know how the business has been doing when you were in charge. The only way to do this is through the financial statements.

It's tempting to procrastinate, but the best time to set up these systems is right at the beginning, or even just before you start.

Establish Bookkeeping Procedures

If you're a sole proprietor, you'll need to take a crash course in bookkeeping basics to gain an overview of these procedures. If you're running a small business with partners or investors, you may want to hire a bookkeeper to handle your books.

Basic bookkeeping starts on a day-by-day, sale-by-sale level. Whether you're using a software program or doing the bookkeeping manually, you'll need to keep a journal of sales and cash receipts. This will allow you to see your sales totals and keep track of when you received payment for each item. Your cash expense journal will provide you with information on how much you're spending and to whom you're paying the money. You'll also need to keep a general journal for listing unusual entries or those made annually.

ALERT

It's absolutely critical that you save supporting documents to back up your journal entries. You will need all bank deposit slips, credit card slips, cash register tapes and receipts, invoices, credit card receipts, cancelled checks, bank statements, and petty cash vouchers.

Bookkeeping for online businesses is different from bookkeeping for bricks-and-mortar businesses in one important way. Because your sales are online, there is an opportunity to have transactions automatically entered into your bookkeeping program, or at least downloadable into a file that you can import into it. As you design your system—and choose a bookkeeping program—it is important to keep this integration point in mind.

ALERT

Be wary of any online offers or come-ons from professionals that offer dramatic shortcuts to handling the tasks of record keeping. While technology can speed up your accounting methods, anything that appears to be too fast or takes too many shortcuts is probably missing some vital steps that will come back to haunt you later.

The attitude that "We'll let the gang in accounting handle it" or "You'll have to ask my bookkeeper" can lead you into trouble. Bookkeepers are hired to provide you with accurate books, and accountants will help you prepare financial statements and make recommendations. But it's up to you to make the final informed decisions. Therefore, it's important that you meet with your accountant and/or bookkeeper regularly to review your financial statements. In the case of uncommon situations, such as buying a new building, a merger, or even an audit, you need to spend even more time in these meetings to understand the financial picture of your company.

ALERT

As an online business, you might be tempted to try and do everything on the web, including your bookkeeping. Before you do this, however, make sure that the web version of the bookkeeping program has all of the features that you need.

Keeping Track of Your Business

Choosing an accounting system is one thing. But after you've made that decision, you need to know what to keep tabs on—otherwise, your accounting system won't do you any good.

Accounts Receivable

You'll need to keep track of all accounts receivable, which is the money owed to you by customers. For each customer, you'll keep an individual list of accounts receivable. This will allow you to know how much you're owed in total and how much each customer owes you.

Accounts Payable

The money that you need to pay (your bills) is your accounts payable. You may owe money to suppliers, vendors, or others from whom you've purchased merchandise, equipment, or services. If you keep a separate ledger account for each supplier or vendor, you'll be able to see exactly who is owed money and how much you owe at any given time.

Balance Sheet

One of your key financial statements is the balance sheet. This will provide you with a snapshot overview of your business at any moment in time.

Included on a balance sheet are all your assets and liabilities. As the name would imply, the balance sheet will need to balance, meaning your assets will equal your liabilities plus your capital. If the totals don't balance, you'll have to look for a discrepancy or error.

ESSENTIAL

Besides finding a competent and trustworthy bookkeeper and accountant, you may need to have administrative assistance in your office, especially if you don't want to do this work yourself. It's very important that you find someone whom you can trust with confidential information.

Profit-and-Loss Statement

This is the statement that will generate the most attention from prospective investors. It's also the one that you're most eager to read, simply because it shows your net income or loss and gives you an overall perspective on where the business stands. Also known as an income statement, this is very simply a summation of what you've spent in each of several areas and what you've earned. Generally you will list the following:

- Sales.
- Cost of goods sold: this will include the cost to buy the goods you sold during the period for which you're preparing the statement. If you are selling services, cost of goods sold will include the salaries of the people directly involved in delivering the services.
- Gross profits: this is the difference between the sales and the cost of goods sold.
- Expenses: this includes any other salaries, contractor fees, advertising, rent, payroll taxes, insurance, depreciation, repairs, office supplies, and all other expenses.
- Net income: this is your gross profit less your expenses.

If nothing else, profit-and-loss statements will show you how quickly expenses can cut into your profits.

Choosing Accounting Software

An accounting software package should be easy to learn and include features pertinent to your particular business. You should discuss your choice of software with your bookkeeper or accountant to make sure you're using the same program, or at least one that's compatible.

There are numerous programs and online services available, ranging from ones under $20 to high-end programs costing several thousand dollars. Here is a list of a few of the more well-known ones:

- **QuickBooks Pro:** *www.quickbooks.intuit.com*, or 1-800-548-0289.
- **Sage 50:** (formerly Peachtree Accounting): *www.na.sage.com*, or 1-877-495-9904.
- **Netsuite:** *www.netsuite.com,* or 1-877-NETSUITE.

Spend some time on the websites of each of them (and any others that come recommended to you) to familiarize yourself before you actually make the purchase.

ALERT

In your eagerness to get your bookkeeping onto your computer, don't forget to review carefully the system's requirements for any software package you purchase. Do the same for upgrades. The last thing you need is to invest a lot of money in software that your computer is too outdated to run.

Record Keeping and Administrative Needs

Besides all the financial records, you'll need to maintain other records, including the names and addresses of your suppliers, accurate client records, and up-to-date employee data.

Your personnel files should include:

- All necessary tax information for each employee, including Social Security numbers
- Personal contact information
- Employment history (resume, initial job application, and so on)
- Employment record with your company, including pay rate and vacation days accrued

For clients and customers, you will also need to maintain files, including:

- All up-to-date contact information
- Tax exempt certificates if applicable
- Correspondence
- Record of transactions

Even though a lot of business is transacted through e-mail, it's very important to take the time to print hard copies of all key documents and store them safely in your files. Businesses that rely solely on their computers are taking enormous risks. Backing up data is not just about making a copy of computer files!

Other files that should be on hand include:

- Permits, licenses, and registrations
- Equipment leasing contracts or receipts for purchases
- Correspondence with landlords, regulatory agencies, and any government officials
- Legal papers including claims you've made and claims made against your company

One of the biggest, yet least discussed, causes of business failure is poor record keeping. This doesn't refer strictly to financial records. Businesses have been shut down because they let licenses and registrations lapse, and companies have found themselves in financial trouble because they neglected legal matters.

Who Should Do the Administrative Duties?

At the very beginning, you may decide that, since you have the extra time and since you need to have a handle on all of the details, that you should do all of the administrative work. Eventually though, you will realize that if you are to grow the business, then you won't have time to do the admin required to keep the business running. When this happens, you will have three choices:

- **Automate:** Because of the nature of your online business, you may be able to have some of the record keeping partially or fully automated. Sales from your e-commerce system can be sent directly to your bookkeeping program—as can bank statements.
- **Delegate:** Many hands make light work. Instead of one person doing the admin work for everyone on your team, ask everyone to do his own. Split some of your admin work with one or two trusted staff members or partners. Doing this gives them ownership over the task, while also reducing your personal administrative commitments.
- **Outsource:** What can't be done internally, outsource. Beyond your bookkeeper, accountant, and attorney, there are a growing number of people who specialize in doing admin work remotely. Some might be found on sites such as *www.elance.com* and *www.odesk.com*, but also check out the International Association of Virtual Assistants, at *www.ivaa.org.*

Remember that a choice that you make need not be a forever one. You may start by doing everything yourself, then delegating it to an employee, then eventually automating it or outsourcing it.

Daytime Is for Delivery

The question of who should do the work is straightforward, but as an online entrepreneur, how do you know when to do your administrative work? The mantra daytime is for delivery, nighttime is for admin is a useful guideline, as it sets priorities for how you spend your prime business hours. For online businesses, however, this is somewhat less useful: customers might be reaching out via e-mail 24/7. Your discussion forums and public social media connections may require your attention at any hour of the day or night—or you may miss the sale. In other words, daytime is for delivery, and nighttime may be too. Depending on your business, there may be very little that you can do about this, except for one thing: schedule time each week to focus on the admin. If you can't measure it, you can't manage it—and if you can't schedule time to do it, then it simply won't get done.

Record keeping in general is critical for two other reasons. Your financial statements determine how much tax you pay. And if you have to make an insurance claim, your records will often impact the size of the payment to you.

CHAPTER 26

Insurance and Tax Information

No matter how you are structured and how much (or little) you generate in sales or net profits, you will need to prepare and file taxes, and you will want to reduce your risks through purchasing appropriate insurance. In this chapter you will find a broad overview of what you need to do to stay on top of these obligations.

What You Need to Pay and When

You will be obligated to pay federal and state income tax based on what you earn during the year, minus expenses and deductions. As opposed to individual personal tax returns, which are due every year by April 15, you will be required to pay quarterly estimated taxes if you are incorporated. Quarterly taxes are due on April 15, June 15, September 15, and January 15. (These dates will be different if your business is operating on a different fiscal year.) Check with your accountant to find out exactly when your estimated taxes are due, and how much you should pay. If you have any questions about estimated taxes, check out the IRS website at *www.irs.gov.*

ESSENTIAL

If your company depends on retail sales that are heaviest during the end of the calendar year and into the beginning of the new year with merchandise returns, it might be prudent to set up your fiscal year to begin and end in your lighter season, perhaps May through April. This will take pressure off during the tax preparation season.

Proper Deductions Help Profits

The IRS uses the words "ordinary," "necessary," and "reasonable" to determine which expenses they consider to be helping you to earn income from your business. The concern is not how much a particular piece of equipment helps you earn, but that the purpose, or reason for buying the item, is business related.

If it relates to your business, it's deductible. If it's for personal use, it isn't. If it's for both, such as a car, then you'll have to determine the amount of mileage for personal use and the amount of mileage for business use. For business purposes, you can deduct fifty-five and a half cents for each business mile as of 2012. (Up-to-date numbers are available at *www.irs.gov/Tax-Professionals/Standard-Mileage-Rates.*) Keep tallies of how much you use your car or any item for business, and how much you use it for personal needs. The bottom line is justification. If you put something down as a business expense, be able to justify it with backup paperwork. Include the date, the name of the person or business that received the payment, the total amount, and the category of business expense into which you have listed this deduction.

Home offices have increased steadily over the past decade. If you operate your business from your home, and you conduct the administrative or management activities of the business there, you can claim a deduction for the portion of the home used for business. Accordingly, you can also claim a percentage of your utilities and insurance costs.

ALERT

When you prepare your tax form you will notice a place where you are asked to insert a six-digit code to classify your business. If you are unsure of how to classify yours, you can use the generic code 999999. Be cautioned, however, as using this code will draw attention and your return may receive closer scrutiny.

If you're seeking to deduct business expenses, you need to be engaged in what the IRS considers a trade or business, which is an activity carried out with a profit motive—even if you haven't made a profit in the past year. Generally, the IRS looks to see if a business has made a profit in three consecutive years out of five, meaning you can show losses in those always-difficult first two years. The IRS may also use their nine-step profit motive test to determine whether or not your business is a business and not a hobby. The nine factors include:

- The manner in which the business is run
- Your expertise
- Time and effort involved in running the business
- Appreciation
- Success with previous businesses
- History of income or loss
- Amounts of occasional profit
- Financial status of owner, other than this business
- Whether the activity is usually considered for personal pleasure or recreation

When listing your deductions, always refer to the IRS guidelines, since not all expenses are equally deductible.

Employment Taxes

Unless you are a sole proprietor, you will need to hire employees. This means that you'll be required to have an employer identification number (EIN). You can obtain an EIN by filing an SS-4, Application for Employer Identification Number, online at the IRS website.

Your principle concerns when paying employees are the following:

- Withholding taxes
- Social Security and Medicare (FICA)
- Unemployment taxes
- Disability taxes

Withholding taxes are calculated depending on the filing status of the individual and are withheld from each person's salary. You will determine both federal and state income tax payments.

Paying these taxes can get a little tricky, as the rates and caps are all different—and changing. You'll also find that people working for you change their marital or dependent status. In addition, individuals are putting money away in tax-free retirement plans and you need to calculate the taxes after this money is invested into their individual plans. Is it any wonder why you need to hire a good accountant?

ESSENTIAL

All full- and part-time employees should be paid on the books. An IRS audit could prove costly if it is determined that you are paying people and not recording it, reporting it, and paying their withholding taxes. Likewise, if you are avoiding paying sales tax amounts you can be hit with heavy fines.

When you hire an employee, you will ask that person to fill out a W-4 form. The employee will include her income tax filing status, which you will use to calculate the amount of income taxes.

You're also responsible for having employees fill out I-9 forms from the U.S. Citizenship and Immigration Services, proving that the employee is eligible to work in the United States. Noncitizens must have work visas. For more information about these forms, contact the USCIS at 1-800-375-5283 or check out *www.uscis.gov*.

Keep in mind that you need to define which individuals are considered your employees and which are considered independent contractors. In general, an individual is considered your employee if:

- He receives his primary income by working for you.
- He receives direction from you on a regular basis.
- He has his pay rate controlled by your decisions.

Also, if you've specifically trained the person to perform a task or job, including procedures and methods by which the work is to be done, this generally indicates an employee.

QUESTION

What is the common-law test for determining the status of an employee? According to the IRS, you can determine if a person is an employee or an independent contractor based on behavioral control, financial control, and your relationship with the individual. Check with the IRS for more details.

An independent contractor is hired by you to do a specific job, or several jobs, but has his own established business and pay rate and also works elsewhere to make his income. In short, an independent contractor isn't under your control as an employee. If you pay an independent contractor more than $600 in a given year, you're required to send him a 1099 form. There are no withholdings that you're required to pay, and the contractor is, therefore, responsible for including the income in his own personal income taxes.

Payroll taxes are due either semiweekly or monthly, depending on the size of your payroll, not on when you issue checks. The IRS will dictate the schedule—you can't make the choice. If your total payroll is less than $2,500 for the quarter, you can file quarterly. If you do not pay your payroll taxes on time, you can be hit with fines and penalties. The IRS takes this very seriously!

Tax Planning with a Pro

You can't avoid paying taxes, but you can strategically plan to structure and conduct your business in such a manner that it reduces how much you have to pay. While you don't want to focus so much attention on minimizing your tax bite that you neglect your business, you can work with a tax professional to choose the best options for your individual situation. Whatever you do, do it legally. Fraud will result in serious consequences.

A good tax plan evaluates your current situation and looks forward over the next several years to determine what your anticipated earnings will look like. The better you estimate your sales revenue, income, and cash flow over the coming years, the better you'll be able to plan accordingly. Choices of claiming deductions, hiring employees, selecting a business structure, and setting up your fiscal calendar year are all aspects of your business that you can plan, in part, around tax payments.

A tax professional who understands online business and the special tax challenges they may face can mean the difference between success and failure.

ESSENTIAL

As an employer, you must annually report wages, tips, and all other compensation paid to an employee on a W-2 form. Also, report the employee's income tax and Social Security taxes withheld. You provide copies of the W-2 to your employees and to the Social Security Administration.

Insurance and Risk Management

Of all the hats you wear when starting up a business, being a risk manager may not be the first that comes to mind. Yet you have to be one. Risk management is broader than just insurance. It requires you to look carefully at all of the possible exposures in your business and then figure out the best way to handle them. Insuring yourself and your business is certainly an obvious way to manage risk, but there are also steps you can take that are more efficient and economical.

Covering Assets and Earning Power

When planning for loss, many folks think of protecting their assets. Yet, there are a great number of intangibles that contribute to the success of your business that cannot be overlooked. Here are seven broad areas most risk management professionals would advise you to evaluate: real and personal property, processes, product information, advertising claims, liability exposures, loss of key people, and the possibility of indirect losses.

Risk Control

Once you have a handle on the specific risks for your particular business, you can start finding ways to handle them. Some can be eliminated. For example, you may want to make payments by check rather than cash to provide proof. In some cases you can shift responsibility for some functions by subcontracting them. Clearly, any time you can completely eliminate a risk at little or no cost, that is the path to follow. In some cases you might not be able to completely eliminate a risk, but you can take steps to reduce it; terms and conditions of use and privacy policies are examples.

Retaining or Transferring Risk

As strange as it may seem, there may be instances when you choose to assume a particular risk in whole or in part. Retaining the risk may make sense when the risk of the potential loss is small, or the cost of insurance is high, or you can amortize it over a number of years.

If you cannot reduce or eliminate risk in your business, or if you are unwilling to ignore it, your third option is to transfer the risk to an insurance company. The key instance in which you should opt to buy insurance is when your loss could not be paid from current earnings due to its catastrophic dimensions. The two-part golden rule for deciding whether to insure or not is this: Do not risk more than you can afford to lose regardless of the odds, and do not risk a lot to save a little.

Evaluating Your Insurance Needs

Now that you have an idea of where and when to assume risk, let's take a look at the various facets within your business where insurance may be appropriate. There are three broad areas, each with its own distinctive characteristics. Some of these may be optional, and some may be required (such as workers' compensation insurance, which is legislated in every state for all of your employees, including you!). The following checklists will give you a jumping-off point for things to consider insuring. Your particular business may have others.

Property	Liability to Others	People Coverage
Real Property	General Liability	Group Health/HMO
Broad Form	Fire Legal Liability	Individual Disability
Business Interruption	Professional Liability	Pension/Profit Sharing
Inland Marine	Errors and Omissions	401(k)
Crime	Fiduciary Employee Benefits Liability	Group Life
Contents/Inventory	Internet Liability	Buy Sell/Stock Business Continuation
Boiler/Machinery	Environmental Impairment Liability	
Data Processing	Umbrella/Catastrophe	Key Man
Bonds	Workers' Compensation	Overhead Expense
Fidelity	Products/Completed Operations	
	Directors and Officers	
	Garage Liability	
	Employment Practices Liability	
	Product Recall	
	Intellectual Property	
	Business Auto (hired/nonowned)	

With so many different types of insurance, spending time with an insurance professional is critical.

General Coverage Considerations

The first consideration for how much insurance to buy is a determination of the value of what you need to protect. Will your insurance coverage replace what you have? You will want to select replacement valuation in your coverage. A common choice policy owners make to save on premiums overlooks this very important standard. You want whatever repairs or replacements of damaged items are necessary to restore your operations to the same quality you had before your loss.

ALERT

Don't dismiss third-party liability coverage as extraneous just because you are a small business. If someone has a grievance against your business they may come after you with the same expectation for retribution as if you were a giant corporation. A judge and possibly a jury will rule on these claims in court. They tend to be tougher on businesses than individuals.

Deductibles are the first dollars paid when a loss is incurred. Once the deductible is paid, the balance of the responsibility for the loss is transferred to the insurance company. The higher the deductible, the lower the premium. As the buyer of an insurance policy you drive the choice of deductible levels.

ALERT

One out of every three business failures is caused by employee theft. To protect yourself, do four main things: (1) install security cameras, especially in a retail store; (2) keep an inventory list of all key items; (3) perform background checks when hiring employees; (4) keep up-to-date records and a watchful eye on bookkeeping.

Real Property

Real property is the nuts and bolts, brick and mortar, the tangible stuff of your business. You may think its loss or damage would be the most obvious, but there are some areas that are not; work with your insurance professional to ensure that you have the right amount and type of coverage.

Contents Inventory Coverage

As with real property, contents inventory can have enhanced coverage with specialized insurance. Here are a few examples:

- **Loss of income—business interruption:** How long could you stay in business if you experience the perfect storm of income loss and devastatingly expensive repairs following a fire or some other calamity? Even if your property coverage takes care of the big items, the loss of income can drive you into some serious debt pretty quickly.
- **Valuable papers—accounts receivable:** Imagine a client who, realizing your records have been destroyed in a fire, develops amnesia about money she owes you. This coverage can help keep you whole after you have proven that your efforts to collect have been thwarted as a result of the loss.
- **Selling price coverage:** Similar to replacement value on real property, this coverage protects not only the cost of your goods but also your profit margin.

Should you purchase these coverages? The answer is fairly simple: what would be the impact on your business if something happened and you had no coverage? While insurance sometimes seems expensive, it is significantly cheaper than the potential of financial ruin.

Workers' Compensation

Workers' compensation insurance coverage is required of employers in all fifty states. Rates may vary and may be updated periodically. If yours is a very small, perhaps a one-person, sole-proprietor operation, it is possible to ask for a waiver from this requirement. To do so will entail signing releases, but it may be worth researching.

This coverage must be provided to all employees. If you use subcontractors, one simple test to determine if they could be viewed as employees is this: Do you exercise control over their work? If the answer is yes, they could be considered an employee. In every case you should firmly establish that your vendors carry workers' compensation insurance or you may one day be supporting a claim of one of their employees.

Liability

Liability exposure is an area of "open exposure" where the boundaries of a claim may not be known. At one time insurance product liability policies were written to provide reasonable coverage for use by a responsible person. Today, it is often the courts who determine whether there is liability and the amount: the reasonable person standard has disappeared. As a result, there have been a plethora of additional liability coverages that are now available.

Catastrophe Umbrella

This is the biggie. Because of the uncertainty of liability exposure you will want to carry the largest policy you can reasonably afford with the largest deductible you can absorb in the event of an award against your business. The limit of the protection should be enough to cover the assets of the business. This coverage is specifically needed to protect the business from large judgments as well as more typical claims.

Internet Liability

With an online business, there may be special risks that you are exposed to. You might be sued because someone believes that you've used their intellectual property without permission. Or because they believe you violated their privacy rights. Or because they believe that your web transmitted a virus into their computers. Internet liability insurance is designed to protect you from web-oriented risks that may slip between the cracks of a general policy.

Directors and Officers Liability

This type of policy offers protection for the decisions made at the highest executive and board level. This would include allegations and claims from stock or shareholders or employees and third-party class action suits. If you serve on any boards, for charity or otherwise, and they do not provide directors and officers liability protection, you might want to seriously reconsider your involvement. Holding a board position means you share in the legal responsibility for the direction and decisions of that organization.

It's exciting to set up a business and focus on selling, but the back-office plumbing of the business—from record keeping to insurance to supply chain—needs just as much focus, particularly in the start-up phase of the business. Once this is in place, then you can focus on growth—and being a winner.

A Winner's Checklist— Tips and Tricks

Once you are up and running, your identity established, your legal status in place, inventory and service issues humming, and happy clients spending more, you cannot just sit back and coast. Every day continues to be a challenge— both exciting and nerve-racking. To stay on top of your game you will need to stay sharp.

Customer Service

Customer service is not just responding to complaints. It is a way to show your customers that they're important. It can help enhance your reputation far more effectively than hiring the best public relations firm. For every customer who shares your story, you'll gain free advertising and profile. For this reason, retaining customers is actually more important than attracting new ones—don't take them for granted.

Make Relationships the Highest Priority

Poor managers look only at the immediate profit regardless of the long-term ramifications. If you work to make a sale at the cost of a satisfied customer or at the expense of a staff member, you may lose both in the end. Likewise, if you don't take time to establish relationships with vendors or wholesalers, you may lose them and your competition will benefit. A good business manager can prioritize all areas of the business.

Employee Development

Before you spend money on training, spend time recruiting the right person for the right job. Assess a person's general skill level and see how close he is to meeting your needs. It's unfortunate to lose business because your employees simply don't know how to do their jobs. If this happens, it is a reflection on you and your leadership. Managing a business, unless you're on your own, means developing and maintaining a team of competent employees who will work together for the good of the business. If you can maintain a team that is motivated, you're more likely to have a successful business.

Stay Abreast of Industry Changes

Building a sustainable business means being connected to industry changes and being open to new opportunities. This flexibility means adapting to change, taking in what you hear, and using it constructively.

Do ongoing research on your demographic base, changes in your industry, and changes in the market. Keep track of government policies and regulations, local business news, and environmental concerns that could affect your business. It's vital that you know your consumers. If their needs are changing, you have to be aware; there is no substitute for knowledge. Analyze the data you've gathered to determine how it impacts your business.

To maintain your market position and improve upon it, you must not only keep tabs on your direct competition, but evaluate where you stand. Compare the data you gather on your competitors with your own company facts and figures. What is their pricing? Are you able to match their prices, beat them, or provide something that justifies your price being higher?

Make Your Company a Leader

Your business sits within an industry and a community—what would it take to make it a leader? Unique products, great service quality, a motivated workforce, and more. Learn from others, and benchmark yourself against the other leaders in your market.

At the same time, walk the walk as a community leader. Sponsor local teams, charities, or grass roots initiatives. The media can also help or hurt a business, depending on the stories they broadcast or articles they write; the more leadership, the more respect you will earn with the media. This is especially helpful when it comes to potentially controversial stories that involve your business. You want the media on your side.

Monitor Cash Flow

Monitor your cash flow very carefully. If employees aren't getting paid—they'll quit. Not being able to pay your vendors won't endear you to them either. Maintain as much cash in your bank account as possible. Try to turn all sales into cash as quickly as possible. Offer incentives for cash payments or for paying off a line of credit quickly. Make some of your own purchases on credit. If you combine the two ideas by offering a discount if a customer pays in thirty days and then buying on credit that is due in forty-five days, you give yourself a two-week gap to collect and then make payments.

Planned Expansion

Expansion requires that you balance the revenue to cost equation every step of the way. Before adding a new sales team, add a salesperson or two. Before launching your second website, add product offerings to your first. Manage and control your expansion. Many businesses have tried to expand too fast, taking a successful small business and growing it into an unsuccessful larger one.

Not unlike starting a business, expanding your business requires financing. However, if you're in a position to expand, it's likely that you're successful. If you've proven your worth, you should have established a solid line of credit, making loans easier to get.

No One Knows Your Business Better Than You

It's tempting to outsource as much as possible to offshore workers, contractors, virtual assistants, and consultants, but remember that they don't know your business the way you do. While they may be professionals in their own right, at best they are "hired hands" to do specific work on your behalf. Choose your advisors carefully, and remember that while they can help, the buck will always stop with you.

Hold On to Your Sanity

So, you lead with both a gentle touch and a forceful hand. You try to maintain a steady base of customers while constantly seeking to expand upon that base. The business is growing, but with Herculean effort. You put in forty, fifty, sixty, seventy plus hours each week. Are you overworked? Yes. Underpaid? Yes. Underappreciated? Yes. It goes with the territory.

Whether you walk away to the golf course for a few hours, spend a day at the beach, or take a weekend away, you need to shut the cell phone off periodically and clear your head. Put someone else in charge and instruct her to reach you only in an emergency. Time spent away is time to refuel your body and your mind. Don't think about the office.

Know When to Hold, Know When to Fold

No entrepreneurial venture is risk-free. Taking that leap of faith is part of the thrill of starting something new. Businesses that make it over the long haul go through cycles of renewal, expansion, and all the attendant issues associated with starting something new. If you have the stomach for operating with a fair degree of uncertainty, and the willingness to learn what you don't know and make the most of the knowledge and resources you already have, then go for it.

Yet if, despite all of your hard work, the results don't seem to materialize, you may have had an idea ahead of its time, a shortage of capital to make the entity viable, or any of a host of other issues. A sensible person will accept the reality of disappointment before too much financial damage scorches all available resources.

APPENDIX B

Case Templates

There are hundreds of different variations of online businesses; in this appendix, we provide a few pointers on three: making a few extra dollars on the side, starting an online-only business from scratch, and moving an existing business online. Are these lists complete? Absolutely not. But they may help you think of the order of operations as you start your own online business.

Making a Few Dollars on the Side

Picture this scenario: you are working during the day, and you are looking to make a few dollars selling crafts online. Inventory isn't a problem: the challenge is selling them online at the same time as keeping your day job.

In this particular case, cash is at a premium; in fact, the entire reason for the part-time business is to generate more of it. As a result, it makes no sense—at least at the beginning—to invest in a custom website, complete with e-commerce. Instead, the decision should be to sell the products on others' stores: eBay, Craigslist, Kijiji, Etsy, and others. If you are reselling a well-known product, setting up a marketplace account on Amazon might even make sense. Eventually, you will earn enough money to afford a custom site: first using a low-cost (or free) template design from an Internet hosting company, and later a custom design that better reflects your products—and your unique brand.

Marketing can be done cheaply and easily in three ways: linking from other sites, being active in social media, and using your real-world network to drive traffic to the product pages. What is critically important for any product sales site is that each page contain appropriate keywords, so that it is easily indexed—and found—using Google.

While it might be tempting to think of this as bonus pocket change, your efforts are actually a business, and you need to treat them as such. Put together a budget, keep business records, and pay your taxes; doing this not only helps you track your progress—it's the law.

Building a Business All Online

In this scenario, you are looking to devote 110 percent of yourself to your new enterprise. While you may have a financial cushion from savings, severance, or family, you don't have unlimited funds, so you can't afford a misstep. Many people are able to transition from making a few dollars on the side to doing it full-time, but this case template is a bit more aggressive. You have decided to build something a bit bigger than just you by yourself—you have a unique product that you're hoping to introduce and sell online.

The most critical thing to do is to define your business tightly: who are you selling to, what do they need, and what are they willing to pay. Where will you source your products, and how will you deliver them to your customers? Once you've done some basic market research to test your assumptions, a business plan with complete financials is mandatory. How much capital will you need? What will you do with this money? And when will your business become profitable? If you are self-funded, then your budget can be used to track progress, giving you an early warning sign if things begin going off track. If you need to find external funding (investors and bankers), then a detailed business plan is the first thing they'll ask for.

Give your business a unique and memorable name, and then properly register the name (and the business itself) with all of the relevant authorities. At the same time, register the website domain names (.com, .net, .org, etc.) so no one else can get them first.

While it seems to be fashionable to create online businesses that foster "communities" (Twitter being an example), this type of undertaking is highly risky, as it requires continuous funding until the business is eventually sold. And such an effort assumes that the venture will actually be successful in generating "eyeballs." It's far better to develop a site that has a viable business model, based on that time-honored strategy: buy low/sell high.

Implementing a shopping cart and a WordPress-based website is relatively easy for most developers. The only question is what unique features do you want built in to differentiate yourself from the competition. And once these features are decided, what does your branding look like? While you are developing your site, make sure that social media and SEO are built in from the get-go. It's far easier to build these capabilities in at the beginning than adding them in later.

As you are starting from scratch, you don't need to worry about making an online business "fit" a real-world one—you can chart your own path. That being said, don't skimp on your branding or marketing. This is the number one area of connection between your prospects and you.

Marketing and sales are critical for any business. Budget enough to drive prospects to the site, using pay-per-click ads, links from partners, and off-web initiatives. Before spending a nickel, set goals for conversion (the percentage of browsers that turn into buyers).

Moving a "Real World" Business to the Web

In this case scenario, you have an already-existing business, and it's doing well. Your brochure-style website, however, hasn't changed in many years, and you are thinking of ways to use the web both to sell online—and to drive these customers to your real-world location.

The rationale for investing in your online business is both strategic and a competitive necessity: your customers are beginning to shop online . . . elsewhere. Better you serve them than someone else does.

It is too easy, as a successful business, to forget about your business plan, and just concentrate on your growing cash balance. Opening up an online division is something completely new, so building a new plan is actually quite important. It's the mechanism to force you to think through how to integrate your online and offline activities. The plan will help you measure progress—and ROI.

Low-Hanging Fruit

What is low-hanging fruit? Basically it's some quick and easy activities (listed here) to get you started.

1. Set up a detailed company page on LinkedIn (and a personal one, if you haven't yet done so). Depending on your business, you may also wish to set up a Facebook "fan page" as well. The goal is to increase your Internet presence beyond your older website, and provide a venue for your customers and prospects to interact with you.
2. Set up a Twitter account and begin tweeting information that would be of interest to your customers, including any sales, new products, free white papers, etc. Post similar status updates on Facebook and LinkedIn. The goal is to develop a group of followers who value your company and its products, then empower these people to spread your news to their friends. Think about how Apple has fostered customer loyalty—you should be striving to do the same over time.
3. Update your site to be on a "social" platform (e.g., WordPress), then begin a blog. WordPress will automatically send your content both to the social web and also directly to any person who subscribes to it. Build in the capability to sell—which means both a shopping cart and a credit card gateway. Don't forget to train your staff on how the website can be used—they need to know as much about the site as your prospects and customers.
4. Begin using a CRM to capture your prospects, and drive their conversion into customers. This can be done using web-based lead generation forms, marketing automation and campaigns, newsletters, and the like.

The key marketing goal is to use the web to build the relationship with your real-world customers, so they transact online, or they come to your business in the real world and transact there. At the same time, the web should be used to collect new prospects and have them either transact online, or if they are in the same geography as you, transact in person.

Your real-world location gives you a significant head start: purchasing, inventory, fulfillment, marketing, and human resources all are an extension of something that is running already—you don't have to start from scratch. They also give you a competitive edge. Consider the possibilities:

- In addition to online delivery, you can also offer in-store pickup.
- Customer training with real-world instructors can take place on your premises.
- Your history is valuable: "Since 1995" means that you know more about your products, industry, and area of expertise than a pure start-up.

Without web traffic, you will not sell an appreciable volume of products. You'll need to promote them if you want the sales. In-store ads, QR codes on brochures, traditional and online ads, and social media all can be used to drive users to your site. And depending on your budget, implementing a CRM system can tie it all together.

One of the challenges of a new online division is the assumption that everything is "the same," but just online. This isn't exactly the case. Customer service expectations may be higher, and if you are not responsive, any dissatisfaction will be broadcast on Facebook, LinkedIn, YouTube, and Twitter. Fraud needs to be monitored differently online versus off. And the profile of your online staff may be different than that of those you are used to hiring.

Once these basics are taken care of, your online business can look to getting to the next level. Are there any new products that can be sold to the same customers? Are there any of your products that can be converted to a digital format and sold as a downloadable file, or as part of a monthly membership site? Can you create a loyalty program that works both online and off?

Finally, make sure that your business systems (online and offline) are working in tandem: if you are out of a product on your shelves, it shouldn't show as available on your website. And of course, your financials need to reflect both online and offline operations.

Additional Resources

There are numerous organizations, websites, and associations that can help you research answers to questions regarding any aspect of business. The following list is only a small subset of the many sources that you might have. In a certain sense, Google has become the ultimate directory of resources.

Government and Association Sites

- **American Association of Franchisees and Dealers**
  www.aafd.org

- **American Society of Association Executives**
  www.asaecenter.org

- **Chamber of Commerce**
  www.USChamber.com

- **Dun & Bradstreet Corporation**
  www.dnb.com

- **Federal Trade Commission**
  www.ftc.gov

- **Internal Revenue Service**
  www.irs.gov

- **International Franchise Association**
  www.franchise.org

- **National Association for the Self-Employed**
  www.nase.org

- **National Association of Women Business Owners**
  www.nawbo.org

- **National Institute for Occupational Safety and Health**
  www.cdc.gov/niosh

- **Occupational Safety and Health Administration (OSHA)**
  www.osha.gov

- **U.S. Census Bureau**
  www.census.gov

- **U.S. Department of Commerce**
  www.commerce.gov

- **U.S. Department of Labor**
  www.dol.gov

- **U.S. Patent and Trademark Office**
  www.uspto.gov

- **U.S. Securities and Exchange Commission**
  www.sec.gov

- **U.S. Small Business Administration (SBA)**
  www.sba.gov

Other Reference Sites

- **AllBusiness.com**
  A comprehensive site with resources for small and medium-sized businesses.
  www.allbusiness.com

- **BizWeb.com**
  A guide to some 46,000 companies.
  www.bizweb.com

- **Bplans.com**
  Numerous sample business plans for various industries.
  www.bplans.com

- **BusinessFinance.com**
  A major online source for finding potential investors.
  www.businessfinance.com

- **Business Owners' Idea Café.com**
  A good place for news, tips, expert advice, ideas, and schmoozing with other small business owners.
  www.businessownersideacafe.com

- **Hoovers**
  Provides detailed business and company information, industry reports, links, professional help, business news, and more.
  www.hoovers.com

- **Inc.com**
  A wealth of articles and advice about starting and growing your business from the folks at Inc. magazine.
  www.inc.com

- **iPower.com**
  A web host for setting up your own website.
  www.ipower.com

- **morebusiness.com**
  Articles, tips, sample business and marketing plans, legal forms, contracts, a newsletter, and more are offered to entrepreneurs.
  www.morebusiness.com

- **My Own Business, Inc.**
  Free online course on how to start a business.
  www.myownbusiness.org

- **National Association of Small Business Investment Companies (NASBIC)**
  Promotes growth in the business sector through numerous programs.
  www.nasbic.org

- **Thomas Publishing Company, LLC**
  Publishers of industry trade directories, which include listings of manufacturers and distributors.
  www.thomaspublishing.com

- **Whois?**
  Site can be used to research ownership of domain names.
  www.whois.com

- **Women's Business Development Center**
  Many valuable resources on writing a business plan and going after funding.
  www.wbdc.org

Index

Shakespeare's
JULIUS
CAESAR

ROBERT LITTMAN
COLUMBIA UNIVERSITY

Edited by

FRANCES BARASCH
ASSISTANT PROFESSOR OF ENGLISH
STATE UNIVERSITY OF NEW YORK

MONARCH
PRESS

Published by
MONARCH PRESS
a Simon & Schuster division of
Gulf & Western Corporation
Simon & Schuster Building
1230 Avenue of the Americas
New York, N.Y. 10020

MONARCH PRESS and colophon are trademarks of
Simon & Schuster, registered in the U.S. Patent and
Trademark Office.

Standard Book Number: 0-671-00632-0

Library of Congress Catalog Card Number: 65-7227

Printed in the United States of America

CONTENTS

INTRODUCTION

SHAKESPEARE'S LIFE AND WORKS.   Shakespeare was born in Strat-
ford-on-Avon, a town not far from London, in April, 1564. His father,
a successful merchant, sent him to the local grammar school, where he
studied a considerable amount of Latin and somewhat less of Greek. He
probably acquired his first interest in English history at this time, and
an interest in drama, that was never to leave him. In 1582, at the age
of eighteen, Shakespeare married Anne Hathaway. Their first child
was born six months later; three children in all were born to them in
the space of three years.

Shakespeare came down to London sometime between 1585 and 1591,
when his play *The Comedy of Errors* probably was performed. During
this time he established himself as an actor and writer. He collaborated
on the three history plays of *Henry VI,* which were probably acted between 1590 and 1592. Soon after he wrote *Richard III* (published in
1594) and became a member of the acting company called the Lord
Chamberlain's Men. During this period, Shakespeare also wrote a number of light comedies and histories, which catered to the popular taste for
sensational effects and farcical situations. Toward the end of his first
decade as a dramatist, Shakespeare wrote a set of historical plays:
Richard II (c. 1593), *Henry IV* in two parts (1597-98), and *Henry
V* (1599). These chronicle plays reveal a loose and irregular structure,
but they also demonstrate Shakespeare's incrasing powers as a creator
of character and a recorder of life-like speech.

The tragedy of *Julius Caesar,* written in 1599, was perhaps the first of his
plays produced in the Globe, a theater which was built in the same
year and in which Shakespeare owned shares. *Julius Caesar* is generally
regarded as a transitional play between the early histories and the great
tragedies, *Hamlet, King Lear,* and *Macbeth,* which were written during
the following years. As a transitional play, *Julius Caesar* combines the
historical approach of Shakespeare's earlier works with the tragic mode
of his later plays. As in the earlier historical plays, the structure of
Julius Caesar is loose and episodic, the theme is political, and the ruler
dies before the end of the play. As other characters in the later tragedies,
so Brutus in *Julius Caesar* experiences inner conflict, makes the wrong
decisions, and brings destruction upon himself and upon those he loves.
Brutus' psychological struggle is Shakespeare's first great achievement in
portraying the inner conflict of a tragic character and anticipates the
development of his art in the direction of *Hamlet,* which is, perhaps, the
greatest of his tragic plays.

In the middle of his career, Shakespeare realized his full powers of
characterization in the plays *Hamlet* (1602), *Othello* (1604), *King Lear*
(1605), *Macbeth* (1606), and *Antony and Cleopatra* (c. 1608). His
work in this period also demonstrates a new philosophic turn of mind,

and the questioning spirit of *Hamlet* marks the "Problem Comedies": *All's Well that Ends Well* (1601-02), *Troilus and Cressida* (1603), and *Measure for Measure* (1604). Near the end of his life, Shakespeare returned to the comic genre with which he had begun his career and wrote *Pericles, Cymbeline, The Winter's Tale,* and *The Tempest.* These later comedies, however, are delicate and romantic pieces with a strong element of the fantastic which the early farces do not possess. In 1611, Shakespeare retired to his home in Stratford, where he died on April 23, 1616.

HISTORY OF THE PLAY. The earliest extant edition of *Julius Caesar* is in the First Folio edition of the works of Shakespeare, published in 1623. The date of its writing is generally determined as 1599. Meres' *Palladis Tamia,* published on September 7, 1598, lists Shakespearean plays which had already appeared but does not mention *Julius Caesar.* This indicates with a fair degree of certainty that the play was written after this date. The terminal date set for the writing of the play, 1599, is based on a reference to the speeches of Brutus and Antony over the body of Caesar (III.ii) in John Weever's *The Mirror of Martyrs,* which was written in 1599. The best corroborating evidence for this date is the journal of Thomas Platter, a Swiss traveler to England who saw a production of the play on September 21, 1599. Contemporary allusions to the play make it clear that it was well received. Performances of it are said to have taken place in the courts of James I, Charles I and, later, Charles II. Extremely popular in its own time, *Julius Caesar* has pleased countless audiences up to our own day.

SOURCES. It is widely acknowledged that Shakespeare borrowed the bulk of his material, both plot and characters, from Plutarch's *Lives of the Noble Grecians and Romans,* translated from the Greek into French by Jacques Amyet in 1559 and from French into English by Thomas North in 1579. The characters of Brutus, Cassius, Antony, Portia, Calpurnia, and others are much as Shakespeare found them in Plutarch's original, but it is generally agreed that Shakespeare's portrayal of Caesar differs widely from the noble, courageous, politically astute, amiable, cultivated, and sophisticated hero, described by the ancient Greek biographer, Plutarch, although the Victorian scholars Georg Brandes and Sir Mungo MacCallum have attempted to prove otherwise. Professor Ayres was one of the first to point out that the source of Shakespeare's characterization of Caesar was probably in popular Elizabethan conceptions of the stage Caesar or in characters of the conquering hero, which had frequently been portrayed on the Tudor stage. The resemblance between Shakespeare's Caesar and the Senecan Hercules type or the Marlovian Tamerlane character type is extremely close. All are valiant, boastful, almost superhuman characters, whose long habits of military conquest, success, and prosperity produce a false sense of security of their own invulnerability. Their overconfidence leads to the "judicial blindness," which makes them fatally ignore the precautions ordinarily taken by men.

HISTORICAL BACKGROUND.   The events of the play occur in 44
B.C. during a period of crisis in the Republic of Rome. Rome had been
plagued by political revolution and reform from the second century
B.C. until the fall of the Republic and the establishment of the Roman
Empire by Octavius in 27 B.C. During the second century B.C., a new
class of rich men had risen among the governors and generals of Rome's
expanding territories, while soil erosion and heavy taxation at home
had caused the rapid growth of a class of landless men. This economic
revolution spurred attempts to make political changes, notably by Tiberius and Gaius Gracchus, tribunes of the people, whose strong sense
of civic responsibility had been handed down to them from their heroic
grandfather, Scipio Africanus. The political and social reforms attempted by the Gracchi, who were hostile to the patrician Senate of
Rome, were ended by Tiberius' murder in 133 and by Gaius' suicide in
121 B.C. But a reform party emerged from the democratic efforts of the
Gracchi, and it remained hostile to the Senate for the remainder of the
Republic. Both reformers and senators looked to the military for support of their different causes, and the power shifted between reformers
and conservative generals for several decades before Caesar's rule. The
Senate appointed th general Sulla to fight Marius, a general who sup-
ported the Gracchan tradition. Marius remained in control until 86
B.C., but with his death, Sulla became the power in Rome and by 84
B.C., had become its absolute dictator.

After Sulla's retirement the old political issues were revived. Those who
followed the Gracchan tradition wished to extend democracy and decrease the powers of the Senate and of the wealthy patrician class,
while conservative Romans continued to exalt the Senate. The pattern
of allowing generals to seize control of the state, established by Marius
and Sulla, was followed by Caesar, the most competent and most
ambitious of the Roman generals. In 60 B.C., Caesar became a member
of the first triumvirate, a coalition ruling body composed of Caesar, Pompey and Crassus, who were to act with the counsel of the Senate. In
49 B.C., Caesar made his move to become supreme ruler of Rome by
defying Senate orders and leading his army across the Rubicon in
pursuit of his Republican enemies. He defeated Pompey, his fellow
triumvir and champion of the Senate, at Pharsalia in 47 B.C. Then he
pursued Pompey to Egypt in order to make the defeat final. Pompey
was already dead when Caesar arrived in Egypt (where he had his
famous liaison with Cleopatra). Pompey's sons were slain in the battle
at Munda, Spain in March 45 B.C., and by the end of the year Caesar
was back in Rome, a conquering hero. With the backing of the people
he established himself as dictator, and served until his assassination in
March of 44 B.C.

Caesarism, which the assassins had hoped to exterminate by the murder
of Julius Caesar, had only begun to be formulated during the dictator's
lifetime. Caesar had succeeded in totally subverting the decaying institutions of the Republic. He ended the system of checks and balances

among the various assemblies and officials, assumed all powers as con-
sul, tribune of the people, ruler, and chief priest. The Senate became
Caesar's tool, adopting his proposals without opposition. (The hero-
worship of Caesar anticipated his deification during a later regime.)
Octavius, Caesar's grand-nephew, adopted son and heir, continued his
uncle's aims. To achieve complete power, he pursued Antony to Egypt,
where, in the face of defeat, Antony and Cleopatra committed suicide.
In 30 B.C., Egypt was annexed to Rome, and the Republic, soon after
the death of Antony, expired at last.

Octavius called himself the restorer of the Roman Republic, but he
had, in fact, established the Empire of Rome. He lived simply and pre-
tended to prefer the modest title *Princeps* (first citizen) to the more
grandiose *Augustus* (revered one). He established a dyarchy, that is, a
rule of two, himself and the Senate. In practice, however, the government was a monarchy rather than a republic. He retained the Senate
but purged it of reformers, deprived it of control over the army and
taxes, and made it a tool of his whims. In 42 B.C., the Senate declared
Julius Caesar a god, making Octavius the son of a god as well as the
supreme monarch over Rome.

All effective and potential opposition was wiped out by Octavius, so
that the spirit of Caesarism survived in the empire he had established,
and the spirit of the Republic was extinguished. Shakespeare's play *Julius
Caesar* recreates the last days of the Republic, when Caesar, the man,
is killed and Caesarism, the spirit of the Empire, is born. Brutus and
Cassius, the last of the great republicans, struggle hopelessly against
the second triumvirate and destiny, and are conquered by the heirs and
the spirit of Caesar.

SHAKESPEARE'S USE OF HISTORY.   To those who are familiar with
Roman history, Shakespeare's method of telescoping events, incorporating anachronisms, and using license in his historical portraits may prove
confusing. Shakespeare was a dramatist, not a historian, and chrono-
logical or historical accuracy was less important to him than the creation of a single unified draamtic effect. With this end in mind,
Shakespeare condensed history wherever and whenever such condensa-
tion suited the character, plot, or passions he chose to create. Historically, the events enacted in *Julius Caesar* took place over a period of
years. Dramatically, these events occur in six days.

Caesar began his pursuit of Pompey in 49 B.C. and finally defeated
the sons of Pompey at Munda in 45 B.C. He returned to Rome in
October of that year, months before the celebration of the Feast of
Lupercal, which was held on February 15, 44 B.C. Caesar was murdered
on the ides of March, 44 B.C., a month after the Lupercalia, and his
adopted son Octavius did not reach Rome for two more months. The
meeting of the second triumvirate was held on November 43 B.C., and
it was an entire year later that the battle of Philippi took place. At this
battle both Brutus and Cassius committed suicide.

It can be seen that history moves slowly. The emotional impact of Caesar's death, the timely arrival of Octavius, and the swift retribution which descends upon the assassins is heightened by the rapid sequence in which these events are presented in the play.

If Shakespeare was careful to condense history to suit his dramatic purposes, he was careless about historical details and more than once introduces anachronisms into his play. In Julius Caesar, a clock chimes before the clock was invented, and Brutus discovers Cassius' body at sunset, after which he engages in battle on the afternoon of the same day. The costumes, trades, and habits of many of the characters are Elizabethan; some of these will be pointed out in the commentary which accompanies the summary of the play.

Shakespeare also used license in his portrayal of historical characters, at times borrowing information and often whole lines and passages from his biographical source, and at other times ignoring large bodies of fact, which he must have known, but which he did not choose to use. Shakespeare's portrait of Caesar, for example, is an interpretive rather than a historical one. Caesar is shown as degenerating when, bloated by conquests, he returns to Rome as an arrogant demagogue. His nobility and courage, his political astuteness, his charm and gaiety, all of which are recorded in Plutarch, are submerged in the pompous manners and language of Shakespeare's Caesar and appear only occasionally during the first half of the play. After the assassination takes place in the play, however, Antony's eulogy portrays the Caesar who has come down to us in history as the conqueror, true friend, and lover of the people.

BRIEF SUMMARY OF *JULIUS CAESAR*

As the play opens, the Roman people have turned out to celebrate the triumphal return of Caesar from his victory over Pompey (a member of the first triumvirate and champion of the Republic). Flavius and Marullus, two tribunes (officers appointed to protect the interests of the people from possible injustice at the hands of patrician magistrates) disperse the crowd of commoners, arguing that Caesar's triumph in civil war is no cause for celebration and that the people had much better weep for Pompey, who they had formerly adored.

Accompanied by fanfare and a large following, Caesar arrives to witness the race traditionally held on the Feast of Lupercal, which is being celebrated on the same day. A soothsayer warns Caesar to beware the ides of March, but Caesar peruses the man's face and dismisses him as a dreamer. Meanwhile, Cassius tell Brutus of his resentment of Caesar's growing power. As Caesar emerges from the race, he eyes Cassius and tells Antony that he does not trust men with a lean and hungry look. Casca joins Brutus and Cassius and describes how Caesar had reluctantly refused the crown offered to him three times by Mark Antony. Brutus promises to think over Cassius' fear that Caesar's ambition is a danger to the democracy of Rome and agrees to meet him the next day. Casca is invited to join them.

During a violent storm, Casca and Cicero meet and discuss the great wonders that have occurred that night. After Cicero leaves, Cassius arrives, explains the omens of the storm and discusses a conspiracy against Caesar. They both plot how they might win Brutus over to their side completely, for he is already inclined against Caesar.

Alone in his garden, Brutus debates with himself over the threat that Caesar poses to the Republic. At last he decides that Caesar must be killed because he might become a tyrant. The conspirators, Cassius, Casca, Decius, Brutus, Cinna, Metellus Cimber, and Trebonius arrive at this point, and Brutus sanctions the decision to kill Caesar the next day when he is to receive the crown of king. They decide that only Caesar is to die. Portia, Brutus' wife, enters after the conspirators have left. She entreats Brutus to tell her what is happening, but as he is about to reveal the conspiracy to her, another conspirator, Ligarius, arrives and takes Brutus away.

Caesar, meanwhile, spends a restless night. His wife, Calpurnia, begs him not to go to the Senate meeting that day because she has dreamed that she saw a statue of him, spouting blood like a fountain, and because of the ominous events which have occurred during the storm. Caesar sends his servant to the seers to make a sacrifice and to determine what the gods are trying to say. The augurers tell Caesar to stay at home, and Caesar decides to comply, especially since his wife has urged him so strongly. However, one of the conspirators, Caesar's good friend, Decius Brutus, persuades him to go to the Senate by pointing out how ridiculous he would seem to heed his wife's superstitions.

The same morning, Artemidorus, a teacher of rhetoric, prepares a letter for Caesar, warning him of the conspiracy. The Soothsayer also prepares to stop Caesar outside the Capitol to warn him of harm, and Portia, who now knows Brutus' plan, anxiously anticipates its outcome.

Caesar is given two warnings; he ignores them both, goes into the Senate, and after a speech in which he arrogantly praises himself, he is stabbed by the conspirators.

Mark Antony, who has been lured out of the Senate by Trebonius, returns after the murder and pretends to join the conspirators. When left alone with the body of Caesar, however, Antony vows to avenge the murder, even if he has to throw all Italy into civil war to do it. Meanwhile, Octavius, Caesar's heir, arrives near Rome. Antony and a servant carry Caesar's body out to the Forum. Brutus addresses the crowd first, telling them that Caesar was killed because he was too ambitious. The crowd reacts favorably to Brutus and is ready to make him a second Caesar, but Brutus orders them to listen to Antony's funeral oration for Caesar.

In a brilliantly ironic speech, Antony inflames the crowd against the conspirators. The crowd runs wildly through the streets, determined to burn the houses of the conspirators. The mob comes upon Cinna the poet who happens to have the same name as one of the conspirators, and for the sake of destruction, they tear him to pieces. Brutus and Cassius flee from Rome. Antony, Octavius, and Lepidus unite forces, calling themselves the second triumvirate. They prepare to put to death those whom they suspect will be hostile to their cause.

Brutus and Cassius, meanwhile, have gathered their forces in Sardis in Asia Minor. Their destruction is forecast when the Republican leaders begin to quarrel with each other. Brutus rebukes Cassius because the latter has permitted an officer to take bribes and because he has not been sending money to Brutus, who has ben unable to raise his own funds. His anger spent, Brutus apologizes for his ill-temper and informs Cassius that Portia has killed herself. By the time official word is brought that Portia is dead, Brutus has accepted the news with quiet resignation. During the night, Brutus sees the ghost of Caesar, who says that they will meet again at Philippi.

Cassius and Brutus then march to Philippi in Greece to meet the armies of Antony and Octavius. The generals meet and exchange insults before the battle begins. In the first engagement, Antony overcomes Cassius, while Brutus overcomes Octavius' wing. Cassius retires to a nearby hill, and when he mistakes approaching horsemen for enemies, he runs upon a sword held by his servant, Pindarus. Brutus and not the enemy arrives, finds Cassius' body, and sends it away for burial. There is another skirmish and Brutus' forces are defeated completely. Unwilling to endure the dishonor of capture, Brutus commits suicide with the aid of his servant, Strato. Antony and Octavius find Brutus' body, over which Antony states, "This was the noblest Roman of them all." Octavius declares that Brutus will receive burial befitting his virtue, and calls an end to battle as the play concludes.

DETAILED SUMMARY OF *JULIUS CAESAR*

ACT I: SCENE i

The play opens in a street in Rome. Two tribunes, Flavius and Marullus, are dispersing the crowds that have gathered there. The tribunes have trouble extracting an explanation from a cobbler who appears to be leading the mob, for the cobbler gives equivocal answers to the direct questions of the officials. He claims to be a "mender of bad soles," "a surgeon to old shoes," and one who lives by the "awl." Finally, he admits that the workingmen have left their shops and have assembled "to see Caesar and to rejoice in his triumph."

COMMENT. Although the scene is Rome, the atmosphere is Elizabethan, and the workers here behave like pert Tudor craftsmen. In his portrayal of crowds and of workingmen, Shakespeare frequently relied on humor to establish the unruly atmosphere and vulgar tone of the scene. The cobbler's humor is typical of his craft, and he puns on the words of his trade: "all" (awl), "cobbler" (shoemaker, bungler), "sole," (soul), "out" (out of shoes, out of temper), "recover" (save, mend).

Elizabethan trades were ranked according to the dignity of the craft, and although the shoemaker's trade was among the lowest, Shakespeare has the cobbler lead the mob, partly to show how vulgar the leadership is, and partly because of the popular legend of the shoemaker who became the leader of the people and the mayor of London.

Flavius and Marullus are Tribunes of the People, officers who were appointed to protect the interests of plebeians from injustices that might be perpetrated by patrician magistrates. They could reverse a magistrate's judgment or inflict punishment on a plebeian. In Caesar's time, however, their powers were nominal. In this scene, the tribunes are trying to protect the democracy of Rome by preventing their charges from installing a dictator in office.

Marullus is incensed by the reason he is given. He rebukes the commoners for gathering to honor Caesar. What territories has Caesar conquered for Rome, the tribune asks; what prisoners has he led home? He reproaches the people for their hard hearts and senseless cruelty in forgetting Pompey so soon after they had cheered him. He reminds the mob of how they had lined the streets and climbed the battlements of buildings, sitting there all day with babes in arms to get just a glimpse of Pompey when he returned after a victory. "And do you now strew flowers in his way/That comes in triumph over Pompey's blood?" Marullus harangues. He warns the unfeeling mob that their ingratitude will be repaid by plague if they do not disperse immediately and pray mercy of the gods. Flavius enjoins the people to run to the Tiber and weep for Pompey until the river is filled with tears up to its highest bank.

> **COMMENT.** The tribunes' harangues are spoken from the point of view of the Republican who is sickened by the conquest of a Roman over a Roman. Caesar's triumph was not over a foreign nation but over Pompey and his sons, all fellow Romans. Pompey had been a member of the first triumvirate, formed in 60 B.C. by Pompey, Caesar, and Crassus. They were a coalition group, holding supreme political authority over Rome, subject to the advice and veto of the Senate, a legislative body, comprised mainly of noblemen or patricians. Pompey was married to Caesar's daughter by a former wife, but after the daughter's death, disagreement flared out between Caesar and Pompey. As champion for the Senate, Pompey fought Caesar when he sought to overthrow the triumvirate, disobey the Senate, and establish himself as dictator of Rome. Pompey was assassinated in Egypt, but his sons continued his fight at Munda in Spain. The death of Pompey's sons, that is, "Pompey's blood," meant the death of the Republic, for which the plebeians should have no cause to rejoice.

> The commoners, however, are more concerned with personal favors than with abstract political principles and the interests of the mainly patrician Senate. They have been won over to Caesar's side by his previous gifts to the people. After his triumph of 46 B.C., for example, Caesar entertained the people with feasts and shows and gave one hundred denarii to each citizen. The capricious nature of the mob is established at this point when Marullus complains about their ingratitude and the fickle transfer of their affections from Pompey, whom they had formerly adored, to Caesar.

When the commoners leave, Flavius remarks, "They vanish tongue-tied in their guiltiness." Then he instructs Marullus to go through the city and "disrobe the images," that is, remove the decorations intended to honor Caesar. Marullus asks if it would not be sacrilege to remove the decorations for the Feast of Lupercal, which is being celebrated on this same day, but Flavius replies that it does not matter. He also orders Marullus to drive the vulgar from the streets so that the absence of the people (who grew like feathers on Casaer's wing and enable him to fly higher than he otherwise could) will keep Caesar's ambitions in check.

> **COMMENT.** The idea of desecration is suggested at this point in connection with the removal of the decorations for Caesar's triumph and the Feast of Lupercal. The Lupercalia was an annual festival, celebrated in honor of the god Pan or Faunus and ad-

ministered by the members of two ancient families of Rome. In 44 B.C., the Luperci Iulii was instituted in honor of Julius Caesar, which probably explains why Shakespeare condensed history so that Caesar's triumph and the Lupercalia would fall on the same day.

The purpose of the feast held in February was to secure expiation, purification, and fertility for the spring planting. The rites included a race around the Palatine by two youths carrying thongs made from a sacrificed he-goat. Women who stood in the path of the runners would receive blows from the thongs, which were believed to be a charm against barrenness.

Shakespeare achieved special effects by telescoping history. In this scene, he makes Caesar's return coincide with the Lupercalia, suggesting thereby that Caesar, the astute politician, had timed his arrival for a day on which the streets would be crowded with a cheerful public and the statues adorned for the feast as well as for his return. In this way, objections that the people were not at work or that the statues were adorned in his honor would be answered by the feast. At the same time, Caesar would be associating his return with a religious occasion and work on the superstitions of the people who would eventually proclaim him a god and accept him as their dictator. It was in this month, in fact, that Caesar was proclaimed *Dictator Perpetuus* (dictator for life) and that the Lupercalia was named in his honor.

The idea of Caesar's ambition is introduced in Flavius' metaphor of the bird, in which he states that the people's adulation allows Caesar to place himself above other citizens of the Republic and that there is danger he will become a king and keep "us all in servile fearfulness."

SUMMARY. This first scene works as a skillful introduction to the major action of the play. It represents the crowd as a vulgar and capricious mob, who will be important in the political action which ensues. It supplies the background of events to come by representing the civil disorder which exists in Rome and the differencs which exist between two main factions of the city; the commoners who favor Caesar and the tribunes who are Republicans. The case for the Republicans is stated by Marullus, who is angry at the "senseless" mob for celebrating Caesar's triumph over Pompey, another Roman. Flavius establishes the fact that Caesar is ambitious, that he flies too high, and that he is a danger to free men. It is suggested that Caesar is a shrewd politician for arranging his arrival to coincide with the Feast of Lupercal, when crowds would be available to cheer him and when images would be adorned to honor him as well as the god Faunus. The idea of desecration is suggested when Flavius orders the disrobing of the images.

ACT I: SCENE ii

Shortly after the crowds have been dispersed by the tribunes, a procession arrives. There is music and pageantry as Caesar, Antony, Calpurnia, Portia, Decius, Brutus, Cicero, Brutus, Cassius, and Casca, dressed in elegant attire, march through the street. A large crowd follows the procession which is on its way to the race traditionally held on the Lupercal.

Caesar calls to his wife, Calpurnia, and tells her to stand directly in Antony's way, as he runs through the streets. He orders Antony to strike her since "the barren touched in this holy chase, / Shake off their sterile curse." Antony replies to Caesar's command, "When Caesar says 'do this,' it is performed."

> **COMMENT.** At the Feast of Lupercal, young noblemen ran naked through the streets, striking women, who deliberately stood in their way, believing that if they were pregnant, they should deliver well, and if they were barren, that they would become pregnant. Antony's comment shows that he is Caesar's devoted and obedient follower.

From the crowd a Soothsayer emerges and cries to Caesar, "Beware the ides of March!" Caesar asks the Soothsayer to come forward and repeat what he has just said. He peruses the man's face, hears the warning again, and decides, "He is a dreamer; let us leave him."

> **COMMENT.** The Soothsayer's prophetic warning is heavy with dramatic irony, for the audience knows that Caesar will be killed on the ides (the fifteenth) of March, while Caesar, who studies the man and his words, exercises poor judgment in dismissing both.
>
> In ancient Greek drama, the solution of an oracle or riddle brought about the tragic resolution of the play at the point when the hero learned the true meaning of the oracle. The ambiguous prophecy of the Soothsayer works in a similar way. It creates dramatic suspense as the audience anticipates Caesar's discovery of the tragic import of the riddle.

As Caesar and his followers go off to the feast, Cassius and Brutus remain behind. Brutus tells Cassius that he will not follow the course of the young men (as they race around the city), for he is not "gamesome" and has not Antony's "quick spirit." Cassius expresses his fear that his good friend Brutus disapproves of him, for his looks no longer show his former love. Brutus assures Cassius that he is not vexed with his friend but with himself. He is, in fact, "with himself at war" and "forgets the show of love to other men."

COMMENT. The friendship and love between Brutus and Cassius is established in this conversation, and indication is given for the first time that Brutus is in a state of inner conflict. The face as a reflection of the feelings and thoughts of men is a recurrent theme in this scene. Caesar has scanned the soothsayer's face and has misjudged him as a dreamer, and Cassius has misjudged Brutus' "ungentle" eyes as a sign of his own disfavor.

Next, Cassius will read Brutus' face to him as if he were holding up a mirror before him. The mirror as a reflection of the moral nature of man was a popular device in the literature of Tudor England. The book called *A Mirror for Magistrates*, consisting of a series of morally edifying biographies of famous princes, went through eight editions in the years between 1555 and 1587. Its theme, copied by such notable writers as George Gascoigne, Samuel Daniel, and Michael Drayton, had a powerful influence on the chronicle plays of the 1580's and 1590's, Shakespeare's included. The idea was to present stories or biographies of important men who, through some flaw of character, worked out their destinies in a tragic way. The retelling of these tragedies was expected to have a moral influence on the reader.

In addition, poems like Gascoigne's *Steel Glass* and Sir John Davies' *Nosce Teipsum* used the mirror device as a means of reflecting the abuses of the times and the horrors of man's own sinful nature. It was important for man to learn to "know thyself," these poems taught; man was to search his own nature for the causes of evil. Cassius' desire to show Brutus his reflection in other men's eyes has a Machiavellian cast to it. He wishes to influence him to join a conspiracy. Morally speaking, Brutus must discover his own nature by himself.

The various characters who participate in this scene are also described as reflections in other men's eyes, and it should be noted that Shakespeare unites dramatic exposition, characterization, and dialogue through the use of the mirror metaphor.

Relieved to learn that he is still in Brutus' favor, Cassius tells his friend that he had misunderstood his emotional state and had refrained from discussing important matters with him. He asks Brutus if he can read his own character, which shines in his own face, revealing that Brutus is a just man. Many men, "except immortal Caesar," are now enslaved by Caesar's rule and wish that Brutus had Caesar's eyes so that Brutus could see his own nobility as Caesar sees his own.

COMMENT. Cassius has uttered the first in a series of persuasive remarks designed to win Brutus to the anti-Caesarsist cause. His reference to "immortal Caesar" is a sarcastic and covert allusion to the dictator's wish to be declared a god and to his ambitious desire to rise above his fellow Romans, who consider themselves his equals. Brutus is self-effacing, apparently, and Cassius works on his natural humility by reporting the praise other men have given him. At the same time, he is suggesting that many respected men of Rome compare Brutus to Caesar, wishing that Brutus had a higher opinion of himself so that he might take action against the self-esteeming dictator. Thus, the characters of Brutus and Caesar are juxtaposed from the conspirator's point of view; Brutus' humility is contrasted with Caesar's presumptuousness and arrogance.

Having thus complimented Brutus, Cassius prepares to tell Brutus the subject of his argument. But first, he testifies to his own honest character, his veracity, his sobriety, his loyalty to friends.

COMMENT.   Cassius is following rhetorical procedure in the persuasive argument he is about to deliver. He fails to come straight to the point, but first greets and compliments his audience, then attempts to establish the authority of the speaker. (Brutus will use this device in his address to the mob after Caesar's death.) Cassius' oratory is cut short, however, when a fanfare is sounded from the market-place, but after the interruption, Cassius announces his subject and proceeds to develop it.

Shouts are heard and a sennet is sounded (a series of bars played on a trumpet, symbolizing sovereignty). Brutus blurts out his fear that the people have chosen Caesar for their king. Cassius latches on to Brutus' expression of fear: "Ay do you fear it"/Then must I think you would not have it so." Briefly, Brutus answers that he would not have Caesar king, and yet he loves him. Then he urges Cassius to go on with his message and promises that if it concerns the general good, even the fear of death will not permit him from doing what is honorable.

COMMENT.   Caught unaware, Brutus states his inner conflict between his duty to the Republic and his personal love for Caesar. He admits, however, that he loves honor more than he fears death, and that he will act in the public good at any cost. Cassius' course is now clear to him. He must convince Brutus that the removal of Caesar is in the public interest.

Elizabethans associated the ancient Romans with the idea of noble friendship and dedicated statesmanship. Shakespeare expected his audience to realize the deep perturbation which would arise in a man when these two ideals came into conflict.

Returning to his speech and taking his cue from Brutus' remark about honor, Cassius announces his subject is honor. He cannot tell what other men think, but speaking for himself, Cassius states his preference for death to subjugation under a man who is no better than he. Caesar is just another such man, Cassius argues. He and Caesar were born equally free, were nurtured equally and endure the cold in the same way. In fact, Cassius claims, Caesar cannot swim as well as he, for once in a swimming contest, Cassius, like Aeneas (founder of Rome, who bore his father Anchises on his shoulders to save him from the flaming city of Troy), bore Caesar to safety on his shoulders. Another time, when Caesar was afflicted by fever in Spain, he cried for water as a sick girl might. Cassius is angered at the thought that a man of such "feeble temper" should now rule the majestic world alone, while Cassius, his equal, must bend to Caesar's slightest nod.

> **COMMENT.** Cassius' reasons for hating Caesar are all personal ones and are, therefore, considered ignoble and envious. Cassius has indicated, however, that other noble Romans prefer death to slavery, although he does not pretend to be able to advance their motives. The portrait of Caesar is painted from a Republican's point of view, it should be remembered. Cassius emphasizes the physical deterioration, which Caesar actually displayed in the declining years of his life, but he ignores the heroic parts of the conquering hero. Cassius' amazement at Caesar's success reveals his own blindness to an important point. It is not Caesar's physical strength which has made him a dictator, but the spirit of Caesar, an intangible idea, which has raised him above his fellows.

The crowd roars and the trumpet flourishes a second time. Brutus surmises that some new honors are being heaped on Caesar. Cassius compares Caesar to a Colossus and calls Brutus and himself "petty men," who walk under the legs of this giant. "The fault, dear Brutus, is not in our stars./But in ourselves, that we are underlings," Cassius states. Then he asks: "Why should that name be sounded more than yours." Once more he alludes to Caesar's physical attributes and asks by what virtue he has become great: "Upon what meat doth this our Caesar feed/That he is grown so great?" The reputation of Rome rests in the fact that it does not esteem "one only man." He ends his exhortation to Brutus by reminding him of his namesake, Lucius Junius Brutus (a Roman hero who had expelled Rome's last king, Tarquin, five hundred years earlier).

> **COMMENT.** Cassius' reference to Brutus' namesake links Brutus with the ideal of liberty and the Republic. Cassius shows that he is concerned with the reputation of Rome and that he does not want Caesar's position for himself when he argues that "since the great flood" Rome "was famed with more than with one man." It has been argued, however, that Cassius is motivated solely by the desire for personal power and envy of Caesar. Antony says this too in the closing scene of the play. We should view Cassius, however, not as a black or white figure, but as a gray one, who is noble, although not the "noblest."

Brutus replies to Cassius' argument point for point. He assures Cassius that he is not suspicious of his love and that he is somewhat inclined toward Cassius' sentiments. But exactly what he thinks of conditions in Rome must be discussed at another time. Brutus promises to consider what Cassius has already said, to listen to him further and to answer him at a later time. For the present, Brutus tells Cassius, "chew upon this: "Brutus had rather be a villager/Than to repute himself a son of Rome/Under these hard conditions as this time/Is like to lay upon us."

> **COMMENT.** The "villager" to whom Brutus refers was neither a patrician nor a plebeian and not have rights as a citizen of Rome, but Brutus rhetorically asserts that even the villager's position is preferable to a Roman's under a monarchy. Brutus is not easily persuaded or inflamed by Cassius' passions. He shares Cassius' sentiments but has not yet decided if action is called for. Cassius, we shall see, is aware of Brutus' reflective nature and will use means other than argument to win Brutus to his cause.

The conversation is concluded by Caesar's return from the race. Brutus detects anger on the face of the dictator; he notices the paleness of Calpurnia's cheeks and the fires that burn from Cicero's eyes as if he had been "crossed in conference by some senators." Caesar, on his part, spies Cassius standing by, and turning to Antony, he tells him that he trusts fat men above lean ones. "Yond Cassius has a lean and hungry look! /He thinks too much, such men are dangerous." Antony urges Caesar not to fear Cassius, for he is a noble Roman of excellent disposition. Caesar asserts that he has no fear, "for always I am Caesar," but if he had, he would avoid Cassius more than any other man. He contrasts Cassius with Antony, who loves plays and music and laughter. Cassius, on the other hand, is never entertained; he reads a great deal, watches men, and penetrates the motives behind their deeds. He rarely smiles, except as if in self-mockery. Such men are dangerous, Caesar warns Antony, insisting that he says this by way of instructing Antony in the ways of men and not because he is expressing his own fear. As Caesar leaves with his train, he bids Antony come to his right side, because he is deaf in the left ear, and tell him what he really thinks of Cassius.

> **COMMENT.** The reading of faces is continued in this episode, and the respective observers interpret character from the appearance and habits of the man in question. Brutus observes the spot of anger on Caesar's brow and remarks that the whole company looks like a "chidden train." He deduces that something has happened which they do not like. Caesar characterizes Cassius as dangerous because he is observant and perceptive, traits which are appropriate to Cassius' lean and hungry look. Antony is apparently fatter, loves pleasure more than Cassius and values the noble arts of poetry and music; as a follower, Caesar implies, he is a man to be trusted.

This is the second of Caesar's brief appearances onstage since the opening of the play. Much has been said about him from the Republican point of view. The tribunes and Cassius fear Caesar's ambition, and Brutus indicates that he has similar trepidations

himself. Apart from Caesar's costume and the pomp and ceremony which accompany his appearance, Caesar so far displays
none of the special virtues which have made him a conqueror and
dictator and beloved by the common people of Rome. His physical
condition is in a state of decay. In his first appearance we learned
that his wife is sterile, which suggests Caesar's own aging im-
potence. Now we see that he is deaf in one ear. According to
dramatic chronology and Cassius' report, Caesar has recently
suffered from fever in Spain and that he has never been especially
adept in physical feats. Disease and infirmity will continue to be
associated with Caesar until his tragic death scene. These infirmities reflect the diseases of his times; factionalism, civil disorder,
and sacrilege, which finally overcome Caesar, but not his spirit,
which lives on in Octavius. (Compare Caesar's infirmities with
those of the king in Shakespeare's *2 Henry IV*.)

Also worthy of notice is Caesar's protestation that he does not
fear Cassius, "for always I am Caesar." This has been interpreted
as a cover for Caesar's real fear of Cassius, as a sign of Caesar's
arrogance for disdaining the emotions which other men have,
and also as a mark of real fearlessness which is associated with
the regal and courageous nature of the man.

When Caesar leaves, Brutus grasps Casca's cloak and asks the cause
of Caesar's anger. Casca replies that Antony had offered him the crown
three times and that three times Caesar refused it. Each time Antony held
out the crown, Caesar fingered it, but discerning the mood of the mob
which rejected monarchy, he put it aside. To Casca's thinking, however,
he refused the crown more reluctantly each time. Then, Casca relates,
Caesar fainted. Brutus remarks that Caesar has the falling-sickness (epi-
lepsy). Cassius ironically replies that it is not Caesar, but they, who
have the falling-sickness (that is, the Republic is falling). Having thrice
refused the crown and thrice seen how glad the people were at his
refusal, Casca continues, Caesar opened his doublet and offered them
his throat to cut. Casca admits that if he had had a weapon, he would
have taken up Caesar's offer. Casca goes on to say that when Caesar
recovered from his fainting spell, he blamed his actions on his infirmity,
and the mob forgave him. Casca ends his description with the words:
"If Caesar had stabbed their mothers, they would have done no less."

COMMENT.   We learn shortly that Casca is a "blunt fellow,"
who had a "quick mettle" (a good wit) at one time and which
he still has when noble action calls for it. However, he has learned
to put on "tardy form" (to act like a fool) and to appear to be
rude in order to add "sauce" to "his good wit" so that men can
better receive the truth he utters. Casca himself calls the business
at the race "foolery," and so it was, according to Plutarch, who
was Caesar's biographer. Like Plutarch, Casca suggests that Antony's offer of the crown and Caesar's refusal was a prearranged
plan, designed to test the reactions of the crowd toward the ele-

vation of Caesar from dictator to monarch. The crowd loves Caesar as dictator, but it is not ready to install him as monarch. The disappointment at having been cheered for refusing the crown explains Caesar's anger as he leaves the race.

Casca is a Republican, however, and he later joins the conspirators against Caesar. His interpretations of Caesar's refusal of the crown, as Casca repeatedly insists, is "to my thinking," "to my thinking," "and for mine own part." Shakespeare emphasizes that the description of events is being given from Casca's points of view and suggests that Caesar is more noble than Casca (or Plutarch) believes.

Casca's report and opinion roughly follows that of Plutarch's in his treatment of the episode in which Caesar offers his throat to be cut. In Plutarch, there is no doubt that Caesar wanted the crown and that he used ruses to test the people's reactions to his ambition. But in Shakespeare, the description of events is put into the mouth of a fool (who may not be a fool), and the entire subject of Caesar's ambition is thus put open to question. Was he ambitious, as Brutus later states, or did he put by the crown sincerely, as Antony implies.

In reply to Brutus' question on Cicero's reaction to the events at the Lupercalia, Casca answers that Cicero spoke Greek to his friends, but "it was Greek to me." He states further that Marullus and Flavius have been "silenced" for pulling garlands off Caesar's statues.

COMMENT.   We learn that the images disrobed by the tribunes were really statues of Caesar bedecked with scarves of honor. The suggestion is that Caesar has allowed the people to treat him as a diety and that he has punished the tribunes for attempting to prevent their action. There is no doubt from Casca's point of view that Caesar is ambitious and presumptuous.

Seeing that Casca feels the same way toward Caesar as he does, Cassius invites him to dinner. After Casca leaves, Brutus comments that Casca is unpolished, but Cassius explains that Casca's rudeness is a mask behind which he can speak the truth freely. Repeating his promise to talk more the next day, Brutus leaves.

Alone on the stage, Cassius states that Brutus is a noble man, but that he sees Brutus can be diverted from his natural inclinations. Reflecting that noble minds should always keep company with other noble minds lest they be seduced, Cassius also observes that no one is so firm that he cannot be persuaded to change his course. He acknowledges that he is in Caesar's disfavor and that Brutus is loved by Caesar, but if he were Brutus, Cassius asserts, he would not let Caesar's love prevent him from following his principles. Cassius then announces his plan to win over Brutus completely. He will forge letters from leading citizens in which he will praise Brutus' name and hint covertly at

Caesar's dangerous ambition to overthrow the Republic. After the letters have been thrown into Brutus' window and he has read them, Caesar should beware, for "We will shake him or worse days endure."

COMMENT.   Cassius speaks the play's first soliloquy, a monologue in which the speaker reveals his thoughts to the audience. Since no dramatic interaction takes place during the soliloquy, it is a traditional dramatic convention that the speaker always utters the truth.

We learn Cassius' real feelings, motives, and plans from this speech. Brutus is indeed noble, but he can be moved. Cassius' reflection on the company noble minds should keep may mean that Brutus has made a mistake in befriending him, but it is more likely that Cassius feels Brutus is lucky to have him as a friend, for Cassius will lead him to "noble enterprise" (of the sort Casca will also participate in).

Cassius reveals, however, that he is capable of using devious means to achieve his "noble" end, the suppression of tyranny, but he raises the question, just how noble is that enterprise? Cassius is being portrayed as a careful and deceitful conspirator. As a lean and hungry man, he has already been identified as a Machiavellian type, whose cold statesmanship knows expediency, not honor. This was the common Elizabethan view of Machiavelli, author of *The Prince,* a book in the tradition of mirror-of-princes literature, which was extremely popular in the latter decades of the Tudor dynasty. The intellectual spirit of Machiavelli's book, however, did not reflect the moral teachings of English works in the same tradition. Machiavelli rejected metaphysics, theology, and idealism, and emphasized the necessity of political realism if the prince was to achieve and maintain his power. Deception, lies, and forgeries were all part of the Elizabethan conception of Machiavelli's statesmanship, and this conception is precisely what Cassius is meant to convey at this point. His cause may be honorable, but since his methods are not, he dishonors his cause. Cassius, however, will not always be seen as the practical, shrewd opportunist who would betray his friend (Caesar) if he were loved by him, for his character changes as the play progresses, and he commits suicide at the end, partly because he believes "his best friend" has been captured.

SUMMARY.   Scene ii develops the political conflict already introduced in the first scene between the commoners who love Caesar and the tribunes who fear for the safety of the Republic. The mob and tribunes manifest the state of conflict in Rome on the plebeian level. Cassius, Brutus, and Caesar, in Scene ii, display political factionalism on the patrician level.

The major characters of the play are introduced in this scene, and their dispositions are examined from varying points of view. Caesar is seen amid all his pomp as a man concerned with religious ritual, the sterility of his wife, and the envious looks of Cassius. He shows his failing powers of perception when he dismisses the Soothsayer; he insists that he knows no fear; and he shows his wisdom of men and manners when he correctly diagnoses Cassius as a dangerous man. However, he admits to infirmity when he tells Antony to avoid his deaf ear and speak into his good one, and he suggests a growing hesitation in his own judgment when he asks Antony to give him his opinions of Cassius.

Antony, a member of Caesar's train, is a "gamesome" fellow who runs in the race of the Lupercal. He is unlike Brutus who has no inclination to participate in popular festivities, and he is opposite Cassius in that Antony is not lean and enjoys plays, music, and laughter. Caesar implies he is a loyal fellow, which he is indeed.

Cassius' character is opposed both to Antony's and Brutus'. He reads a great deal, fails to participate in entertainments, stands apart watching and thinking, and rarely laughs. He is a jealous man, uneasy at seeing another in power. He is a man to be feared. Cassius, moreover, is admittedly capable of betraying those who love him for the sake of his particular principles. He would use dishonorable means to achieve ends which he judges to be honorable.

Brutus' noble character is established by both Cassius and Caesar. Brutus is a reflective man, dedicated to the principles of the Republic, to love and friendship, to duty, and to honor. For the sake of honor, he will even face death (as, in fact, he does at the end of the play). But as strongly as he holds his ideals, he is just as strongly torn by conflicting loyalties to those ideals. Brutus makes decisions deliberately, and he is not quickly influenced by persuasive and passionate argument. He is torn between his love for Caesar and the anti-Caesar sentiments he admittedly shares with Cassius.

Casca has a rude manner and saucy wit, which he uses to disguise his satirical commentary on political events. He does not sympathize with Caesar and tends to interpret Caesar's behavior in the worst possible light. As a result of his denigrating interpretations of Caesar's ambition, he is invited to join the conspiratorial meeting which Cassius is planning.

Cicero is seen but not heard. He has a fiery look in his eye of the sort he has been known to show when arguing with senators. It is reported by Casca that he spoke Greek to the commoners who (since Casca cannot understand Greek) were not expected to understand Cicero. Those who did comprehend Cicero's Greek simply smiled at one another and shook their heads. Casca's implication is that Cicero is a pedant, who does not choose to speak in the language of the people.

Shakespeare foreshadows Caesar's assassination through the prophecy of the soothsayer and in the dialogue among Brutus, Cassius, and Casca.

Thus, this scene lays the foundation for the conflicts, characterizations, and tragedy which will be developed throughout the play.

ACT I: SCENE iii

It is the eve of the ides of March. Lightning flashes through the sky and thunder roars. On a street in Rome, Casca is seen with drawn sword, frightened out of his wits by the storm. He meets Cicero on the street and tells him that either there is "civil strife in heaven" or else men have offended the gods. He then describes other prodigies he has seen that night. A common slave's left hand was burned with flame, yet remained unscorched; a lion roamed loose near the Capitol; a hundred women have sworn they saw men walk in fire up and down the streets, and the birds of the night hooted and shrieked at noonday. Cicero philosophically replies, "Indeed, it is a strange-disposed time," but men interpret things absolutely contrary to the meaning of the events themselves. He asks Casca if Caesar is coming to the Capitol tomorrow, and Casca says he will be there. Declaring that "this disturbed sky/ Is not to walk in," Cicero departs.

> **COMMENT.** Cicero is stoically calm in face of the storm and the fantastic events related by Casca. Casca's credibility is called into question by Cicero's refusal to discuss the meaning of these wonders and in his dispassionate statement that men often err in their interpretations of unnatural phenomena. Casca's report of the Lupercalia may be reexamined in the light of this conversation. Cicero questions Casca's interpretation of events, and so may we.

Casca hears someone coming and issues a challenge. It is Cassius, who recognizes Casca by his voice. Casca asks why the heavens are so menacing. Cassius replies that he has been walking through the storm, exposing himself to the lightning, and asserts that these unnatural events are heaven's instruments of fear and warning that something unnatural is happening on earth. Then he compares the storm to a man no mightier than himself or Casca, a man who roars like a lion in the Capitol. Casca replies, " 'Tis Caesar that you mean."

> **COMMENT.** Having just been advised by Cicero that men tend to interpret events in their own fashion, that is, according to some personal predisposition that they may have, Casca proceeds to ignore this piece of Stoic wisdom and demands an explanation of the wonders from Cassius, the next man he meets in the storm.

Unwittingly confirming Cicero's statement, Cassius explains the monstrous wonders produced during the storm as a warning from heaven that something monstrous is going on on earth. The monstrosity he has in mind, of course, is Caesar's ambitious bid for the crown. Cassius may not believe his own interpretation of the supernatural events because he is an epicurean (later in the play he says he has renounced his epicureanism) and does not believe that gods concern themselves with human affairs. He may only be pretending such concern in order to persuade Casca to join the conspiracy. But Cassius, apparently unsuperstitious, has walked "unbraced" (with doublet open), exposing himself to the storm as he intends to face Caesar.

Casca remarks that on the morrow the senators plan to establish Caesar as king over all lands of the empire except Italy. At this Cassius delivers a tirade against tyranny and hurls abuse at the servile Romans for following "so vile a thing as Caesar!" Cassius declares that he is armed and ready to fight Casca should he turn out to be one of Caesar's men. But Casca gives his hand as a pledge of his cooperation, telling Cassius he will join his cause. Cassius then tells Casca that he has already enlisted some of the "noblest-minded Romans" to join him in the deed, "most bloody, fiery and most terrible."

> **COMMENT.**   Although it has been seen that Cassius cannot stomach Caesar's power, that he personally cannot bow to a man who was formerly his equal, we learn from his speech on tyranny that Cassius' feelings are noble ones. It is his methods that are reprehensible, such as the seduction of Brutus from his natural inclinations and the forged letters which he hopes will do the trick.

As Cassius and Casca conclude their pact, Cinna, a member of the conspiracy, arrives. He begins to talk of the storm, but Cassius cuts him short, anxious to know if the conspirators are waiting for him. Cinna says they are and adds how beneficial it would be to their cause if Cassius could "but win the noble Brutus to our party." Cassius orders Cinna to put one of the forged letters on Brutus seat of office, to throw another in his window, and to place a third on the statue of Lucius Junius Brutus (the ancient and heroic namesake of Marcus Brutus). Then Cinna is to meet him at Pompey's theater. Cassius then tells Casca that Brutus is three-parts won to his cause, and at their next encounter he will be entirely persuaded. Casca remarks that Brutus "sits high in all the people's hearts," and that what would appear to be evil if done by them, would appear virtuous if done by Brutus. Cassius agrees with Casca's judgment that Brutus is of great worth and is much needed for their cause, and he bids Casca join him in securing Brutus for their party.

SUMMARY.   This scene advances the conspiracy against Caesar. Cassius has already enlisted many noble Romans to his cause, and the plotters are anxious to have Brutus as a "front." In the first scene, we saw the conflict betwen the people and the Republicans; in the second, the major characters began to take sides in the impending power struggle. In the third, it becomes obvious that the conspiracy against Caesar has grown, and the noblest of the Romans, Brutus, is being drawn into it. The development of Brutus' character continues. In

Scene ii, he was a respected and honorable man, who was hardly aware of his own worth. In this scene, he is judged the most honored of men in Rome who, because of his virtue, can make black appear white. Cassius continues to be characterized as a schemer who is able to manipulate men, but also as one who has a passionate hatred of tyranny and the courage to prefer death to a life of servility.

ACT II: SCENE i

Brutus is seen in his orchard at three o'clock in the morning of the ides of March. He cannot sleep because he is troubled by the conflict between his love for Caesar and his love for freedom and Rome. He bids his servant, Lucius, to bring him a candle, and muses over what must be done. He resolves that the only way to stop Caesar is to kill him. Brutus has no personal motive for murdering him; he believes that Caesar must die for the general good. Since he can find nothing in Caesar's past conduct which would justify murder, Brutus projects his thoughts into the future. He considers the possibility of Caesar receiving the crown, changing his nature, and becoming a tyrant. It would be better not to give Caesar this opportunity, not to give the adder its chance to strike. Brutus resolves to "think him as a serpent's egg/Which, hatch'd, would as his kind grow mischievous,/And kill him in the shell."

COMMENT. Brutus' soliloquy reveals that he has no personal grievance against Caesar but that he fears Caesar may become a danger to the "general good," the public welfare. He has a strong sense of honor and deep feelings of responsibility to protect the freedom of his native city. Reason as he may, he can find no grounds in Caesar's past behavior for believing that he will abuse his power once he is crowned monarch. Yet, Brutus knows, it is the nature of tyrants to disjoin "remorse from power," that is, to rule without conscience or mercy. So, while he can find nothing in reason to argue against Caesar's coronation, he decides to base his reasoning on possibility. As a monarch, Caesar *may* run to "extremities" and become excessive in his despotic rule. On the basis of this possibility, which would ruin the Republic, he must be killed. Brutus is an idealist, but he confuses treachery with honor when he decides to kill Caesar for no existing reason.

Lucius reenters with a letter he has found while lighting the candle in Brutus' study. It is the forged note which Cinna has tossed into the window and bears the cryptic message, "Brutus, thou sleepst. Aware, and see thyself!/Shall Rome, etc. Speak, strike, redress!" Brutus interprets "Shall Rome, etc." to mean "Shall Rome stand under one man's awe?" Lucius returns to report that tomorrow is the fifteenth of March. When the servant leaves to answer a knock at the gate, Brutus continues his thoughts. He says that since Cassius has "whet" him against Caesar, he has not slept a wink. His wakefulness has been a nightmare of conflict between "the genius and the mortal instruments" which work on the human condition as insurrection does on a kingdom.

COMMENT.   The letter contains an ironic comment on Brutus' disturbed condition; it exhorts him to awaken when, in fact, Brutus has not slept since his conversation with Cassius. And like Cassius, he has become dangerous to Caesar, who, we recall, preferred "sleek-headed men, and such as sleep o' nights" (I.ii). Brutus' dangerous line of thinking is made even clearer when he interprets the incomplete but suggestive sentence, "Shall Rome, etc." as a complaint against the potential tyranny of Caesar. The seeds of insurrection, which Cassius had sowed, have taken root in the fertile soil of Brutus' rebellious mind. Brutus' description of the "hideous dream" he is experiencing, in which his mind ("genius") and his body ("mortal instruments") suffer an inner turmoil comparable to the effects of insurrection in a kingdom, reflects the moral philosophy of the Renaissance. In that philosophy the relationship between the body and the mind (or the body and the soul) and the correspondence between the human condition and the body politic were basic assumptions. Shakespeare carefully designed Brutus' personal emotional upheaval to reflect and foreshadow the political chaos which would follow Caesar's assassination.

The word "insurrection" still rings on the stage as Lucius enters to announce the arrival of "your brother Cassius" (Cassius is married to Brutus' sister). Others are with him, but their hats are pulled low over their ears and their faces are buried in cloaks so that they cannot be identified. Brutus comments on the shamefulness of conspiracy that fears to show its monstrous face even in a state full of evil. But he quickly overcomes his sense of shame by reasoning that even if the conspirators continued in their normal ways, the blackness of Erebus (the path to hell) could not hide them from Caesar's tyranny ("prevention").

Cassius, Casca, Decius Brutus, Cinna, Metellus Cimber, and Trebonius enter. Before introducing these men, Cassius tells Brutus that each one is acquainted with and honors him. Brutus and Cassius whisper to each other as the rest of the conspirators engage in small talk, disagreeing over the direction in which the sun is rising. The conclave finished, Brutus takes their hands one by one as fellow conspirators. Cassius proposes that they swear an oath, but Brutus says it is unnecessary, since "the sufferance of our souls, the time's abuse" are strong enough motive to assure their good faith. Honesty and the promise of a Roman is enough, Brutus patriotically asserts.

COMMENT.   Brutus overcomes his natural sense of shame over the idea of conspiracy by using more of the fallacious reasoning which he has already demonstrated in his soliloquy. He allows himself to believe that the evils Caesar *may* inflict *if* he becomes monarch actually exist at the moment. However, he shows his own integrity, although misguided, when he rejects Cassius' proposal of the oath. Brutus is convinced that the souls of free men suffer by the "time's abuse" (Caesar's potential coronation), and that the conspirators are all honest Romans nobly concerned with the good of the state.

The apparently insignificant talk about the direction of the rising sun is a humorous and meaningful incident in which Shakespeare characterizes the conspirators as a discordant group who cannot agree on a simple issue and suggests that they are ill-equipped to decide political issues as well.

The oath rejected, Cassius then proposes that Cicero be included in their group. Casca and Cinna agree, and Metellus Cimber reasons that Cicero's dignity and age will win them the good opinion of the masses. "It shall be said his judgment rul'd our hands," Cimber states. Brutus rejects Cassius' second proposal, arguing that Cicero "will never follow anything/ That other men begin." Cassius grudgingly agrees to leave Cicero out. Decius proposes to kill Antony as well as Caesar. Cassius readily agrees, on the grounds that Antony is a "shrewd contriver" and may harm them later. For a third time, Brutus opposes Cassius on the grounds that "Antony is but a limb of Caesar. / Let us be sacrificers, but not butchers." As for Caesar, "Let's carve him as a dish fit for the gods,/ Not hew him as a carcass fit for hounds." Naively, Brutus adds, "We shall be call'd purgers, not murderers. And for Mark Antony, think not of him;/ For he can do no more than Caesar's arm/ When Caesar's head is off."

COMMENT. Brutus has taken Antony's love of pleasure and his loyalty to Caesar as a sign of political weakness. He conceives of the murder of Caesar as a religious sacrifice rather than a slaughter and is blind to the possibility that his sacrifice may, in fact, be sacrilege, because the gods have ordained that Caesar rule. Brutus also fails to realize that, although he personally may be fearful of Caesar's power, the people are not. He is acting out of a patrician and Stoic sense of duty to the state, which according to his philosophy is the highest motive from which men may act.

Unlike Brutus, Cassius observes and understands men. He perceives that Antony is a "shrewd contriver" and that he has a large force which, if increased, could endanger the conspirators' cause. Cassius errs against his own judgments by acceding to each of Brutus' three decisions.

The clock strikes three, and Trebonius says it is time to part. Cassius finds it doubtful that Caesar will come forth because of the "apparent prodigies" and unaccustomed terrors of the night, "for he is superstitious grown of late." But Decius promises to get Caesar to the Capitol by flattering him with praise of his hatred for flatterers. Cassius proposes that, instead, all the conspirators go and fetch Caesar. Metellus Cimber bids them include Caius Ligarius in the plot, and Brutus assents, asking that Caius Ligarius be sent to him. Their plans concluded, the conspirators adjourn. Brutus calls his servant, but finding him asleep, he tenderly wishes him sweet dreams and reflects on the sound slumber of those unburdened by care.

COMMENT. In Elizabethan philosophy, superstition was a sign of the diseased senses. Thus, by calling Caesar superstitious, Cassius adds to the portrait of Caesar as a decaying and declining man. Caesar's susceptibility to flattery suggests that his moral sense is decaying as well as his mental power.

Brutus' address to Lucius his servant expresses his affection for the boy and reveals his own gentle nature. Shakespeare frequently uses the unburdened sleep of humble people as a contrast to the restless state of the leaders of men, particularly insurgents.

When the conspirators have gone, Brutus' wife, Portia, comes to inquire why Brutus is up in the middle of the night. She wants to know what has been absorbing him so much of late. Brutus replies that he is not well. Portia retorts that Brutus is not acting like someone sick in body but like someone with a troubled spirit. She implores him on her knees to tell her what is wrong and asks about the visitors who had come in with their faces hidden. She declares that by failing to share his secret, Brutus excludes her from part of the marriage and makes her his harlot rather than his wife. Brutus insists she is his honorable wife, but Portia continues to protest her good repute, by virtue of her father, the noble Cato, and by her own act of courage, a self-inflicted thigh wound that was intended to prove her worth as Brutus' wife and the sharer of his secrets.

COMMENT. The theme of disease is continued in this dialogue in Brutus' feigned excuse for his behavior and in Portia's accurate and ironical diagnosis that there is "some sick offense within your mind." Physical and mental diseases repeatedly figure as symbols of the disease of civil rebellion, which Caesar's murder and its results represent.

The nobility and courage of Portia are expressed in this passage. She is the daughter of Marcus Porcius Cato, who killed himself at the battle of Utica in the civil war against Caesar rather than fall into Caesar's hands. Plutarch wrote that Portia cut her thigh with a razor to prove her courage, and this is undoubtedly the meaning of her "voluntary wound" in the thigh.

Brutus is touched by his wife's devotion and is about to tell her his plans when he is interrupted by the entrance of Ligarius. Ligarius has been ill but is ready to throw his bandages aside if Brutus proposes some exploit worthy of the name of honor. Brutus says such an exploit is planned, and at these words, Ligarius throws aside his bandages and presents himself ready for action. Brutus says that the plot is one which will make sick men whole and that he will tell Ligarius of it as they walk. Ligarius replies that even though he is ignorant of the plot, it is enough for him that Brutus leads it.

COMMENT. The theme of sickness or disease is continued in this interview. Ligarius, literally ill, says he will become well when a deed of honor is proposed. Caesar's later remark that Ligarius' illness has made him lean (like dangerous men) is a dramatically ironic reference to Ligarius' statement here. Equally ironic is the fact that the plot against Caesar which should make "sick men whole" has disturbed Brutus' quiet mind and turned it from health to sickness. The entire conspiracy is, thus, associated with the disease of insurrection, and Caesar's own rule is given a similar unhealthy cast through its association with the infirmities of Caesar.

SUMMARY.   The main purpose of this scene is to show the change which takes place in Brutus after his first conversation with Cassius. The seeds of insurrection having been planted, Brutus is torn by inner conflict as he decides to join and head the conspiracy. His motives are honorable, but he mistakes treachery for honesty and murder for sacrifice. He finds oaths unnecessary among noble Roman; he vetoes an invitation to Cicero to join the conspiracy, and he objects to Antony's murder, underestimating the shrewdness and potential danger in the man. Each of these judgments is based on high civic and moral principles, and, in contrast with Cassius' suggestions, they are impractical and unrealistic, as we shall see.

The conspirators show their true colors when they disagree over a trifling matter such as the direction of the sun's rising and when they invite Ligarius to join the conspiracy because he hates Caesar, not because he loves Rome. Their desire to enlist Cicero for the dignity he will bring their "youths and wildness" is similar to the reason for choosing Brutus for the virtue with which he will coat their offenses (I. iii).

Cassius shows skill in judging men and opposes the naive decisions of Brutus. Nevertheless, he is influenced by Brutus' principled behavior and betrays his own judgment in yielding to Brutus' wishes. The noble and courageous Portia is introduced in this scene, and her reference to Cato her father (who fought for Pompey against Caesar) suggests that she will endorse her husband's plot.

ACT II: SCENE ii

The storm is still raging as the scene shifts to Caesar's house. It is three A. M. in the morning of the ides of March. Caesar, like Brutus, is spending a restless night. He exclaims that neither heaven nor earth is peaceful on this night; even Calpurnia, his wife, is having disturbed dreams and has cried out three times in her sleep, "Help, ho! They murder Caesar!" Caesar sends a servant to the priests and orders them to make a sacrifice and send him the results. Calpurnia enters and begs Caesar not to stir out of the house that day, but Caesar fatalistically replies, "What can be avoided Whose end is purposed by the mighty gods?"

Calpurnia says that she is not normally upset by prodigies, but that the unnatural occurrences of the proceding night have disturbed her: a lioness was seen giving birth in the streets; the dead rose from their graves; and fiery warriors fought in the clouds so fiercely that blood drizzled upon the Capitol. There were also reports that horses neighed. that dying men groaned, and that ghosts shrieked and squealed along the streets.

> **COMMENT.**   The appearance of the lioness, the warriors, and the dying men are foreshadowings of Caesar's death and the civil chaos which will follow his death. Caesar's resigned acceptance of the will of the gods is the position taken by the Stoic philosophers who purged their minds of all fear and passion to leave them free for virtuous thought and action.

Calpurnia interprets the comets in the air, also seen during the night. as a prophecy of the death of a prince, for comets are never seen when beggars die. Caesar firmly encourages his wife with the now famous lines, "Cowards die many times before their deaths;/The valiant never taste of death but once." He finds it strange that men should have fears, since death is a necessity which "will come when it will come."

> **COMMENT.**   Calpurnia's superstitious interpretations of the wonders of the night express her fears for Caesar's life; they are projections of the thoughts which trouble her most just as Cassius' interpretation of the prodigies reflect his greatest fear, that Caesar will become king. Caesar's courage is asserted here; it is the characteristic courage of a man who has known war and conquest and is confident of his own bravery. But Caesar also shows that he has lost touch with ordinary men and no longer understands their passions.
>
> Calpurnia's dream has already foreshadowed Caesar's murder, and the dramatic irony of the situation continues as she warns Caesar not to leave the house and Caesar replies that the only real threats that can be made to him are those made to his back, that is, through conspiracy, which is now being organized behind his back.

The sacrifice Caesar had ordered earlier has been done, and the servant returns to report that the priests advise Caesar to stay at home, for the beast, when opened, was found to have no heart. Caesar defies this answer of the gods sent by the priests, and like Cassius and Calpurnia, he gives his own interpretation of the sacrifice, which is colored by his personal predilections. The heartless beast, Caesar asserts, is a chatisement of the gods against cowardice. If he should stay at home this day, Caesar would be a beast without a heart. (The heart was regarded as the seat of courage in Renaissance physiology and philosophy.) He calls himself the brother of danger; metaphorically, he and danger are two lions born on the same day, and of the two, Caesar is the more terrible. (The lion, the king of the beasts, traditionally represented the king of men, the masculine spirit, and male courage.) "Caesar shall go forth," the intemperate ruler declares.

> **COMMENT.** Caesar's defiance of the priests and of the gods themselves is immoderate and even blasphemous. His judgment fails when he sacrilegiously defies the advice of the priests and the "ceremonies" (religious superstitions) which frighten Calpurnia. He is, indeed, tempting the gods, and his fate awaits him.
>
> The likeness of men and animals was the basis of the study of physiognomy during the Renaissance, and the lion metaphor repeatedly reflects this habit of comparison. Cassius, Calpurnia, and now Caesar himself interpret the appearance of the lion in the Capitol as the animal corresponding symbolically to Caesar.

When Caesar declares himself braver than danger itself, Calpurnia exclaims that Caesar is losing sight of his wisdom in his overconfidence. She implores him to send Mark Antony to the Senate to say Caesar is not well. According to her "humor," Caesar agrees to send the message and to remain at home.

> **COMMENT.** The reason for Caesar's concession to Calpurnia's fears has been a point of critical contention. Either Caesar is hiding his real fears by seeming to consent to Calpurnia's "humor" or he means just what he says and grants his wife's wish out of tenderness for her. (Brutus in a parallel scene with his wife also grants her wish, although his granting of it does not become apparent immediately.) Calpurnia's accusation that Caesar has become overconfident is the first clear indication that Caesar has been afflicted with that state of mad arrogance which in ancient Greek theology was believed to arouse the wrath of Nemesis, the goddess of moderation who hated every transgression of the bounds of temperance and restored the proper and normal order of all things through chatisement and vengeance.

Decius Brutus enters to fetch Caesar to the Senate. Caesar asks Decius to bear his greeting to the senators and tell them that he will not come today. He adds that to say he cannot come is false, and to say he dares not come is even falser. Calpurnia tells Decius to say that Caesar is sick, but Caesar insists that he will not send a lie. He bids Decius again to say simply that he will not come. Craftily, Decius asks Caesar to give him some cause so that Decius will not be laughed at when he delivers the message. Arrogantly, Caesar answers that it is enough to tell the Senate that Caesar will not come, but because he loves Decius, for his personal satisfaction, he will give him the reason: Calpurnia keeps him at home because she dreamed she saw his statue like a fountain with a hundred spouts, pouring forth blood in which smiling Romans bathed their hands.

Decius protests that Calpurnia's dream has been misinterpreted, that it really means that Rome sucks reviving blood from Caesar and through him regains its vitality. Decius adds that the Senate has decided to give Caesar a crown this day. If he does not come, the Senate may change its mind. Decius argues that the dream as a reason for his absence "were a mock/Apt to be rendered for someone to say/'Break up the Senate till another time,/When Caesar's wife shall meet with better dreams." That is, Caesar's excuse might be interpreted as an insult by one of the senators. Furthermore, if Caesar does not appear, senators will say that Caesar is afraid. Caesar is persuaded to see that Calpurnia's fears are foolish ones and tells his wife to get his robes, for he will go.

> **COMMENT.**   Caesar is a man of personal tenderness as well as public ambition, courage, and virtue. Personally unafraid, he is nevertheless capable of conceding to the fears and wishes of those he loves. Such softness at this point in his life is a sign of his age and growing infirmity, for the conquering hero of Caesar's youth was more decisive and more firm in his convictions. It has been argued that Caesar's words are not to be trusted and that he is really a frightened man, covering his fears with a show of bravado, and using Calpurnia as an excuse to act out his own cowardly inclinations. Decius' argument may then be interpreted as the crafty manipulation of an arrogant, conceited, and fearful old man.

Publius, Brutus, Ligarius, Metellus, Casca, Trebonius, and Cinna enter to escort Caesar to the Senate, and Caesar graciously welcomes them. Alluding to their former enmity, Caesar also notes that Ligarius' illness has made him lean. The clock strikes eight as Antony enters. Caesar remarks that despite the fact that Antony revels all night, he is able to get up in time for his duties in the morning. Caesar apologizes for keeping his escorts waiting and bids Cinna, Metellus, and Trebonius to sit near him in the Senate. Trebonius replies in an aside that he will be so near Caesar that Caesar's best friends will wish he had been further away. Caesar invites the men to drink wine with him and then "like friends," they shall be off together. In response to Caesar's show of trust, Brutus mourns, in an aside, that every "like" is not the "same."

> **COMMENT.**   Caesar is portrayed among his apparent friends as a gracious, polished and courteous host. (He is neither arrogant nor pompous as in his other appearances.) When Brutus sees Caesar behave in his usual generous and gracious manner, his personal love for Caesar comes to the fore, and he grieves ("earns") over Caesar's assumption that they are all "like friends" Punning on several meanings of the word "like" (love, the same as, apparent), Brutus regrets that all meanings of "like" are not "same," and that all loving friends are not what they appear to be, nor do they remain the "same" in their loyalty. Caesar's wish that the conspirators remains close to him in the Senate is another instance of draamtic irony, for as Trebonius implies in his aside

(intended only for the audience's hearing), he will be close enough to murder Caesar.

SUMMARY. This crucial scene serves many purposes in advancing the plot and characterizations of the major figures. First, this scene is carefully balanced with the one immediately preceding in which Brutus meets with the conspirators and with his wife Portia. Here Caesar and his devoted wife Calpurnia are seen, then the conspirators arrive as guests. Like Portia, Calpurnia petitions her husband on her knees and at first wins her point that he remain at home. Like Portia, Calpurnia is fearful, restless, concerned for her husband. Both wives are well-suited to their husbands. Portia and Brutus are young, strong, and courageous; Calpurnia and Caesar are aging, infirm, and superstitious.

Both Brutus and Caesar entertain the same guests. Ironically, however, the guests arrive in friendship in Brutus' garden, concealed by hats and cloaks, to form a conspiratorial alliance, while the same men visit Caesar as enemies, wearing no disguise at all. They simply mask their monstrous visages under "smiles and affability" as Brutus had planned in the preceding scene (II. i. 85-6).

Both Brutus and Caesar are seen as tender and yielding husbands and gracious and courteous hosts. Both trust the honesty of the conspirators; both succumb to their flattery. Brutus, however misguided, relies on his reason and his sense of duty, and is firmly decisive in dealing with the plans for the assassination. Caesar's behavior has been vacillating in dealing with the omen of Calpurnia's dream and the advice of the priests whose augurs he had demanded. The assured rashness of Brutus' youth in the preceding scene is contrasted with the vacillation and over-confidence of the aging Caesar in the present scene.

The themes of prodigies, dreams, augurs, and their interpretations are carried on in this scene, establishing an atmosphere of unrest, insurrection, and foreboding which is so essential to the building of suspense for the crucial murder scene and the subsequent events.

ACT II: SCENE iii

In a street near the Capitol, Artemidorus appears reading a paper. Artemidorus places himself in a spot where Caesar must pass on his walk to the Capitol, and rereads the letter he plans to thrust into Caesar's hands. The letter warns Caesar to beware of Brutus, Cassius, Casca, Cinna, and other members of the conspiracy because they are plotting against his life. It warns Caesar that unless he is immortal, overconfidence opens the way for conspiracy. His letter ends, "If thou read this, O Caesar; thou mayst live;/If not, the Fates with traitors do contrive."

COMMENT AND SUMMARY. Artemidorus was a "doctor of rhetoric in the Greek language, who, because of his profession, associated with certain of Brutus' confederates, knew most of their practices against Caesar," according to Plutarch. This explains how Artemidorus was in a position to learn of the plot. Suspense is created by establishing the fact that the plot against Caesar is in danger of failure. The letter suggests that Caesar's failure to recognize the conspiracy will be a result of *hubris or* overconfidence, of presuming to be immortal like the gods, who alone are secure in their immortality. Calpurnia has already warned Caesar against overconfidence, but he has chosen to ignore her. This presumptuous sense of security on Caesar's part will prevent him from reading the second warning.

ACT II: SCENE iv

On the morning of the ides of March, Portia stands before the house of Brutus, directing her servant Lucius to run to the Senate House. Having been informed of the assassination plot by Brutus, she is visibly distraught over the possible danger to her husband should his plans miscarry. The boy asks what errand he is to perform at the Senate, and Portia realizes that she cannot tell. How hard it is for a woman to keep a secret, Portia reflects, for although she has a man's mind, she has only a woman's might. The bewildered servant asks if he must run to the Capitol and back again and do nothing else, but Portia, now composed, orders him to bring her word if Brutus looks well, for he seemed sick when he left.

Portia imagines she hears a "bustling rumor" (uproar, report) from the Capitol, but it is only the Soothsayer who arrives on his way to the Capitol. Hoping to get news of him, Portia asks the Soothsayer which way he has been, but when she learns that he has just come from home, she asks him the time and inquires whether or not Caesar has gone to the Capitol. The Soothsayer replies that Caesar has not gone yet; he adds that he himself is going to find a place to see Caesar pass on the way to the Senate. Portia wants to know if he has a suit with Caesar, to which, he replies that he is going to "beseech him to befriend himself." Fearfully, Portia asks if the Soothsayer knows of any harm intended toward Caesar, and she is told that the Soothsayer *knows* of no harm intended but *fears* there will be some. He excuses himself, saying that he must find a good spot before the crowds gather.

After he leaves, Portia complains about the weakness of the woman's heart, "O Brutus!/The heavens speed thee in thine enterprise." Fearing that the boy has overheard her prayer, she adds that "Brutus hath a suit /That Caesar will not grant." She grows faint and, forgetting her former errand, tells the boy to run to Brutus, inform him that she is well, and return with word of what he says.

COMMENT AND SUMMARY.   This brief scene serves as another stage in the building of suspense for the crucial action of the assassination. The dramatization of Portia's anxiety creates a sympathetic emotional response to her own impatience and fears over the outcome of the plot, as she nearly gives the plans away several times during this brief interval. The arrival of the Soothsayer and the disclosure of his prophetic warning adds to the cumulative effect of the suspense which is being created. The prophet's warning to Caesar in the following scene is prepared for at this point, and it is seen that Caesar will have still another opportunity to "befriend himself," as mortals must. By the time that Caesar overconfidently rejects each of the warnings prepared for him, it will be clearly understood that Caesar has been chastised (warned by the gods) and that vengeance is in order. Caesar, as much as Brutus, is responsible for his own tragic fate.

ACT III: SCENE i

Brutus, Cassius, Casca, Decius Brutus, Metellus, Trebonius, Cinna, Antony, Lepidus, Popilius, Peblius, and others accompany Caesar through the streets to the Capitol. A crowd has gathered to watch the procession, among them Artemidorus and the Soothsayer. As Caesar and his train pass, Caesar sees the Soothsayer in the crowd and confidently reminds him that "the ides of March are come." "Ay, Caesar," replies the Soothsayer, "but not gone." Artemidorus then comes forward and begs Caesar to read his note, but Decius hastily intervenes with another note, asking Caesar to read Trebonius' suit at his leisure. Impetuously, Artemidorus demands that Caesar read his first, for it is of personal importance to Caesar. Magnanimously, Caesar replies, what concerns Caesar himself will be read last. When Artemidorus insists again, Caesar indignantly exclaims, "What! is this fellow mad?" Cassius steps in and chides Artemidorus for presenting petitions in the streets; the Capitol is the proper place for such things.

> **COMMENT.** Caesar has just gone down for the third time. He has overruled Calpurnia's fears, confidently mocked the Soothsayer, and now indignantly rejects Artemidorus' plea that Caesar think of himself. His arrogance on these matters is his own contribution to the tragedy which must now ensue.

Caesar goes up to the Senate House, followed by the crowd. Popilius whispers good luck to Cassius on his enterprise, but when the startled Cassius asks, "What enterprise, Popilius?" the senator simply replies, "Fare you well" and advances toward Caesar. Cassius tells Brutus of Popilius' ambiguous remarks and express his fear that their conspiracy has been discovered. He vows that if the plot is unsuccessful, he will kill himself. Brutus tells Cassius to be calm, for Popilius is smiling as he talks to Caesar and Caesar's face shows no sign of change.

> **COMMENT.** Popilius' ambiguous remark brings the play to its height of suspense, for Cassius' guilty conscience causes him to give the most fearful interpretation to the senator's good wishes. As Popilius walks to Caesar's side and speaks to him, attention is

focused on Cassius who watches Caesar. The fear of disclosure makes Cassius vow his own death, but at the peak of excitement, Brutus reads Caesar and the senator's faces. Be calm, Brutus urges, and we learn that the plot is still on. (According to Plutarch, Popilius told Cassius that their enterprise had already been betrayed, but Shakespeare, who certainly knew this historical fact, artfully rephrases Popilius' words so that their ambiguity will create a most intense dramatic moment.)

Cassius notices that the plan is beginning to work, for Trebonius is drawing Antony out of the way. Antony and Trebonius leave as the senators take their seats. Cassius asks for Metellus Cimber so that he can present his suit to Caesar, while Brutus urges the conspirators to press near Caesar and aid Metellus. Cinna tells Casca that he is to be the first one to strike Caesar. As Caesar calls the Senate to order, Metellus kneels before Caesar and begins a flattering address. Caesar cuts him short with a lengthy reply in which he asserts that Caesar is not like ordinary men who succumb to flattery and make childish decisions. He cannot be melted by praise from the "true quality" of a suit. He says that if Metellus is pleading for his brother who has been banished, Caesar will "spurn thee like a cur out of my way." Metellus asks if anyone else will aid his suit for his banished brother. Brutus comes forward and kisses Caesar's hand, saying that he does this not in flattery, but out of desire for Caesar to repeal the banishment of Publius Cimber. Next, Cassius humbly entreats Caesar, falling "low as to thy foot." But Caesar remains adamant.

In a piece of over-extended self-eulogy Caesar asserts, "I am constant as the Northern Star,/Of whose true-fixed and resting quality/There is no fellow in the firmament." Among men on earth, Caesar continues, "men are flesh and blood, and apprehensive;/Yet in the number I do know but one/That unassailable holds on his rank,/Unshaked of motion; and that I am he." Publius Cimber shall remain banished, for Caesar cannot be moved. Cinna and Decius implore Caesar, but he dismisses them, uttering the most arrogant statement of all, "Hence! Wilt thou lift up Olympus?" Casca signals the attack, "Speak, hands, for me!" He stabs Caesar, and one by one, the other conspirators add their blows. Seeing Brutus among their number, the stricken Caesar cries, *"Et tu, Brute?* Then fall, Caesar."

COMMENT.   The assassination is one of the most dramatic moments on the Shakespearean stage. Metellus begins the action by petitioning for his brother's repeal from banishment. One by one, the conspirators join in the plea, kneeling abject and humble before the merciless ruler who shuns their petitions with arrogant boasts of his own firmness of decision and constancy. As Caesar extravagantly compares himself to the brightest star of all, he is surrounded by kneeling figures who seem to inflate the already immoderate sense of his own worth. Caesar's self-praise grows stronger and more intemperate; he above all men is "unassailable."

The assailants bide their time. Ignobly dismissed by Caesar, who now reaches the height of arrogance and blasphemy as he likens himself to an Olympian god, Casca signals the attack.

Caesar's merciless response to his petitioners, his abuse of power, his arrogant self-praise, have worked on the passions of the audience as well as the conspirators, and Casca's death blow comes as a welcome relief from the madness of self-inflation which Caesar has imparted. Once stricken, however, Caesar becomes the object of total sympathy. *"Et tu, Brutè?"* Even you, Brutus, The pathetic query of the fallen leader, three words, counteracts all the injury Caesar has done by his outrageously hubristic boasts. His friend's betrayal ends his will to live. "Then fall, Caesar." From this point on, Caesar's sins will be forgotten and only his noblest attributes will be remembered, suggesting that the play may be pointing to a political lesson, that a tyrant, however intolerable, is a force against disorder, which is far worse than tyranny.

As Caesar dies, the senators and people retreat in confusion. Cinna cries out, "Liberty! Freedom! Tyranny is dead!/Run hence, proclaim, cry it about the streets." Cassius bids the conspirators to run to the common pulpits and call out "Liberty, freedom, and enfranchisement!" Casca encourages Brutus to go to the pulpit, and Decius urges Cassius to go also. Brutus and Cassius advise the senator Publius to leave, lest the people attack the conspirators and harm the aged senator. Brutus adds that no man should bear the consequences of the deed, except the conspirators themselves. Trebonius returns and tells his fellows that Antony has fled to his house amazed and that "Men, wives, and children stare, cry out, and run,/As it were doomsday."

Brutus asks the Fates what is in store for the assassins now. Agreeing with Cassius that life involves the fear of death, Brutus declares that they are Caesar's friends for having cut off his life from years of fearing death. Then Brutus exhorts the conspirators to bathe their hands and arms in Caesar's blood, and with their swords besmeared with the blood, to walk into the market place, shouting "Peace, freedom, liberty!" Cassius envisions that in ages to come this noble scene will be enacted by nations yet unborn and in languages yet unknown. Brutus wonders how many times plays will be held portraying the bleeding of Caesar, who now lies by Pompey's statue, "No worthier than the dust!" And Cassius adds that in these plays of the future, they will be remembered as the men who gave liberty to their country.

COMMENT.   The chaos and disorder which reigns immediately after the assassination is narrated by the conspirators. The silently amazed Publius, venerable senator of the Republic, represents the astounded confusion of the general public. Brutus' noble concern for Publius' age and safety, even in the passionate aftermath of the slaughter, reveals the truly noble nature of the man, as does his claiming responsibility for the assassination and his willingness to yield to the decision of the Fates. Brutus' exhortation to the blood-bath is not expressive of the blood lust of the man but of his desire to treat the assassination as a sacrifice by the ritualistic smearing of the victim's blood on the priests of liberty and by showing the public that an offering has been made in the name of "Peace, freedom, and liberty."

Infused by the lofty purpose of their deed, Cassius and Brutus envision themselves as heroes of liberty who will be immortalized on the stages of nations (like England), which are yet unformed. Thus, the effects of the murder are shown from two points of view. The senate and the public flee in confusion or are paralyzed by astonishment, while the conspirators are inspired by the lofty purpose of their deed, which they imagine has ennobled their names and will receive the acclaim of all posterity.

The structural unity imparted to the play by the device of the dream and the arrangement of events is embedded in this scene. The blood-bath fulfills and explains Calpurnia's dream of the statue pouring blood, and the death of Caesar at the foot of Pompey's statue complements the initial reference in the play to Caesar's triumph over Pompey's blood. Visually, the statue of Pompey can now be seen standing in triumph over Caesar's blood.

The conspirators have decided to leave the Senate House with Brutus at their head when a servant of Antony's arrives. The servant says that Antony instructed him to kneel before Brutus and deliver the message that Antony loves and honors Brutus, that he feared, honored, and loved Caesar, and if Brutus can show him why Caesar deserved to die, "Mark Antony shall not love Caesar dead/So well as Brutus living; but will follow/The fortunes and affairs of noble Brutus." Brutus at once replies that his master is a wise and valiant Roman. He instructs the slave to fetch Antony to the Capitol to learn the cause of Caesar's murder and to tell him that by Brutus' honor, he will depart unharmed. While the servant runs to get Antony, Cassius tells Brutus that he fears Antony and that his fears very often prove correct.

Antony arrives, and ignoring Brutus, he addresses Caesar's body, "O mighty Caesar! Dost thou lie so low?/Are all thy conquests, glories, triumphs, spoils,/Shrunk to this little measure?" Then Antony asks who else must die and says that if he is marked for death, he will never be more ready than now. If he lived a thousand years, he would find no place, nor hour, nor weapon more pleasing than those which have accompanied Caesar's death, nor would he find executioners more fitting than those who are now "the choice and master spirits of this age."

COMMENT.   Antony's arrival on the scene of the crime is partly out of loyalty to his master Caesar and partly out of the desire to effect a reconciliation with the assassins until he can muster the force to oppose them successfully. Although he says he is prepared to die, he has first made certain through his servant that Brutus promises him safe conduct. His flattering address to the killers then may be interpreted as the first cautious step in a counter-rebellion, and Cassius' misgivings over Antony seem to be falling "shrewdly to the purpose," to be proving true. Antony from this point on begins to display the dangerous and shrewd political judgment which Cassius has perceived in him. He is more than the lover of plays and music and all-night revels; he will be seen to be as calculating as Cassius, as persuasive as Decius Brutus, as noble and far more loyal than Brutus.

Brutus tells Antony not to beg for death, for although the conspirators appear to be bloody and cruel, their hearts are actually filled with pity for the general wrong done to Rome by Caesar. Antony is welcome to join their ranks. Cassius adds that Antony will have as much power to dispense favors in the new state as the conspirators do. Brutus asks Antony to await an explanation patiently until the people, who are beside themselves with fear, have been appeased; then he will explain why he who loved Caesar struck him down.

COMMENT. Once again we see the sharp contrast between Brutus and Cassius. The idealistic Brutus has been explaining Caesar's murder and Antony's welcome in terms of "our hearts" and "all kind love, good thoughts, and reverence." On the other hand, the practical Cassius realizes these words mean little to Antony and offers him some of the powers the insurgents have won.

Pretending to be satisfied with the assassins' wisdom in overthrowing Caesar, Antony takes the bloody hand of each of the men. Antony realizes that to the conspirators he must appear to be either a coward or a flatterer, and turning to the dead body of Caesar, he begs its forgiveness for befriending Caesar's enemies. He declares how unbecoming it is to the love he bore Caesar to make peace with the assassins in the very sight of the corpse; it would be more fitting to weep at the fall of Caesar, whom Antony now compares to a noble deer, run down and killed by a pack of hounds.

Cassius interrupts Antony's apology to Caesar, at which Antony begs his pardon for praising the dead man before his slayers. Still, Antony points out, his praise is slight; Caesar's enemies will do him as much credit. In a friend, however, Antony's words are merely passionless understatement. But Cassius is not prepared to blame Antony for praising Caesar; what he wants to know is can Antony be counted on as one of his allies, or shall the conspirators go along their way without depending on Antony's support. Antony explains that he shook their hands in order to indicate his alliance with their cause, but the sight of Caesar did indeed sway him from that resolution. Therefore, Antony qualifies his pledge of friendship; he will join their ranks if they are able to supply reasons why and in what way Caesar was dangerous.

Brutus promises that the reasons he will give Antony would satisfy him even if he were the son of Caesar himself.

> **COMMENT.**   Antony's eulogy over the body of Caesar includes a simile in which Caesar is compared to a hart and his murderers to hounds. The figure, however covert to the conspirators, is that Antony has likened them to dogs. We shall see shortly that this is exactly how he feels about them.
>
> There may be a touch of historical irony in Brutus' promise to give reasons so satisfactory that even a son of Caesar would be satisfied. Although in this play Shakespeare makes no use of the fact that Caesar and Brutus' mother were lovers during the time when Brutus was born, the phrasing of Brutus' promise may be a subtle allusion to the unconfirmed report that Brutus was Caesar's bastard son.

Antony asks if he can deliver the funeral oration over Caesar's body in the market-place. Without any hesitation, Brutus agrees to Antony's request. Cassius pulls Brutus aside and cautions him not to allow Antony to speak. "You know not what you do," Cassius warns. Antony easily may stir up the people. Convinced of the justice of his crime, Brutus answers that he will speak first and tell the people the reasons for the murder of Caesar, and that Antony speaks with their permission, since they want Caesar to have "true rites and lawful ceremonies." Brutus is sure "it shall advantage more than do us wrong." Cassius says he still doesn't like it. Brutus then orders Antony not to blame the conspirators during his oration, but to speak good of Caesar without condemning his killers. Furthermore, he is to say he speaks with the insurgents' permission, and he must agree to speak after Brutus. Antony assents, And Brutus bids him to prepare the body and follow them. The conspirators go off, leaving Antony alone with the body.

> **COMMENT.**   Brutus is not a subtle man; he cannot imagine that Antony may be lying about joining their cause. Besides, he has such confidence in his own powers of reasoning that he believes he can convince Antony, the people, and even Caesar's son, if he had one, of the justice of his deed. Cassius continues to be suspicious and finds it more and more difficult to concur with Brutus' decisions. His strongest arguments, however, are based on feelings not reasons, and his only course in view of Brutus' idealism is to submit to it entirely.

Alone with the body, Antony speaks his true feelings to the corpse. He begs pardon for being so meek and gentle with Caesar's butchers. "Thou art the ruins of the noblest man/That ever lived in the tide of time," Antony declares. He swears an oath so strong that he calls it "prophecy" over the gaping wounds of Caesar which "like dumb mouths, do ope their ruby lips/To beg the voice and utterance of my tongue." The limbs of men shall be cursed for Caesar's death, domestic fury and civil strife shall spread through Italy. Blood, destruction, and other monstrosities of war will become such a familiar sight in the land that mothers will merely smile when they see their infants cut up by the hands of war. Caesar's spirit, with Ate (the hellish god of discord) at his side, shall range through the land and "Cry 'Havoc.' " And "this foul deed shall smell above the earth/With carrion men, groaning for burial."

COMMENT. The soliloquy reveals Antony's true purpose in seeming to befriend the conspirators. He is anxious to give his prince a ceremonial burial before he musters forces and ranges through the land carrying destruction to the farthest reaches until Caesar's death has been avenged. The imagery in this speech is, perhaps, the most revolting imagery to be found in Shakespeare. It is designed to show the full extent of Antony's hatred and rage against "this foul deed." The images of civil chaos are grotesque and grisly in the extreme; mother's smiling at their quartered babes and dead men rotting above the ground, crying out for burials, are the horrible conceptions of an impassioned brain. These are the feelings of Antony as he looks at the gaping wounds of Caesar, which seem to him like repulsive yet appealing ruby lips, begging Antony for revenge.

Once more Cassius' suspicions fall "shrewdly to the purpose"; Antony intends to betray his new-made friendship. Brutus' judgment has been wrong again. There can be no good reasons to satisfy the angry spirit Antony has just displayed. The remainder of the play is foreshadowed by Antony's "prophecy"; civil strife and destruction will follow; Caesar's spirit will seek revenge.

Antony's harangue is ended by the arrival of a messenger who Antony recognizes as the servant of Octavius Caesar. The messenger begins to relay his message, but when he sees the body of Caesar, he cries out. Tears welling in his eyes, Antony asks the slave if his master is coming and learns that Octavius is only seven leagues from Rome. Antony orders the slave to tell his master what has happened and to warn him that Rome is not safe for entry. On second thought, Antony decides to have the servant wait until after the funeral oration. After they see how the people react to the murder, the slave may report to Octavius on the state of things. Then Antony and the servant carry Caesar's body off.

COMMENT. A new character, Octavius Caesar, is introduced just at the point when Julius Caesar is carried off. Octavius was the grand-nephew of Caesar, his son by adoption, and his first heir. He actually arrived in Rome a month after Caesar's demise and took his name Caesar only after he heard the terms of his uncle's will. His arrival at this point, however, as another Caesar, has obvious dramatic significance; he is meant to convey the idea that "Caesar" is not dead. (The king is dead; long live the king.)

Octavius is generally known as Augustus (the revered one) after the title given him later by the people of Rome. Shakespeare ignores the exact chronology of historical facts, although he knew them well, because adherence to them would clearly interfere with the development of the plot and destroy the dramatic effect and thematic significance of Octavius' timely arrival.

SUMMARY.   This scene brings the play to its first climax. The first two acts dealt with the events leading up to Caesar's death; the remainder of the play deals with the events leading to the death of Cassius and Brutus. The stage is set here for the action which follows the assassination.

Once Caesar has been killed, the focus of the play shifts to Brutus, whereas it has previously been on Caesar as well as Brutus. Brutus has been shown as a noble, honorable, and virtuous man who, because of these very qualities, is blind to reality and practicality. Brutus' role now changes from conspirator to victim, hunter to fugitive, and Antony's role expands as he plans action against Brutus. Brutus' blindness becomes more and more evident after this point. Caesar's excessive courage had made him blind to the normal precautions taken by men, while Brutus' excessive idealism now obscures his view of the practical reality of politics. Brutus' stubborn naivete, his tragic flaw, leads to his destruction, for his quick acceptance of Antony's friendship, despite the warnings of Cassius, is neither the first nor the last mistake in judgment that Brutus makes.

In this scene, Antony emerges as a loyal friend, but he is also a wily, conniving, vengeful, and ambitious man. He declares that he will plunge all Italy into civil war in order to avenge Caesar and actually does this in the play, while Brutus has been anxious that only the conspirators suffer for the assassination.

The death of Caesar so early in the play raises a legitimate question— who is the main character of *Julius Caesar?* Some critics maintain that Caesar is the focus of the entire play, the man being replaced by the spirit or ghost of Caesar after the assassination. Others insist that Brutus is the real tragic hero, that the focus is on him throughout the .play, that the assassination is the first climax of his career, and that the remainder of the play leads to a second climax in Brutus' downfall and death. Still others suggest that this is a play without a hero, that Shakespeare's point of view was ambigious, and that he was examining the many aspects of civil insurrection. The decision finally falls into the hands of each reader, for Shakespeare, above all else, was conscious of his audience, an extremely mixed breed of men comprised of members from all levels of social, economic, and intellectual life. His plays communicate with people on all levels because Shakespeare designed them to do just that and their durability may be directly attributed to the fact that Shakespeare had the genius of ambiguity, the power to suggest different meanings to different men of different times. Perhaps the problems of the climax, the play's hero, and its unity, should be confronted stoically with the thoughts Shakespeare put into the mouth of Cicero: "But men may construe things after their fashion, Clean from the purpose of the things themselves" (I. iii).

ACT III: SCENE ii

Later on the same day, the ides of March, throngs of citizens crowd the Forum of Rome. They are angry and fearful at Caesar's death. When Brutus and Cassius arrive, some among them cry, "We will be satisfied! Let us be satisfied." Brutus divides the crowd so that some stay to hear him speak, while others go off to listen to Cassius. Brutus begins to speak in a dry, emotionless prose. Logically and coldly, he appeals to the wisdom and judgment of the crowd, asking them to trust his honor so that they may believe his reasons. First he addresses "any in this assembly, any dear friend of Caesar's," to whom Brutus says that his own love for Caesar was no less than his. If then that friend demand why Brutus rose against Caesar, this is the answer: "Not that I loved Caesar less, but that I loved Rome more." He declares that Caesar would have enslaved them if he had lived, and asks them if they would rather be slaves and have Caesar alive or be free men and have Caesar dead. He tells the mob: "As Casar loved me, I weep for him; as he was fortunate, I rejoice at it; as he was valiant, I honor him, but as he was ambitious, I slew him." He asks any so base as to be a slave to speak up, or any so rude as to be other than a Roman, or any "so vile as will not love his country?" Brutus then asserts that the reason for Caesar's death is a matter of official record in the books of the Senate.

As Antony appears with the body of Caesar, Brutus announces that Antony, although he had no part in the slaying, will receive all the benefits of Caesar's death, a place in the commonwealth, as shall all the crowd. Finally, he closes his speech with the words, "As I slew my best lover for the good of Rome, I have the same dagger for myself, when it shall please my country to need my death." Moved by Brutus' oratory, the crowd cries, "Live, Brutus! Live, live!" Some of the citizens suggest that they build a statue of Brutus. Another exclaims, "Let him be Caesar." Brutus silences the mob and asks them all to stay and hear Antony praise Caesar. Before he leaves, he orders that none depart before Antony' finishes his speech, save himself.

COMMENT. Brutus' speech is typical of his own fallacious reasoning. He naively believes that by claiming honor for his name his deed will be accepted as honorable. He feels that by calling Caesar ambitious, he has given clear and cogent reasons for Caesar's death. He believes that the mob will be won over by the simple explanation of his motives, and, indeed, they are. But the mob is not won by any reasoning they have heard; Brutus has flattered them by addressing them as equals, by claiming his concern for their liberty, and by forcing them to deny that they are base, uncultivated, unpatriotic slaves. He has moved the passions of the crowd by his theatrical promise to kill himself if it should please the country, and he hopes to show the mob how noble and just he really is by demanding that Caesar's funeral oration gets a respectful hearing. As for the reasons for Caesar's murder, the mob learns only that Caesar was "ambitious." They are easily persuaded by the tricks of oratory, although Brutus has made a sincere speech which he thinks reasonable. The crowd, however, has missed Brutus' point, for although he has intimated that he has freed them from the bondage of a monarch, shouts are raised that Brutus should be crowned, immortalized by a statue, or be made Caesar himself. They have no idea of the point of the murder and are only aware that Brutus is an honorable and agreeable man who likes Romans and hates ambition.

Antony, however, is not a man of the crowd. He listens carefully as Brutus speaks, finds no satisfaction in Brutus' "reasons," and prepares a shrewd and ironic rebuttal for his funeral speech.

Brutus' naive political judgment is nowhere more evident than at the moment when he turns the mob over to Antony, when he gives Antony the last word and leaves the scene entirely, foolishly trusting that all will go as he has ordered it without his personal supervision, and foolishly believing that his personal idealism and fallacious reasoning will prevail with Antony as well as with the crowd.

As Antony makes his way to the pulpit, one citizen exclaims, " 'Twere best he speak no harm of Brutus here," while another cries out, "This Caesar was a tyrant," and another answers, "Nay, that's certain,/We are blest that Rome is rid of him." Antony mounts the pulpit and begins his speech: "Friends, Romans, countrymen, lend me your ears;/I come to bury Caesar, not to praise him." Antony declares that the evil which men do lives after them, not their good; "So let it be with Caesar." Pretending thus to agree with Brutus, Antony continues, "The noble Brutus/Hath told you Caesar was ambitious: If it were so, it was a grievous fault." (He does not state it was so.) Antony repeats again and again that Brutus has called Caesar ambitious, "and Brutus is an honorable man." The speech continues to relate how Caesar wept when the poor cried out. "Ambition should be made of sterner stuff: /Yet Brutus says he was ambitious;/And Brutus is an honorable man." Antony reminds the crowd that Caesar had refused the crown three times at the Lupercal. "Yet Brutus says he was ambitious;/And sure, he is an honorable man." Antony reminds his listeners that they all loved Caesar once and not without cause. What keeps them from mourning him now, Antony exclaims, crying, "O judgment, thou art fled to brutish beasts,/And men have lost their reason!" Bursting with emotion, Antony mourns, "My heart is in the coffin there with Caesar, /And I must pause till it come back to me."

As Antony weeps, the plebeians comment on his remarks. There is reason in them, one plebeian observes. "He would not take the crown; /Therefore 'tis certain he was not ambitious." Another, totally converted to Antony's cause, asserts, "There's not a nobler man in Rome than Antony."

> **COMMENT.** Antony's skill in verse and dramatic presentation displayed throughout the oration may be attributed to his love for plays and music. These arts were regarded as important aspects in the education of a Renaissance prince or statesman-orator, a value effectively displayed in Antony's verbal victory over the mob.

Antony does not present a direct line of reasoning at first but uses irony, implication, and constant repetition. Hoping to strike home his point that the only proof of Caesar's ambition which Brutus has offered is that Brutus, a man of honor, says that Caesar was ambitious, Antony works the idea of Caesar's ambition and Brutus' honor into every other line. He alternates ironical allusions to Brutus' honor with concrete instances of Caesar's generosity, public concern, and lack of ambition. Then he applies reason to the emotional brew he is concocting. If Caesar was ambitious, why did he refuse the crown three times. The crowd is in no position to consider the question rationally for they had actually forced him to reject it by cheering his refusals. Instead, they draw the conclusions which Antony desires. To make the dam of public opinion burst, Antony theatrically weeps over Caesar's coffin. He appeals to the sympathy of the crowd, dropping real tears and growing red in the eyes. Many plebeians are moved; one is totally won over, but the speech goes on until every last man in the crowd is a frenzied avenger.

Having composed himself, Antony begins to speak again. He says that he means not to inflame them against the conspirators, for they are all honorable men. Then he produces Caesar's will from his cloak, and holds it up for the people to see. Antony says he cannot read the will, since if he does, "they would go and kiss dead Caesar's wounds,/ And dip their napkins in his sacred blood." A citizen shouts out for Antony to read the will. He refuses again, saying that if he reads the will, they would find out how much Caesar loved them, and the knowledge would inflame them and make them mad. The same citizen cries out again for the will to be read. Antony calls for patience and ironically says that he has gone too far: "I fear I wrong the honorable men/Whose daggers have stabbed Caesar: I do fear it." Another citizen cries, "They are traitors. Honorable men!" Still another shouts, "They were villains, murderers. The will! Read the will!" Antony finally consents to read the will and tells the crowd to make a ring about Caesar's body so that he can show them him who made the will.

> **COMMENT.** Part of the crowd had already been won over when Antony paused to weep. Recovering his composure and con-

tinuing in an ironic vein, Antony claims that he doesn't want a counter-rebellion, while this is actually his very desire. But Antony draws from a large bag of rhetorical tricks and next produces Caesar's will, which he refuses to read. Thus, he works on the curiosity of the crowd until they are eating out of his hand. When the citizens persist long enough, Antony promises to read but does not do so at once. The reading requires staging to be most effective, Antony knows. The plebeians must gather around the corpse, and they eagerly do so. Thus, the hostile crowd has been subdued and seduced. Brutus' argument for Caesar's killing has been successfully undermined by Antony's insinuations by the time the citizens, like children anxious to hear a story, form a circle around the coffin.

Antony descends from the pulpit and comes down to Caesar's body. He takes Caesar's cloak in his hand and begins to speak. He says that Caesar first put on this cloak on the day he conquered the Gallic tribe, the Nervii. He points to a tear in the cloak and says, "Look in this place ran Cassius' dagger through./See what a rent the envious Casca made." Then he points to the wound that Brutus made and explains, "Brutus, as you know, was Caesar's angel:/Judge, O you gods, how dearly Caesar loved him!/This was the most unkindest cut of all:/For, when the noble Caesar saw him stab,/Ingratitude, more strong than traitors' arms,/Quite vanquish'd him. Then burst his mighty heart,/And, in his mantle muffling up his face,/Even at the base of Pompey's statue/(Which all the while ran blood), great Caesar fell." Then Antony openly calls the bloody deed treason. The crowd is weeping now over Caesar's mutilated clothing, and Antony asks why they weep over mere clothing. "Look you here! Here is himself, marred as you see with traitors." Dramatically, Antony reveals Caesar's corpse to the horror-stricken view of the public.

COMMENT. Now that Antony knows the crowd is on his side, he proceeds to arouse their wrath against the conspirators. He uses visual aids to illustrate well-known anecdotes. He displays Caesar's cloak, torn by foul wounds and tells them it was worn against the Nervii to remind the crowd of Caesar's glories. Next Antony makes them visualize the slaughter by describing how the rents in the cloak were made and by naming a conspirator for each hole. The fact that Antony did not witness the murder has no bearing on his oratory. Antony's indictment of the conspirators becomes open at this point, and the plebeians who had warned him not to speak ill of Brutus are now ready to tear Brutus limb from limb. Effectively and completely, Antony has won over the mob, but he is not finished yet. He must direct them to action.

At the point when Antony drops his irony and openly calls the conspirators traitors, the crowd becomes angry and ugly. The citizens shout, "Revenge! About! Seek! Burn! Fire! Kill! Slay! Let not a traitor live!" But Antony cries halt and, resuming his irony, he says this murder was the deed of honorable men. He adds that he is not an orator like Brutus and that he speaks with the leave of the conspirators, who know very well that Antony has "neither wit, nor words, nor worth, /Action, nor utterance, nor the power of speech to stir men's blood." He only tells the crowd what they already know and shows Caesar's wounds so they can speak for him. He adds, "But were I Brutus, /And Brutus Antony, there were an Antony/Would ruffle up your spirits, and put a tongue/In every wound of Caesar, that should move /The stones of Rome to rise and mutiny." The suggestion planted, the citizens shout out, "We'll mutiny." One citizen suggests, "We'll burn the house of Brutus." As the citizens are about to leave the Forum and begin the pillaging of the murderers' houses, Antony calls halt again, for they have forgotten the will which Antony was going to read. Antony then reads: "To every Roman citizen he gives/To every several man, seventy-five drachmas" (about one hundred fifty dollars in modern purchasing power). A citizen calls out, "Most noble Caesar! We'll revenge his death." Antony continues, "Moreover, he hath left you all his walks,/His private arbors, and new-planted orchards,/On this side Tiber; he hath left them you,/And to your heirs for ever—common pleasures,/To walk abroad, and recreate yourselves./Here was a Caesar! When comes such another?"

The citizens are now wild with fury; they pile up benches, tables, and stalls from the Forum to use as fuel for Caesar's funeral pyre, which they plan to erect in a holy place. The crowd leaves with the body of Caesar to bring it to the holy place for cremation. Antony muses to himself over the results of his speech, "Now let it work. Mischief, thou art afoot,/Take thou what course thou wilt."

> **COMMENT.** Antony has played the crowd as he might a flute, sounding them and stopping them at will. He has used wit, words, worth, action, utterance, and "the power of speech to stir men's blood" (all the rhetorical tricks which, ironically, he claimed he did not have) to work the crowd into a frenzy of passion, to set mischief afoot, as he remarks in his Machiavellian aside.

A servant enters with a message that Octavius has already arrived in Rome. He and Lepidus are at Caesar's house. Antony replies that he will come at once, that Octavius' arrival is like the granting of a wish. "Fortune is merry," Antony remarks, and so is Antony. The servant reports that he has heard that Brutus and Cassius "are rid like madmen through the gates of Rome." To this, Antony remarks, "Belike they had some notice of the people,/ How I had moved them." Antony and the servant leave for the house of Caesar where Octavius awaits them.

SUMMARY. The first climax of the play having been reached and the action having been pointed in the direction of revenge and civil disorder, as Antony had prophesied, the second scene of Act III works as a transition between the two phases of the plot, the murder and the revenge.

The capriciousness of the mob had been prepared for in the first scene of the play. Thoughtlessly, the mob had turned out to celebrate Caesar's triumph over Pompey whom they had formerly loved. Now they are moved by Brutus, the betrayer of Caesar, not by reason but out of thoughtless respect for Brutus' honor. Just as rapidly as they turned to Brutus' views, so do they turn to Antony's. But Antony has the shrewd judgment of a practiced orator and public manipulator. He does not let his audience go until they are so enraged that they will not listen to the simplest reason or answer the simplest plea for mercy. Worked to a frenzy by Antony's "mischief," the mob goes off crying "havoc." Antony's prophesy over the body of Caesar has moved toward fulfillment, and the plebeians' irrational behavior in the next scene has been prepared for amply.

The two speeches given in this scene are designed to contrast their speakers and their oratorical styles. Brutus' speech, in prose, is terse, emotionless; it appeals to the cool judgment of men, although its reasoning is questionable. Antony's speech, in verse, is emotional, lengthy, dramatic; it makes use of wit, repetition, action, visual effects. Antony makes his listeners participate in the development of his argument by pausing frequently to give them time to react, by drawing them into a circle around Caesar's body, by making them recall a famous victory in which, as Romans, they had shared Caesar's glory.

A new powerful side of Antony's character is revealed in this scene. This is a far shrewder Antony than we have seen before, when he followed at the heels of Caesar, a fat, sleek-headed fellow, given to pleasures. Then he was simply a man to be trusted, but his taste for the arts suggested his nobler parts; now his loyalty in friendship, his skill in oratory, his ability to know men (perhaps, learned from Caesar) come to the fore.

Brutus is seen in the first stages of his decline. His faulty reasoning and his poor judgment of men combine with his overconfidence in the virtues of reason and lofty idealism and make him reject the minor vices which must be practiced in persuasive oratory. His prose reflects his dry, rational approach to life and contrasts sharply with Antony's musical verse, his use of dramatic effects, and his moist appeal to emotionality which is the secret of his rhetoric.

Caesar or the spirit of Caesar is the subject of both orations. From Brutus's point of view, we hear that Caesar was ambitious; from Antonys' that he was glorious, victorious, tender, generous. Caesar speaks to the people once more when Antony reads his will aloud. Although dead in body, Caesar's spirit remains, and his shrewd political judgment is revealed in his final bequest. The good that Caesar does will live after him in the gift of money, parks, and pleasures that he bequeathes the people.

At the close of the scene, the meeting of Antony, Lepidus, and Octavius hints at the force which is mustering to destroy the conspirators and prepares us for the action of Acts IV and V.

ACT III: SCENE iii

Later that day on the ides of March, Cinna the poet is seen on a street near the Forum. As he walks along, he muses over a dream he has had in which he feasted with Caesar. Now omens of evil are charging his imagination. He does not wish to go out of doors, but something leads him forward. A band of citizens suddenly appears and question Cinna; asking his name, where he is going, where he lives, and if he is married or a bachelor. Wittily Cinna replies that he is "wisely . . . a bachelor." An enraged citizen interprets this as an insult to married men and promises to beat Cinna for calling him a fool. Cinna then reports that he is going to Caesar's funeral as a friend. When he answers that his name is Cinna, one citizen cries; he is a conspirator, tear him to pieces. Cinna protests that he is Cinna the poet, not Cinna the conspirator. But another citizen, completely unreasonable, shouts, "Tear him for his bad verses." When Cinna again pleads that he is the poet, still another plebeian answers, "It is no matter; his name's Cinna! Pluck but his name out of his heart, and turn him going." Madly they set upon the helpless poet, and when they have finished rending him, they charge off to burn the houses of Brutus, Cassius, Decius, and the rest.

COMMENT AND SUMMARY. Cinna was a distinguished poet, a close friend of Caesar, and a tribune of the people. He is not portrayed here in his historical personage but as the Elizabethan stereotype of the court poet of ancient Rome. The poet, it was held among the ancients, had powers of prophecy and the ability to envision the future in their imaginations. Cinna the poet, musing over his ominous dream, shows these legendary powers.

The ancient poet was also a satirist of the people and his times. Cinna in this scene indulges in some trivial foolery over the wisdom of remaining a bachelor, a familiar jest both in ancient times and in our own.

The crowd is in no humor to be amused, and Cinna's wit is taken as an insult to married men. Even so, no reason is necessary to turn the inflamed mob against the first victim they find in the streets. Antony had promised Caesar revenge and a quota of horrible slaughter, which the plebeians are now prepared to take. The spirit of the mob, created in the preceding scene, is dramatized in the tearing of Cinna. In addition, Cinna's ominous dream introduces the theme of murder just as Calpurnia's dream anticipated Caesar's slaughter. Omens will continue to be used as forecasts of death and destruction for the remainder of the play.

ACT IV: SCENE i

The scene now shifts to a room in Antony's house where Antony, Octavius, and Lepidus are holding council. They are found in the middle of their discussion, deciding who is to be killed in the reign of terror which they are about to begin. Octavius tells Lepidus, "Your brother too must die. Consent you, Lepidus?" Lepidus consents "upon condition that Publius shall not live,/Who is your sister's son, Mark Antony." Antony calmly agrees to this. Antony then sends Lepidus to Caesar's house to fetch Caesar's will in order to see if they can eliminate some of the heirs.

> **COMMENT.**   The meeting of the Caesarist party parallels the earlier meeting held by Brutus' faction. Here as there, an elimination list has been proposed; it is being decided who may be hostile to the party and must die because of it. Unlike Brutus, Antony is calmly prepared to execute his enemies, even his own sister's son, Publius.
>
> (Historically, it was Lucius Caesar, Antony's uncle, who was marked for death in this way. Shakespeare's distortion of this historical fact serves the special purpose of emphasizing the inhumanity and villainy which insurrection fosters. By making Antony condemn his own nephew, Shakespeare shows the cruelty of which Antony is capable, for in ancient Rome, a sister's son was generally raised and adopted by men of repute and often became the heirs of their uncle's great estates. Hence, Antony's consent to Publius' death is as unnatural as a father's execution of his own son.)
>
> In view of Antony's Machiavellian behavior, the deals he makes over the lives of Lepidus' brother and his own nephew calls Antony's honor into question, and his ironic regard for Brutus who "is an honorable man" begins to suggest this double irony that Brutus is really honorable, and that Antony does think so, although he pretends not to for the political purpose of rabble-rousing.

As Lepidus leaves, Antony tells Octavius that Lepidus has little merit as a man and is only fit to do errands. He asks if it is right that this man should get a third part of the world. Octavius answers that Antony seemed to think well of Lepidus when he asked his advice about the proscription lists. But Antony replies he has been using Lepidus as a scapegoat on whom the blame for the murders may be placed later on. Lepidus follows where they lead, or leads where they tell him to go. He will be discarded like an ass set to pasture when it has delivered its burden. Octavius leaves these plans up to Antony, but interjects that Lepidus is a tried and valiant soldier. Antony insists once more that Lepidus can only be regarded as property like a horse. Then he reports that Brutus and Cassius are beginning to gather their forces and that now is the time for unity and for taking council. Octavius assents and they leave to make plans.

COMMENT.   The meeting of Antony's party, which has been taken up at mid-point, is to be understood as the one in which the second triumvirate was formed. That is, the three men were to govern Rome with the advice of the Senate.

Antony's machine-like mind continues to be portrayed in his feelings over Lepidus. He shows how little he values men, even those whose service has been courageous and loyal. He believes in using men as he uses animals to serve his own ambitions and needs.

In contrast to Brutus' meeting with the conspirators earlier in the play, Antony has his cohorts well in hand. When suggestions are raised, he yields and consents to them. There are no half-way measures for the practical ruler. At the same time, Lepidus agrees fully to Antony's proposals, and Octavius accedes to Antony's plan to discard Lepidus even though he regards him as a tried and valiant soldier. However brutal the triumvirate may seem, there is far more unity and promise of success in their alliance than was seen among Brutus' conspirators.

SUMMARY.   In this scene, Antony is revealed as a cruel, conniving and ambitious man, an opportunist who will seize the first chance he gets to gain full control over Rome. The cruelty of the entire triumvirate is manifest in the ambitious nature of each of its members, and their plan to attack Brutus and Cassius is motivated as much out of the desire for power as for revenge. Thus, Antony, once the friend and pupil of Caesar, is now seen in the light of his unscrupulous ambition; Octavius who is docile for the moment is shown as the willing accomplice in the quest for power; Lepidus who goes off on his errand like the mule Antony calls him promises to be little competition to the two dominant members of the triumvirate. Caesar's ambition, the spirit of Caesarism, lives on in these two.

The triumvirate's council works as a contrast and balance to the meeting of the conspirators in Brutus' garden. The differences to be noted are that Antony shows the powers of calculation which Cassius has, but he has the power to influence his cohorts which Cassius does not have. Octavius takes things at face value as Brutus does, but he is acquiescent to the political wisdom of the acknowledged leader of the triumvirate.

Two new characters are introduced in this scene as complements to Antony and as a balance and contrast to Brutus' team. Antony's cool nature resembles that of Cassius; Octavius' naivete is balanced by Brutus'; and Lepidus' fatuity parallels Casca's.

ACT IV: SCENE ii

The scene now shifts to a camp near Sardis where Brutus' army has pitched its tents. Drums are sounded as Brutus arrives before his tent accompanied by Lucilius, Titinius, and other soldiers. Lucius, Brutus' servant, is also present. Lucilius has just returned from a visit to Cassius' camp, accompanied by Pindarus. Brutus tells Pindarus that his master Cassius has given him some cause to wish "things done, undone." Pindarus replies that his master will appear "such as he is, full of regard and honor." Brutus then asks Lucilius how he was received by Cassius, and Lucilius explains that he was received with courtesy and respect, but not with the old familiarity that Cassius used to show. Brutus tells Lucilius that he has witnessed a "hot friend cooling," and he compares Cassius to a horse which seems spirited at the start but quickly falls under trial of battle. He then learns from Lucilius that Cassius' army will be camping at Sardis that night.

> **COMMENT.**   Attention is shifted from the triumvirate planning its action against Brutus to Brutus' camp, where the insurgents are preparing to fight Antony's forces. Servants arrive to report Cassius' arrival and information is exchanged which suggests that discord between Cassius and Brutus has grown since our last view of them. Brutus' feelings toward Cassius are expressed when he compares his ally to a horse, hot at the start, unreliable in the finish, and the comparison works as a link to the previous scene in which Antony compared Lepidus to a horse and as a foreshadowing of subsequent events in which Cassius will prove unreliable in battle, quick to admit complete defeat, and overly hasty in suicide. Such figures of language force comparisons to be made, work as binding elements among the scenes, and supply much of the unity of the play, which is often difficult to see on the surface. It is intended next that the conflict between the Republican conspirators be compared and contrasted with the momentary harmony of the triumvirate.

Cassius enters with several soldiers and greets Brutus with the words, "Most noble brother, you have done me wrong." He accuses Brutus of hiding his wrongs under "this sober form of yours." Brutus reminds Cassius of his hasty temper and tells him not to wrangle in front of their two armies. Both armies are led off some distance as Brutus and Cassius enter the tent where Brutus regally promises, "I will give you audience."

COMMENT AND SUMMARY.   The argument which ensues in the next scene is anticipated by Cassius' greeting to Brutus and his charge that Brutus hides his wrongs under the appearance of virtue. Cassius has changed since his last appearance; his irascible behavior during the subsequent argument is predicted when Brutus alludes to Cassius' rash temper and urges Cassius not to speak before their men. Brutus is seen to be in control of the situation; he is more confident and self-assured than ever, but his political naivete shows no improvement here or in the subsequent scene. This hint of discord between the conspirators will be confirmed and the suggestion of defeat, which accompanies discord, will prevail from this point on.

ACT IV: SCENE iii

Inside the tent, Cassius tells Brutus he has been wronged because Brutus has condemned Lucius Pella for taking bribes from the Sardians, even after Cassius had sent letters entreating him not to dismiss Pella. Cassius adds that this is not the time to scrutinize and rigidly censure every petty or trifling offense. Brutus reproaches Cassius for selling offices to undeserving men for gold. At this, Cassius becomes infuriated and says that if anyone but Brutus had told him this, he would have been killed on the spot. Speaking of corruption, Brutus says that Cassius himself has set the example among his men and has escaped punishment only because of his high position. Brutus reminds Cassius of the ides of March, how they had struck down Caesar, the foremost man of all the world, for the sake of justice. He asks if they should now "contaminate our fingers with base bribes." Brutus argues, "I had rather be a dog, and bay the moon, /Than such a Roman." "Brutus, bait not me;/I'll not endure it," Cassius warns. He adds that Brutus forgets himself when he attempts to restrain Cassius' actions, for Cassius is a more experienced soldier and more able "to make conditions," that is to make bargains with men and officers. Indignantly, Brutus retorts that Cassius is not more able; Cassius insists he is; Brutus contradicts. Cassius warns Brutus to provoke him no farther, but Brutus insists that Cassius had better listen, since he will not be silenced by Cassius' rash temper. When he asserts that he cannot be frightened by a madman, Cassius exclaims, "O ye gods, ye gods! Must I endure all this?" Viciously, Brutus warns Cassius that he will defy him until "you shall digest the venom of your spleen," and he promises that Cassius will be the object of his ridicule from this day forth. Sarcastically, Brutus urges Cassius to prove he is a "better soldier," for he is anxious to learn from "noble men." Cassius protests, "I said, an elder soldier, not a better." He asserts that Caesar dared not treat him so, and Brutus replies that Cassius had not dared to provoke him as he dares Brutus now. Now at the peak of his anger, Cassius threatens, "Do not presume too much upon my love;/I may do that I shall be sorry for." Brutus replies arrogantly that Cassius has already done what he should be sorry for and that his threats have no terror for Brutus, "for I am arm'd so strong in honesty/That they pass by me as the idle wind." Next Brutus complains that Cassius did not send him any of the gold which he had badly needed, for he cannot raise money by vile means, that is, by extorting it from local peasants. Cassius claims that he did not deny Brutus the gold but that the messenger who delivered his reply was a fool. Cassius charges that Brutus no longer loves him, for he refuses to tolerate Cassius' weaknesses and makes them even greater than they are. Cassius unsheathes his dagger, and, handing it to Brutus, he says, "I, that denied thee gold, will give my heart:/Strike, as thou didst at Caesar, for, I know,/When thou didst hate him worst, thou lovedst him better/Than ever thou lovedst Cassius."

COMMENT. During the entire argument, Brutus shows that he is still incapable of managing men. He is too truthful, too "sober," too noble to resort to practical necessities of war. He has become arrogant and overconfident, on the one hand, denying Cassius' superiority as a soldier and as a raiser of funds, and on the other hand admitting that he is unable to raise his own money, which he regards not as a soldierly weakness but as a sign of his noble nature. Cassius' methods of appointing officers and raising money are corrupt but practical. The incorruptible Brutus, however, will not engage in practical immorality.

The argument of the two men follows the childish pattern of insistence, denial, insistence, denial. "You did," "I didn't," children might say. The heroic assassins of the mighty Caesar behave like children who have lost a tyrannical father and unconsciously suggest that Caesar, at least, had maintained harmony among these children. The irrational argument, furthermore, displays both men in a state of angry madness, which, the ancients believed, was inflicted upon men whom the gods would destroy.

The pride Brutus takes in his unassailable honesty is reminiscent of Caesar's pride in his unassailable constancy just before he was killed and presages the imminent destruction of Brutus himself. Brutus taunts Cassius with his own virtuous honesty and his immunity to threats: "I am arm'd so strong in honesty," etc. To the audience, the effect is shocking; to Cassius, it is maddening. Pressed to his limit, Cassius bares his breast and, like Caesar, is prepared to die because he has lost Brutus' love. The harshness Brutus had displayed in his ability to subordinate his personal feelings to his ideal of good in the slaying of Caesar is reasserted in his cruel abuse of his friend Cassius.

This famous Quarrel Scene is one of the best exhibits in Shakespeare of his knowledge of human nature; it has won the praise and interest of critics through the ages and has moved even those who did not like *Julius Caesar* as a whole.

Seeing Cassius with his bosom bared and his dagger offered for his death, Brutus apologetically tells Cassius to sheathe his dagger and "be angry when you will." Brutus compares himself to a lamb that carries anger only briefly as a flint afire one moment is cold the next. Brutus is sorry he has laughed at Cassius' weakness of temperament, promises to tolerate it in the future, and the friends are reconciled.

Suddenly, there is a disturbance outside the door. A poet is trying to gain admittance to the tent on the grounds that he must stop the quarrel within, for the two generals should not be alone at such a time. Lucilius, who has been guarding the entry, refuses to admit the poet, but the poet insists, "Nothing but death shall stay me." Cassius appears and inquires the poet's errand and learns, through some doggerel verses, that someone who is older than either of the generals knows it is not fitting for them to fight. Cassius laughs at the poet and at the inferior quality of the rhymes, but Brutus is annoyed and says that foolish poets are out of place in war. Although Cassius is tolerant of the new fashion of taking poets to war, Brutus orders the poet to be gone. Then Brutus orders Lucilius and Titinius to bid the officers to make camp for the night, and Cassius adds that Messala is to be brought to them immediately.

> **COMMENT.** The reconciliation having been effected when both parties admit they have been ill-tempered, the tension is released by the poet who bursts in and anti-climactically attempts to effect the reconciliation which has already been made. The poet's exaggerated vow to enter the general's tent or die is funny in itself, and his doggerel verses add to the comedy of the moment. However, the gist of the verses suggests the childishness which has been displayed during the quarrel, for the poet affects a kind of paternal authority over the disputants by claiming to "have seen more years" than they.

> Cassius' response to the poet is characteristic. Although we have been told that Cassius rarely smiles, we have also learned that when he does, he smiles as if in self-mockery. The poet, whom Cassius calls a cynic (one who satirizes men), has enabled Cassius to smile at himself. Brutus, however, is a Stoic of sorts, who has never been "gamesome." Here he shows his complete lack of humor and his priggish sense of decorum when he orders the "saucy fellow, hence."

The poet gone, Brutus asks Lucius, his servant, for a bowl of wine. Cassius remarks that he did not think it was possible to make Brutus so angry. But Brutus explains that he hears many griefs. Cassius reminds Brutus to make use of his philosophy in facing evil events. Then calmly Brutus tells Cassius that Portia is dead. Amazed at this news, Cassius wonders how Brutus prevented himself from killing Cassius when he had crossed him so. He asks of what sickness Portia had died. Brutus replies that, impatient of his absence and seeing Mark Antony and Octavius grow strong, she killed herself by swallowing fire. Appalled, Cassius cries, "O ye immortal gods!"

> **COMMENT.** The philosophy to which Cassius refers is Stoicism, a creed by which men accepted human events with resignation and quietude. Brutus' uncharacteristic anger is thus explained as the diversion of his grief over Portia's death. This is the first sign that Brutus is in a state of mental deterioration. Soon he will

see spirits, which is how Shakespeare commonly dramatized the condition of the unhealthy mind.

Lucius reenters with wine and tapers. Brutus says he buries all unkindness in a bowl of wine, while Cassius says, "I cannot drink too much of Brutus' love." Titinius and Messala arrive and are told that Brutus has received letters saying that Octavius and Antony are marching with a mighty force toward Philippi. Messala says he has had letters to the same effect and adds that Octavius, Antony, and Lepidus have murdered a hundred senators. Brutus remarks that their letters differ in this point, since his report says seventy senators had been killed, Cicero among them. Messala asks if Brutus has received any news from his wife. Brutus replies he has not and asks Messala if he has heard anything. Messala reports that Portia is dead. Brutus, with philosophic quietude, states, "With meditating that she must die once, /I have the patience to endure it now."

Messala compliments Brutus on his stoical acceptance of Portia's death; this is the way great men should endure their losses, he says. Cassius states that he knows as much about the theory of Stoicism as Brutus does, but his nature (rash and choleric) could not bear grief with the resistance of the Stoic.

COMMENT. The discrepancy in the reports over the number of Senators killed by Antony is a realistic device frequently used by Shakespeare to suggest the confused nature of things during time of war and to introduce the theme of false report which later will be so vital to the tragedy of Cassius.

Brutus allows Messala to tell him Portia has died, although he has already heard this news. We have been shown that messages delivered over long distances are often unreliable and contradictory. Brutus realizes this when he patiently listens for confirmation of Portia's death. When the first report is confirmed by the second, Brutus' response is, "Why farewell, Portia." This may be taken to mean that Brutus was reluctant to bid farewell until he was absolutely certain of her death.

Other explanations have been offered for the double report of Portia's death. One attributes it to the carelessness of the compositor, who failed to remove the second report, which was marked for deletion. Another, within the context of the play, claims it to be the consideration of Brutus, who lets Messala deliver his report out of respect for his office.

Brutus' reaction to Portia's death is reminiscent of Caesar's belief that "the valiant never taste of death but once." A comparison is forced upon the reader who recalls the verbal and philosophic resemblances between Caesar's statement and Brutus' stoical idea that Portia "must die once." As Messala observes, this stoical resignation to death is the mark of a great man. Cassius, purportedly an Epicurean at this point in the play, admits that he is unable to bear grief like a Stoic, suggesting that he is not a great man. However, he will shortly renounce his Epicurean philosophy and die a Stoic. The implication is that Cassius' character becomes ennobled as the play progresses.

Anxious to leave the subject of Portia's death, Brutus suggests that they march to Philippi with their armies, but Cassius is against this plan. He feels it is better to let the enemy come to them, wearying their troops in the long march, while Brutus and Cassius' men are rested and ready to defend themselves. Brutus counters Cassius' suggestion by asserting that the enemy will gather fresh troops along the way among the people Brutus and Cassius have antagonized by extorting their money. Silencing Cassius, Brutus argues further that the morale of their troops is at its highest, and that if they wait, the morale will decrease. Cassius reluctantly agrees to march to Philippi. Brutus announces that it is time for rest, and Cassius begs Brutus that such a disagreement as had begun that night may never again come between their souls. Brutus replies, "Everything is well," and as Cassius, Titinius, and Messala leave, each in turn addresses him as "my lord" or "Lord Brutus."

COMMENT. Brutus' will has been asserted among his allies, who are forced to accept his decision to march against the enemy rather than wait for the enemy to attack. Cassius offers some feeble opposition to this plan, but, anxious to prevent any further discord, he quickly concedes to the stronger man. By the time the council is over, Cassius acknowledges Brutus as "my lord," as do Titinius and Messala. Thus, Brutus' poor judgment in military affairs prevails over the sounder advice of Cassius, the more experienced soldier, and draws closer the tragic end that awaits the two men.

Preparing for rest, Brutus calls for his gown and asks Lucius to find his instrument (lute). Paternally, he notes that Lucius is drowsy from having served all day. He sends for Varro and Claudius to sleep in his tent in the event that messengers to Cassius are needed during the night. The two soldiers offer to stand guard all night, but Brutus considerately insists that they sleep until they are called. From the pocket of his gown, Brutus produces a book he had blamed Lucius for misplacing and apologizes to his servant for being so forgetful. Still apologetic, Brutus asks the tired boy to play a tune and promises to reward him if Brutus lives. Music and a song follow before Lucius falls asleep. Tenderly, Brutus removes the lute from Lucius' hands. Then, finding his book, Brutus begins to read.

COMMENT. Brutus' obstinate will and his poor military judgment give way to another side of the man. Here he is considerate of his men, who, in return, serve him loyally. To Lucius, his young servant, he is paternal and tender, and his promise to be good to Lucius if he lives is unquestionably a sincere one. The qualification to the promise, however, introduces a new idea. There is doubt in

Brutus' mind and, perhaps, fear of death. The contrast between Brutus' treatment of his men and Antony's attitude toward Lepidus may be noted at this point.

As Brutus picks up his book to read, the ghost of Caesar, unnoticed by Brutus, appears in the tent. Brutus observes that the taper burns poorly. Then, suddenly, he sees the apparition, which he tries to attribute to the weakness of his eyes. As the spirit draws closer, Brutus asks, "Art thou some god, some angel, or some devil,/That mak'st my blood cold and my hair to stare?"/Speak to me what thou art."

The ghost answers, "Thy evil spirit, Brutus." Brutus asks why the spirit has come, to which the ghost replies, "To tell thee that thou shalt see me at Philippi." Then I shall see you again, Brutus asks? "Ay, at Philippi," the ghost replies. The ghost disappears as suddenly as it has come. "Now that I have taken heart, thou vanishest," Brutus exclaims.

COMMENT.   The taper flickers; Brutus is not certain what he sees, but he is frightened by the apparition, whatever it may be. His blood runs cold, his hair stands on end. The question of whether or not the spirit is an angel or devil reflects the divided opinion held during the Renaissance on the existence and the nature of ghosts. Physicians and realists of the age attributed apparitions to an excess of the melancholic humor or the "melancholy adust," produced under the influence of a hot passion like anger. Others who believed in the supernatural thought that ghosts were spirits of the dead released from purgatory. Some thought they were good angels sent by God; still others that they were evil angels sent by Satan.

The fact that the ghost speaks should not be taken as proof that it has objective existence. It may simply be a superstitious projection of Brutus' mind, which has recently been heated by a passionate anger against Cassius and turned melancholy by grief over the death of Portia. Brutus himself admits that his mind has been disordered of late when he apologizes to Lucius for forgetting the book, and he seems to be in doubt over whether or not he will live. (The book, incidentally, is another anachronism; Romans used scrolls.) Caesar too had become superstitious in his declining days. The appearance of ghosts and the occurrence of supernatural events is repeatedly associated in Shakespeare with diseases of the mind, sometimes accompanied by somatic disabilities, as in Caesar.

That the ghost tells Brutus he is his "evil spirit" may be taken as a foreshadowing of the tragedy at Philippi; it is also a reflection of Brutus' subconscious misgivings over the death of Caesar and his present venture, which Brutus may consciously be incapable of acknowledging. Those in Shakespeare's audience who regarded the ghost as an objective spirit would have seen that supernatural forces were united to the natural ones of Antony to work against Brutus for Caesar's revenge.

In either case the spirit of Caesar, whether real or imagined, has come to plague Brutus. The effect of the ghost is the same; Brutus is frightened, and the death he fears is foreshadowed by the ghost. When Brutus exclaims that the ghost vanishes "now that I have taken heart," the balance swings in favor of a subjective ghost, which is conjured up in the imagination of a troubled mind and disappears when Brutus pulls himself together.

Brutus wakes Lucius, Claudius, and Varro. Lucius, dreaming he is still playing, says, "The strings, my lord, are false." Brutus asks him if he had dreamed and cried out in his sleep, but Lucius says he did not know he cried out and that he saw nothing in the tent. Brutus asks the same questions of Varro and Claudius, and their replies are as negative as Lucius'. Immediately, Brutus sends Varro and Claudius to tell Cassius to set out with his forces promptly and that Brutus will follow close behind.

COMMENT. Brutus' first reaction to the ghost is to find out whether it was real or imagined. He questions his men to see if any of them spoke in his sleep or saw anything. Since they have perceived nothing, Brutus may suspect that the ghost is a figment of his disturbed imagination, or he may believe that the ghost has made its appearance only to him, as was reportedly the case in a good deal of Renaissance demonology.

Brutus' decision to go to Philippi at once may be explained as characteristic of the behavior which Brutus has revealed earlier in the play during his inner struggle before the murder of Caesar (II. i). At that time, the anticipation of action against Caesar had made him sleepless, and his mind in turmoil was described by Brutus himself as a kind of nightmare, a state of insurrection: "Between the acting of a dreadful thing/And the first motion, all the interim is/Like a phantasma or a hideous dream./The genius and the mortal instruments/Are then in council, and the state of man,/Like to a little kingdom, suffers then/The nature of an insurrection." Now, in IV. iii, Brutus has decided to march to Philippi. Having made the decision to do so, he must await the time of action; but for Brutus this is a time of nightmare, a time of mental insurrection. Brutus is anxious to get to Philippi. His troubled mind seems to conjure up a nightmare, a ghost who will appear at Philippi. When he rouses from his vision or visitation, he orders Cassius to march at once, because, whether he realizes it or not, Brutus cannot bear the state of suspense "between the acting of a dreadful thing,/And the first motion . . . ."

SUMMARY. This lengthy scene, which takes place in the rebel camp, may be divided into four stages. In the first stage, Brutus and Cassius engage in a heated argument which stems from the essential differences between the two friends; Brutus' stoical virtue and incorruptible idealism is opposed to Cassius' cynical and practical militarism. The quarrel, however, turns into a childish battle of wills over who is the better man and ends with the total capitulation of Cassius to Brutus, who has shown the stronger will. The theme of discord among the assassins is intended as a contrast to the cold-blooded harmony of the newly-formed triumvirate, which is masterminded by Antony. Brutus' character, during the argument, shows several unfortunate changes. He has become petty and arrogant, self-confident and obstinate in asserting his misguided judgments on his cohorts. Cassius has become a rash, fearful, and beaten man. By the end of the argument, the man who loved freedom so much calls Brutus "my lord."

The second stage of the scene deals with the reconciliation of the quarrelers and the double disclosure that Portia is dead. Cassius now interprets Brutus' anger as having stemmed from grief over Portia, but Brutus is a Stoic, who remains unaffected by the external events of life, and he seems to accept his loss with resignation, as becomes a great man.

The third state of the scene concerns the decision to attack the enemy at Philippi. Cassius' sensible opposition to Brutus' plan is feeble, and it is quickly dropped when it seems that dissension may be renewed between himself and Brutus, whom he loves.

The fourth stage of the scene is marked by the appearance of Caesar's ghost, which Elizabethans interpreted variously as an objective or subjective spirit, angelic or diabolic, or simply as the spirit of the dead risen from purgatory. The ghost vanishes when Brutus' courage returns, so that it seems to be a projection of his troubled mind, heated from the argument with Cassius, depressed by the news of Portia's death, and fearful of the outcome of the battle of Philippi. Rather than endure the nightmare of a delayed departure, Brutus orders Cassius to march at once toward Philippi, and he himself prepares to follow shortly to meet his destiny.

ACT V: SCENE i

The action now shifts to the plains of Philippi where Antony, Octavius, and their armies are encamped. Octavius tells Antony that their prayers are answered since the enemy is coming to meet them on the plains rather than keep to the hills as Antony had imagined. Antony replies that he knows why the conspirators do this. They are trying to make a show of courage, which Antony does not believe they really have. A messenger enters to announce the enemy's approach. Antony tells Octavius to take the left side of the field, but Octavius demands the right. Antony asks, "Why do you cross me in this exigent?" Octavius ominously replies, "I do not cross you; but I will do so."

COMMENT.   Antony's tone is marked with confidence here; he gives orders to Octavius who is technically his peer, and Octavius shows signs of balking at Antony's command. He demands the right side when ordered to the left and concedes with an ominous warning that while he does not cross Antony now, he will do so in the future. (See Shakespeare's *Antony and Cleopatra,* where the central conflict concerns Octavius' pursuit and victory over Antony.)

The fact that Brutus has forsaken his vantage point in the hills to fight the enemy on the plains is another mark of his poor military judgment and a foreboding of his defeat.

At the sound of drum, Brutus and Cassius lead their army to the field. Lucilius, Titinius, and Messala join them. Brutus notes that Antony and Octavius stand as if to invite a parley. Antony, observing the same hesitation on Brutus' part, decides to answer the enemy's charges before doing battle. Cassius and Brutus advance to meet Antony and Octavius, while the armies wait for a signal from their generals to begin the fray. The rivals exchange insults over Brutus' love of good words and Octavius' penchant for giving bad strokes (in fighting). A master of the discourteous retort, Antony tells Brutus, "In your bad strokes, Brutus, you give good words;/Witness the hole you made in Caesar's heart,/Crying 'Long live! Hail, Caesar!' " Antony gets as good as he gives when Cassius reminds him that Antony is yet untried in battle, although his speech is gifted and his honeyed words rob the bees of Mount Hybla. Parrying Cassius' thrust neatly, Antony replies, "Not stingless too." Antony becomes angry as the insults continue, and his taunts become more venomous. "Villains!" he cries. "You did not waste words when your daggers struck Caesar while some of you smiled like apes, fawned like hounds, bowed like bondmen, kissing Caesar's feet, while damned Casca". . . stabbed him in the back. "O you flatterers!"

Failing an answer, Cassius turns to Brutus, arguing that if his advice had been followed instead of Brutus', they would not now be listening to Antony's abuses. Octavius draws his sword and swears that he will not sheathe it, "Never, till Caesar's three-and-thirty wounds/Be well aveng'd; or till another Caesar/Have added slaughter to the sword of traitors." Brutus replies that Octavius cannot die by traitors' hands unless he himself brought those hands with him. When Octavius says that he was not born to die on Brutus' sword, Brutus replies that he could not die more honorably if he were the noblest of his strain, that is, if he were his uncle, Julius Caesar. In a final insult, Octavius bids Cassius and Brutus to come to the field if they dare to fight that day; if not, they may come when they have the stomachs for a fight.

COMMENT. This verbal battle in which the rival generals engage before entering physical combat was a medieval rather than a Roman practice, but it serves an important function in this scene, which overrides any annoyance the anachronism may cause. It establishes the animosity between the two armies and substitutes verbal combat for physical combat which is difficult to enact onstage. The generals' abusive wit, moreover, was a source of delight to the Elizabethan audience, which regarded the clever insult as a form of art.

Cassius shows that he still resents Brutus for rejecting his battle plan; Antony and Octavius make it clear that they plan to avenge Caesar, and Brutus still insists on the merits of Caesar's murder.

As Antony, Octavius, and their armies leave the field, Brutus and Lucilius, his lieutenant, go aside to talk, while Cassius and Messala confer in the foreground (downstage). Cassius says that this day is his birthday, and he calls Messala to witness that he is compelled, against his will, to risk everything on one battle, just as Pompey was. Cassius confides that although he had formerly believed in Epicurus, he has now changed his mind and believes, to some extent, in portents and omens. He relates how, on their way from Sardis, two eagles swooped down, ate from the hands of the soldiers, and followed them all the way to Philippi. Now, however, the eagles have flown away, and in their stead, ravens, crows, and kites look down upon them as if they were sickly prey. Advised not to believe in the omen, Cassius admits that he only partly believes in it, for at the same time, he is "fresh of spirit and resolved/To meet all perils very constantly."

COMMENT. At the battle of Pharsalia (48 B.C.), Pompey was persuaded against his will to fight Caesar and was decisively defeated. Cassius feels that, like Pompey, he is being forced by Brutus to stake everything on one poorly planned battle and that he too will be defeated by a Caesar, that is, Octavius Caesar.

Cassius explains that he had formerly believed strongly in the philosophy of Epicurus (a materialist who believed that the gods did not interfere in human events so that omens were to be ignored). Now, however, his deep forebodings of doom in the coming battle have led him to discard his former philosophy. On the other hand, although he senses his forthcoming defeat, he is "fresh of spirit and resolved/To meet all perils," that is, he has purged his mind of fear and anxiety and has apparently taken the Stoic position of resignation to one's fate. In his conversation with Brutus, which follows, Cassius remarks that "the gods today stand friendly," indicating that he does, indeed, believe that gods concern themselves with human events.

Brutus and Cassius finish their conversations with their respective lieutenants and rejoin each other. Cassius suggests that although the gods are favorable, he and Brutus might hold a final conversation before battle. If the worst befalls them, this conversation will be their last, Cassius states; therefore, he asks Brutus what he proposes to do should they lose the day. Brutus replies that he would arm himself with patience and live by the same rule of philosophy he had followed when he had condemned Cato for his "cowardly and vile" suicide. Cassius asks if this means Brutus would be content to be led captive through the streets of Rome, and Brutus arrogantly replies, "No, Cassius, no.

Think not, thou noble Roman,/That ever Brutus will go bound to Rome./He bears too great a mind." Without revealing how he could escape humiliation and still avoid suicide should he be defeated and taken prisoner, Brutus asserts, "But this same day/Must end that work the ides of March begun." He bids a final farewell to Cassius and the two part friends. As they go off to battle, Brutus impatiently wishes, "O that a man might know/The end of this day's business ere it come!"

COMMENT. Cato, Portia's father, committed suicide at the battle of Utica (46 B.C.) rather than fall into Caesar's hands. In Stoic doctrine, which Brutus presumably follows, suicide in the interest of the public good was condoned. The philosophic principle which Brutus lives by and which holds that suicide is a transgression against the high powers that govern men's lives is really a Platonic (and Christian) one. According to Shakespeare, Brutus has combined Platonism with Stoicism to form his philosophy.

Cassius tries to make Brutus realize that the alternative to death is to be led through the streets of Rome in triumph, but Brutus asserts that he will never face this indignity. At the moment, he is not contemplating suicide, which he regards as "cowardly and vile." He believes that the Fates will pass final judgment at the battle of Philippi for the work that was begun on the ides of March. On that day, just after the assassination, Brutus had called upon the goddesses of destiny: "Fates, we will know your pleasure. /That we shall die, we know, 'tis but the time,/And drawing days out, that men stand upon." Convinced that the Fates will grant him victory or death, Brutus refuses to face the possibility of defeat and capture, which would force him to choose between humiliation and the betrayal of his philosophic idealism.

The talk of suicide and of parting forever reflects the general pessimism the two men feel and foreshadows both their deaths by suicide. Each man faces possible defeat with characteristic resolution. Cassius, practical and realistic, gives up his former philosophy and embraces a form of Stoicism. He is prepared to commit suicide rather than be taken captive. Brutus still impractical, unrealistic, immutably idealistic, refuses to face the real possibility of defeat without death. Ironically, Brutus will betray the principles he holds so strongly when he commits suicide at last, but he will be honored, nevertheless. Cassius will be honored somewhat less, but his expedient change of creeds before his death allows him to maintain his integrity and die by the principles he has newly embraced.

SUMMARY. This scene juxtaposes the rival generals and shows the prevailing mood in each of the two camps. Antony and Octavius are optimistic and united, although the shadow of disagreement passes over their camp. Their mood foreshadows victory. Brutus and Cassius are also united but pessimistic; they still disagree both in their military and philosophic decisions, but they exchange farewells in perfect harmony and friendship. The talk of omens, suicide, and philosophy foreshadows the death of Cassius and Brutus by suicide.

ACT V: SCENE ii

On the battlefield at Philippi, Brutus and Messala exchange hasty words. Brutus orders Messala to ride to the legions on the other (right) side of the field to deliver written orders to Cassius. He is to make an immediate attack on Antony's wing. Then Brutus observes that Octavius' wing shows signs of weakening and orders a sudden attack to overthrow it completely.

COMMENT AND SUMMARY.   Since it is impossible to depict a full-scale battle onstage, playwrights in various eras have used a variety of devices to convey the idea of battle without actually showing it. In ancient dramas, battles took place offstage, and messengers relayed information concerning the outcome of the battle. Shakespeare uses this classical method of establishing the atmosphere of battle without actually showing it, but he combines it with several other devices: short scenes, shifting from place to place on the field of battle to produce the effect of confusion and rapid action; some hand-to-hand combat enacted onstage; and verbal dueling, as among the generals in the preceding scene. The entire battle of Philippi is presented from the conspirators' point of view. In this scene, only Brutus and Messala are seen, but Brutus' orders describe what is taking place elsewhere on the field.

ACT V: SCENE iii

Cassius and Titinius appear on another part of the field of Philippi. Cassius, seeing his men deserting, tells Titinius how he slew his ensign who was turning to run. Titinius cries that Brutus gave the word to attack Antony too early. Meanwhile, Brutus' men, having overcome Octavius, were busy plundering the enemy's camp instead of assisting Cassius' flank, which was surrounded by Antony's soldiers. Pindarus enters to warn Cassius to flee, for Antony and his men have reached his tents. Cassius answers that he has retreated far enough. Looking across the plain, he asks, "Are those my tents where I perceive the fire?" Titinius replies, "They are, my lord."

COMMENT.   The attack ordered by Brutus has been a failure for Cassius, who has slain his own flag-bearer for deserting the field. Now Cassius rests on a hill at one end of the Philippian plain. He shows his courage and resignation by refusing to retreat farther even though the enemy is in close pursuit.

Cassius sees a body of horsemen in the distance and asks Titinius to ride to them and learn whether they are friends or foes. As Titinius rides off, Cassius orders Pindarus to climb higher on the hill to watch what is happening to Titinius, for his own "sight was ever thick" (near-sighted). As Pindarus climbs the hill, Cassius expresses his complete resignation to death: "This day I breathed first; time is come round,/And where I did begin, there shall I end;/My life is run his compass." Pindarus yells back to Cassius that Titinius has been surrounded by horsemen and exclaims, "He's ta'en! And hark! They shout for joy." Cassius bids Pindarus to come down, grieving that he is a coward to live so long and to see his "best friend" captured before his face. When Pindarus returns, Cassius reminds him how he had spared his life in Parthia when he had taken him captive on the condition that Pindarus swore to do whatsoever Cassius demanded. Cassius declares Pindarus a free man and orders him to take his sword, the same which ran Caesar through, and strike him in the bosom. As Pindarus guides the sword into his heart, Cassius cries, "Caesar, thou art reveng'd Even with the sword that kill'd thee." And with these words, Cassius dies. Pindarus sighs, "So I am free; yet would not so have been,/Durst I have done my will. O Cassius!/Far from this country Pindarus shall run,/Where never Roman shall take note of him."

COMMENT. Cassius has already resigned himself to death before he is misinformed that Titinius has been captured. Ironically, he has set Pindarus to watch because his own sight is short. Equally ironic is his grief over having lived to see his best friend captured "before my face," when, in fact, he has not seen a thing. It is Cassius' pessimistic resignation and his short-sightedness which moves him to commit suicide before he has confirmed Pindarus' report. The emphasis on the fact that Cassius dies with the same sword that pierced Caesar expresses the theme of retribution and is an example of poetic justice, in which an ironic ending, suitable to the crime committed, is provided for the wrongdoer. Still another irony is suggested by Cassius' suicide, which shows his complete and misguided rejection of Epicureanism, a philosophy which held that the senses were often deceptive and created illusions which, if they produced pain, were to be rejected. Cassius as an Epicurean would have been forced to reject the false report of Titinius' capture, at least until it had been confirmed absolutely. In his final words, Cassius addresses Caesar, leaving the impression that the spirit of Caesar hovers over the field of death and has participated in his own vengeance.

Pindarus' final words before parting adds a touch of bitter humor to the somber scene by suggesting that the civilized Romans are far more barbaric than the semi-civilized Parthians.

As Pindarus leaves the Roman world for good, Titinius returns with Messala. Messala tells Titinius that they have exchanged Brutus' victory over Octavius for Antony's victory over Cassius, leaving the situation the same as at the start of the day. Titinius remarks that these tidings will comfort Cassius. Messala asks where Cassius is and learns that he is on that same hill, just as he discovers a body on the ground. When Titinius sees that it is Cassius', he cries, "Cassius is no more. O setting sun!/As in thy red rays thou dost sink to night, /So in his red blood Cassius' day is set;/The sun of Rome is set. Our day is gone;/Clouds, dews, and dangers come; our deeds are done./Mistrust of my success hath done this deed." Messala, however, blames Cassius' suicide on his lack of confidence in their victory for Rome and on the imaginary fears produced by Cassius' melancholy and despondent nature. Titinius then asks where Pindarus is. Messala tells him to look for Pindarus, while he returns to tell Brutus the bad news.

When Messala leaves, Titinius addresses the body of his noble lord Cassius, mourning, "Alas, thou has misconstrued everything." He takes the victory garland which Brutus had given him for Cassius and places it as a sign of honor on the head of the corpse. Then, asking leave of the gods (for ending his time before their appointed hour), he expresses his duty as a Roman, picks up Cassius' sword, and kills himself.

> **COMMENT.**   Titinius has taken personal blame for the death of Cassius, who upon learning that Titinius his "best friend" had been captured, ended his own life. Following Cassius' example, Titinius takes the death of his friend as a sign that all is lost for their cause. He shows the loyalty and personal devotion of a true friend and proclaims it his duty as a Roman to die with Cassius. The theme of friendship even unto death is not a major one in this play, but it crops up from time to time as a sign of the great interest the Renaissance audience had in the concept of friendship among the ancients.

Messala returns bringing Brutus, young Cato, Strato, Volumnius, and Lucilius. Brutus asks where Cassius' body lies, and Messala points to where Titinius kneels in mourning. Brutus discovers that Titinius is dead and cries, "O Julius Caesar, thou art mighty yet!/Thy spirit walks abroad, and turns our swords/In our own proper entrails."

> **COMMENT.**   The theme of vengeance for Caesar's murder, echoed in Cassius' dying words, is expressed again in Brutus' cry. The battle and destruction which Antony had prophesied at Caesar's death, has, indeed, come to pass, and the spirit of Caesar has relentlessly tracked the murderers "and turns our swords/In our own proper entrails." Brutus' own death by suicide is now ominously predicted in his last remark.

In a final tribute to his dead friends, Brutus exclaims, "Are yet two Romans living such as these?/The last of all the Romans, fare thee well!" Brutus then orders that Cassius' body be sent to Thasos for the funeral, lest his funeral at Philippi destroy the morale of the soldiers. He bids young Cato, Lucilius, Labeo, and Flavius prepare for another battle before the night, since it is only three o'clock.

SUMMARY.   The importance of this scene is the death of Cassius as the result of his own nature and his ironic misunderstanding of events. Cassius' last hours are courageous and noble ones. He has rescued his battle flag, killed a coward, refused to retreat, and grieved over a captured friend. He dies not as a coward or base murderer but as a noble if misguided man, the victim of an avenging spirit, his own melancholy fears, and his own tragic flaws. The work begun on the ides of March is nearing its end. The man who devises the conspiracy against Caesar is dead. The monster of "domestic fury and fierce civil strife which Antony had set loose (III. i) is writhing to its end. Brutus and Labeo (who, according to Plutarch, had also stabbed Caesar) are the only conspirators left alive. We can expect to see the end of them in the remaining two scenes of the play.

ACT V: SCENE iv

Brutus, Cato, Lucilius, Messala, and Flavius are seen on another part of the battlefield of Philippi. In the midst of battle, Brutus passes quickly across the stage, encouraging his men to fight bravely.

As Brutus goes off, young Cato stoutly proclaims he is the son of Marcus Cato, "a foe to tyrants, and my country's friend."

Enemy soldiers appear and engage Cato and Lucilius in single combat.

Echoing young Cato's cries, Lucilius shouts, "And I am Brutus, Marcus Brutus, I." The fighting continues. Lucilius sees young Cato fall. As he continues to fight, Lucilius pays tribute to his comrade, "O young and noble Cato, art thou down?/Why now thou diest as bravely as Titinius."

Commanded to yield, Lucilius ceases to do battle and offers his captors gold to kill him instantly and to be honored by having slain Brutus in battle. The soldier declines the bribe, for it is a far greater honor to take the noble Brutus prisoner.

Antony arrives at this point and is told that Brutus is captured. Addressing Lucilius, Antony asks where Brutus is. Loyally, Lucilius answers, "Brutus is safe enough," He adds, "When you do find him, alive or dead,/He will be found like Brutus, like himself" (that is, as noble as ever).

Antony informs his men that Lucilius, although he is not Brutus, is a worthy prize. He orders them to take Lucilius prisoner and to treat him kindly, for Antony would like to have him as a friend. Then others are ordered to pursue Brutus and to report to Antony at Octavius' tent.

COMMENT AND SUMMARY.   The second engagement in the battle of Philippi is portrayed with a good deal of physical movement. Brutus rushes across the stage. There is hand-to-hand combat. Cato falls. Lucilius is captured. Lucilius follows a practice of medieval warfare in proclaiming he is Brutus. He does not wish to assume honors that are not rightfully his, but attempts to protect his generals by confusing the enemy and preventing their pursuit of the real target, Brutus. In some editions of the play, this speech is attributed to Brutus, in which case, Brutus makes an exit just before Cato falls. Plutarch makes it clear that Lucilius does impersonate Brutus.

Brief as it is, the scene shows that Brutus' men are loyal, fight courageously to the end, and are still devoted to the cause of the Republic. It shows that Brutus is slowly being defeated. His brother-in-law, young Cato, is killed; his lieutenant, Lucilius, is captured; and he himself is in flight with the enemy in hot pursuit. Antony appears briefly as shrewdly politic as ever and attempts to sabotage the rival army by expressing his desire to have Lucilius for a friend.

ACT V: SCENE v

Brutus, Dardanius, Clitus, Strato, and Volumnius appear in another part of the field. Brutus and the remnants of his army rest on a rock. Clitus reports that Statilius has sent a signal, but since he did not come back he has evidently been captured or slain. Pessimistically, Brutus replies, "Slaying is the word;/It is a deed in fashion." Leaning closer, Brutus whispers into Clitus' ear, and Clitus responds to the message, "What, I, my lord? No, not for all the world!" Brutus then turns to Dardanius, who replies, "Shall I do such a deed?"

Clitus and Dardanius compare notes and reveal that Brutus has requested each of them to kill him. They watch him as he meditates quietly apart. "Now is that noble vessel full of grief,/That it runs over even at his eyes," Clitus observes.

Brutus calls Volumnius to him and tells him about the ghost of Caesar, which has appeared to him twice, once at Sardis and again last night at Philippi. "I know my hour is come," Brutus declares. Volumnius tries to argue Brutus out of his depression, but Brutus is convinced that the enemy has beaten them to the pit like wild beasts. It is better, he decides, "to leap in ourselves/Than tarry till they push us."

An alarm is sounded and Clitus warns Brutus to fly. Brutus bids his men farewell, declaring, "My heart doth joy that yet in all my life/I found no man but he was true to me." Now he is tired and his bones crave rest. The alarm is sounded again, and warnings to fly are shouted from within. Brutus sends the others off, promising to follow. Only Strato is asked to remain.

Brutus confronts his servant Strato with the same request he had made of his friends, and Strato agrees to hold the sword and hide his face, while Brutus ends his life.

Servant and master take hands and say goodby. Then, with the words "Caesar, now be still;/I killed not thee with half so good a will," Brutus runs upon his sword and dies.

A retreat is sounded as Brutus dies. Antony and Octavius arrive on the scene. They have with them Messala and Lucilius who have been taken prisoner. Octavius speaks first, "What man is that," he asks, pointing to Strato. Messala identifies Brutus' servant and asks Strato where Brutus is. "Free from the bondage you are in, Messala," Strato replies. Brutus has killed himself, "and no man else hath honor in his death." Lucilius praises Brutus' suicide, which proves to him that Brutus was as honorable as he had thought.

Octavius offers to take Brutus' men into his service, and Strato agrees to go if Messala gives him a recommendation. Learning that Strato held the sword for Brutus, Messala urges Octavius to take this good servant as his follower.

Antony, who has been silent all the while, speaks now over the body of Brutus: "This was the noblest Roman of them all./All the conspirators save only he/Did that they did in envy of great Caesar;/He, only in a general honest thought/And common good to all, made one of them." Antony concludes his eulogy of Brutus by describing his nature as gentle "and the elements/So mixed in him that Nature might stand up/And say to all the world, 'This was a man!' "

It is Octavius who has the last words in the play. He orders that Brutus be given "all respect and rites of burial" and that within Octavius' tent "his bones tonight shall lie,/Most like a soldier, ordered honorably."

COMMENT AND SUMMARY.   The last climax of the play is reached with Brutus' death. His presumptuousness and arrogant virtue disintegrated in death, Brutus has honor and dignity restored to him in his last hours. He has fought courageously and has faced death with the resignation becoming a great man. In the last scene, he is seen as the object of devotion of his surviving friends, who refuse to hold the sword on which he dies. He is rid of his obstinate constancy to impracticable ideals and acts by human impulse when he decides on suicide. Lucilius, Messala, and Strato applaud his honorable death, and Octavius promises funeral rites in which Brutus' honor as a soldier will be recognized. Antony sums up the character of Brutus as it has been seen throughout the play. Brutus was "the noblest Roman of them all," the only one of the conspirators who killed Caesar out of a concern for the public good and not for envy or in the hope of personal gain.

The avenging spirit of Caesar is never seen again, except as Brutus reports it as an omen of his defeat. Clearly, it is Brutus' belief as he dies that the work begun on the ides of March has been finished, the pleasure of the Fates has been decided, and the spirit of Caesar has been avenged.

The final episode of the play is like a prologue to another. It shows Octavius emerging as the most dominant member of the triumvirate. He speaks first and last and gives all the commands for the disposition of Brutus' men and his body. Then, for the first time in the entire play, Antony praises Brutus. There is a touch of pathos in the fact that his eulogy of the man he had pursued to his death had its counterpart in previous and subsequent events. Brutus has so praised Caesar, the man he had slain; now Antony praises the man he has hunted to the pit; and later, Octavius praises Antony after he has hounded him to his death. This eulogy over his victim suggests that Antony will take over Brutus' role as the man marked for extinction by the gods, just as Brutus had taken over Caesar's, and the clash between Antony and Octavius, which is dramatized in Shakespeare's *Antony and Cleopatra*, is foreshadowed in this closing scene of *Julius Caesar*.

CHARACTER ANALYSES

JULIUS CAESAR in Shakespeare's play is not the Caesar of the Gallic wars, described in Plutarch's *Life of Caesar* and reflected in Caesar's own *Commentaries*. He is the aging Caesar, physically infirm, but successful and overconfident, who, according to Plutarch, had overreached himself, insulted his peers, and incurred the wrath of patricians, Republicans, and the gods. According to the dramatic chronology and Cassius' reports, Caesar has recently suffered from fever in Spain and is now deaf and epileptic. At the opening of the play, apart from his costume and the pomp and circumstance which accompany his appearance, Caesar displays few of the special virtues which had made him a conqueror and dictator and favorite of the common people. Of late, he has begun to stand on ceremony (religious ritual and superstition), which is a sign of his mental deterioration. He is concerned with sacrifice and augury, with prodigies, and with Calpurnia's dream. He is subject to flattery and is vain and boastful. But to call him a coward is to do him an injustice. He agrees to stay home from the Senate out of consideration for Calpurnia's fears, but when he is told the decision would be misconstrued, or ridiculed, or that he might never be offered the crown again, he alters his decision. His human tenderness is subordinated to his public image and his ambition.

Despite his shortcomings, some of the heroic traits and gracious attributes which belonged to the historical Caesar come through in Shakespeare's characterization. His insight into Cassius shows he is still a shrewd judge of men, and his public bequests betoken his political wisdom even after his death. His friends attest to his military powers, his justice, and his generosity; Brutus, his murderer, finds no fault in his past actions; and even Cassius, his worst enemy, admits that Caesar never abused him as Brutus has. Caesar is almost tender in his dealings with Calpurnia and Decius; he is paternal to Antony when he instructs and praises him, and he is urbane and hospitable to the conspirators when they call at his home.

In the Senate, on the day of his death, Caesar reaches the height of his ruthlessness and self-assurance, which had once made him a hero. He has forgotten his human limitations in his rise to power. He tempts the gods when he declares himself above "ordinary men," comparing his own constancy with that of the North Star, and he enrages his friends when he obstinately refuses their petitions, although they implore him on their knees to grant mercy to a banished Roman.

After he is stricken, his humanity is restored to him. The dying Caesar is not the infatuated man who has just spoken from the throne. For a moment, he is an Elizabethan idealist who cherishes the noble love of a friend more than anything in the world. When he sees Brutus, whom he loves best, among his betrayers, he relinquishes his hold on the world: "Then fall Caesar."

BRUTUS is first seen in the play as the bemused observer of Caesar's procession as Caesar marches to the Lupercalia. He is not a "gamesome" fellow and does not choose to join the festivities. Of late, he has shown ungentle looks and has made Caesar fear he has lost his love. Upon hearing shouts from the market-place where Caesar is presiding, Brutus inadvertently expresses his fear that Caesar has become king. From that moment on, he is forced to end his contemplations and make a decision for action.

His conflict consists of his love for Caesar on one hand, and his concern for the public good and the welfare of the Republic on the other. Persuaded by Cassius to join a conspiracy against Caesar, Brutus spends a restless night making his decision. He can find no justification for Caesar's murder in Caesar's past actions; therefore, he finds justification for it in what Caesar might become. He assumes that Caesar will become an unbearable tyrant if he is made king, and on the basis of this assumption he decides to murder him. The flaw in his reasoning is that Brutus does not raise the question of whether or not a moral end justifies immoral means, nor does he consider that his action may be met with public disfavor. He is blindly convinced in the power of reason and believes that the public, when they have heard his reasons, will support his action.

Because he has little practical knowledge of life, he is blind to the real motives and characters of men and is ignorant of the practical means of conducting a war. He trusts Antony who betrays him, rejects Cicero who is as loyal to the same Republican cause as he, and mistrusts Cassius who loves him. He refuses to obtain money by unjust means at Sardis, yet becomes indignant because Cassius has not sent him some of the tainted money that Cassius has obtained. He even falsely accuses Cassius of personal corruption.

He is seen at the height of his arrogance and self-confidence, obstinate idealism, and incorruptibility when, like Caesar, he is being least merciful, least human, least yielding to his friend, Cassius. Despite his show of confidence during this quarrel with Cassius, Brutus spends a restless night in his tent. Disturbed over the reaction of the mob to the murder of Caesar, empassioned by the argument he has had with Cassius, and grieving over the death of his noble wife, Portia, Brutus sees an apparition. The ghost, which is either a subjective projection of Brutus' disturbed mind, or the existing spirit of the unavenged Caesar, tells Brutus that he is his "evil spirit" and will see him again at Philippi.

Courageously, Brutus decides to meet his destiny at once. He is no longer in torment when he sets out for Philippi, for the resolution of his conflict is in sight. Either he will be victor of the day or he will be killed in battle, and the work begun on the ides of March will have been done. It is this impatience to see the end which causes Brutus to act impetuously, bringing about destruction to Cassius, to the cause of the Republic, and finally to himself.

His death by suicide is in opposition to the philosophic principles he has professed all his life, and which he claimed he would continue to follow even if defeated. This suicide is the one compromise with his ideals that Brutus is known to make in the play, for it is an act which he had previously regarded as "cowardly and vile." Yet this act wins him continued honor among his friends and the praise of his enemy, Antony, for the first time in the play.

CASSIUS is an able soldier and a shrewd politician. He is the real organizer of the conspiracy against Caesar, which he enters out of his love of freedom as much as out of his hatred for Caesar and tyranny. When he is first seen in the play, he expresses his fear that he has lost the friendship and approval of Brutus, whom he loves and respects. Assured of Brutus' continuing love for him, Cassius tries to persuade his friend to join the anti-Caesarist cause. Cassius' imprecations against Caesar show a certain blindness to the spirit of leadership, which Caesar still has, and an overemphasis on physical strength, which Caesar no longer possesses.

Seen next from Caesar's point of view, Cassius "has a lean and hungry look;/He thinks too much." He is a man to be feared because "he reads much,/He is a great observer, and he looks/Quite through the deeds of men. He loves no plays,/. . . he hears no music;/Seldom he smiles, and smiles in such a sort/As if he mocked himself and scorned his spirit/That could be moved to smile at anything./Such men as he be never at heart's ease/Whiles they behold a greater than themselves,/And therefore are they very dangerous." Caesar's description is that of a melancholy man, who is also a cynic (in our sense of the word). Cassius is a silent type, observant, penetrating, quick to anger, slow to smile. He abjures the sensual pleasures of life such as Antony enjoys, but he is well-read and thoughtful. He knows the philosophy of Stoicism, but claims he could never live by its ideals, and he knows that he cannot accept Portia's death with stoic resignation as Brutus does. He is by admission (and historically) an Epicurean, who believes in friendship as one of the highest forms of good and disbelieves in the divine intervention in human affairs. His interpretation of the amazing prodigies on the eve of the ides of March must be regarded as a ruse to attract Casca to the conspiracy, for surely, as an Epicurean, he cannot believe in omens. On the other hand, Cassius announces late in the play that he has discarded Epicureanism and now accepts omens as warnings from the gods to men. Perhaps the conversion is supposed to have taken place prior to the events of the play. (Although Shakespeare does not provide this information, Cassius' philosophic conversion is said to have taken place just before the assassination of Caesar (see Plutarch). If this is true in the play as well, then, as the play progresses, Cassius' character changes philosophically as well as psychologically.)

Early in the play, Cassius' plan to persuade Brutus to join his cause makes him seem like a Machiavellian villain who seduces the noble Brutus in order to use him as a puppet; thus, Brutus appears to be exalted by this contrast with the conniving Cassius, and when he wins decisions over Cassius, his victories seem to be just. Shakespeare makes it clear, however, that Brutus' decisions are based on impractical ideals and Cassius' suggestions, although ignoble, are workable ones. As the play progresses, Brutus' character deteriorates; he becomes overconfident, obstinate, cruel, and taunting. Cassius, meanwhile, begins to display the "rash choler" of his melancholy nature. At the same time, he reveals that the love, respect, and honor he shows for Brutus are unquestionably real. Cassius ultimately submits to chastisement for practicing certain military expediencies which Brutus regards as corrupt, and acknowledges his subordination to Brutus by calling him "my lord." His submission is so complete that he follows Brutus to Philippi against his better judgment, changes his philosophy to Stoicism in order to meet his destiny with greater resignation, and ends his life in a burst of melancholic depression in which imaginary fears and delusions of imminent defeat overcome him entirely. Already depressed over the ill-timed venture at Philippi, Cassius seizes upon the supposed capture of his "best friend" Titinius as a final reason for ending his life. His trusted slave Pindarus "guides" the sword, which had killed Caesar, and Cassius dies, guiltily crying, "Caesar thou art revenged."

MARK ANTONY was one of the foremost opportunists of his day. Historically, he was interested in only one thing, political power. In the play, however, Antony is portrayed as a well-rounded Roman or a perfect Elizabethan gentleman. He is an athlete, likes music, and enjoys plays. He is given to all-night carousing, but does not shirk his duties by sleeping late. He is loyal and devoted to Caesar, almost subservient to the man he loves, honors, and fears. He is misjudged by Brutus as a harmless fellow and a mere lover of pleasure, but he is seen as shrewd and dangerous by the more perceptive Cassius. Antony wisely pretends to throw in his lot with the conspirators in order to gain time and favors, but as soon as he can, he plans to let loose an unholy reign of terror to avenge the death of his beloved lord. The mischief he sets afoot is so clever and cruel that he becomes a Machiavellian figure for a time. His gifts of oratory, his political acumen, and his knowledge of mob psychology have been hidden from men, but they are all disclosed during his famous funeral oration, delivered in verse over the body of Caesar. It is seen during the oration that Antony's indulgence in the company of men and in the arts, especially poetry and drama, have served as an education in political leadership.

Antony is next seen ruthlessly signing death warrants of political enemies—seventy or one hundred, according to the reports, including Cicero and his own nephew. He displays Machiavellian statesmanship in these political murders and in his plan to get rid of Lepidus when he has finished using him. His ambition and greed come forward when he flinches at sharing a third of the world with a mulish dullard like Lepidus.

At the end of the play, Antony shows his skill in verbal and physical combat. He is confidently, even smugly, assured of victory over the conspirators, and he still speaks of avenging Caesar, despite his previously expressed interest in gaining control over Rome. Octavius begins to show his teeth, however, and in the final scene of the play, takes full command over the business at hand. Antony is silent in Octavius' presence, but he delivers a final eulogy over the body of Brutus in which he praises his enemy for the first time in the play, suggesting that since Octavius has taken over, Antony has had some cause to sympathize with Brutus' fight against tyranny.

OCTAVIUS, the grand-nephew of Caesar, was adopted as Caesar's son and heir, inheriting Caesar's name, three-fourths of his estate, and Caesar's lust for power and control over Rome. Octavius first appears in the play after Caesar's death. He joins the triumvirate formed by Antony and Lepidus and follows the plans and directions of Antony, even agreeing to eliminate Lepidus. Privately, however, he feels that Lepidus is a tried and valiant man, who deserves to be rewarded for good service. At his second appearance at the battle of Philippi, Octavius is beginning to balk at Antony's command, accepts orders this time, but threatens to cross Antony at a later date. By the end of the battle and the play, Octavius is in full command. He does most of the talking, gets no opposition from Antony, gives orders for Brutus' funeral, recruits men from Brutus' ranks, and calls the field to rest, all in the presence of Antony, who remains silent except for a final, pathetic eulogy over the body of Brutus.

PORTIA is a heroic example of the devoted Roman wife. She has a noble husband, Brutus, and a noble father, Cato, whose courage and wisdom she feels she has inherited. Concerned for her husband, she explains in great detail the reasons for her anxiety and implores him to tell her the cause of her grief. She is not put off by pretexts and uses reason and flattery to get to the truth, which she claims it is her right to know.

As she says, she is more than an ordinary woman, for she is Brutus' wife and Cato's daughter, and has proved her constancy and resolution by spilling her own blood when she thought it necessary. Although she wins the argument and learns of Brutus' plans, she has great difficulty the next day in keeping herself from divulging the plans inadvertently. She admits that it is hard for women to keep counsel, but manages to do so. She becomes a study in anxiety as she awaits news of the outcome of the assassination. Later, her anxiety over Brutus' absence causes her to commit suicide. Her death is received with stoic resignation by Brutus.

Because of her spirited and intelligent argument, her occasional use of legal terminology, and her delicate sexual conversation, Portia's characterization is sometimes taken as a prototype of the later Portia, heroine of *The Merchant of Venice*.

CALPURNIA is the superstitious and barren wife of Julius Caesar, whom she loves and obeys. Her fears of omens is recently acquired, for she "never stood on ceremonies" in her earlier days. Now, however, strange dreams, ominous prodigies, and fateful augurs have frightened her. She fears for her husband's life and implores him to stay at home and guard his safety on the ides of March. She thinks of Caesar as a prince and believes that the falling meteors are warnings of a prince's death. When she hears her husband boast that he is more dangerous than danger itself, she recognizes that this is foolish arrogance and tells him so; "Alas, my lord/Your wisdom is consumed in confidence." In response to her criticism and humble petitions, Caesar momentarily agrees to satisfy her whim. However, she is last seen accepting chastisement silently ("How foolish do your fears seem now") and obediently fetching Caesar's robe as he flouts her wishes and leaves for the Senate.

DECIUS BRUTUS is a member of the conspiracy against Caesar. His real name was Decimus Brutus, but Shakespeare followed North's translation of Plutarch where Decius had appeared. Decius volunteers to assure Caesar's arrival at the Senate on the ides of March. He is aware of Caesar's assumed disgust for flattery and plans to flatter Caesar by praising this disgust. He uses his friendship with Caesar and Caesar's love for him to elicit Caesar's excuse for absenting himself from the Senate. Then he cleverly reinterprets Calpurnia's dream, which prevents Caesar from going out, and shrewdly converts it to an auspicious one. Decius manipulates Caesar through the latter's fear of ridicule, his ambition for the crown, and his fear of insulting the Senate. When he finally gets Caesar on his way, Decius contrives to keep him from reading Artemidorus' warning by interposing another letter, purportedly from Trebonius. Thus, he prevents Caesar from reading one letter by giving him a second, and seems to know that Caesar will be easily confused and decide to read none. After the assassination, he disappears from the play, but it is presumed here, as it occurred in history, that Antony has Decius murdered.

CASCA is an amusing and informative conspirator. He first appears as a member of Caesar's train who has attended the Lupercal and observed the attempted coronation and Caesar's reactions to it. He describes these events to Cassius and Brutus in a ludicrous satirical style with more than a hint of rudeness and vulgarity. The whole coronation episode, to Casca's thinking, is "mere foolery," a phrase he repeats more than once during his description. Brutus views him as a "blunt fellow" who used to have a "quick mettle" when they went to school together, but Cassius explains that Casca still has a lively disposition when it is needed for some bold or noble enterprise. (It is Casca, in fact, who strikes the first blow at Caesar.) According to

Cassius, Casca's rudeness and sluggish appearance are donned to disguise his good intelligence so that when he speaks the truth, men will be slow to take offense at an apparent fool.

Not long after this, however, Casca is seen as a trembling clown, amazed, confused, and frightened by the wonders of the night and unable to make sense out of the portents. He fears that the gods are angry and that the end of the world had come. Cassius easily persuades Casca, whom he calls "dull," that the impatience of heaven is a warning of the abnormal state of affairs in Rome, and that an ordinary man like Caesar has become a fearful monster.

Fear and Casca are often found together. Casca believes "it is the part of men to fear and tremble," and he regards one who dies early as one who "cuts off so many years of fearing death." Casca is associated with cowardice when Cassius tells him that he lacks courage ("those sparks of life That should be in a Roman,") or else that he does not use it, and again when Antony sarcastically calls him "my valiant Casca" and when Antony claims that Casca stabbed Caesar in the back. Although Casca signals the attack against Caesar and strikes the first blow, it may be inferred that Casca's participation in the "bold or noble enterprise" of Caesar's assassination is the act of a coward. (Shakespeare does not reveal Casca's fate after the assassination, but history records that he killed himself after the battle of Philippi.)

OTHER CONSPIRATORS are *Trebonius* who lures Antony away from the Senate while Caesar is being murdered; *Metellus Cimber* who had a personal grudge against Caesar for exiling his brother, Publius Cimber; *Cinna*, a messenger for the conspirators, who had the same name as Cinna the poet; *Ligarius* who gets out of a sickbed to join the conspiracy.

CICERO has a minor role in the play and is used mainly to create the atmosphere of the period in which the play takes place. Cicero was well known to Elizabethans as a famous orator and an ardent Republican; his absence from the conspiracy is given some explanation in the play.

LEPIDUS is the third and weakest member of the triumvirate, consisting also of Antony and Octavius. He appears only briefly, and is rather a subject of discussion between Antony and Octavius than a character in the play.

MEMBERS OF BRUTUS' ARMY AND HOUSEHOLD include *Lucilius*, a trusted and loyal lieutenant; *Lucius*, a devoted young slave and lute player; *Strato*, the slave who assists in Brutus' death; *Volumnius, Cato the Younger, Varro, Clitus, Claudius, Dardanius,* and *Messala*, a loyal follower who joins Antony after Brutus' death.

MEMBERS OF CASSIUS' TROOP AND HOUSEHOLD include *Titinius,* Cassius' "best friend,' whose capture is the immediate cause of Cassius suicide; *Pindarus*, the Parthian slave of Cassius, who assists in his death.

OTHER MINOR CHARACTERS include *Publius*, the venerable Roman senator, who is terrified by the assassination and says not a word in the play; *Flavius* and *Marullus*, tribunes of the people, followers of Pompey, and defenders of the Republic, who chastise the mob for celebrating Caesar's triumph; *Cinna the Poet*, a friend of Caesar's who is torn apart by the mob for having the same name as Cinna the conspirator; *Artemidorus*, a teacher of rhetoric, who tries to warn Caesar; the *Soothsayer*, who also tries to warn Caesar of the conspiracy; *Popilius Lena*, the senator who wishes Cassius good luck on his venture and then walks off to speak to Caesar, terrifying the assassins with possible betrayal; a cynical poet, who attempt to reconcile Cassius and Brutus after their quarrel.

THE MOB has an important role in many of Shakespeare's plays, especially *Coriolanus*, but is nowhere more significant than in *Julius Caesar*. Here they are seen as an Elizabethan rather than as a Roman mob. They are a capricious lot who love holidays and pageants. They turn out early, climb high towers with babes in arms, and sit all day waiting for a procession to go by. They hiss what offends them and cheer what they like. They have a mass will and a mass mind which can easily be persuaded and easily enraged. Once it is enraged, it is impossible to reason with the mob. Then they are quick to take insult and merciless in their punishment of slight offenses. No individual in the mob would kill a man because of his name, but as a mob, they kill for a name or for no reason at all. They have "chopt hands" and "sweaty night-caps," and utter such a deal of stinking breath (onions were staples in the diet of lower-class Elizabethans) because Caesar refused the crown, that it almost choked Caesar; "for he swounded and fell down at it."

CRITICAL COMMENTARY

INTRODUCTION. *Julius Caesar* is one of Shakespeare's most popular and enduring plays. It has been so for nearly four hundred years and has withstood the changes of time and taste. Different ages had different reasons for enjoying the tragedy, but for each, the play had some special appeal. For Elizabethans, that special appeal was the resemblance betwen Caesar and some of their more tragic kings. For our own age, the political, ethical, and psychological implications are of primary interest.

The play was almost certainly produced originally in 1599 at the Globe theater. Contemporary allusions to it, and the frequency of its production, make it clear that it had a profound effect on its early audiences. During the seventeenth century, it was performed at the courts of James I, Charles I, and, later, Charles II. It was one of the few plays which was not revised to meet the so-called classical standards of the Restoration era, although critics of both the Restoration and Augustan eras of English literature had difficulty in reconciling *Julius Caesar* with the Aristotelian unities and rules of decorum. Romantic critics of the nineteenth century turned their attention on the characters of the play, and in the liberal spirit of the age tended to favor Brutus as the hero of the play over Caesar the tyrant and villain of the piece.

In our own time, critics have taken many new approaches in attempting to answer fundamental problems, raised in the play, which have vexed thinkers since the play was first produced. The structural unity of the play, the identity of the hero, the real theme of the play, and the author's moral attitude toward insurrection, have all been open to question. Its genre, too, has been questioned, and has been identified by some modern critics as a "problem play" in which the central interest is a moral-political-psychological problem rather than a tragic hero.

THE STRUCTURE OF THE PLAY. If *Julius Caesar* was produced in 1599. it was performed not long after Shakespeare's chronicle play *Henry V* had been seen on the boards. It is easy to see the chronicle's influence on the loose construction and episodic treatment which the Roman tragedy received. Because of its loose composition, critics have argued that there are two parts to the play and two heroes, Brutus and Caesar. Others like George Lyman Kittredge have insisted on the structural unity of the play, pointing out that Caesar's spirit takes over after Caesar's death and remains in the background for the remainder of the play.

The historian and literary critic Louis B. Wright, who has probed deeply into the character of the Elizabethan audience, agrees with Kittredge that Caesar is the central interest and provides the unity of the play: "To Elizabethans, Caesar was a character of consuming interest. They were vastly interested in strong men who could impose order in a chaotic world. . . . Caesar had been a leader with the capacity for rule such as Elizabethans understood and approved."

The Victorian critic R. G. Moulton produced an elaborate analysis of the structure of the play as the movement of Passion. In doing so, however, he could not avoid the inevitable issue of the hero of the play. Moulton chose Caesar as the hero, for he believed that the climax of the play occurs in the center rather than at the end. Such an early climax, Moulton declared, might create a tediously long conclusion in the work of other writers, but Shakespeare's dramatic genius prevents this loss of interest in the remainder of the play by making Antony appear immediately after the murder as the avenger of his dead lord. There is a transitional stage in which the play lags somewhat after Antony's oration, but new interest arises when Cassius and Brutus quarrel and become reconciled. In this master stroke of human characterization, Moulton declared, Shakespeare revives audience interest in the decline of the two chief conspirators and prevents a lag of interest in the waning action of the play.

Ever since the eighteenth century, critics have felt that Brutus, not Caesar, was the central interest in the play and provided its structural unity from beginning to end. Voltaire was among the first of many who believed that *Julius Caesar* was a misnomer and that the tragedy should rightly be called *Marcus Brutus*. Sir Mungo William MacCallum (1910), supported by Dover Wilson, also saw Brutus as the character who determined the unity of the play. MacCallum argued that *Julius Caesar* was a transitional play between Shakespeare's histories and his tragedies and pointed out that in a number of Shakespeare's historical plays, the titular hero dies before the end of the play. In 2 *Henry IV*, for example, the play continues for an entire act after King Henry's death, while in all of Shakespeare's tragedies, the hero remains in focus until the end of the play.

When modern critics approach the problem of the structure of *Julius Caesar*, they often base their analyses on the assumption that the hero of the play is deliberately made ambiguous and that the theme of rebellion or insurrection is the real focus of Shakespeare's interest. Under these circumstances, the unity of the play is not found in a single hero, but in its ironic contrasts of characters and events and in its style and imagery. Brents Stirling (1951), for example, finds that the theme of religious ritual dominates the assassination scene and that Brutus' failure to make a sacrifice out of the murder is the result of Shakespeare's intention to give the theme satirical treatment. Leo Kirschbaum (1949) tried to put Brutus back into the perspective from which he was removed by Romantic critics, who had concentrated on character analyses, believing that characters were the most important interests in Shakespeare's plays. Kirschbaum argued that Shakespeare deliberately "invented the blood-bath" in order to shock us into seeing that "murder is in the act savage and inhuman" and that regardless of its purpose "the merciless rending of a man is an obscene performance."

In his study of style and imagery in Julius Caesar, R. A. Foakes (1954) discovered that the themes of superstition, sickness, noise, and names, which run through the play and comprise its fabric, also determine that the unity of the play is to be found in the theme of rebellion. There is a good deal of concurrence among moderns like Harley Granville-Barker (1947) and Leonard F. Dean (1961) that the political theme of the play constitutes its focus and provides its unity. (From the point of view of staging the play, however, Granville-Barker finds that Shakespeare's sympathy rests with Brutus, although he does not wish to justify Caesar's assassination.) In an essay by Ernest Schanzer (1955), *Julius Caesar* is declared "one of Shakespeare's most perplexing plays," for Schanzer believes that Shakespeare created a deliberately ambiguous Caesar to show up the futility of assassination. In other words, the moral and political theme of assassination determines its unity for Schanzer and provides the frame of reference for understanding the ambiguous natures of the characters in the play.

THE CHARACTER OF CAESAR. It is inevitable that Caesar himself should be the subject of wide critical interest. As has already been seen, the attitude of the critic toward the structural unity of the play is always brought to bear on his interpretation of the characters in the play. The conservative opinion, represented by George Lyman Kittredge, is that Caesar is central to the play from start to finish. Another conservative in his approach to Caesar is James E. Phillips, Jr. (1940), who finds that "in the character which he gives Caesar as a ruler, Shakespeare makes it clear that such autocracy was a blessing to the state. Caesar is represented as ably qualified, according to Renaissance standards, to exercise 'the specialty of rule.' There are, to be sure, personality weaknesses. . . ."

There is very little argument about the fact that Shakespeare depicts Caesar's physical infirmities, but there is considerable debate on whether or not Shakespeare creates a general impression of Caesar's greatness at any point in the play. MacCallum argued that Shakespeare's Caesar was a heroic figure to the audience for whom he was originally intended and that it is only through minute analysis that his defects are discovered. Professor Harry Morgan Ayres (1910) supported the argument for Caesar as the central figure of the play, but showed that he was created in the Renaissance stage tradition of the Marlovian or Senecan stage tyrant, a great and ambitious man whose heroic success produced a mad arrogance which presaged his destruction. Louis B. Wright (1958), insisting on the historical approach, asserts, "If Caesar on Shakespeare's stage sounds pompous to us, his manner was not objectionable to the spectator at the Globe." Nevertheless, observers like Maynard Mack (1960), who interprets Caesar's superstitions as signs of his childishness, continue to find Caesar defective, while others like Ernest Schanzer stress the ambiguity and pathos in Caesar's portrayal. The questions still remain: Is Caesar simply the heroic and ambitious figure of history; is he purely a defective creature who deserves his bloody fate; or is he the pathetic, complex, and ambiguous figure who symbolizes the theme of insurrection in a problem play?

THE CHARACTER OF BRUTUS. Brutus has always aroused more interest among critics than any other character in the play. As early as the eighteenth-century, Brutus was considered by some to be the central figure of the play and the character for whom the play should be named. Samuel Johnson, the great eighteenth-century editor of Shakespeare's works, who found Julius Caesar "cold and oppressing" on the whole, was moved by "the contention and reconciliation of Brutus and Cassius." Coleridge (c. 1812) was perplexed but decidedly interested in Brutus' mental processes and in his anxiety to harmonize Brutus with his "historical preconception" of him. Coleridge probed the question, "How . . . could Brutus say he finds no personal cause for the murder; i.e. none in Caesar's past conduct as a man? Had he not passed the Rubicon? . . ." Equally romantic and sympathetic in his approach to Brutus, William Hazlitt (1817) views the character as a demonstration of Shakespeare's "penetration into political character." The whole design of the play, according to Hazlitt, is Brutus' attempt to liberate Rome, an attempt which "fails from the generous temper and overweening confidence of Brutus in the goodness of their cause and the assistance of others. Thus it has always been. Those who mean well themselves think well of others and fall a prey to their security."

The Danish biographer and critic Georg M. Brandes brought events in Shakespeare's life and times to bear on his interpretation of the play and also chose Brutus as the true hero. Brandes believed that the unsuccessful conspiracy against Queen Elizabeth by Southampton and Essex, two of Shakespeare's friends, had shown Shakespeare how "proud and nobly-disposed characters might easily be seduced into political error." In addition, Brandes maintained, Shakespeare, then at the height of his career, had begun to show an interest in noble characters like Brutus and Hamlet, whose fortunes had turned against them. Moreover, Brandes asserted, Plutarch did not appreciate Caesar's greatness, and Shakespeare, who followed Plutarch so closely in other respects, adopted Plutarch's attitude toward Caesar as well. Brutus, therefore, was selected as the tragic hero of *Julius Caesar.* As a result Caesar was belittled into a "miserable creature" of a tyrant in order to supply Brutus with a reliable motive for murder. According to Brandes, Caesar is a villain for attempting "to introduce monarchy into a well-ordered republican state," and Brutus is made "simple and great" at Caesar's expense.

Like Brandes, MacCallum found justification in Plutarch for Shakespeare's exaltation of Brutus and downgrading of Caesar. He believed, as Voltaire had more than a century earlier, that the proper title of the play should have been *Marcus Brutus,* for he felt that Shakespeare had made Brutus the spokesman for the Republic, which the playwright favored, and Caesar the spokesman for imperialism, which

Shakespeare opposed. According to MacCallum, "Shakespeare wishes to portray a patriotic gentleman of the best Roman or the best English type. . . ." Brutus' only flaw (as Hazlitt also saw it) is his too strict adherence to the virtues he possesses. The career of Brutus, according to MacCallum, is one of disillusionment and defeat, which reaches its climax in the quarrel he has with Cassius. Echoing Hazlitt, MacCallum wrote, Brutus has been "impractical and perverse, as every enthusiast for abstract justice must be, who lets himself be seduced into crime on the plea of duty, and yet shapes his course as though he were not a criminal." At the end, MacCallum declares, Brutus dies a martyr.

MacCallum's extreme justification of the nobility of Brutus is received with disfavor in many quarters, even among critics like Granville-Barker (1927), who felt that Shakespeare's sympathies were with Brutus. Granville-Barker tempers his interpretation of Brutus by insisting that Shakespeare did not intend to justify Caesar's assassination when he gave Brutus sympathetic treatment. Sir Mark Hunter approaches the play as a study in character, an approach generally rejected by younger critics, but Sir Mark does not make Brutus a stereotype of virtue as MacCallum had. He finds Brutus "noble-hearted and sincere beyond question, [but] he is intellectually dishonest." He is fanatical, self-righteous, and inconsistent. Sir Mark perceives that Brutus' "own conduct, apart from the capital crime, is sometimes at strange variance with principles simultaneously professed."

More recently, however, the studies of John Palmer (1948) have led him to conclude that Shakespeare has made Brutus the object of ironic satire. Cassius is the foil who first brings out Brutus' deficiencies; later Antony replaces Cassius in this function. Brutus, according to Palmer, is the portrait of an ineffectual politician whose confused thinking is "sharply divorced from political reality." But Brutus has a double nature, a private personality as well as a public image. His scenes with Portia show his private tenderness and his quarrel with Cassius reveals his real disturbance over her death, while his public show of resignation to the news of her death is in the "high Roman fasion" which Brutus assumes as his public image.

In spite of John Palmer's complex handling of the dual character of Brutus, there are still critics who view Brutus as the Romantics had. However, increased knowledge of Elizabethan history and thought has now been brought to bear on these arguments, supporting the nobility of Brutus. Bernard R. Breyer (1954), for example, expresses this view: "Brutus is, according to my theory, the good tyrannicide [and], it cannot have made the audience very happy to see him fall at the hands of the tyrant's avengers. . . ."

ESSAY QUESTIONS AND ANSWERS FOR REVIEW

1. What is the relationship between Brutus and Cassius?

ANSWER. Brutus and Cassius are friends of long standing who, as opposite types, have apparently fallen out with each other many times. When they are first seen in conversation, Cassius expresses the fear that Brutus no longer loves him; he suggests that he is the more dependent member of the friendship when he is happy to learn that Brutus' "ungentle" eyes are not directed at him. Apparently inconsequential, this subtle exchange between the two men sets up the relationship they continue to have with each other for the remainder of the play. Cassius is an intelligent man, a keen observer of human nature; he makes practical decisions of questionable morality, but he admires and honors the virtue and reputation of his friend Brutus and is too dependent on his love to oppose his friend for very long.

Although their conflicting natures are never forgotten, there are two major scenes in which the differences between the men are brought into sharpest focus. The first is the meeting of the conspirators in Brutus' garden, where Brutus rejects without compromise three of Cassius' proposals. He refuses to kill Antony, refuses to swear an oath, and refuses to invite Cicero to join the conspiracy. In each case, Cassius' suggestions are based on sound practical reasons. In each case Brutus' rejections are based on his constancy to moral principles. In every case, Cassius submits to Brutus' decisions, not without some argument.

The second scene in which the idealistic and practical natures of the two men are contrasted is the famous Quarrel Scene, which takes place in Sardis. Here Cassius' emotional dependence on Brutus' love is most visible, and Brutus' coldly rational appraisal of his friend's behavior is given its most extreme expression. The argument concerns practical corruption vs. absolute morality in the conduct of war. Despite his conviction that a general must overlook petty corruption and sometimes use unjust means for obtaining funds, Cassius finds his own position untenable in the face of the higher morality of Brutus, whom he reveres. Brutus is immovable to his friends' frailties of judgment and nature. He provokes Cassius' choleric disposition to greater shows of rashness and cruelly taunts him with a promise to mock (reject) him, which he knows Cassius cannot endure. Cassius is brutally pushed to the point where he asks Brutus to kill him. Having reached its nadir, the argument can go no farther, and a reconciliation takes place in which Cassius makes most of the apologies. At the close of the scene, Cassius' opposition is completely enfeebled. He protests only once more to Brutus' decision to attack the enemy on level ground rather than take the defensive from the vantage point in Sardis. At the close of the scene, Cassius addresses Brutus as "my lord." His submission is so total that he never argues with Brutus again. In the final moments before battle, he asks Brutus how he plans to face defeat if it should come. When he cannot make Brutus realize that his choice may be capture or suicide, he simply bids him a fond farewell.

Thus, the relationship between Brutus and Cassius is that of friendly antagonists. Allies in the conspiracy, they differ in every other respect. Their humors, philosophies, morals, and ideals are at odds at every point. There can be little doubt that Cassius and Brutus are intended as foils for each other, through which the characters can be examined in all their complex ramifications.

2. What is Antony's function in the play?

ANSWER. Although Antony appears briefly in the early part of the play as the loyal follower of Caesar, he does not emerge as an important participant until after the assassination of Caesar.

Before the assassination, careful suggestions are planted about Antony's nature, which do not take on meaning until later in the play. He is a man who enjoys plays, music, games, and the company of men, but he is unfailing in his duty and rises early to attend to affairs of state even when he has been reveling all night. He spends a good deal of time with Caesar, and seems to be taking lessons from him on the natures of men. After the assassination, it appears that Antony has learned his lessons well. He has judged Brutus wisely as an honorable man and accepts his promise of a safe conduct in order to gain the shrewd advantage of speaking to the crowd. Left alone with the body of Caesar, Antony's soliloquy reveals that he has taken upon himself the role of Caesar's avenger. Thus, along with Caesar's ghost, Antony is to function as an agent of revenge against the group of insurgents who have assassinated the ruler of Rome.

During his funeral oration, Antony reveals that he has tremendous powers as an orator and political manipulator, which had long been hidden under his apparent role as a lover of pleasure. Like young princes in Shakespeare's history plays (especially Prince Hal in *Henry IV Part I*), Antony has feigned profligacy while he bided his time. Now he bursts forth in all his glory as the leader and manipulator of men. The funeral oration shows Antony's superiority over Brutus not only as a politician but as an orator of the first rank. He has learned how to move men by having kept company with them; he has learned from music the power of moving men through the use of verse; he has learned from plays the power of moving men through action and utterance, and he has learned from Caesar how to be ruthless and deceitful to achieve his purposes. At this point in the play, Antony clearly functions as a contrast to Brutus.

Antony's handling of the triumvirate is meant to contrast with Brutus' handling of the conspirators. Antony kills men freely when it suits his purpose; he compromises to maintain unity among his cohorts; he deceives and uses men to achieve his ends. His conduct of the triumvirate is immorally practical. Brutus, on the other hand, refuses to kill men who may harm his cause, refuses to make compromises to maintain unity, and refuses to deceive or use men to achieve his ends. His conduct of the conspiracy is moral and impractical, and it is through Antony's behavior that we learn how to judge Brutus' character.

Antony is used as a foil for Brutus for the last time in the play during the verbal battle which precedes his victory at Philippi. There Antony is shown at the peak of confidence, but Brutus is an equal match for him. Antony's courage and optimism in the face of battle is juxtaposed to Brutus' courage and pessimism in his anticipation of the decisive fight. Brutus' courage is made clear when he is seen as the equal opponent in the verbal duel and when his victory over Octavius is matched by Antony's over Cassius. Finally, Antony is made to deliver the eulogy over his enemy Brutus, so that the honor of Brutus becomes most emphatic when Antony admits, "This was the noblest Roman of them all."

3. Who is the hero of *Julius Caesar?*

ANSWER. For centuries perplexed critics have wrestled with the question, who is the hero of the play? The tangled results of their considerations have left the question unanswered, or, at the most, with many answers. Let us then examine three suggestions among the many submitted. A) Caesar is the hero of the play. B) Brutus is the hero. C) Neither is the hero; the central interest of the play is its theme of rebellion.

A) Caesar may be regarded as the hero of the play not only because of the title or because historians have informed us of the profound interest Elizabethans had in the character of Caesar, or because there was a stage tradition of tyrant-kings who resembled Caesar, but because the play itself points to the fact that Caesar is its hero. The entire action of the play centers around Caesar's being, both corporeal and in spirit. The opening scene presents opposite views of Caesar, expressed by the tribunes, who hate him, and by the mob, which adores him. Subsequently, Caesar is seen marching in triumph, accompanied by pomp and pageantry which captivated the Elizabethan eye. (The audience paid rapt attention to tragedies of fallen monarchs of classical periods because of their resemblance to heroes of their own history, and they were accustomed to give first place in their minds to their own monarchs.) Caesar is the picture of a king, who, although seen infrequently, makes his presence felt continuously, and is the more honored because he is rarely seen.

Caesar's presence is next felt and visualized by Casca in his narrative of the events of the Lupercal. Next, Caesar is the center of Brutus' thoughts; what Caesar had been and what he may become is the problem which confronts the troubled patriot. Caesar is next seen in his domestic environment, then in the procession to the Senate. He is the focus of interest as Artemidorus petitions him and the Soothsayer warns him. All eyes are on Caesar when he opens the Senate on the fateful ides of March; his stature grows as his petitioners kneel before him. Overwhelmed by his self-importance, Caesar swells, reaches for the stars, falls. He is the target of the daggers in the hands of the outraged petitioners. And when the assassins step back, Caesar is dead center at the base of Pompey's statue.

After his assassination, his success and ambition are carried on in his image in the persons of Antony and Octavius, and his ghost visits his assassin seeking revenge. Finally, when the assassins die one by one, they die with the name Caesar on their lips. Thus, Caesar and the spirit of Caesar may be said to dominate the play, and the character of Caesar may be described as the tragic hero of the play.

B) If Brutus is to be called the hero of the play, the character of Caesar must be viewed in a different light. With Brutus as the hero, Caesar must be seen as pompous, arrogant, superstitious, infirm, overweening, and tyrannical. Brutus, the chief assassin, then can be seen as the hero, who out of duty to the Republic and in the spirit of freedom sacrifices his personal love for Caesar for the sake of the common good. He kills Caesar, whom he loves as a friend, because Caesar's ambitions endanger the freedom of all Romans. The tragedy of the noble Brutus becomes the tragedy of a man who was too true to his ideals to be good at the job of statecraft, which requires compromise. Brutus was too moral to execute the men who might harm him or to accept proposals which were tainted with self-interest or corruption. He was too noble to see that other men were not like himself, too eager to put his fate into the hands of the gods, whom he trusted. That Brutus was an honorable man was known by all men. Even Antony, an opportunist, who turned the mob against Brutus, knew that "this was the noblest Roman of them all."

C) If Shakespeare has written a problem play in which his principle concern is to examine the state of insurrection, the immorality of the act itself, and the evil which comes after, then *Julius Caesar* is play without a hero. It is a play of men who as individuals are both good and bad, men with mixed motives and mixed emotions, men with private as well as public needs, and men put to confusion by the disorder they have created. If the theme of rebellion is the central interest in the play, then Caesar is a courageous and heroic figure, who, inflated by success and weakened by age and physical and mental infirmities, forgets those who have helped him (both men and gods), and, through his outrageous arrogance in seeking the crown, tempts the gods and invites his own death at the hands of angry men.

Brutus, under these circumstances, is an insurgent, who, for just cause, does an immoral act and brings disaster to the Republic, which is greater than that which he had hoped to prevent. Caesar's rule, however despotic, must be seen as a unifying force in the Republic. He was destined to become king and found an empire. Brutus tried to interfere with destiny and slew Caesar, but, ironically, Caesar lived on. The spirit of Caesar or Caesarism survived the tyrant's death, and the empire, destined to be founded by "Caesar," was born under Octavius, who adopted the spirit and the name of Caesar.

SUBJECT BIBLIOGRAPHY AND GUIDE TO RESEARCH PAPERS

The most important thing in the study of Shakespeare's plays is the selection of a suitable text. Most modern texts of *Julius Caesar* are based on the First Folio edition of his works (1623), which is a particularly good one and one of the few left intact when Shakespeare's texts were being altered and revised during the eighteenth and nineteenth centuries. There are numerous good editions of the play available in inexpensive bindings with notes, glossaries, and critical commentaries. The New American Library edition, the Folger Library edition, and the Bantam Classic Books edition are among the best. Students may prefer the Folger Library edition, which is printed in an attractive format with notes and pictures facing the text pages they explain. The reader wishing a more permanent edition might purchase the Arden Shakespeare. The most thorough and comprehensive version of the play is in the New Variorum edition of Shakespeare's Works. This work includes the complete text with all its variants as well as extensive excerpts from the sources and major critics, exhaustive textual notes, and an elaborate bibliography. The student will find in the Cambridge edition of the play, edited by W. A. Wright and W. G. Clark, the most authoritative text of the play. The Cambridge Shakespeare and a special version of it, published as the Globe edition, are generally regarded as the standard reading text for *Julius Caesar*.

Listed below is a selective bibliography of the more significant books and articles dealing generally with Shakespeare and his era, many of which contain references to the play. There are also listed more important critical analyses of the play itself. They are arranged alphabetically by author within key research topics.

SHAKESPEARE'S LIFE

Alexander, Peter. *Shakespeare's Life and Art*. 1939.
Bentley, Gerald E. *Shakespeare: A Biographical Handbook*. 1961
Brandes, Georg M. *William Shakespeare: A Critical Study*, trans. W. Archer. 1902.
Chambers, Sir E. K. *William Shakespeare: A Study of Facts and Problems*. 2 vols. 1930.
Chute, Marchette. *Shakespeare of London*. 1949.
Van Doren, Mark. *Shakespeare*. 1939.

SHAKESPEARE'S TIMES

Byrne, M. *Elizabethan Life in Town and Country*. 1961.
Craig, Hardin. *The Enchanted Glass*. 1936.

Raleigh, Sir Walter. *Shakespeare's England: An Account of the Life and Manners of His Age.* 2 vols. 1917.

Tillyard, E. M. W. *The Elizabethan World Picture.* 1944.

Wright, Louis B. *Middle-Class Culture in Elizabethan England.* 1935.

SHAKESPEARE'S THEATER

Adams, John C. *The Globe Playhouse.* 1961.

Beckerman, Bernard. *Shakespeare at the Globe, 1599-1609.* 1962.

Chambers, E. K. *The Elizabethan Stage.* 4 vol. 1923.

Harbage, Alfred. *Shakespeare's Audience.* 1941.

Nagler, A. M. *Shakespeare's Stage,* trans. Ralph Manheim. 1958.

Venezky, Alice. *Pageantry on the Shakespearean Stage.* 1951.

GENERAL CRITICISM

Bradby, Anne, ed. *Shakespeare Criticism.* 1919-1935. 1936.

Bradley, A. C. *Shakespearean Tragedy.* 1904; 1955.

Campbell, L .B. *Shakespeare's Tragic Heroes.* 1930.

Granville-Barker, Harley. *Prefaces to Shakespeare.* 2 vols. 1946-7.

Moulton, R. G. *Shakespeare as a Dramatic Artist.* 1929.

Smith, D. N., ed. *Shakespeare Criticism.* 1916; 1947.

Spurgeon, Caroline T. E. *Shakespeare's Imagery and What It Tells Us.* 1935.

Traversi, D. A. *An Approach to Shakespeare.* 1956.

CRITICISM AND INTERPRETATION OF JULIUS CAESAR

Ayres, H. "Shakespeare's *Julius Caesar* in the Light of Some Other Versions," *PMLA,* XXV (1910), 183-227.

Boas, F. S. *Shakespeare and his Predecessors.* 1896.

Bonjour, Adrien. *The Structure of Julius Caesar.* 1958.

Brooke, C. F. Tucker. *Shakespeare's Plutarch. Vol. I: Containing the Main Sources of Julius Caesar.* 1909.

Charney, Maurice. *Shakespeare's Roman Plays.* 1961.

Coleridge, Samuel Taylor. *Coleridge's Writing on Shakespeare,* ed. T. Hawkes, 1959.

Dean, Leonard F. "*Julius Caesar* and Modern Criticism," *The English Journal* (October 1961), 451-6.

Dennis, John. *On the Genius and Writings of Shakespeare.* London, 1711. Reprinted in D. N. Smith, ed. *Eighteenth-Century Essays on Shakespeare,* 1903.

Dorsh, T. S., ed. *Julius Caesar.* 1955.

Foakes, R. A. "An Approach to Julius Caesar," *Shakespeare Quarterly,* V (Summer, 1954), 259-70.

Hazlitt, William. *The Characters of Shakespeare's Plays.* 1817.

Hudson, Henry Norman. *Lectures on Shakespeare.* 1848.

Hunter, Sir Mark. *Transactions of the Royal Society of Literature.* 1931.

Kittredge, George Lyman, ed. *Julius Caesar.* 1939.

Knight, G. Wilson. *The Imperial Theme.* 1951.

MacCallum, M. W. *Shakespeare's Roman Plays and Their Background.* 1910.

Palmer, John. *Political Characters in Shakespeare.* 1945.

Phillips, James E., Jr. *The State in Shakespeare's Greek and Roman Plays.* 1940.

Schanzer, Ernest. "The Problem of *Julius Caesar,*" *Shakespeare Quarterly,* VI (Summer, 1955), 297-308.

————. *The Problem Plays of Shakespeare.* 1963.

Smith, Gordon Ross. "Brutus, Virtue and Will," *Shakespeare Quarterly,* X (1959), 367-8.

Stirling, Brents. "Or Else This Were a Savage Spectacle," *PMLA,* LXVI (1951), 765-74.

————. *The Populace in Shakespeare.* 1949.

NOTES

MONARCH® *NOTES* AND STUDY GUIDES

ARE AVAILABLE AT RETAIL STORES EVERYWHERE

In the event your local bookseller
cannot provide you with other
Monarch titles you want —

ORDER ON THE FORM BELOW:

TITLE #	AUTHOR & TITLE	(exactly as shown on title listing)	PRICE
	PLUS ADDITIONAL $1.00 PER BOOK FOR POSTAGE		
		GRAND TOTAL	$

MONARCH® **PRESS, a Simon & Schuster Division of Gulf & Western Corporation**
Mail Service Department, 1230 Avenue of the Americas, New York, N.Y.   10020

I enclose $ .... to cover retail price, local sales tax, plus mailing
and handling.

Name _____

(Please print)

Address _____

City _____ State _____ Zip _____

Please send check or money order. We cannot be responsible for cash.